The Dragon Strikes

THE
DRAGON
STRIKES

China and the Korean War:
June–December 1950

Patrick C. Roe

PRESIDIO

Published by Presidio Press, Inc.
505 B San Marin Drive, Suite 160
Novato, CA 94945-1340

Library of Congress Cataloging-in-Publication Data

Roe, Patrick C.
    The dragon strikes : China and the Korean war, June–
December 1950/Patrick C. Roe.
        p. cm.
    Includes bibliographical references and index.
    ISBN 0-89141-703-6
    1. Korean War, 1950–1953—China. I Title.
DS919.5 .R64 2000
951.904'242—dc21
                                                    00-028566

Printed in the United States of America

Contents

Preface

Entry of the Chinese Communist Forces (CCF) into the Korean War in late October 1950 drastically changed the course of the war. In a little less than five months, the war had gone from near-disaster to almost certain victory. Most of North Korea was occupied. Only fragmented remnants of the North Korean People's Army (NKPA) remained. Final victory was at hand.

The Chinese Communist Forces reversed the situation, inflicted serious punishment on forces of the United Nations Command (UNC), drove them back into South Korea below the Han River, threatened to drive them from Korea, and extended the war for two and a half years. The People's Republic of China (PRC) was transformed from a rogue regime of questionable legitimacy and doubtful stability into a major power. Asian nations learned that America could be successfully challenged.

These are decisive results. The course of history was changed. The initial battles with the Chinese along the Chongchon River and at the Chosin Reservoir deserve to be included among the decisive battles of the twentieth century. General Douglas MacArthur was right when he radioed the Joint Chiefs of Staff (JCS), saying, "We face an entirely new war." It was the end of one war—one that ended in failure to reunite Korea. It was the beginning of another that ended in stalemate.

I was the young intelligence officer of the 3d Battalion, 7th Marines, during the Chosin operations. As we advanced northward into the mountains, the information we had from civilian refugees, from patrol contacts, and from the occasional deserter indicated that the Chinese were present in ever-increasing numbers but hanging back out of contact. Ever since, I have had a keen interest in knowing why the Chinese chose to enter the war at that point, why we were so ill-informed of their increasing presence, and how they were able to avoid detection.

The history of modern China provides more than enough reason for the Chinese to suspect American intentions, enough motivation for them to enter the war. The single great thrust of modern Chinese history is the effort of that country to overcome foreign colonialism and regain its independence. In Chinese eyes, America was the foremost of the colonial powers. I believe this was such a major factor in the Chinese entry into the war and in the conduct of the war—and a factor that still persists today—that I have taken an entire chapter in an attempt to summarize it.

Americans in general, and most American military officers, particularly those who had served in China, never understood this. We had a badly warped view of the Chinese in those days. Much of what many of those "old China hands" thought they knew was wrong. Franklin Delano Roosevelt thought he knew and understood China. The Delano family fortune was made by his grandfather in the China trade. His romantic view of China was a poor basis for our China policy. Henry Luce, the powerful and influential publisher of *Time* magazine, was born in China of missionary parents. He viewed China through the rosy goggles of the missionaries and fostered that view in his magazines. Luce had spirited and often bitter disagreements with Theodore White, his correspondent in China during World War II. White wanted to report on China and Chiang Kai-shek as he saw it, realistically. Luce wanted to print it as he saw it, in rosy retrospect. The "China hands," a small group of foreign-service officers who did report objectively and recommended changes in policy, were treated disgracefully and punished for their candid reports.

General MacArthur boasted of his understanding of the "Oriental mind." But the "Oriental mind" he believed he understood, as with many other China experts, was the mind of the submissive and opportunistic Oriental who had been colonialized. He was startled indeed when the Chinese offensive forced him to look into the minds of passionate Chinese patriots, freed of the constraints of Confucian convention and determined to rid China of foreign domination.

Behind a screen of advance Chinese Communist Forces, believed by UNC intelligence to be merely a token effort, the Chinese were able to assemble, undetected, a huge but primitive force. Their appearance in overwhelming numbers was a shock to UNC forces and a stunning failure of UNC and U.S. intelligence.

General Omar Bradley called it the worst intelligence failure since the Battle of the Bulge in 1944. Bradley underestimated it. The Battle of the Bulge was a temporary setback. The battles in North Korea changed the course of the war. Attempts to reunify Korea were given up. We settled for a return to the prewar status. Our future relations with Asian nations changed.

Much of the answer to the intelligence failure is to be found in analysis of the day-to-day intelligence reports of the Far Eastern Command (FEC), the Eighth Army, and X Corps in the National Archives, plus other sources noted in this book. However, some key information in the hands of the National Security Agency and the Central Intelligence Agency has not been declassified and, given our strained relations with the Chinese, may never be.

From a detailed study of the available material, and my own experience, it is clear that if the information provided by front-line units had been properly evaluated by intelligence officers who knew the Chinese, and who knew Korea, it would have provided more than sufficient intelligence to prevent such a stunning surprise. It appears that two things occurred to much of the intelligence provided by front-line units. First, evaluation of that information was warped by the predisposition of so many senior officers who were unfamiliar with the Chinese Communist Army and viewed it disparagingly. Second, the front-line reports were contradicted by other intelligence still classified, such as communication intercepts, which would have been closely held. The circumstantial evidence is strong that the Chinese, aware their radio traffic might be read, transmitted misleading information as a deliberate part of a well-planned deception program.

That deception plan, one of the most successful in modern warfare, enabled the Chinese to achieve near-total surprise. In fact, they did it twice—once with the initial clash in late October (what they referred to as their Phase I offensive) and then again in late November with their all-out offensive. The Red leaders may well have been dedicated Communists. They were also dedicated Chinese and avid students of the works of Sun Tzu. The proverb "Fool me once, shame on you; fool me twice, shame on me" comes to mind.

It is most unfortunate that the full intelligence story is not yet available. Existing histories of the Korean War do not address this key question. In the ceremonies connected with dedication of the Korean War memorial, I sat through a two-day symposium on the war where the intelligence failure was not once mentioned. The intelligence failure was the key element in the disastrous outcome of the battles in North Korea. Military histories are of limited value as learning tools if they do not include the intelligence available to the commanders when decisions are made.

The trend in Korean War history has been to hold General MacArthur and his intelligence officer, Gen. Charles A. Willoughby, responsible for the reverses in North Korea. Whatever culpability they may bear, the Joint Chiefs, the members of the National Security Council, and the Central Intelligence Agency (CIA) have to share a substantial part of the responsibility. Using the available records, I have attempted to provide the background of the discussions and decisions at the national level in responding to the entry of the Chinese.

I have not dealt in detail with the two crucial accomplishments leading up to our advance into North Korea. The success of the Eighth Army in halting the North Korean offensive along the Naktong River and the complete reversal of the course of the war that came with the successful Inchon landing were great achievements. The contribution of those campaigns to the outcome of the war is a separate story that has been told elsewhere and surely will receive further attention in the future. Brief mention of these is made in the following story only as a way of setting the background for the battles in North Korea.

This book began in 1994, when I was asked to be historical chairman for our group of veterans of the Chosin Reservoir campaign—

a group known as the "Chosin Few." In reviewing the history of that great feat of arms, I felt that the day-to-day story has been told well. What seemed to be needed was a comprehensive story of how we got into that situation, what the Chinese were doing, what decisions were made on both sides during the battle, and what the outcome was. It was obvious from the start that the entire effort in North Korea, both at Chosin and along the Chongchon River, had to be included.

The Chongchon battles have not received the historical attention they deserve. The best and most detailed information on the initial Chinese entry was produced in the Eighth Army sector. It was one of the great tragedies of the war that the desperate shortage of qualified Chinese linguists and scholars prevented that information from being properly evaluated. Veterans of those actions deserve a more thorough study. There are lessons to be learned from a worthwhile study of an army under great pressure and the decisions made at the time.

Few of those still alive played key command or staff roles during these events. Thus, with scant opportunities for interviews, I have had to rely almost entirely upon the written records contained in published histories, in records of the time located in various archives, and in interviews of key players done earlier by other researchers. That makes the interest and contribution of Lt. Gen. William J. McCaffrey, USA (Ret.), and Lt. Gen. Alpha L. Bowser Jr., USMC (Ret.), particularly valuable and deeply appreciated.

The results follow. I hope this will provide a new perspective on the Korean War and, perhaps, a somewhat different perspective on the Chinese.

Among the many to whom I am indebted for their interest and assistance is the staff of the MacArthur Library in Norfolk, Virginia, and in particular Jim Zoebel, the archivist. Rick Boylan at Archives II was of immense help in locating records of the various military organizations. Kerry Strong at the Marine Corps Research Center, Quantico, Virginia, was helpful in providing information from Marine Corps records. Thanks are due to David A. Keough, U.S. Army Military History Institute, Carlisle, Pennsylvania, for providing information from that amazing treasure trove of history.

Thanks are also due to Col. George Rasula, USA (Ret.), for getting me involved in this project and for our often-spirited discussions of the North Korean operations. Colonel John Counselman, USMC (Ret.), a classmate and valued friend, read the manuscript and offered encouraging comments.

   And, finally, thanks are due to Edith Blomberg at the Lopez Island Library for her help in obtaining much of the needed reference material.

List of Abbreviations

AA antiaircraft
AAA antiaircraft artillery
AAA-AW (SP) antiaircraft artillery automatic weapons, self-propelled
BARs Browning automatic rifles
CCF Chinese Communist Forces
CCP Chinese Communist Party
CIA Central Intelligence Agency
CIC Counterintelligence Corps
CinC Commander in Chief
CINCFE Commander in Chief, Far Eastern Command
CINCUNC Commander in Chief, United Nations Command
CMC Central Military Commission (Chinese)
CMC Commandant of the Marine Corps
CNA Chinese Nationalist Army
CO Commanding Officer
COMNAVFE Commander, Naval Forces Far East
CP command post
CPV Chinese People's Volunteers
DA Department of the Army
DIS Daily Intelligence Summary (Far Eastern Command)
DPRK Democratic People's Republic of Korea (North)
EUSAK Eighth U.S. Army, Korea
FA field artillery
FEC Far Eastern Command

GMD Gumomindang (Chinese Nationalists)
JCS Joint Chiefs of Staff
JSPOG Joint Strategic Plans and Operations Group (FEC)
KATUSA Korean Augmentation Troops, U.S. Army
KIA killed in action
KMAG Korean Military Advisory Group, U.S. Army
MIS Military Intelligence Service
MSR main supply route (lifeline)
NEFF North Eastern Frontier Force (Chinese)
NKPA North Korean People's Army (also Inmun Gun)
OI Operational Instruction
PIR Periodic Intelligence Report (daily)
PLA People's Liberation Army
PRC People's Republic of China (Communist)
PW prisoner of war (also POW)
RCT regimental combat team
ROC Republic of China (Nationalist)
ROK Republic of Korea (South)
ROKA Republic of Korea Army
SCAP Supreme Commander, Allied Powers
UNC United Nations Command
USSR Union of Soviet Socialist Republics

1
Prewar: The U.S. Situation

The best doggone shooting army outside the United States.
—Brigadier General Lynn Roberts,
chief of the Korean Military Advisory Group, 1950

When Kim Il Sung's T-34 tanks rolled southward across the thirty-eighth parallel on 25 June 1950, a precarious balance of world forces was suddenly and drastically tilted. The tangled chain of world events leading up to that attack and the subsequent entry of the Chinese into the war formed the attitudes of the major participants and provide the background for their responses. Those events are worth reviewing.

The Threat of Communism
The end of World War II had promised an era of world peace benignly protected by the American nuclear monopoly. Instead, the menace of a monolithic, worldwide, Communist imperialism threatened.

What Winston Churchill described as an iron curtain had slammed shut across Eastern Europe. Berlin had been isolated and blockaded by Soviet forces in mid-1948. For nine months, Berlin had survived only through the largest continuous airlift in history. In Greece, Communist insurgents infiltrating from neighboring Yugoslavia had barely been beaten back. In the Middle East, Soviet subversion and overt pressure on Iran threatened the rich Middle East oilfields upon which the United States and the rest of the world were becoming more and more dependent. The State Department looked on the situation in the Far East as more complex, more turbulent, and, in the spring of 1950, more disheartening.

Much of the Far East had been under Western domination at the start of World War II. With the end of the war, Western powers at-

1

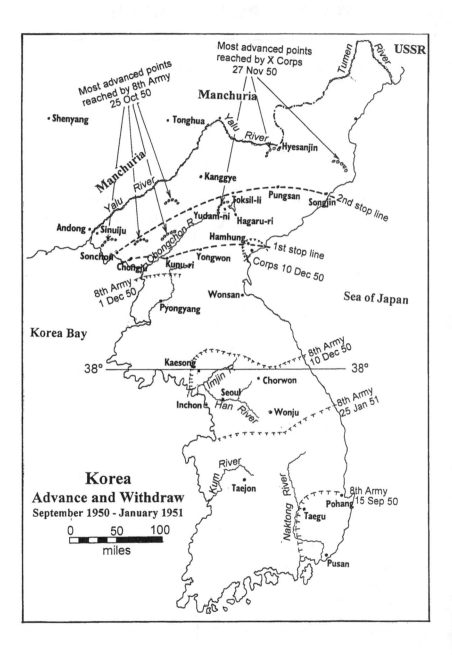

Most advanced points
reached by X Corps
27 Nov 50

USSR

Most advanced points
reached by 8th Army
25 Oct 50

Manchuria

• Shenyang

• Tonghua

Yalu River

Hyesanjin

Manchuria

Yalu River

• Kanggye

Toksil-li   Pungsan

Yudam-ni Hagaru-ri   Songjin 2nd stop line

Andong • • Sinuiju

Chongchon R.

Hamhung   1st stop line

Sonchon

Yongwon   Corps 10 Dec 50

Chongju   Kunu-ri

8th Army
1 Dec 50

Wonsan •

Sea of Japan

• Pyongyang

Korea Bay

8th Army
10 Dec 50

38°   Kaesong   38°

Imjin   • Chorwon

Seoul

Inchon   Han River   • Wonju   8th Army
25 Jan 51

River

Korea
Advance and Withdraw
September 1950 - January 1951

Kum   • Taejon

Naktong River

8th Army
15 Sep 50

Pohang

• Taegu

0   50   100
miles

Pusan

tempted to reestablish their position. Indigenous forces strongly re-sisting Western attempts to reestablish control of their Asian colonies found Communism, with its powerful anticolonial doctrine, to be a useful ally. In much of the Asian turbulence, called "wars of national liberation" by the Communists, Communism played some role. To the Western powers, this was evidence of Communist imperialism. To the locals, it was a legitimate move toward national independence. Western observers wondered if many Asian countries were simply ex-changing one form of imperial domination for another.

Communist guerrillas appeared to be making headway against the British in Malaya. In the Philippines, the Communist Hukabalahap rebels were a serious threat to the future stability of those islands. French forces in Viet Nam were fighting a gradually losing war against the Communist Viet Minh rebels. In Korea, the nominally democratic leader of South Korea and the Communist leader of North Korea were making threatening noises at each other.

Most alarming of all was the situation in China. By the autumn of 1949, the Chinese Communists had decisively beaten the National-ist forces under Chiang Kai-shek and had driven them from the main-land to the offshore island of Taiwan (then Formosa). The People's Republic of China (PRC) had been proclaimed in Beijing (Peking). Chinese Communist forces were actively training for an invasion of Taiwan. Its fall to the Communists was expected in the near future.

To an observer from the North American continent, it seemed as if Communism was menacing Europe and a triumphant wave of in-ternational Communism was sweeping across all of East Asia. It was widely and devoutly believed to be part of a monolithic global con-spiracy, planned and directed from within the walls of the Kremlin. The lone non-Communist outpost on the Far Eastern mainland was that portion of the Korean peninsula below the thirty-eighth parallel.

American Strategy

Pursuing the pleasures of peace, the United States was slow to per-ceive the menace of Communist imperialism but soon responded with an escalating series of measures. In April 1947, aid to the Greek resistance against Communist guerrillas was approved. The follow-ing year, the European Recovery Act, known as the Marshall Plan, was approved. And in the summer of 1949, the North Atlantic Treaty Organization (NATO) was established for the defense of Europe.

These measures were part of the American political strategy of containment—the determination to resist the expansion of Soviet influence. The assumption was that with Soviet expansion contained, it would internally transform into a less-threatening system.

George F. Kennan, then the director of the State Department's Policy Planning Staff and the architect of the containment policy, elaborated on this in a lecture to the National War College. Kennan stated that there were only five vital power centers in the world: the United States, the Soviet Union, Great Britain, the Rhine Valley, and Japan. The task of containment was to see to it that the four not then under Soviet control remained so. If this were so, Kennan said, ". . . you do not need to hold land positions on the Eurasian land mass to protect our national security. If that is true, you can theoretically content yourself with permitting most of these land areas to be in the hands of people who are hostile to ourselves as long as you exercise that power of inhibiting the assembly and launching of amphibious forces from many Asian ports."[1] Kennan's comments were directed principally to the effects of the revolution in China.

Under these conditions, American policy was first to protect Europe from Soviet domination. Admiral Forrest Sherman, then Chief of Naval Operations and a member of the Joint Chiefs of Staff (JCS), expressed the priorities of that policy by pointing out that if the Soviets took Europe, they would immediately double their industrial capacity. Sherman believed that if we lost Western Europe we would have an increasingly difficult time in holding our own. If we lost all the Asiatic mainland, we could still survive and build up and possibly get it back again. The situation in Europe was straightforward, the lines clearly drawn.

Devising strategy for the Far East was more difficult. Western efforts to contain Communism were often looked upon as covert colonialism or, as the Communists put it, imperialism. Finding a stable base for a workable strategy in the turbulent Far East was difficult.

General Douglas MacArthur, who was Commander in Chief, Far East Command (CINCFE), Supreme Commander Allied Powers

(SCAP), in Japan and virtually an American proconsul there, strongly believed that the future lay in the Far East. As far back as 1944, he had viewed the Orient as the region of rising power: "Europe is a dying system. It is worn down and will become an industrial and economic hegemony of Soviet Russia. . . . The lands touching the Pacific with their billions of inhabitants will determine the course of history for the next ten thousand years."[2]

MacArthur was quite distressed with the Eurocentric orientation of American policy. In a meeting with Carlos Romulos, he expressed himself freely: "This group of Europhiles just will not recognize that it is Asia which has been selected for the test of Communist power and that if all Asia falls Europe would not have a chance—either with or without American assistance. In their blind and stupid effort to undermine public confidence in me as something of a symbol of the need for balanced thinking and action, they do Europe the gravest disservice and sow the seeds to its possible ultimate destruction."[3]

The American Far East strategy that evolved was anchored upon Japan and required converting Japan from an occupied nation into an ally. MacArthur described this strategy, a containment line, in an interview with a British newspaper in March 1949: "Our defensive dispositions against Asiatic aggression used to be based on the west coast of the American continent. The Pacific was looked on as the avenue of possible enemy approach. Now the Pacific has become an Anglo-Saxon lake and our line of defense runs through the chain of islands fringing the coast of Asia. It starts from the Philippines and continues through the Ryukyu Archipelago, which includes its main bastion, Okinawa. Then it bends back through Japan and the Aleutian Island chain to Alaska."[4]

Two places of vital strategic importance lay outside this line: One, Taiwan, was recognized as important; the other, Korea, was not.

The policy of containment required constant watchfulness by Americans. It was a new and unfamiliar burden. Secretary of State Dean Acheson expressed the situation this way: "We have got to understand that all our lives danger, the uncertainty, the need for alertness, for effort, for discipline, will be upon us. This is new to us. It will be hard for us."[5]

American Resources

The United States was the only country in the world that had ended World War II stronger than it began. It was the only remaining Western power strong enough to stand up to the threat of world Communism. That responsibility rested uneasily on Americans and their leaders. The financial burden of that role conflicted with American desires to enjoy the prosperity and peace that victory in World War II had promised.

To meet its responsibility, the United States obviously would have to maintain a strong military force. But despite these new worldwide commitments, President Harry Truman was determined to reduce the size of the armed forces. In a move to increase efficiency and economy, the armed forces had been "unified" under the Department of Defense (DOD). The JCS had been formally created with a chairman to advise on military matters. The National Security Council (NSC) had been established to coordinate and advise the president on defense policy. The Central Intelligence Agency (CIA) had been created to coordinate the production of national intelligence. As the summer of 1950 approached, these new institutions were all slowly beginning to adapt themselves to their roles. None had been tested in a major national crisis.

The pressure for economy resulted in bitter struggles over the roles and missions of the services. Decisions made by the JCS and the DOD, now under Louis Johnson, precipitated the "Revolt of the Admirals." The admirals took their case directly to Congress, complaining of the undue emphasis on Europe and arguing that hostilities could start anywhere in the world; heavy cutbacks would signal to foreign powers that Americans were not able or willing to intervene overseas. The "revolt" was countered by a speech by Gen. Omar Bradley referring to the Navymen as "fancy Dans."

The dominant American military strategy that evolved was heavy reliance on the Air Force and the delivery of atomic weapons. The bulk of the limited funds went to the Air Force, with the Navy the second highest recipient. The Army's conventional ground forces were drastically reduced. With the advent of the atomic bomb, it seemed as if air power could go a long way toward replacing conventional military power, and at much less cost in money and manpower. It was an attractive proposition.

By the spring of 1950, the great American ground forces created to fight the Germans and Japanese had shrunk to the equivalent of eleven understrength divisions. The Army had the equivalent of ten divisions. The two Marine divisions amounted to the equivalent of one understrength division. Four of the Army divisions were in Japan; about one and one-third were in Europe; two and two-thirds were in the United States. The remainder were fragments scattered in the Caribbean and various Pacific locations. Secretary of Defense Louis Johnson, acting on instructions from President Truman to limit the size of the military budget, promised further cuts,[6] vowing to cut the fat from the American armed forces. In doing so, he had taken great chunks of bone and muscle.

Korea

Korea had been occupied by Japanese troops in 1905, then annexed by Japan in 1910. During World War II, it was considered enemy territory. At the Cairo Summit in November 1943, President Franklin Roosevelt endorsed a policy of a free and independent Korea in due course. That policy was reiterated in 1945 at the Yalta Summit. It was further agreed that until Korea became independent, it would be under the joint trusteeship of the United States, China, and the Soviet Union.

The world's first atomic bomb was dropped on Japan on 6 August 1945; Russia entered the war on 8 August; and the Japanese surrendered on 14 August.

With the sudden and unexpected Japanese surrender, there was great haste to cobble together plans to accept the surrender of Japanese field forces and to disarm them. The opportunistic Soviet declaration of war on Japan, coming two days after the first atomic bomb was dropped, made it necessary to agree on a line of demarcation between the zones within which the United States and the Soviets would accept the Japanese surrender. The U.S. State Department wanted the American zone to be as far north on the mainland of China as possible, including key points in Manchuria. The

Army did not want to go into an area where few other forces were close at hand.

In the planning for the surrender, two young American colonels, Dean Rusk and Charles Bonesteel, from the War Department's Operations and Plans Division (OPD), were assigned the task of finding a line. Neither was particularly knowledgeable about Korea or the Far East, although Rusk had served briefly with Gen. Joseph W. Stilwell in China during the war. They retired to an office and pondered over a *National Geographic* map. The Army wanted to have two ports, Inchon in the north and Pusan in the south. North of Inchon, there did not seem to be any natural geographic division. They settled on the thirty-eighth parallel. The Soviets agreed. Later Rusk learned that in the early 1900s, the Russians and Japanese had, initially, proposed the thirty-eighth parallel as the dividing line between their respective spheres of influence. There has since been suspicion that the Soviets took agreement on the thirty-eighth parallel to be an acknowledgment of their historic sphere of influence.[7]

The U.S. XXIV Corps came ashore at Inchon to carry out the U.S. occupation mission. The Soviet Army moved down from the north, closed on the thirty-eighth parallel, and sealed the border. All subsequent attempts to proceed with a coordinated policy toward Korea failed.

The occupation was not a happy task. Lieutenant General John R. Hodges, the XXIV Corps commander, called it the worst job he ever had. The troops disliked it intensely. In Japan, one commander addressed his incoming troops, warning them to behave and saying that they had only three things to fear—diarrhea, gonorrhea, and Korea. In the south, the Koreans were not willing to wait for "due course" to achieve freedom and independence. They wanted it right away. And there were competing groups of all political stripes ready to take on the job.

The wisdom of maintaining American troops in Korea was questioned almost from the very start. To the Joint Chiefs, the troops were needed elsewhere. In the years that followed, with the Cold War becoming more frosty, force levels dropping, and other needs increasing, the question became more urgent. It was not a decision easily made. An ongoing discussion of the subject continued from 1947 to 1949. It revolved around the strategic value of Korea, its political importance, and its importance in contributing to U.S. prestige. In April 1947, the Joint Strategic Survey Committee noted, "This is one country within which we alone have for almost two years carried on ideological warfare in direct contact with our ideological opponents so that to lose this battle would be gravely detrimental to the United States prestige and therefore security."[8] The State-War-Navy Coordinating Committee (prior to the formation of the Joint Chiefs of Staff) concluded: ". . . the U.S. cannot at this time withdraw from Korea under circumstances which would inevitably lead to Communist domination of the entire country." That concern was echoed and reechoed in the next two years.

The strategic considerations were equally convincing. In June 1947, the Joint War Plans Committee concluded that existing forces in southern Korea could not repel a Soviet attack. Reinforcements from Japan would only weaken the security of Japan without being able to match the size of forces the USSR could deploy. "A withdrawal from Korea immediately after the outbreak of hostilities is indicated." Withdrawal under those conditions would be difficult if not impossible. The newly formed Joint Chiefs concluded in September that, "in the light of the present severe shortage of military manpower, the corps of two divisions . . . now maintained in South Korea, could well be used elsewhere."[9]

General George Marshall, then secretary of state, was not so sure. At a meeting in his office, the following conclusions were reached: "It was agreed that (a) ultimately the U.S. position in Korea is untenable even with expenditure of considerable U.S. money and effort; (b) the U.S., however, cannot 'scuttle' and run from Korea without considerable loss of prestige and political standing in the Far East and in the world at large; (c) that it should be the effort of the government through all proper means to effect a settlement of the Korean problem which would enable the U.S. to withdraw from Korea as soon as possible with the minimum of bad effects."[10]

The solution adopted was to ask the United Nations (UN) to take over U.S. responsibilities in Korea, followed by a gradual withdrawal of troops. This would give the new supranational body an opportunity to perform a task for which it was created. A UN Temporary

Commission on Korea (UNTCOK) was organized. UNTCOK attempted to arrange elections in both the north and the south. It too failed. As a result, two separate governments contending for control of the peninsula had been created in Korea by the fall of 1948.

In the south, after a bitter and possibly fraudulent campaign, the Republic of Korea (ROK) was formed, with Syngman Rhee as president. A month later, in September, the Democratic People's Republic of Korea (DPRK) was formed in the north, with twenty-eight-year-old Kim Il Sung as its head. The UN recognized the Republic of Korea as the only legal government on the peninsula. The Koreans are sometimes called "The Irish of the Orient"—tough, stubborn, and combative; Kim and Rhee both vowed to unify Korea, by force if necessary. In the following years, guerrilla bands and raiding parties crossed the border from both sides.

Then, with a North Korean government in existence, the Soviets offered to participate in a mutual withdrawal of troops, leaving Korea to the Koreans. So, if the Soviets were withdrawing troops from North Korea, it appeared safe to withdraw U.S. troops from South Korea.

The first U.S. troops left in March 1948. The headquarters of the XXIV Corps was transferred to Japan for deactivation in January 1949. The last troops left on 30 June 1949. But as the scheduled departure of the remaining troops approached, the subject was once again anxiously reviewed. In February 1949, the CIA had concluded that "U.S. troop withdrawal could probably result in a collapse of the supported ROK" and suggested a continued presence of a moderate number of American forces in the area to discourage invasion as well as to boost morale in the south. A month later, the National Security Council observed: "The overthrow by Soviet dominated forces of a regime established in South Korea under the aegis of the UN would . . . constitute a severe blow to the prestige and influence of the UN; in this respect the interests of the U.S. are parallel to if not identical with those of the UN."[11]

But the military continued to oppose keeping troops there, for two primary reasons: the pressure of other commitments and the conviction that Korea would not provide favorable fighting terrain should war come. An Army study, for the first time using the phrase *police action,* stated: ". . . police action with UN sanction" in Korea, including U.S. military units, would "involve a militarily disproportionate expenditure of U.S. manpower, resources and effort at a time when international relations in Europe are in precarious balance." Active military support of Korea "would require prodigious effort and vast expenditures far out of proportion to the benefits to be expected."[12] The clinching argument seemed to be the possibility that the United States would become heavily and unnecessarily involved if the bellicose Syngman Rhee should attempt an attack northward to unify Korea on his own.

The last troops were withdrawn. To replace them, the Korean Military Advisory Group (KMAG), under Brig. Gen. Lynn Roberts, was established to train the newly formed Army of the Republic of Korea.

The strategic value of Korea was viewed rather narrowly. The problems of defending were certainly not overestimated. That became very clear in the next few years. But Korea certainly has strategic value comparable to or perhaps exceeding that of Taiwan. While subsequent debate on the value of Taiwan raged in public, Korea's strategic importance to the United States was overlooked both within the government and in public.

Korea was a historic avenue of approach, a land bridge between Japan and the mainland of China. It was the route taken by the Japanese in 1895 when they defeated China at Pyongyang and the Battle of the Yalu and gained a toehold in Manchuria. It was the route the Japanese took in 1905 when they defeated the Russians, strengthened their position in Manchuria, and prepared for the full-scale invasion of China in 1937. Korea led straight into the heart of Manchuria, the most highly industrialized and productive area in China. If Germany was considered the cockpit of Europe, Manchuria was the cockpit of East Asia. It was the place where, historically, Chinese, Russian, and Japanese interests had collided.

Conversely, in hostile hands Korea was a dagger pointed at the heart of Japan. From bases in Korea, hostile aircraft could reach areas where they could do far more damage than those based on Taiwan. Korea was the closest and quickest route from the Asian mainland to the industrial heart of Japan. If, as MacArthur said, Taiwan was an unsinkable aircraft carrier, so too was the Korean peninsula, and it was much closer to a vital center of American interest.

In January 1950, Secretary of State Dean Acheson gave a speech to the National Press Club that, among other things, repeated MacArthur's explanation of U.S. Far Eastern strategy. Acheson went just a bit further. In response to a specific question, he stated that the United States had no strategic interest in Korea. But, he continued, "so far as the military security of other areas in the Pacific is concerned, it must be clear that no person can guarantee these areas against military attack. . . . Should such an attack occur . . . the initial reliance must be on the people attacked to resist it and then upon the commitments of the entire civilized world under the Charter of the United Nations, which so far has not proved a weak reed to lean on by any people who are determined to protect their independence against outside aggression."[13]

After the North Korean attack, Acheson's speech was blamed by some for encouraging the attack. Acheson amplified and corrected his remarks in a session before the Senate Foreign Relations Committee: "The estimate that we have . . . is that South Korea could now take care of any trouble that was started solely by North Korea, but it could not take care of any invasion which was either started by the Chinese Communists or powerfully supported by them or by the Soviet Union."[14]

The estimate to which he was referring was based on reports by General Roberts, the KMAG chief. The Korean Army had been increased to 100,000 men and was equipped with American weapons. Training was commenced, but it progressed slowly. There were serious deficiencies in weapons and equipment as well as deficiencies in training junior and senior officers. Despite this, and for reasons unknown, Roberts, who had been passed over for major general and was due to retire at the end of the year, embarked on an extensive public relations program touting the capabilities of the Republic of Korea Army (ROKA). In an article in *Time*, 5 June 1950 Roberts called it the "best doggone shooting army outside the United States."

MacArthur sent Gen. Leland S. Hobbs to inspect the ROKA. After the visit, Hobbs went away enthusiastic about the work of KMAG and the Korean Army. Author John Gunther in Tokyo was told by

General Headquarters (GHQ) that if war came in Korea, "The South Korean forces, 'The best Army in Asia,' could wipe out the North Koreans with no difficulty." GHQ in Tokyo was convinced—as were the Army General Staff in Washington and numerous influential politicians who visited Korea. John J. Muccio, the U.S. ambassador to the Republic of Korea, was convinced by Roberts's assertion and passed on Roberts's view to Acheson that the Korean Army had the capability of containing the North Korean forces.

Not everyone was content with the condition of the ROKA. During a diplomatic dinner in Tokyo, the ROK defense minister confided to Ambassador William J. Sebald, MacArthur's political adviser, that much work needed to be done before the ROKA could match the North Koreans. On the same occasion, General Roberts was talkative, confident on the subject of South Korea's defenses. He emphasized: "I can hold the Commies if they attack."[15]

In reality, the ROKA lacked an air force, adequate artillery, and antiaircraft weapons. Roberts, an armored officer, decided that Korea was not good tank country. Therefore, adequate antitank weapons, including mines, were not needed, requested, or supplied. Training of the ROKA also fell behind. By 15 June 1950, only 25 percent of the Korean Army had completed battalion-level training, 35 percent of the vehicles were out of commission for lack of spare parts, and 10 to 15 percent of the weapons were unusable.

The resource-rich and industrialized north of the Korean peninsula was nicely balanced by the agricultural south. Korea was the one country in Asia that had the potential to be economically balanced and self-sufficient. President Syngman Rhee was determined to reunite the nation. To keep Rhee from launching an improvident adventure, the United States ensured that the ROKA received no weapons that could be used offensively. Kim Il Sung was equally determined to reunite Korea. But, like Rhee, he was dependent upon the support and approval of his patrons.

Relations with China

Dean Acheson's belief that the Chinese situation was more complicated was certainly justified. Even today, knowledgeable authorities differ strongly on the historical realities.

American policy had been to support Chiang Kai-shek and the Guomindang (GMD, also Kuomintang) as early as 1937. Prior to Pearl Harbor, the U.S. government had indirectly provided money and arms for Chiang's fight to resist Japanese aggression. It was in our own interest to have someone tie down rampant Japanese military power. Chiang was publicized as "man of the year," perhaps the Asian man of the century, the only one who could unify and lead China. Americans, strongly influenced by the Christian missionary movement in China and the efforts of *Time* publisher Henry Luce, were enthralled that this stalwart defender had married one of the daughters of China's leading Westernized family and converted to Christianity. President Roosevelt believed China would be one of the four great powers that, together with the United States, Great Britain, and Russia, would guarantee the peace in Asia after the war.

The reality of Chiang Kai-shek's China was quite different from the public perception. The Chinese government was, in fact, little more than a loose coalition. The central government was in firm control in two provinces and had partial control in eight provinces. In the other eighteen provinces, warlords, nominally cooperating with Chiang, were in control. The weak and divided Chinese government was under attack from two directions. The Communist uprising, beginning in 1927, had grown into a serious internal threat, consolidating in a strong base around Yanan in Shaanxi (Shensi) Province.

Then, in 1937, after occupying all of Manchuria and nibbling at the northern Chinese provinces, the Japanese launched a full-scale offensive to occupy all of China. By 1941, the Japanese occupied nearly all of the coastal provinces and much of the Yangtze Valley. Chiang Kai-shek's Nationalist government had been driven inland to Chongqing (Chungking). There, exhausted, increasingly corrupt, and dictatorial, it settled down to await rescue from abroad. Pearl Harbor Day, 7 December 1941, a day of infamy in the United States, was a day of celebration in China's wartime capital of Chongqing. General Stilwell was sent to China with the basic mission of keeping China in the war in order to keep the Japanese occupation troops pinned down while the Pacific campaigns went forward.

Far from cooperating in the war, Chiang was content to hold his position and let someone else win the war. Then he would turn on the Communist rebels and destroy them. The Communists were following a similar strategy—avoiding, with one exception, full-scale clashes with the Japanese. But the Reds were maintaining a steady guerrilla pressure, tying down large numbers of Japanese.

The Chinese Communists were a new and mysterious phenomenon on the world scene. Were they simply agrarian reformers, as one trend of thought held? Were they Nationalists? Were they just another version of the Chinese bandits, as the GMD called them? Or were they hard-core Communists subservient to the will of the Soviet Union? General Joseph Stilwell, commanding the American Army in China, needed to know their military potential. Under pressure from President Roosevelt, Chiang finally permitted Stilwell to send an observer mission to the Communist headquarters in Yanan.

The group—called the "Dixie Mission" because they were going into rebel territory—was the first systematic contact by Westerners with the Chinese Communists. The observers soon learned that the Reds were a very different kind of Chinese from those found in the dispirited, corrupt, and incompetent Nationalist armies. Most of the observer group were men with long and intimate experience in China. The entire atmosphere of Yanan was so different that one officer, born and brought up in China, complained he was continually trying to find out just how Chinese the people at Yanan were.

Reports from the mission commented very positively on the strength and effectiveness of the Communists and stated that they could be a powerful asset in the war with Japan. The Communists held nearly one-third of the country, if their strength behind the Japanese lines was counted. The observers recommended that American military aid be shared with the Communists. It was also apparent to them that if the attempts to reconcile the Nationalists and Communists failed and civil war resulted, the Communists were very likely to win.

This was not welcome news in Chongqing or in Washington. For the Communists, this was an opportunity to gain important recognition and assistance now and possible economic assistance after the war. In Yanan, Mao Zedong argued that military assistance to the Chinese Communist Party (CCP) would make the Communist armies strong enough so that Chiang Kai-shek would not attack and would be forced to create a coalition government. Civil war would be averted.

Mao vigorously asserted to the mission that the Communists were really not as radical as believed: "The policies of the Chinese Communist Party are merely liberal. . . . Even the most conservative American businessman can find nothing in our program to take exception to." He realized, he said, that China would need to industrialize and that it would need free enterprise and foreign capital. He emphasized that American and Chinese interests were correlated and similar, that they fit together, economically and politically. China and America could and had to work together: "America does not need to fear that we will not be cooperative. We must cooperate and we must have American help. . . . We cannot risk crossing you—cannot risk any conflict with you."[16]

As a result of the Western exploitation of China in the preceding hundred years, all Chinese—whether Nationalists or Communists—were strongly anti-foreigner and anti-imperialist. The Communists were even more strongly opposed to those whom they considered to be imperialist powers. The United States was clearly in the imperialist block. For Mao to court the United States ran counter to basic Communist theory. Mao had to find an ideological rationale. He rationalized it by claiming that the liberal elements in the United States were overcoming the reactionary and imperialist elements and that soon the United States would evolve into a more progressive nation.

Mao's approach to the United States was certainly a tactical diversion. On a practical basis, he realized that after the war, the United States would be the dominant power in the Pacific. He also realized that the United States would be one of the few countries whose economies had been strengthened rather than weakened by the war. In pursuit of American favor and assistance, he offered to go to the United States as a representative of a major Chinese political party and talk personally to President Roosevelt.

Whatever insights were gained by the military and diplomatic observers at Yanan were not only lost in Washington, but later, when the Communists triumphed, their reports became the basis of charges of treason for the so-called loss of China. The myth of the loss of China and a "sellout" was to bedevil U.S. policy toward China for the next twenty years. Echoes of it remain today.

With the Japanese surrender, the Nationalist government was to accept the surrender of Japanese troops in China and disarm them. But the Nationalist forces were poorly positioned to do so. Communist forces, in the areas they controlled, began to disarm Japanese. Conflicts with the Nationalists began, and civil war broke out. General George C. Marshall was sent to China with instructions to arrange a cease-fire and reconciliation between the Nationalists and the Communists, leading to a coalition government. Despite herculean efforts, Marshall failed.

The United States has proclaimed that it was neutral in the civil war. Even so, the mythically heroic figure of Chiang Kai-shek, the staunch fighter against the Japanese, the man of the year, the potential savior of China, was a figure in whom much emotional capital had been invested. Americans, and Congress in particular, would not let go. So, while overt military support of the GMD ceased, America continued to provide the GMD with "nonmilitary" trucks, communication equipment, medical supplies, and provisions. An American military advisory group remained with the Nationalists and was authorized, on an informal basis, to provide military advice to the Nationalist government. All of this infuriated the Communists.

With the conclusion of the Battle of Huai-Hai, the decisive battle of the Chinese Civil War, on 10 January 1949, the fate of the Chiang government was sealed. It was not unexpected. In the two years since the failure of General Marshall's attempt to reconcile the GMD with the Chinese Communist Party, it had been clear that the Nationalists would lose. Although the general public in the United States was still unaware of the extent of the Nationalist losses, the State Department was increasingly concerned with the need to come to some sort of terms with Mao Zedong, the Chinese Communist Party, and whatever government they would sooner or later form.

American diplomatic personnel remained at their posts as the victorious People's Liberation Army (PLA) marched southward. In early June of 1949, Consul General O. Edmund Clubb in Beijing was approached in a roundabout fashion by Zhou Enlai, who indicated he was a member of a "liberal" faction seeking ties with the United States. That approach was not followed up. At Nanjing later in June, U.S. ambassador Leighton Stuart was approached with the suggestion that he visit Beijing and confer with Mao and Zhou Enlai. It seemed like a promising possibility for some sort of accommodation with the Communists.

Unfortunately, in the meantime Mao Zedong made his famous "leaning to one side" speech, in which he said there was no middle ground, no neutrality between the socialist and the imperialist nations. China would lean toward the USSR. Stuart was informed by the Communists that the speech was a tactical move and should not interfere with an accommodation with the United States. Plans were made for Stuart's visit, but President Truman ordered him not to go. The Chinese had been rebuffed again.

The decision on whether to let Stuart visit Beijing was complicated by U.S. reaction to the case of Angus Ward, U.S. consul general in Shenyang, who had remained at his post when the Communists entered in November 1948. Initially, Ward was treated cordially by the Reds and recognized as a representative of the U.S. government. Then, on orders of Mao, the Communist authorities terminated any diplomatic treatment of Ward and he became just another displaced American. Later it was charged that Ward was concealing a spy ring. Communist authorities entered his compound and seized his transmitter. Several Chinese members of his household were arrested and Ward was placed under house arrest. On 19 June 1949 he was tried for espionage, convicted, and expelled from the country. Despite U.S. protestations of innocence, there was some basis for the Chinese charges. Ward was cooperating with the U.S. Navy "External Survey Detachment No. 44," which was attached to the Commander, West Pacific. The detachment was a remnant of the intelligence-gathering organization established by Adm. Milton E. Miles during the war. Nevertheless, President Truman was incensed at the treatment of Ward.

Meanwhile, the Communist armies rolled southward, crossing the Yangtze on 20 April. Red troops entered Shanghai on 27 May and by fall were deep into Sichuan Province. On 1 October 1949, Mao proclaimed the establishment of the People's Republic of China in Beijing. By the end of the year, the remaining intact Nationalist forces had withdrawn to Taiwan.

Commencing in late 1949, Communist propaganda became increasingly strident and critical of the United States, which was accused of turning Japan into a permanent American base. The line delineated by MacArthur and Acheson, running through the offshore Asian islands, was a defensive line to Americans. To the Chinese, it was an offensive line, with Japan as its central bastion. American aid to Viet Nam was viewed by the Chinese Communists as an attempt to establish a position from which China could be encircled from the south. The U.S. "defensive line" was far more valuable as a series of bases for offense against the mainland than Taiwan ever would be as a base to threaten the defensive line. The Communist propaganda theme of "encirclement" did have more than just a little substance to it.

Chinese criticism of the United States puzzled Americans. We simply could not conceive of ourselves as evil and aggressive imperialists bent on dominating China. We were the "good guys" fighting for liberty and justice. We were the friends of the Chinese. Hadn't we sent thousands of missionaries to rescue them? It was upsetting. After years of stories about China—the mystery, the adventures of the missionaries, the heroism of China's great leader Chiang Kai-shek—few people could understand how the Chinese could voluntarily embrace godless Communism. How could they say such hateful things about America and Americans?

Few Americans realized that beneath the submissiveness of the rickshaw coolie, the house amah, the shopkeeper, and the compradore lay a smoldering resentment of Western exploitation of China and the Chinese. They regarded the Americans and other foreigners as inferior barbarians, the "long noses." Whereas the overriding American viewpoint was that of a superior toward an inferior and backward culture, the Chinese had exactly the opposite view. They were members of the Middle Kingdom, heirs of an unbroken 5,000 years of recorded history. Most Americans, their attitude based on a romantic, paternalistic, and largely mythical view of China, never understood this.

Then, in January 1950, Mao and Zhou Enlai traveled to Moscow and negotiated a treaty with the Soviet Union. That seemed to end any possibility of a reasonable U.S. relationship with the Chinese. While the United States had worked hard to shore up the eastern flank of our defense against Communism with the Marshall Plan, aid to Greece, and the creation of NATO, the western flank in China had totally collapsed.

From 1947 onward, U.S. policy in the Far East had been based on the assumption that China would fall and that nothing America could do within the reasonable limits of its capabilities would change that. The political problem was how to deal with the Communist takeover and the new government.

The first question was how much of a threat was the Communist takeover of China. Within the U.S. government, there were divergent views of the Chinese Communists. The view that prevailed within the military was that the Chinese Communist Party was not basically different from other Communists. They were Moscow-inspired; they advocated the same policies; they should be regarded as tools of Moscow. This view held Communism to be a monolithic, worldwide movement tightly controlled by Moscow. The military view was that the Communist takeover in China would seriously alter the world balance of forces. In particular, Taiwan was a critical factor. Much of the subsequent internal debate focused on how to deal with Taiwan.

Within the State Department, the viewpoint was somewhat more pragmatic. The State Department realized that the Chinese had many differences with the Soviet Union. For instance, the Soviets had extracted demeaning economic and extraterritorial concessions from Chiang Kai-shek. There were border problems in Manchuria and Xinjiang. Soviet occupation troops had sacked Manchuria and drained it of much of its industrial capacity. It appeared to the State Department that friction between the USSR and China was inevitable. The question was *when*. American policy toward China was to disengage gradually from the losing Nationalists and to do whatever possible to drive a wedge between the Chinese and the Soviets. Acheson argued that the potential friction between the USSR and the PRC was the one important asset we had.

The State Department did not view the "loss" of China as the disaster it appeared to be. Acheson told a congressional committee: "We must not minimize but not exaggerate the magnitude of our reversal. China is not a modern, centralized state. China, even under Communism, cannot be a springboard for attack. The Communists face a morass in China. Until some of the dust and smoke of the disaster clear away we must wait and see if there is a foundation on which to build."[17]

In his *Memoirs,* George F. Kennan put it a somewhat more pithy way: ". . . in any war of the foreseeable future China could at best be a weak ally or at worse an inconsequential enemy."[18]

Attempting to put the situation in China in perspective, the State Department published a White Paper on 5 August 1949. It described the background of our attempts to shore up the GMD, the corruption and incompetence that hindered that effort, and the inevitability of the Communist takeover. The White Paper was immediately criticized as an excuse for a "do-nothing" policy. General Patrick Hurley, a former ambassador to China, fanned the flames of the growing concern over possible internal subversion in the government by calling it " . . . a smooth alibi for the Pro-Communists in the State Department who had engineered the overthrow of our ally, the Nationalist Government of the Republic of China, and aided in the Communist conquest of China."[19]

Taiwan (Formosa)

Both the State and the Defense Departments realized that little could be done about China. Taiwan was another matter. Something *could* be done about Taiwan before it was too late. Time appeared to be crucial. It was understood that Taiwan was considered an integral part of China. It had been ceded to Japan by the Treaty of Shimonoseki after the Chinese lost the Sino-Japanese War of 1895. It was reoccupied by the Nationalists at the end of World War II. By late 1949, it appeared that large PLA contingents were assembling in eastern China, preparing to invade Taiwan.

General MacArthur and some conservative politicians argued that, strategically, Taiwan was a break, a salient, in the defensive perimeter the United States had established in the western Pacific. In hostile hands, it would provide a platform from which hostile ships and aircraft could dominate the Philippines, the Ryukyu Islands, and the sea lanes between Japan and southeast Asia. If Mao was a Soviet puppet, Taiwan could be used to extend Soviet power well into the Pacific.

But not everyone agreed with the importance of Taiwan as a vital link in the defensive chain. In the hands of the Chinese, it would extend the range of their aircraft only, at the very most, another 200 to 250 miles, most of that over open sea. It did potentially bring them closer to a position to dominate the Philippines. There were better locations for airfields and naval bases there than on the South China coast. On the other hand, as a location from which to threaten China, it had much greater value. Bases there would extend the range of friendly aircraft as much as 500 miles deeper into Chinese territory. In conjunction with existing bases in Japan, Korea, and Okinawa, it would enable friendly aircraft to completely dominate the major industrial areas and communication lines of China. However stated, the value of Taiwan was much greater as an offensive base than it was as part of a defensive line.

The military was in favor of doing whatever could be done to shore up the GMD defenses and prevent a Communist seizure of Taiwan. The Joint Chiefs recommended sending a survey team. General MacArthur in the Far East was enthusiastically in favor of assisting Taiwan—a locale about which he was particularly sensitive. It was from Taiwan that the Japanese launched the air strikes that caught the bulk of American aircraft on the ground in the Philippines in December 1941.

Opinion was mixed in the State Department. Dean Rusk, the newly appointed assistant secretary for Far Eastern affairs, felt that the fall of Taiwan would put increasing pressure on Southeast Asian countries. Acheson did not feel Taiwan was crucial, nor did he believe Mao was a puppet of the USSR.

The question was examined by the National Security Council. On 30 December 1949, the council produced NSC-48/2, which concluded that the United States had no interest in Taiwan. The Joint Chiefs agreed that the strategic importance of Taiwan did not justify overt military action. On 5 January 1950, President Truman issued a statement saying that no military aid would be given to Taiwan. No military forces were to be used and no designs or special privileges were to be requested. He emphasized that the U.S. government would not pursue a course that would lead to involvement in the civil conflict in China. The matter did not end there, however. Congress exerted intense pressure to come to the aid of Taiwan.

Domestic Concerns
Concern about the Communist advances on the world scene was reflected by similar concerns about Communism in domestic affairs. The revelations by Igor Guzenko in 1945 of Soviet spying in Canada were startling. In the next few years, a series of security breaches rocked the nation. Julius and Ethel Rosenberg were accused, tried, convicted, and executed for giving atomic secrets to the Soviets. Klaus Fuchs, a respected British atomic scientist, was arrested and confessed to giving atomic secrets to the USSR. His colleague Alan Nunn May was also arrested and convicted for the same offense. Alger Hiss, the prototypical eastern establishment model holding a very responsible position in the State Department, was accused of being a Communist. He was eventually convicted on a charge of perjury only because the statute of limitations on espionage had expired. The "loss of China" and the explosion of a Soviet atom bomb in October 1949 aroused suspicion of treachery in high places.

A witch hunt ensued. The author recalls receiving, in a class at the Army intelligence school, a list of some hundred or so well-known Americans who were believed to be either Communists or fellow travelers. In the long run, the list proved to be vastly inflated. Nevertheless, the Venona Project, release of decoded messages from Soviet agents during World War II, has shown that there were more than has been heretofore admitted.

The fear of subversion focused on the State Department, which was beset with internal security investigations. Senate hearings were held. An obscure senator from Wisconsin, Joseph McCarthy, shocked the nation in a speech in Wheeling, West Virginia, where he held up a paper and said, "Right here in my hand I have the names of 253

Communists in government." McCarthy's charge was fraudulent, but the fear of subversion was real.

Americans reacted viscerally to the Communist victory in China. There was a great uproar from what became known as the "China lobby" about the "loss of China." The group claimed that the Nationalists led by Chiang Kai-shek were such staunch and determined defenders of China that their defeat could only have come about through some form of treachery.

Attention focused on that small number of men in the State Department, the "China hands," who had extensive experience in China and firsthand experience with the Chinese Communists; some had participated in the Dixie Mission. They had written objective reports on the strength of the Communist movement and the Red Army—reports that events proved to have been entirely correct. Because they had recommended reaching accommodation with the Chinese Communists they were suspected of bias, or worse. Security investigations concentrated on them, and some endured security reviews several times. As a result, by the outbreak of the Korean War, when their expertise would have been useful in evaluating the Chinese intentions, most of them had been discredited, discharged, shunted off into inconsequential posts, or simply ignored.

Remobilization?

The explosion of a Soviet atomic bomb on 1 September 1949, and the proclamation of the People's Republic of China (PRC) a month later, spurred reexamination of American foreign policy. In January 1950, President Truman authorized work to proceed on the hydrogen bomb. Coincidentally, with that decision he instructed the secretaries of defense and state to review American diplomatic objectives and their effects upon our strategic plans.

The result of that review was NSC-68, presented to the president on 1 April 1950 and approved by him, with reservations, the following week. It recommended an immediate and large-scale buildup of our military and general strength and that of our allies. Its intent was to right the power balance in the hope that through means other than all-out war, we could induce a change in the nature of the Soviet system. NSC-68 was not immediately implemented. President

Truman wanted estimates of its cost. He was not buying any "pig in a poke."

There were other reservations. Would rearmament provoke the USSR? Would it weaken the economy? Pending implementation of the recommendations, Secretary of Defense Louis Johnson continued to slash away at the strength of the armed forces. At the same time, the services and the Joint Chiefs were attempting, for the first time in American history, to prepare a budget for a military force that would support American foreign policy.

Increasing Tension in Korea

Since the founding of the Democratic People's Republic of Korea (DPRK) in September 1948, Kim Il Sung had sought support from his Soviet sponsors for the reunification of Korea by force. In China, Mao Zedong concurrently sought Joseph Stalin's support for the invasion of Taiwan. Stalin was reluctant to assist either effort. Both ventures would improve his strategic position and further isolate China and Korea from the United States, but Stalin feared provoking an American declaration of war. In visits to Moscow in the fall of 1949 and the spring of 1950, however, Kim succeeded in convincing Stalin that, with the support of a huge South Korean block of sympathizers, he could attack and conquer South Korea before the United States could mobilize to help. Stalin gave his consent, contingent on approval by Mao.[20] It has to be considered one of Stalin's most interesting missteps, approving an attack at the one place in the world where the United States had significant troop strength close at hand. Just across the Tsushima Strait in Japan were four U.S. infantry divisions—far from ready, but available nevertheless.

Relations between the new PRC and the DPRK were ambivalent. There was a Chinese trade mission in Pyongyang but no Chinese embassy until August 1950. The Chinese resented Soviet influence in North Korea. Historically, Korea was within the Chinese sphere of influence. From medieval times until 1905, when it was occupied by the Japanese, Korea had been a buffer and a satellite state of China. The Chinese had a keen appreciation of Korea's value as an avenue of approach.

North Korea had been of immense help to the Chinese Red Army during the civil war. In the Manchurian campaigns, Red Army units had withdrawn into the sanctuary of North Korea on a number of occasions. Sinuiju, just across the Yalu River from Manchuria, had been a supply base for Lin Biao's armies. A large number of North Koreans had volunteered to fight with the Chinese in the civil war. So when Kim Il Sung asked the Chinese to return those volunteers, they were sent back to form a part of the North Korean Army.

In May 1950, Kim visited Beijing and obtained Mao's reluctant consent. Although Mao was not enthusiastic, he felt Kim was due fraternal support of a fellow revolutionary. In the discussions, Mao asked Kim if he wanted the Chinese to send troops to the Sino-Korean border if the Americans became involved. Kim told him it would not be necessary. The war would be over within a month and the Americans could not deploy troops before that. There is some belief that Mao agreed to provide assistance if the Japanese became involved.

As preparations for the North Korean attack progressed, Chinese resentment was sharpened by the Soviet and North Korean efforts to conceal from them preparations for the attack on South Korea. In the North Korean Communist Party, in the NKPA, and in the government apparatus were a large number of Koreans who had served in China. During the planning for the attack on South Korea, these "Chinese sympathizers" were isolated and excluded from the preparations.[21] Such efforts went as far as shipping Soviet materiel to North Korea by sea to avoid alerting the Chinese by using railroads through China.

In the years of the U.S. occupation, the Korean Liaison Office had been established. This was the cover name for covert operations into North Korea. When the U.S. troop withdrawal from Korea was complete, Korea was deleted from the area of responsibility of the Far Eastern Command (FEC). But the Korean Liaison Office was maintained, and the FEC continued to monitor the intelligence situation in Korea.

In December 1949, Maj. Gen. Charles A.Willoughby, Far Eastern Command G-2, reported that in his opinion the North Koreans might be ready to act by April or May 1950, because, "with the conclusion of the Chinese Communist campaign in China more troops and supplies could then be made available." But by 15 March he had changed his mind. He foresaw continued guerrilla and psychological war in Korea but stated: "There will be no civil war in Korea this spring or summer."[22] In the Pentagon, the Army G-2, Maj. Gen. Alexander Bolling, echoed this sentiment with an estimate: "Communist military measures in Korea will be held in abeyance pending the outcome of their programs in other areas, particularly Southeast Asia."[23]

As was to be the case later in the war, those speculative and reassuring opinions did not reflect the observations and concerns of the officers on the ground. Captain Joseph Darrigo was the KMAG adviser with the 12th ROK Regiment stationed at Kaesong. In his sector, there had been a continuous string of border incidents from January to early May of 1950. Then they dropped off sharply. North Korean civilians were being evacuated from the border zone. He noticed that information on the North Korean Army showed them to be disposed not on line in a defensive formation but in depth in three major avenues of approach. Then, in June, the North Koreans launched a peace offensive, an effort to convene a constituent assembly in Pyongyang to discuss unification of Korea. Darrigo thought this might be a cover for wartime deployment. His warning reports went unheeded.[24]

Selective, after-the-fact analysis is easy. Not so easy is picking out the significant bits of information from a confusing background of conflicting reports. The command had been saturated with so many reports and alarms; living that close to the edge, all had become desensitized to the threat. Still, there were steps an alert command could have taken to clarify the situation. There is no indication this was done.

So, at 3:30 A.M. on Sunday, 25 June 1950, when seven North Korean divisions, supported by 150 tanks, came thundering across the border in a full-scale invasion, ROK forces and their U.S. Army advisers were caught flat-footed.

In his memoirs, Rusk says the "North Korean invasion came as a complete surprise. Only four days before I had told a congressional committee we saw no evidence of war brewing in Korea." Rusk went on to say that after the attack, some intelligence people thumbed through thousands of bits of information and put together six or seven items that seemed to point to invasion. They wanted to be able to say, "We warned you. . . . That was just damned nonsense."[25]

With the threats abroad and the suspicion verging on hysteria at home, the president and his government were hypersensitive to the advance of Communism and fearful of being considered appeasers. Another Munich was unthinkable. With the North Korean attack, it was time to take a stand.

Notes

1. John Lewis Gaddis, "The Defensive Perimeter Concept," in Dorothy Borg and Waldo Heinrichs, eds., *Uncertain Years: Chinese-American Relations, 1947–1950* (New York: Columbia University Press, 1980), 67–68.

2. David Rees, *Korea: The Limited War* (New York: St. Martin's, 1964), 70.

3. Borg and Heinrichs, *Uncertain Years,* 114n.

4. Quoted in Samuel B. Griffith, *The Chinese People's Liberation Army* (New York: McGraw-Hill, 1968), 111.

5. Quoted in David Rees, *The Limited War,* 56.

6. James F. Schnabel, *Policy and Direction: The First Year.* U.S. Army in the Korean War Series (Washington, D.C.: Center of Military History, U.S. Army, 1988), 43–44.

7. Dean Rusk, *As I Saw It: Dean Rusk as Told to Richard Rusk,* ed. Daniel S. Papps (New York: W.W. Norton, 1990), 124.

8. Borg and Heinrichs, *Uncertain Years,* 103–4.

9. Ibid.

10. Ibid., 104.

11. Ibid., 105.

12. Ibid., 106.

13. Dean Acheson, *Present at the Creation: My Years in the State Department* (New York: W.W. Norton, 1969), 357.

14. Borg and Heinrichs, *Uncertain Years,* 106.

15. William Sebald, *With MacArthur in Japan: A Personal History of the Occupation* (New York: W.W. Norton, 1965).

16. John Stuart Service, *Lost Chance in China: The World War II Despatches of John S. Service,* ed. Joseph W. Esherick (New York: Random House, 1974), 307.

17. Acheson, *Present at the Creation,* 198.

18. George F. Kennan, *Memoirs: 1950–1963* (Boston: Little, Brown, 1972), 47.

19. Acheson, *Present at the Creation,* 196.

20. Sergei N. Goncharov, John W. Lewis, and Xue Litai, *Uncertain Partners: Stalin, Mao and the Korean War* (Palo Alto, Calif.: Stanford University Press, 1993), 136–48.

21. Ibid., 147.

22. Charles A. Willoughby and John Chamberlain, *MacArthur: 1941–1951* (New York: McGraw-Hill, 1954), 352.

23. Clay Blair, *The Forgotten War: America in Korea, 1950–1953* (New York: Random House, 1987), 58.

24. Ibid., 58, quoting correspondence and interviews with Darrigo.

25. Rusk, *As I Saw It,* 124.

2
Prewar: The Chinese Situation

Today the Chinese people stood up!
—Mao Zedong, 1 October 1949,
proclaiming the People's Republic of China

Mao Zedong's declaration establishing the People's Republic of China (PRC) reflected the bitterness with which many Chinese viewed the hundred years of Western intrusion into and exploitation of China. For many Chinese, the period from 1840 to 1949 was the "century of shame." Chinese intervention in the Korean War was a product of many factors—partly in support of another Communist state, partly out of concern for its own borders, but most of all due to the mistrust of Western powers, particularly the United States, resulting from Western domination of China. The very origin and growth of the Communist Party in China came about as a way of ridding China of foreign exploitation and bringing the country into the modern age. The depth of Chinese resentment of foreign influence has never been well understood in the West, particularly in the United States.

A review of the situation from the Chinese perspective is instructive.

Turmoil in China
In the early days of the nineteenth century, China offered the last great chance for colonial acquisition. Until the arrival of the Western traders, China had been secure in its isolation. It was the Middle Kingdom, the center of the Asian world, entitled to respect and tribute from lesser Asian powers. With a highly refined culture but technologically primitive, China was no match for Western military power. When war between the British and the Chinese broke out in

1840 over arguments about opium trading, China proved vulnerable. In the next seventy-five years, the British and then the French, Germans, Russians, and Japanese each in turn negotiated more and more unequal treaties demanding ever-increasing concessions. Missionaries arriving to save the Chinese from their heathen ways also demanded special rights for themselves and their converts. Americans, to their credit, never demanded special concessions for themselves. Instead, they simply piggybacked on the privileges of other nations under the Open Door policy and the "most-favored nation" agreements.

Threatened without and crumbling within, the Manchu dynasty, ruling China since 1662, began to fail. The power of the dynasty, weakened by the foreign demands, was further sapped by the nineteenth-century Taiping Rebellion, which lasted eight years and cost more than twenty million lives. The ignominious defeat of Chinese armies in 1894 by the Japanese weakened the Manchus still further. The dynasty was brought to the edge of collapse by repercussions from the Boxer Rebellion, an ill-advised attempt in 1900 by the "Righteous Harmony Fists" to kill or drive out all foreigners. Hasty attempts at reform came too late.

In 1911, the Manchus were overthrown by a combination of military leaders and Sun Yat-sen's Guomindang Party. The Republic of China was declared but failed. Military leader Yuan Shih-kai was elected president, after which he seized total power and disbanded the elected parliament. Under the leadership of military forces, several provinces declared their independence, initiating the age of the warlords. With the start of World War I, Japan seized German interests in Shandong (Shan-tung). China, in chaos internally, was on the verge of dismemberment.

The outbreak of World War I offered hope of regaining some of the sovereignty lost through the unequal treaties. In 1917, China declared war against the central powers. As belligerents, the Chinese hoped to gain at the peace table. Those hopes were dashed when it was learned on 4 May 1919 that U.S. president Woodrow Wilson, reneging on his principle of self-determination, agreed to award the German concession in Shandong to the Japanese. Rioting against the United States broke out in Beijing, Shanghai, and other cities.

The May 4th Movement was born, renewing efforts to free China from the burden of unequal treaties. Action proceeded along two main avenues. The Guomindang (GMD) movement, led by Sun Yat-sen, was the strongest group, initially offering the most promising road to the "New China." Another, smaller group had been impressed by the Russian Revolution of 1917 and thought that Communism might provide a way to arouse the people and rehabilitate China. The Chinese Communist Party (CCP) was formed and grew rapidly.

Initially, the Communists and the Guomindang cooperated. The Communists joined the GMD base in Canton, took part in recruiting and training officers for the GMD Army, and participated in party affairs. When Sun Yat-sen died in 1925, he was succeeded by Chiang Kai-shek. In 1927, with help from the Communists, Chiang began a military offensive northward from Canton in an effort to defeat the warlords and reunite the country. Shanghai was taken with the help of a Communist-led uprising of workers. But then Chiang turned on the Communists and unleashed the "White Terror." Some, such as the workers who had aided his entry into the city, were shot down in the streets. Others, with the help of Chiang's friends in the Greens, Shanghai's criminal syndicate, were hunted down, arrested, and executed. It has been estimated that as many as three-fourths of the Communists and their sympathizers were killed. Some of the survivors went underground and remained in Shanghai, but many, including Zhou Enlai, fled to the countryside.

The Rise of Communist Power

A small and tattered group, survivors of failed Communist attempts at insurrection, formed around Mao Zedong in the remote Jinggang Mountains (Jinggangshan) on the border between Hunan and Jiangxi Provinces. That group in 1927 began the twenty-two-year effort that would bring the Communist Party to power in China. Over the next seven years, Mao Zedong's tiny band grew into the sovereign Central Soviet, which, by 1934, governed more than three million people and fielded an army of more than 80,000 men.

Initially, the small Communist enclave offered no more threat to the Chiang Kai-shek government than other small bandit groups. By

1930, however, Chiang considered it sufficiently dangerous to begin the first of four "bandit extermination" campaigns. In all four, the Red Army—poorly armed and equipped but with willing soldiers led by Zhu Deh, Peng Dehuai, and Zhou Enlai—used imaginative leadership, mobile tactics, and the advantage of interior lines to ambush and drive back the Nationalist armies.

By the summer of 1934, Chiang had encircled the Central Soviet under a new plan that the Communists realized might succeed. They abandoned the Central Soviet, broke through the encirclement, and started westward with 80,000 troops. Thus began the Long March, one of the most remarkable military feats in history.

Commencing in October 1934, the Red Army marched and fought for 8,000 miles, moving west and north through China. A year later, they reached their objective, a small Communist base in northern Shaanxi Province, with 10,000 men. Only 4,000 of those who started the previous fall reached their goal. They had fought fifteen major engagements, had averaged one skirmish per day, and had marched for 235 days and 18 nights of the 367 days en route. It was a truly remarkable feat that became a legendary example to all future Communist soldiers. A cynic referred to it as the longest armed propaganda tour in history. What the histories of the Long March do not report, however, is the totally merciless way in which the sick and wounded were left behind to a grim fate at the hands of the pursuing Nationalist troops.[1]

By the end of the march, Mao Zedong had emerged as the dominant figure in the CCP. Again the Communists had taken severe losses, but now troops from other scattered and smaller Soviets joined the main body. The Communists concentrated at Yanan (Yenan) in the loess hills of Shaanxi Province, established a base there, settled in, organized training programs, and began building anew. Soon Nationalist forces began closing about them. By late 1936, Chiang's preparations were well under way for what was expected to be the final "bandit extermination" campaign.

After securing most of Manchuria in 1931, the Japanese began extending their control into Mongolia and the provinces of northern China. Chiang was reluctant to fight the Japanese, preferring to deal with the Communists first. To Chiang, the Japanese were a disease of the skin; the Communists were a disease of the heart. But an aroused public demanded action to halt the Japanese. When Chiang arrived in Xian in late 1936 to oversee the start of the final "bandit extermination" campaign, he was arrested by some of his officers, forced to call off the campaign, and forced to agree to form a united front with the Communists to fight the Japanese. The Chinese Red Army became the 8th Route Army of the National Government.

The possibility of a unified national effort alarmed the Japanese. On 7 July 1937, Japan launched a full-scale invasion of China, seizing as a pretext a minor clash between Japanese troops and local militia near the Marco Polo Bridge just outside Beijing. By the end of 1938, Japan controlled the major ports, cities, and lines of communication along the coasts and rivers of China, basically the eastern third of the country.

Secure in their remote and backward Yanan base for the next eleven years, the Communists devoted their efforts toward growing and strengthening, expanding the areas under their control, and preparing for the struggle with the GMD that would come with the defeat of Japan. It was a rich and productive time for the Communists.

A significant effort that escaped the notice of Western observers at the time was the "sinification" of the Chinese Communist Party. At Rujin in the Central Soviet, Mao had been shunted aside and placed under virtual house arrest by Moscow-oriented members who followed often inappropriate and occasionally disastrous advice from Moscow. He determined to "rectify" this situation. In a series of party-rectification movements, he strengthened his hold on the party, distanced the CCP from Moscow, and wrote his own interpretation of Karl Marx as it applied to conditions in China.[2] Moscow-oriented members were eased to the side. By the time of the Seventh Party Congress in April 1945, he had gained tight control of the party. "Thought of Mao" was accepted as the ideology of the Chinese Revolution.

Significant amounts of Mao's time at Yanan were spent developing and writing a theory of military affairs and a conceptual framework for the future. He wrote several treatises on warfare, including *On Protracted War* and *Problems of Strategy in China's Revolutionary War.*

The central question in most of these was, How could a weak force defeat a strong force? The answer, Mao concluded, lay in the moral force. Properly indoctrinated and motivated, men who had an ideal to fight for could overcome materiel superiority. The man-versus-machine philosophy permeated Chinese military thinking then, during the Korean War, and for many years afterward.

Advancing Japanese forces had uprooted millions of people, many ready and willing to fight back. Early successes against the Japanese raised the stature of the Communists. From among this wave of refugees, thousands of eager and idealistic young Chinese made their way to Yanan. Many went into the army. But the most promising were selected to be trained as Communist cadres at the military political university at Yanan. Those from eighteen to twenty-four were considered most desirable candidates, because they were the most receptive to intensive indoctrination. But anyone was qualified as long as he was resolute in resisting Japan and had some schooling. There were many college students in exile from Beijing, as well as some experienced fighters from the ranks of the army.

In training the new cadres, the Communists perfected the *chen feng* method of ideological remolding, known in the West as "brainwashing." The technique was an adaptation of methods used in Russia, but its widespread application was a unique Chinese contribution to political control. In years to come, "ideological remolding," or "thought reform," was applied in one degree of intensity or another to nearly everyone within the People's Republic of China. It was the key to Communist success in gaining control of the country.

The *chen feng* method created intense pressure to read and memorize huge amounts of material, coupled with group confession and criticism. Successfully applied, it resulted in a complete remolding of the subject's outlook. It produced dedicated cadres to perform the political work needed to rouse the "masses." Variations of the procedure were applied to army recruits, to army officers, to "reactionary" citizens, and to prisoners of war. Its use in the Korean War to indoctrinate American POWs caused great concern. Since those days, the techniques have been refined and employed not only in China but also in other countries. Doctor Robert J. Lifton, an American psychiatrist who studied the technique for years, says it might be "the most dangerous direction of the Twentieth Century mind—the quest for absolute or 'totalistic' belief systems."

The curriculum of the military political university included military subjects and political theory coupled with intense indoctrination. From the schools, well-indoctrinated cadres fanned out from Yanan, infiltrated through the thinly held areas behind the Japanese lines, and went to work organizing the villages, recruiting soldiers, expanding the base area, and building new base areas.

From 1927 through 1934, during the Long March and the early days at Yanan, the Communists had developed a set of finely honed procedures for organizing the villages and winning over the "masses"—the Chinese peasants. As a straightforward political proposition, the Communist message was appealing, a sure winner. Basically, the Communists offered more to more people than the GMD offered. Chiang and the GMD bet their future on the money interests. Mao and the CCP bet on the masses. The sheer numbers of the masses outweighed the money interests.

The Communist message was moderate, emphasizing its relation to the ideals of Sun Yat-sen and his three people's principles. It stressed nationalism and an appeal to the patriotism of all Chinese in the fight against the Japanese. Hatred of the Japanese was universal. Peasants, landlords, local gentry, and intellectuals all responded to that appeal.

Village councils, dominated previously by the landlords and gentry, were reformed to include the peasants. Slyly, the "rule of three" was followed. Membership would be one-third Communist, one-third GMD, and one-third representatives of other independent parties, although it was carefully structured to ensure Communist control. Of course, voting privilege was offered only to the "people," not to "reactionaries." For the first time in their history, the peasants had a voice.

So as to not offend the landlords and rich peasants whose support was needed, initially only a mild sort of land reform was adopted. The Reds cleverly carried out a promise the GMD had made to reduce rent and interest—a promise the GMD had not fulfilled. Landlords and money lenders received less money, but the Communists guaranteed they would be paid. Any overeager cadres who advocated or initiated confiscation of land were punished as "left-leaning de-viationists." Nie Rongzhen, who was successful in developing new So-viet areas, described the tactics as "Eat the beef or milk the cow."[3] Holding back on land reform gave the peasants something now and something to look forward to in the future.

Theodore White, at that time a reporter for both *Time* and *Life* magazines, understood the appeal Communism had for the average peasant:[4]

> If you take a peasant who has been swindled, beaten, and kicked about for all his waking days and whose father has trans-mitted to him an emotion of bitterness reaching back for gen-erations—if you take such a peasant, treat him like a man, ask his opinion, let him vote for a local government, let him orga-nize his own police and gendarmes, decide on his own taxes and interest—if you do all that, the peasant becomes a man who has something to fight for, and he will fight to preserve it against any enemy, Japanese or Chinese. If in addition you present the peasant with an army and a government that helps him harvest, teaches him to read and write, and fight off the Japanese who raped his wife and tortured his mother, he develops a loyalty to the army and the government and to the party that controls them. He votes for that party, thinks the way that party wants him to think, and in many cases becomes an active participant.

Despite the shortage of personnel and the counterinsurgency ef-forts of the Japanese, the number and sizes of the liberated areas grew. As early as 1940, the British ambassador, Clark Kerr, was con-vinced the Communists would win. American military and diplo-matic officers were not convinced for several more years.

Four years later, there were a total of fourteen active base areas—five in northern China, eight in central China, and one on Hainan Island. The Communists controlled between 20 and 30 percent of the area and population of China. From the few thousand men Mao had on arrival in Shaanxi in 1935, the Red Army grew to 156,000 by 1938. Six years later, it had reached a strength of nearly 400,000. By the summer of 1945, the Red Army was estimated to have a total strength of about 800,000.

The Civil War

Neither the Nationalists nor the Communists were prepared for the sudden and unexpected end of the war on 14 August 1945, but the Communists reacted more quickly. Most of the Nationalist armies were in south and central China, poorly positioned to accept the surrender of the bulk of the Japanese Army, which was in northern China and Manchuria. The Communists were strongest in north China and in position to interdict the rail movement of Nationalist forces into Beijing and Manchuria. Clashes occurred between Nationalist and Communist. Sustained fighting broke out. The civil war that nearly everyone had anticipated began.

The key areas in the civil war were Manchuria and north China. Soviet troops in Manchuria accepted the surrender of Japanese forces there and disarmed them. Because Communist guerrillas blocked the northward rail movement of Nationalist troops, Chiang was forced to ask the Soviets to remain until American sea and air transportation could move sufficient Nationalist forces to Manchuria. The United States responded. By April 1946, the Nationalists believed they were strong enough for the Soviets to withdraw.

Meanwhile, Lin Biao and 20,000 guerrillas infiltrated northward into Manchuria and began recruiting in the countryside. Lin had time to build his army and arm it with captured Japanese weapons provided by the USSR. When the Nationalists finally arrived, he was ready to battle them. Full-scale fighting between Lin Biao and the Nationalists began when the Soviet forces were withdrawn. For two and a half years, the campaign in Manchuria surged back and forth, but by October 1948, a Communist offensive had isolated Shenyang (Mukden) and forced its surrender. Manchuria was lost. Into this failed effort Chiang Kai-shek had poured 400,000 men, his U.S.-trained and -armed units, the best he had. He lost them all.

General George Marshall was sent to China by President Truman in an effort to halt the fighting and bring about a coalition government. Several truces were arranged but failed. Chiang Kai-shek by that time realized that if he agreed to the Communist terms for a coalition government, they would soon overpower the Guomindang. Both Chiang and Mao decided to submit the future of China to a trial of arms. General Marshall was withdrawn.

With Manchuria secure, the PLA moved south. November 1948 saw the beginning of the Battle of Huai-Hai, the climactic battle of the civil war. It occurred along the Longhai Railroad, centered on Xuzhou (Suchow). Zhu Deh concentrated here 600,000 men of the Red Army, now known as the People's Liberation Army (PLA). The Nationalist force initially was about the same size. Additional GMD reinforcements were thrown in as the battle progressed. More than two million peasants were mobilized to supply the PLA. In a sixty-five-day campaign, the Nationalist defenders were shattered. More than 600,000 men were lost through death or surrender. Entire armies defected. Half the strength of the Nationalist Army was gone.[5] By April, the PLA was across the Yangtze River and moving south. Chiang withdrew to Taiwan with portions of his armies.

Defeat of the Nationalist armies was attributed more to loss of morale, corruption, and inept leadership than it was to the fighting qualities of the Red Army. General David G. Barr, then military adviser to Chiang Kai-shek, reported: "Their [the Nationalists'] military debacles in my opinion can all be attributed to the world's worst leadership and many other morale destroying factors that can lead to a complete loss of will to fight. The complete ineptness of high military leaders and the widespread corruption and dishonesty throughout the Armed Forces, could, in some measure, have been controlled and directed had the above authority and facilities been available."[6]

At the start of the Korean War, Barr's view was widely held in the U.S. Army. With a few exceptions, it was believed that the Red Chinese were not much better fighters than the Nationalists had been.[7]

The People's Republic
While the PLA continued heading southward, Mao commenced preparations to organize a government. To give the new government a veneer of legitimacy, he convened a People's Political Consultative Conference with 662 representatives. It was made up of a cross-section of political groups, GMD excepted, but with the Communists in firm control. On 1 October 1949, the People's Republic of China was proclaimed. The first phase of the revolution was complete. Mao Zedong declared, "Today the Chinese people stood up!"

Few revolutionaries in history had fought so long and hard and endured such privation as had the Chinese Communists. At the center was a tight, tested, and dedicated group, all in agreement and all accustomed to working together. The twenty-two-year fight had shaped their views and formed them into a determined, disciplined, and absolutely merciless team.

A basic aim of the Communists, as it had been of the Guomindang under Sun Yat-sen and Chiang Kai-shek, was to expunge all traces of foreign concessions and unfair treaties that had been wrung from China during the "epoch of national shame." Zhou Enlai stated the viewpoint succinctly in a speech in which he said China had been exploited economically and polluted politically.

Monumental tasks faced the new government. The economy was in shambles. There were still as many as 400,000 Nationalist guerrillas at large in the southern provinces. The PLA had swollen to immense size by absorbing defecting and surrendering Nationalists. Although it represented a rich source of labor needed in the country, it also was a potential counterrevolutionary force. And it was badly in need of reorganization and modernization.

Mao's great concern was to carry the revolution through to the end. He realized that revolutions were vulnerable at this very point. With victory in hand, there would be a tendency to relax. Men who had faced battlefield bullets might be tempted and suborned by flattery and "sugar bullets." Victory was heady, but only half complete. The total transformation of Chinese society still lay ahead.

In foreign affairs, the long-term goal of the new regime was to restore China to its rightful place in the world, to its historical position as the Middle Kingdom. This article of faith rested on the conviction that China was unique, its countless people destined for world-power status.

It was in pursuit of the goal of reestablishing China's "rightful place" in world affairs that theory overcame reality. In reality, the basic economic and military backwardness of China was a huge obstacle to the goal of re-creating national wealth and power. Nevertheless, party theory outlined a road to leadership in Asia.

In theory, China's successful revolution would inspire other Asian nations and provide a model for others to follow. China would become the center of the East Asian revolutionary movement, regaining its status as a central power in Asia. Theory had it that the United States had historically been hostile to revolutionary movements and was especially hostile, and growing more so, to Communist movements. Sooner or later, theory dictated, this would lead to conflict with the United States, which, as "head of the reactionary forces" in the world, would resort to desperate means to prevent such changes in Asia. Conflict was inevitable.

Among the many objectives of the new government was the recovery of Taiwan—a source of shame ever since it was wrested from China at the end of the Sino-Japanese War of 1894. Mao wanted it back. He considered the reconquest of Taiwan to be the last campaign of the civil war.

Relations with the United States

Soon after the opening of the United Front in 1936, a trickle of adventurous journalists began to arrive in Yanan. The Red leadership took great care to make the best possible impression. Mao and his senior officers were interviewed and the reporters came away impressed with what the Communists had accomplished. Edgar Snow was one of these. When he returned to the United States and wrote his complimentary book *Red Star Over China,* he was promptly tagged as a fellow traveler and Communist sympathizer.

Although reporters had been to Yanan, official military and diplomatic observers had not. In the summer of 1944, the Dixie Mission arrived. Mao's efforts in courting the Dixie Mission were not entirely deceptive. In the theoretical framework within which Mao was proceeding, the immediate goal was "new democracy"—an intermediate stage, a coalition of various parties, dominated by the Communists. That intermediate period, which might last as long as ten years, was needed to rebuild the Chinese economy, industrialize, and raise the living standards of the people. Only then, according to theory, could China be transformed into a true Communist regime. To reach this stage would require foreign funding. Communist dogma identified the United States as the foremost among the reactionary imperialist regimes of the world. Still, Mao was flexible enough not to let dogma interfere with the practicality of day-to-day tactics. He knew he would need foreign help and Russia would not likely be in a position to give it to him. John Stuart Service, a foreign-service officer with the Dixie Mission, believed and so reported that the Chinese Communist Party (CCP) was sincere in the desire for friendly relations with the United States: "This does not preclude their turning back toward Soviet Russia if they are forced to in order to survive an American supported Kuomintang attack."[8] Service was not the only one with this view. Nearly the entire diplomatic mission to China, as well as many of the military officers there, felt the same way.

General Patrick Hurley, a former secretary of war, had been sent to China at Chiang's request to act as President Franklin Roosevelt's special representative. Hurley's task was to get the Communists and Nationalists to cooperate. After initially viewing the Communists favorably, he took a strong pro-Nationalist line.

As the leader of a major Chinese political faction, Mao wanted to go to the United States and confer with President Roosevelt, so he asked the Dixie Mission to send a message to that effect. Hurley disapproved the request and warned Roosevelt that disloyal Americans had joined the Communists in a conspiracy against Chiang and Roosevelt. Hurley grew to regard all military and diplomatic officers offering information or opinions contrary to his as disloyal. In early 1945, he ordered the Dixie Mission terminated and all participants withdrawn.

In February 1945, the diplomatic delegation in Chongqing, in Hurley's absence, prepared a lengthy report reviewing the situation. The report stated that the Communists had concluded that the United States would support the GMD exclusively. The report predicted that chaos and civil war would result if present policies were continued. It recommended that aid be given to the CCP, that the Supreme War Council include members of the CCP, and that the Red Army be integrated into the war effort under U.S. command.

Despite increasing internal disorder in the GMD areas, the U.S. commitment to Chiang and the GMD stiffened. Given America's emotional and political commitment to China, policy reappraisal at this point was too painful to contemplate. Mao felt as if he had been rebuffed. If he had reason to be distrustful of the Soviets, the rebuff of his travel request and the withdrawal of the Dixie Mission gave him ample reason to be distrustful of the United States. By July 1945, Mao had given up hope of U.S. goodwill or assistance. He was reported to be saying, "Since I have been able to fight Japan with these few rusty rifles, I can fight the Americans too. The first step is to get rid of Hurley, then we'll see."[9]

Was this our missed opportunity in China? The question has bothered scholars and policymakers alike.[10] The prevailing opinion is that maintaining liaison and direct communication with the CCP then and in the subsequent years would have been of benefit to both. Potential conflict between the United States and China has been described as conflict between two countries with imperfect views of each other. Whatever communication might have been possible would certainly have improved the view each had of the other. As will be seen, in years to follow the Communists did make some gesture toward arranging some communication.

O. Edmund Clubb, then the U.S. consul general in Beijing, pointed out later that the United States was overly concerned with diplomatic legitimacy in not maintaining some contact with the Communists while recognizing the GMD. The Soviets, not so concerned, were able to maintain regular representatives in both the CCP camp and the GMD government in Chongqing throughout the Japanese War and the civil war. Today the United States finds no great difficulty in maintaining relationships with both the PRC in Beijing and the Nationalists, the Republic of China (ROC) in Taiwan.

With the outbreak of fighting, Hurley attempted to obtain a cease-fire and failed. In November 1945, he resigned as ambassador to China, blaming the failure of reconciliation with the CCP on a plot by foreign-service men who worked not to uphold but to cause the collapse of the government of China.

When General Marshall arrived in China with instructions to arrange a truce and a coalition government, the CCP still had some hopes for American goodwill and impartiality. Initially, the CCP was receptive to Marshall's efforts. But other U.S. activities undercut his efforts. Soon after the Japanese surrender, U.S. Marines had been landed at Qingdao (Tsingtao), Tianjin (Tientsin), and Qinhuangdao (Chingwantao), ostensibly to accept the surrender of Japanese troops and disarm them. The real effect was to hold these areas against the Communists pending the arrival of Nationalist troops. To aid the GMD, the United States turned over remaining stocks of military materiel and sent additional shipments of "nonmilitary" equipment, including trucks, radios, and medical supplies. More aid funds were voted. U.S. aircraft and ships continued to be used to move Nationalist troops.

In spite of this, President Truman blandly issued a public statement in December 1946. He pledged not to interfere in the internal affairs of China, saying the U.S. position was clear. While avoiding involvement in their civil strife, the U.S. policy was to help the Chinese people bring about peace and economic recovery in their country.

The American position was certainly not clear to the Communists. As they observed U.S. actions in support of the GMD, any remaining hope for understanding with the United States faded. The CCP was incensed. Zhou Enlai issued a bitter and vehement complaint about U.S. support of the GMD. Anger and frustration were further intensified when General Barr's advisory group was established to help reorganize and train the Guomindang Army with the American weapons that the United States had provided them.

General Marshall's efforts were in vain. He was recalled. On his departure, the Communists issued a long and bitter denunciation of American activities in China, saying, "American imperialists have taken the place of German, Italian, and Japanese fascists in the world." The United States was accused of looking for ways to attack the USSR and of wanting to oppress the American people and those of all capitalist, colonial, and semicolonial countries. The predictions of Communist theory were coming true. Instead of the liberal elements in the United States overcoming the reactionary and imperialist elements, as Mao had told the Dixie Mission, the opposite was happening. The United States, in the Communist view, was regressing.

President Roosevelt's plan to make China a great power able to guarantee stability in the Far East had failed. No substitute policy evolved. In the words of one historian, "The United States was entering into a period, a brief one, when it sought to achieve its purposes by incantation."[11] China did become a great power, but it was not the China that Roosevelt had envisaged.

As the civil war progressed and Communist victory seemed certain, the Reds became concerned that the United States would intervene militarily on behalf of the GMD, especially when Shanghai, with its substantial foreign community and foreign investment, came under attack. When the threat of imminent U.S. intervention faded, attention shifted to possible conflict with the United States in areas beyond mainland China. Korea, Taiwan, and Viet Nam were areas that had been historical avenues into China. They were also areas where the United States held expressed or implied interests. American troops had only recently departed from Korea. In the U.S. press and in Congress, the fate of Taiwan was being discussed. And in Viet Nam, the civil war heated up, with the United States considering assistance to the French.

To the Chinese, the Pacific outpost line General MacArthur had described as a defensive line looked menacingly like an offensive line—a line from which an attack could be launched. It threatened the outer line of Chinese concern, the line along which anticipated conflict with the United States would occur. MacArthur's statement at that particular time, together with the bitter debate taking place in Congress over the "loss of China" and the aggressive anti-Communist loyalty campaign in America, could not help but fuel Chinese apprehension.

Rebuffed by the United States and increasingly bitter, Mao made his "leaning to one side" speech on 30 June 1949. All Chinese had to lean either to the side of imperialism or to the side of socialism. "Internationally," Mao said, "we belong to the side of the anti-imperialist front headed by the Soviet Union." There was no fence-sitting. There was no third way.[12] It was to be expected that China would lean toward the country that was the pioneer on the path to world revolution, even though China and the Soviet Union had some seriously conflicting interests. As Zhou Enlai had told General Marshall earlier, "We will certainly lean to one side. However, the extent depends on your policy toward us."[13] Mao had decided that U.S. policy was hostile.

To provide a public history of American–Chinese relations, the State Department prepared a White Paper that was released on 5 August 1949. The report itself was a relatively straightforward factual account. But Secretary of State Dean Acheson felt compelled by domestic policy pressures to append an inflammatory letter of transmittal. Acheson said the leaders of China "have foresworn their Chinese heritage and have publicly announced their subservience to a foreign power, Russia, which during the last fifty years, under Czars and Communists alike, has been most assiduous in its efforts to extend its control in the Far East." Sooner or later, he said, the Communists in Beijing would have to choose between the interests of their own people and servitude to Moscow.[14]

The White Paper and Acheson's comments provoked strong criticism from Mao. He denounced the United States as the most dangerous enemy of the Chinese people. Shortly thereafter, he launched a countrywide anti-American propaganda campaign. Mao's diatribes against U.S. imperialism apparently struck an unexpectedly responsive chord with the Chinese people. Mao needed an issue to keep the populace agitated, to keep up the momentum of the revolution. Criticism of the United States served well, although he is believed to have held a more realistic view in private.[15]

The June 1949 attempt to make contact through Ambassador Leighton Stuart indicated that the Chinese were not yet ready for a complete break with the United States. But the collapse of that effort was one more rebuff to them. The Communists were not prepared to recognize or do business with foreign nations unless those governments met their terms, which included renunciation of all unequal treaties. The United States was not quite ready to do this.

Relations with the USSR

Rebuffed by the United States, Mao was prepared to lean to the Soviet side, but not without some serious reservations. Despite the fact that the CCP was philosophically aligned with the Soviet Union and shared its goal of worldwide proletarian revolution, the Chinese harbored a number of grievances with the Soviets. Mao remembered the often inappropriate and occasionally disastrous advice the CCP had received from Moscow in the early days. That advice was not much better after the war. Stalin had invited a Chinese delegation to Moscow in 1946. He told them bluntly that he felt the development of the uprising in China had no future, and that the Chinese comrades should join the Chiang Kai-shek government and dissolve their army.

The Soviet Union had continued to recognize and support the Guomindang until nearly the end of the civil war. The Chinese Communists, fraternal revolutionaries, received sparse attention. There were concerns over conflicting interests in Xinjiang and Mongolia. And the Soviets retained rights to Lushun (Port Arthur) and Dalian (Dairen), as well as an interest in the Manchurian railroads—all of which the Chinese considered an infringement on their sovereignty. Given those situations, there is reason to believe that Mao would have welcomed the opportunity to take a more neutral stance between the United States and the USSR. If he were not going to be a Chinese "Tito," he could at least maintain a greater degree of independence. Further, it would have given him the opportunity to play one against the other in the classic Chinese strategy.

Stalin also had concerns about the Chinese. Were they really Marxists? Soviet Foreign Minister V. M. Molotov had told Hurley they weren't real Communists; he had called them "margarine Communists." Stalin wondered if the Chinese revolution might mutate into something else, possibly something anti-Soviet. China was one of the two Communist states that had achieved revolution without Soviet help. The other, Yugoslavia, had shown stubborn independence from Moscow and had been ejected from the Communist community. China also had shown its own independence. In 1945, Stalin was concerned that Mao was courting the Americans and had advised him to expel them from Yanan, but Mao paid no attention. Finally, China and the Soviet Union were two Far Eastern powers. It was inevitable that they should come into conflict.

But with the cold shoulder from the United States, Mao had nowhere else to turn for support. Stalin, despite his reservations, could not ignore a successful Communist revolution. Mao had suggested a visit to Moscow in May 1948, when it became apparent that the CCP would be victorious. He asked again in late 1948. Stalin demurred on both occasions, citing the need for Mao to be in China as the war reached a climax. Finally, in December 1949, a visit was proposed and agreed to. After extensive preliminaries and intense discussion, a treaty was drawn up on 14 February 1950. The key provision was the mutual assistance agreement:[16] ". . . in the event of one of the Contracting Parties being attacked by Japan or any state allied with her and thus being involved in a state of war, the other Contracting Party shall immediately render military and other assistance by all means at its disposal."

The phrase "being involved in a state of war" was crucial. In mutual assistance agreements with other Communist countries, the operative phrase had been "involved in a military engagement." The wording of the Sino-Soviet treaty may have been responsible for the reluctance of either side to escalate the Korean War, which would prompt an official declaration of war and bring in the Soviets.

Zhou Enlai stated: ". . . these treaties and agreements made the Chinese people feel that they were no longer isolated." Later he told an internal audience that the treaty made it less likely that the United States would start a new wave of aggression in the Far East.[17] Nevertheless, the treaty retained Soviet rights to Lushun, Dalian, and the Chinese Eastern Railway. The Chinese considered this an infringement on their sovereignty. There were other portions of the agreement that the Chinese considered demeaning.[18]

The U.S. State Department recognized that the treaty represented a defeat for America. Although the policy of driving a wedge between the Soviets and the Chinese had failed for the present, there was genuine potential for future conflict between the two. And conflict did eventually occur. The Chinese and the Soviets fell out over both geographical and ideological questions. But it didn't happen in time to affect the Korean War.

Shifting Focus to the Periphery

Korea had been discussed during Mao's visit to Moscow. Mao had reservations about Kim Il Sung's plan to reunify Korea by force. Mao told Stalin he thought the United States would consider this an internal affair. That was either an indication of his unrealistic view of the West or a necessary evasion. Mao had to downplay the possibility of American intervention. If the United States might intervene in Korea, it also might intervene in Mao's attempt to seize Taiwan. In addition, Dean Acheson's January speech on the defense perimeter in the Pacific might have convinced Mao that the United States had no further interest in Korea. Mao also worried that Kim's attack, if launched before the Taiwan offensive, would divert Stalin's attention, and his support, from the invasion of Taiwan. Nevertheless, Mao agreed to Kim's plan.

Upon Mao's departure from Moscow, Stalin cabled Kim Il Sung that he was now ready to discuss Kim's plan to seize South Korea and was "willing to help him in this affair." But while Stalin was willing to agree to Kim's plan, he made it subject to Mao's approval. By so doing, Stalin made Mao responsible for failure. He told Kim: "If you should get kicked in the teeth, I shall not lift a finger. You have to ask Mao for all the help."[19]

Elsewhere on the southern approach to China, Ho Chi Minh had been carrying on a guerrilla war against the French in Viet Nam since the closing days of World War II. In January 1950, Ho asked the Chinese for help. To Mao it was an opportunity to help shore up the southern flank. It also was an opportunity for the Chinese to lend aid to a fraternal revolutionary and demonstrate Chinese leadership in Asia. In April, Chinese military advisers were sent to the Vietnamese and a program of materiel aid was established. CCP leaders believed this would be one of the areas where China and the United States would come into conflict sooner or later.[20]

Taiwan was the third area of Chinese concern. Mao looked upon it as "The Last Campaign." Until Taiwan was "liberated," the Civil War could not be considered ended. In the summer of 1949, the PLA Third Field Army, deployed on the east China coast north and south of Shanghai, was ordered to take up the problem of seizing Taiwan. As a preliminary, the PLA launched attacks to seize the island of Dengbu, a small island just to the south of Nationalist-held Maza (Matsu) and Jinmen (Quemoy). Both attacks were repulsed with heavy losses. To the victorious PLA, it was the worst defeat of the war. The sobered CCP leadership realized the seizure of Taiwan would be difficult. Plans were revised and the attack was put off until the summer of 1950, when air support might be available. Practical difficulties kept forcing a postponement. Mao was hoping for materiel assistance (and more) from the Soviet Union. By the time the Korean War commenced, the seizure of Taiwan had been put off to 1951.

On the Eve of War

On the eve of the North Korean attack, a situation of mutual ignorance prevailed between the Chinese and the United States. Some
of the senior Chinese leadership had been abroad as members of a
work-study program. Zhou Enlai was the most experienced and cosmopolitan example of this group. But no one in the top leadership
had any firsthand experience with the United States. There were only
a few second-echelon members of the government who had been educated in China by American missionary schools and universities. To
Mao, their reliability was doubtful. In the final stages of the civil war,
Ambassador Leighton Stuart had given a talk urging those who had
attended Yenching University and other missionary schools not to
flee the advancing Red Army but to remain behind and help build
the new China. The CCP considered this an effort to have them sub-
vert the new regime.

Americans themselves often have great difficulty in understanding conflicting attitudes and untidy policymaking procedures in their
own country. Under the circumstances, then, it is understandable
that the Chinese had even greater difficulty. For all his brilliant insight into the behavior of his fellow Chinese, Mao was burdened with
a badly flawed view of the United States. He and his associates
viewed America through the rigid and warped lens of Marxist theory, which was based upon the harsh conditions that prevailed in
mid-nineteenth-century European industrial strife. He had no idea
of the changes that had come about in the United States since then,
nor did he comprehend American generosity and idealism. He
firmly believed that the United States would soon enter a depression
and that to stave off an uprising of the workers, the reactionary capitalist forces would engage the United States in imperial adventures.

This Chinese parochialism was more than matched by American
parochialism. Those Americans who had some knowledge of China
clung either to the romantic view of the heroic GMD as it existed
during the few years of real progress in the mid-1930s or to the picture of China corrupt and chaotic as it existed from 1945 onward.
The result was that succeeding policy positions were taken and
events unfolded on the basis of mutual ignorance.

The Chinese were focused on Taiwan. Korea seemed a minor matter to them. The United States, for its part, was equally in the dark

about the possibility of the war and had only the sketchiest idea of the internal divisions among the Soviets, the Chinese, and the North Koreans.

Few times in modern history has a war started with combatants so ill informed about each other.

Notes

Much of the background of the growth of the Communist Party in China, the decline of the Guomindang, and the results of the Chinese Civil War is settled history, although more recent research has clarified a number of questions. Unfortunately, there are few English-language studies of the battles of the civil war. They have some very useful lessons for the military professional. In addition to the specific references cited in the footnotes, the books that have been most helpful in preparation of this chapter are Lionel Max Chassin, *The Communist Conquest of China: A History of the Civil War 1945–1949;* O. Edmund Clubb, *Twentieth-Century China;* Bruce Cumings, *The Origins of the Korean War* (2 vols.); F. F. Liu, *A Military History of Modern China, 1924–1949;* Henry McAleavy, *The Modern History of China;* John Stuart Service, *Lost Chance in China;* Edgar Snow, *Red Star Over China.*

1. Harrison Salisbury, *The Long March: The Untold Story* (New York: Harper and Row, 1985).

2. Goncharov et al., *Uncertain Partners,* 16. During the first half of the 1940s there was no formal contact between Yanan and Moscow. A small Soviet liaison group functioned primarily as a communication link.

3. Nie Rongzhen, *Inside the Red Star: The Memoirs of Marshal Nie Rongzhen* (Beijing: New World Press, 1988), 399.

4. Theodore H. White and Annalee Jacoby, *Thunder Out of China* (New York: William Sloan Associates, 1946).

5. Dick Wilson, *China's Revolutionary War* (New York: St. Martin's, 1991), 174.

6. United States Department of State, *United States Relations with China with Special Reference to the Period 1944–1949, with Letter of Transmittal* (Washington, D.C.: Government Printing Office, August 1949), 845–46 (hereafter cited as *China White Paper*).

7. That attitude was not limited to the Army. The author remembers vividly on the night of 2 November 1950, when we first made contact with the Chinese, a senior officer, an old "China hand," saying, "Just give them a carton of cigarettes and they'll surrender."

8. Service, *Lost Chance in China,* 308.

9. Wilson, *China's Revolutionary War,* 127.

10. Ross Terrill, "When America Lost China," *Atlantic Monthly,* November 1969.

11. Herbert Feis, *The China Tangle: The American Effort in China from Pearl Harbor to the Marshall Mission* (Princeton, N.J.: Princeton University Press, 1953), 423.

12. Goncharov et al., *Uncertain Partners,* 44.

13. Ibid., 45.

14. *China White Paper.*

15. Chen Jian, *China's Road to the Korean War: The Making of the Sino-American Confrontation* (New York: Columbia University Press, 1994), 25.

16. Goncharov et al., *Uncertain Partners,* 117.

17. Jian, *China's Road to the Korean War,* 88.

18. Goncharov et al., *Uncertain Partners,* 124.

19. Ibid., 145.

20. Shu Guang Zhang, *Mao's Military Romanticism: China and the Korean War, 1950–1953* (Lawrence: University Press of Kansas, 1995), 44–45.

3
Attack and Counterattack

I order the war to begin. Do you all agree?
—Kim Il Sung, 25 June 1950

Attack

Kim Il Sung's army, led by 125 Soviet-made T-34 tanks, attacked south across the border on the morning of 25 June 1950. The South Korean Army, poorly trained, only partially deployed, and with no tanks or effective antitank weapons, quickly gave way. The North Korean Army soon reached Seoul, crossed the Han River, and headed south. Recent indications of a coming attack had been ignored or misinterpreted. The surprise was total. ROK forces, the Far Eastern Command in Tokyo, and the United States government in Washington were more than surprised—they were all totally unprepared.

Responsible U.S. officials immediately feared this was the start of a worldwide Communist offensive. Was this a diversion for an attack in Europe? President Harry Truman and his advisers hesitated for two days. Then Truman ordered U.S. sea and air units in the Far East to render the fullest possible support to the ROK troops. The same day, the UN Security Council, with the USSR absent, adopted an American-sponsored resolution recommending that UN members furnish such assistance as may be necessary to the Republic of Korea.

In a concurrent move that was to have a powerful psychological impact on the Chinese Communists, Truman, on the recommendation of Secretary of State Dean Acheson, also ordered the U.S. Seventh Fleet to prevent all military action in the Taiwan Strait as a "neutralization" move. Truman explained his action in a public statement on 27 June, saying, ". . . an attack on Taiwan under these circumstances would be a direct threat to the security of the Pacific area and to the United States forces performing their lawful and necessary functions there."[1]

With the collapse of the ROK Army becoming more likely by the hour, Truman, on 30 June, authorized U.S. ground troops to be committed. On 7 July, the UN called on the United States to direct operations in Korea so as ". . . to assist the Republic of Korea in defending itself against armed attack and thus to restore international peace and security in the area."[2] General Douglas MacArthur was appointed Commander in Chief, United Nations Command (CINCUNC).

MacArthur notified the Joint Chiefs that he planned to move one regimental combat team (RCT) to the Seoul–Suwon corridor to block the North Korean attack, then to rush two infantry divisions to South Korea for an early counteroffensive.[3] The 24th and 25th Infantry Divisions would hold the North Koreans while the 1st Cavalry Division would execute an amphibious landing in the North Korean rear at Inchon. This plan reflected the unrealistic view of the ROK Army (ROKA) put forward by Gen. Lynn Roberts. Optimism was so pervasive and opinion of what was assumed to be the abilities of the North Korean Army so disdainful that the Far Eastern Command's chief of staff, Maj. Gen. Edward M. Almond, told the 1st Cavalry Division's commander to expedite the landing "to the utmost limit"; otherwise, the only thing the 1st Cav would hit on landing would be the "tail end of the 24th Division as it passed northbound through Seoul."[4] MacArthur's estimate of the forces needed and the fighting abilities of the North Korean Army were both quickly revised upward.

Three partially trained and understrength divisions from Japan, the 24th, 25th, and 1st Cavalry Divisions—together with the 2d Infantry Division from Fort Lewis and the 1st Provisional Marine Brigade (organized around the 5th Marines) from Camp Pendleton—were committed in Korea.

The initial Army units, inexperienced, ill-equipped, committed piecemeal in small packets, and too often poorly led, engaged in desperate fighting that at times seemed comparable to what American forces had faced in Bataan in the early days of World War II. In two bitter months, U.S. forces were forced back nearly 150 miles. But, gradually, a shaky defense line stabilized along the Nak-tong River. By 7 September, Gen. Walton Walker, commanding the Eighth Army, was able to declare: "Our lines will hold."

Counterattack

The counterattack came at Inchon on 15 September. The U.S. X Corps, with the 1st Marine Division leading, executed a risky but suc-cessful landing. The Marines, together with the 7th Infantry Division, drove inland to recapture Seoul and cut the North Korean lines of communication. The back of the North Korean People's Army (NKPA) was broken. Within days, the Eighth Army broke out of the Naktong perimeter and drove north to link up with the landing force. The bulk of the NKPA was cut off and shattered.

Within the Joint Chiefs of Staff, and within the Navy and Marine Corps, the landing at Inchon had been hotly debated. The seaward approaches to the landing site and the hydrographic conditions at Inchon made it a venture bordering on the reckless. Although it of-fered great possibilities, it also offered the possibility of disaster. MacArthur had held fast in the face of every suggested alternative and every objection. Its success was regarded as the master stroke of a military genius. The opponents were chagrined, the skeptics si-lenced. The Joint Chiefs—all of whom were younger and less expe-rienced than MacArthur and who were already reticent about giv-ing MacArthur direct and specific orders—were, after Inchon, even more reluctant to impose their own judgment upon him.

General Matthew B. Ridgway, then the Army's deputy chief of staff for administration, described it: "A more subtle result of the Inchon triumph was the development of an almost superstitious regard for General MacArthur's infallibility. Even his superiors, it seemed, be-gan to doubt if they should question *any* [Ridgway's emphasis] of MacArthur's decisions. . . . "[5]

Pursuit

Early on, President Truman had been concerned about how this "po-lice action," as he had termed it, should conclude. On 17 July, he posed this question to the National Security Council. Within the State Department, opinion was mixed. The State Department's policy planning staff under Paul Nitze advised restricting ground action to areas south of the thirty-eighth parallel. The staff's opinion was that the Kremlin was unlikely to accept a regime occupying North Korea that it could neither dominate nor control. There also was danger of conflict with Chinese or Soviet forces as the thirty-eighth parallel was approached. It seemed that the risks outweighed the advantages.

Dean Rusk and John Allison, in the Far Eastern Division of the State Department, were more hawkish. The military objective should be to destroy the North Korean Army so that it could not be reorganized to attack again.[6] The Joint Chiefs also favored that option.

The policy, finalized in NSC-81, stated that the United States should persuade the UN to pass a resolution authorizing UN forces to cross the thirty-eighth parallel to destroy the NKPA and provide for unification of Korea by free elections. It was approved by Truman on 11 September. A draft copy of the NSC finding arrived from the JCS just as MacArthur was observing the Inchon landing. It enabled him to commence planning for crossing the thirty-eighth parallel. He was not to execute such plans without the specific approval of the president.

The Joint Chiefs issued their instruction, in the name of the president, on 27 September while the battle for Seoul was still raging:

> Your military objective is the destruction of the North Korean Armed Forces. In attaining this objective you are authorized to conduct military operations, including amphibious and airborne landings, or ground operations, north of the 38th Parallel in Korea, providing that at the time of such operation there has been no entry into North Korea by major Soviet or Chinese Communist forces, no announcement of intended entry, nor a threat to counter our operations militarily in North Korea. Under no circumstances, however, will your forces cross the Manchurian or USSR borders of Korea and, as a matter of policy, no non-Korean ground forces will be used in the northeast provinces bordering the Soviet Union, or in the area along the Manchurian border. Furthermore, support of your operations north or south of the 38th Parallel will not

include Air or Naval action against Manchuria or against USSR territory.

In the event of the open or covert employment of major Soviet units south of the 38th Parallel, you will assume the defense, make no move to aggravate the situation and report to Washington. You should take the same action in the event your forces are operating north of the 38th Parallel, and major Soviet Forces are openly employed. You will not discontinue Air and Naval operations north of the 38th Parallel merely because the presence of Soviet or Chinese Communist troops is detected in a target area, but if the Soviet Union or Chinese Communists should announce in advance their intention to reoccupy North Korea and give warning, either explicitly or implicitly, that their forces should not be attacked, you should refer the matter immediately to Washington.

In the event of the open or covert employment of major Chinese Communist units south of the 38th Parallel, you should continue the action as long as action by your forces offers a reasonable chance of successful resistance. In the event of an attempt to employ small Soviet or Chinese Communist units covertly south of the 38th Parallel you should continue the action.

When organized armed resistance by North Korean forces has been brought substantially to an end, you should direct the ROK forces to take the lead in disarming remaining North Korean units and enforcement of the terms of surrender. Guerilla activities should be dealt with primarily by the forces of the Republic of Korea, with minimum participation by United Nations contingents.

Circumstances obtaining at the time will determine the character of and necessity for occupation of North Korea. Your plans for such occupation will be forwarded for approval to the Joint Chiefs of Staff. You will also submit your plan for future operations north of the 38th Parallel to the Joint Chiefs of Staff for approval.[7]

In the drafting of the final version of the NSC finding, two changes were made that, reflected in MacArthur's orders, were to have a substantial impact on the coming operation. The original version stated that UN operations "should not be permitted to extend into areas *close* to the Manchurian and USSR border." This was changed to say that such operations should not be allowed *across* those borders. In the other change, the original had declared that forces other than those of the ROK should "in no circumstances" be used in the border regions. The final version stated merely that "it should be the policy" not to employ non-ROK forces there.[8]

The Joint Chiefs' instructions proved to be ambiguous in several respects. The possible contingency concerning Chinese intervention *north* of the thirty-eighth parallel was not covered. Restricting non-Korean ground forces from an "area" along the Manchurian border was not a precise definition, nor was the phrase "as a matter of policy" a precise instruction. Most interesting was the provision concerning an announcement of Chinese intention to intervene. As will be seen, the Chinese did make a public and official announcement of exactly this intention just three days after these instructions had been issued and a week before any non-Korean forces had crossed the thirty-eighth parallel, yet there is no record that either MacArthur or the JCS considered it related to this particular instruction.

Also, of subsequent interest, the instructions authorized MacArthur to conduct military operations in North Korea, but nothing in the instructions required him to occupy the entire country.

MacArthur's Plan for Exploitation
Having been given permission to advance north of the thirty-eighth parallel, MacArthur went to work on a plan to destroy the North Korean Army. The demonstrated tenacity of the NKPA in both attack and defense fueled the belief that the North Korean capital, Pyongyang, would be a difficult objective to secure. ROK intelligence had estimated there were six new and uncommitted divisions along three defensive lines at the thirty-eighth parallel.[9]

In final form, the UNC plan was an attack northward to Pyongyang by the Eighth Army, coupled with another amphibious landing by X Corps at Wonsan. X Corps would then attack westward across the peninsula to "juncture" with the Eighth Army, ostensibly sealing off the peninsula and trapping any North Korean forces south of the Pyonggang–Wonsan line.* General Edwin K. Wright, Far Eastern Command (FEC) operations officer, estimated the landing could be executed within ten days of the order—six days to mount out and four days to reach the objective area.[10] At the forthcoming meeting with President Truman at Wake Island, MacArthur compared the plan to Inchon. He believed that X Corps could cut across the peninsula in a week: "When the gap is closed, the same thing will happen as happened in the south."[11] All UN forces would then advance to and halt along the line Chongju–Yongwon–Hamhung. ROK forces would be used north of that line.

MacArthur's plan was greeted with considerable skepticism at the time and severe criticism later. Most of his principal staff officers advised against it, preferring instead an overland attack northeastward along the rail corridor that ran from Seoul through Chorwon and Pyonggang to Wonsan. MacArthur, having demonstrated his judgment at Inchon, was adamant. Outloading of the 1st Marine Division at Inchon took twelve days instead of six. A huge minefield at Wonsan delayed the landing until 25 October, long after Pyongyang had been seized and the opportunity to cut off withdrawing North Korean forces had passed. The two strongest and freshest divisions in the Far East were out of action for nearly three weeks and wound up on the wrong coast.

Long afterward, Gen. Omar Bradley offered his opinion that "had a major at the Command and General Staff School proposed to divide his forces, tie up his logistics and delay vital operations for three weeks he would have been laughed out of the classroom."[12]

---

*On a personal note, the author was S-2 of the 3d Battalion, 7th Marines, at that time, scheduled to be the advance guard for the attack west from Wonsan. We obtained aerial photos of the route and I spent two days with my intelligence chief, SSgt. Christian B. Nicoliasen, studying the route and preparing a report. After discussing it with our battalion commander and Colonel Litzenberg, the regimental commander, it seemed very unrealistic to expect a rapid advance over that tortuous route. Nicoliasen put it succinctly: "A platoon of Boy Scouts could hold us up for days."

Wake Island

Although MacArthur had been able to take time out for a staff visit to Taiwan, he was irritated by the order to meet President Truman at Wake Island on 15 October. Truman's ostensible purpose was to ensure that MacArthur understood U.S. policy; the president wanted to make that clear in person. There is also the general belief that it was a political trip to show respect for a widely admired conservative general just before midterm elections. There is more than a bit of mystery about the discussions at Wake. Truman and MacArthur met privately for the first half hour. When asked later what they talked about, MacArthur said he did not feel at liberty to divulge their conversation. Truman's memoirs simply have a bland reference to that portion of their meeting.

MacArthur's comments during the portion of the meeting at which others were present (General Bradley, Dean Rusk, Philip C. Jessup, and others) reflected the widely held low opinion of the Chinese Communist forces. Asked by Truman about the chances of Chinese intervention, he indicated they were very little:

> Had they interfered in the first or second month it would have been decisive. We are no longer fearful of their intervention. We no longer stand hat in hand. The Chinese have 300,000 men in Manchuria. Of these probably not more than 100,000 to 125,000 are distributed along the Yalu River. They have no Air Force. Now that we have bases for our Air Force in Korea, if the Chinese tried to get down to Pyongyang there would be the greatest slaughter.
>
> With the Russians it is a little different. They have an Air Force in Siberia and a fairly good one, with excellent pilots equipped with some jets and B-25 and B-29 planes. They can put 1,000 planes in the air with some 200–300 more from the Fifth and Seventh Soviet Fleets. They are probably no match for our Air Force. The Russians have no ground troops available for North Korea. They would have difficulty in putting troops in the field. It would take six weeks to get a division across and six weeks bring the winter. The only other combination would be Russian air support of Chinese ground troops.

Russian air is deployed in a semicircle through Mukden and Harbin, but the coordination between the Russian air and the Chinese ground would be so flimsy that I believe Russian air would bomb the Chinese as often as they would bomb us.[13]

In response to Dean Rusk's mention of the Chinese threat to enter the Korean War if UN forces crossed the thirty-eighth parallel, MacArthur told Rusk he ". . . did not fully understand why they had gone out on such a limb and that they must be greatly embarrassed by the predicament in which they now found themselves."

MacArthur told the group that he thought organized resistance would end by Thanksgiving and that he would be able to withdraw the Eighth Army by Christmas. In North Korea he believed he was facing only 100,000 new recruits, poorly trained, led, and equipped, ". . . but," he said, "they are obstinate and it goes against my grain to have to destroy them. They are only fighting to save face. Orientals prefer to die rather than to lose face."[14]

MacArthur later took issue with the report of his views. In his book he said: "My views were asked as to the chance of Red China's intervention." After pointing out that neither the State Department nor the CIA had indicated a Chinese intention to intervene with major forces, he continued: ". . . my own local intelligence, which I regarded as unsurpassed anywhere, reported heavy concentrations near the Yalu border in Manchuria whose movements were indeterminate; that my own military estimate was that with our largely unopposed air forces, with their potential capable of destroying, at will, bases of attack and lines of supply north as well as south of the Yalu, no Chinese military commander would hazard the commitment of large forces upon the devastated Korean peninsula. The risk of their utter destruction through lack of supply would be too great. There was no disagreement from anyone."[15]

Exploitation Commences
MacArthur submitted his plan for approval to the Joint Chiefs on 28 September. Despite General Bradley's subsequent criticism of the Wonsan landing, the plan was approved without change the following day. Eighth Army units began passing through X Corps and mov-

ing forward to jump-off positions north of Seoul. First Marine Division units were relieved beginning on 3 October and assembled in Inchon ready for embarkation, which began on 6 October.

MacArthur's top-secret plan for the advance into North Korea was displayed for all the world three or four days later when the 9 October issue of *Newsweek*, arriving, as all magazines do, several days before its date, hit the newsstands. A large map showed the line from Chongju to Hamhung, labeled the "MacArthur Line," and showed UN forces advancing north in two broad axes—one from central Korea and one up the west coast—converging on Wonsan. The story suggested that Pyongyang would be taken by amphibious assault, as Seoul was.

The MacArthur Line was described as "far more defensible than the 38th Parallel, and on it the UN army can wait, if necessary, while a political solution for all Korea is worked out." Its location, the article stated, was chosen "so as to leave a sizable block of territory between the UN army and the Chinese and Russian frontiers." The article noted Zhou Enlai's threat to help North Korea if the thirty-eighth parallel was crossed and stated: "Line is part of a readiness to face Chinese intervention if it comes, and minimize the danger to world peace."[16]

It is a near-certainty that the *Newsweek* story was a plant, done probably at the instigation of the State Department with the concurrence of the Joint Chiefs, to provide both reassurance and disinformation. Politically, it might reassure the Chinese, concerned as they were about U.S. intentions. Militarily, it would provide a cover plan for the landing at Wonsan. As the next chapter will show, it did provide such a cover. Mao expected the landing to take place at Chinampo, the port for Pyongyang.

The Eighth Army commenced its attack across the thirty-eighth parallel on 8 October 1950. On the east coast, ROK troops had crossed the parallel on 1 October. North Korean resistance crumbled much faster than anticipated. By 10 October, the ROK had secured Wonsan and was advancing northward, reaching and securing Hamhung and Hungnam on 18 October. On the west coast, I Corps troops broke through the North Korean defenses at Kumchon and occupied Pyongyang on 20 October. That same day, the 187th Airborne RCT jumped north of Pyongyang at Sukchon and Sunchon in a vain attempt to intercept fleeing North Korean forces and government officials.

On 15 October, MacArthur was called away to meet with President Truman at Wake Island. On his return, the rapidly changing situation demanded attention.

The jaws of the amphibious trap at Wonsan would snap shut too late to snare the fleeing North Korean forces. So on 17 October, MacArthur cast the net wider. He canceled the proposed attack westward from Wonsan. A new stop line, closer to the Manchurian border, was established. The Eighth Army would advance to the line Songchon–Koin-dong–Pyongwon. X Corps would stay under the direct control of FEC, would take command of I ROK Corps moving up the east coast, and would advance north in its own zone on the eastern side of the mountains, coming abreast of the Eighth Army along the line Toksil-li–Pungsan–Songjin.[17]

Notes

1. Acheson, *Present at the Creation*, 409.
2. Schnabel, *Policy and Direction*, 178.
3. Blair, *The Forgotten War*, 81.
4. Ibid., 88, quoting letter Gay to Appleman.
5. Matthew B. Ridgway, *The Korean War: How We Met the Challenge* (New York: Doubleday, 1967), 55.
6. Omar N. Bradley with Clay Blair, *A General's Life: An Autobiography* (New York: Simon and Schuster, 1983), 558.
7. Joint Chiefs of Staff (JCS) msg 92801, 27 Sept. 50 to MacArthur in U.S. Department of State, *Foreign Relations of the United States: 1950*. Vol. VII, *The Korean* War (Washington, D.C.: Government Printing Office), 781ff. (hereafter cited as *FRUS*).
8. James F. Schnabel and Robert J. Watson, *History of the Joint Chiefs of Staff: The Joint Chiefs of Staff and National Policy*. Vol. III *The Korean War. Part 1* (Wilmington, Del.: Michael Glazier, 1979), 277 (hereafter cited as *HJCS*).
9. Roy E. Appleman, *South to the Naktong, North to the Yalu: U.S. Army in the Korean War* (Washington, D.C.: Center of Military History, U.S. Army, 1992), 624; Eighth Army Periodic Intelligence Reports (8A PIR) 82, 89, and 90, dated 2, 9, and 10 Oct. 50.
10. Schnabel, *Policy and Direction*, 187–88.
11. Ibid., 212.
12. Bradley, *A General's Life*, 568.
13. Substance of statement made at the Wake Island conference, *FRUS*, 949ff. At the start of the conference it was announced that no notes were to be taken. By happenstance a government stenographer in the next room took notes. Copies were provided to MacArthur. However, he later challenged the accuracy of the notes. The conference began at 7:32 A.M. and ended at 9:12 A.M. A footnote says informal discussions among participants on both sides continued for an hour to an hour and a half. Truman and MacArthur met privately for about a half hour prior to the conference. So it is relatively certain that all subjects discussed are not included in the notes compiled by General Bradley.
14. Ibid.

15. Douglas MacArthur, *Reminiscences* (New York: McGraw-Hill, 1964), 362.

16. "New United Nations Line—MacArthur's," *Newsweek,* 9 October 1950, 19–21.

17. Commander in Chief, United Nations Command (CINC-UNC), Operation Order No. 4, 17 Oct. 50.

4
The Chinese React

The key lies in the number of Americans we can kill.
—Mao Zedong

Initial Reaction

The Chinese ideogram for *crisis* is a combination of the ideograms for *danger* and *opportunity*. To the leaders of the People's Republic of China, the Korean War was both.

Conflict with America was danger. American domination of Korea would threaten Manchuria, the most important Chinese industrial region. An American presence in Korea might encourage dissident domestic elements and jeopardize Communist control of China. The prestige of the regime was threatened by American action in Korea. Could the new Communist rulers safeguard China's interests? Could they demonstrate the ability to rule? Did they really have the "Mandate of Heaven"?

Conflict with America was also an opportunity. It was an excuse to carry out an aggressive campaign against domestic dissidents, to eliminate opponents and solidify total internal control. It was a chance to mobilize the masses, to demand extraordinary effort to resist foreign imperialism. The Communist leadership was acutely conscious of how the Japanese threat from Manchuria had galvanized Chinese opinion thirteen years earlier. On the regional scene, it offered the chance to demonstrate Chinese leadership to the people of Asia, to show that China was not afraid to stand up to the most powerful member of the Western imperialist bloc.

Aware of Kim Il Sung's plans, but not the timing, China's attention was focused on its own problems. Liberation of Taiwan was a high priority. The pacification of south China, where there were still some 400,000 Nationalist guerrillas, was a serious problem. On the domestic front, reduction of military expenditures was urgent. A large part of the People's Liberation Army (PLA) needed to be demobilized, the remainder modernized. Battered by years of war, the domestic economy was a shambles.

Overriding nearly all of these was the need to get a firm grasp on the reins of power, to gain control of both the central bureaucracy and the provincial government. In power only eight months, the Communist rulers needed to put all branches of the government into the hands of men and women firm in ideology.

The U.S. response to the North Korean attack was not a total surprise. It came in one of the three places dogma had dictated. The shocking surprises were the speed of the response and the neutralization of the Taiwan (Formosa) Strait. That surprise quickly turned to anger.

In his discussions with Stalin and Kim Il Sung, Mao had downplayed the possibility of U.S. intervention. Korea was a civil war. Why would the United States intervene in a civil war? There must be an evil intention. To the suspicious Chinese, this was part of a long-prepared plan of aggression to subjugate them.[1] U.S. claims that this was a response to defend South Korea were not to be believed. Nor was the claim that neutralizing the Taiwan Strait was as much to prevent Nationalist attacks on the mainland as it was to prevent Communist attacks on Taiwan.

The Central People's Government Council was a group set up ostensibly to give "democratic personages" and parties other than the Communists (excepting the Guomindang) some apparent participation in the government. The day after the announcement about U.S. troops in Korea, Mao appeared before the council and reported:

> The U.S. invasion of Asia can only touch off the broad and resolute opposition of Asian people. On January 5th, Truman said in an announcement that the U.S. would not intervene in Taiwan. Now his conduct proved that what he said was false. Moreover, he shredded all international agreements related to the American commitment not to intervene in China's internal affairs. The U.S. thus reveals its imperialist nature in its true colors. It is very advantageous to the Chinese people and the

people of Asia [to draw a lesson from the U.S. policy toward Taiwan]. The U.S. is unable to justify in any way its intervention in the internal affairs of Korea, the Philippines and Vietnam. The sympathies of the Chinese people and the vast people of the world lie with the countries that have been invaded, and by no means with American imperialism. . . . People throughout the nation and the world unite and make full preparations for frustrating any provocation of American imperialism.[2]

Zhou Enlai went even further, calling the American intervention tantamount to a declaration of war.[3]

Despite U.S. efforts to carry out operations in Korea under the banner of the United Nations, the Chinese never recognized it as a UN effort. Throughout the war, it was referred to as an American effort supported by "puppet" (i.e., South Korean) troops. In China, the term *puppet* had a particularly odious ring, because it was used to describe those Chinese soldiers who deserted the Nationalist cause during the Japanese War and enrolled in forces under Wang Jingwei, who had established a Japanese-supported government in the occupied areas of China.

China's Central Information Bureau took the first step by mobilizing public opinion with a directive to all propaganda organs saying, in part, "All over China, we have to hold this opportunity to . . . start a widespread campaign of propaganda, so that we will be able to educate our people at home and to strike firmly the arrogance of the U.S. imperialist aggressors."[4]

In the following days, the plans for the liberation of Taiwan were postponed until 1951. With Korea demanding Stalin's attention, Mao was certain he would be unable to get the materiel he needed for the campaign. The Taiwan liberation was later postponed until 1952; then, in August, as the Korean War heated up, it was postponed indefinitely. Plans for reducing the size of the PLA went forward, however. On 30 June, in answer to an inquiry from Xiao Jingguang, China's navy chief, Zhou said the present plan was to continue demobilization, continue to strengthening the navy and air force, and postpone the attack on Taiwan.

At the same time, Nie Rongzhen, acting chief of staff of the PLA, proposed that China dispatch a military observation group to maintain contact with Kim Il Sung and observe the course of the war. Chai Chengwen, then director of military intelligence of the Southwest Military District, was his choice. Rather than make it a military mission, Zhou decided that Chai and his group should be attached to the embassy. That would give the mission a diplomatic color and conceal Chinese military interest. Five additional intelligence officers were selected, as well as a communications team. The day following the decisions on the Northeast Frontier Force (NEFF), the group was dispatched with instructions to send back any information on any change in the battleground as soon as possible. They arrived in Pyongyang on 10 July, met Kim Il Sung, and were assured of his full cooperation.[5]

Cautious Preparations

War in Korea might provide both danger and opportunity. It also provided frustration. With war in Korea, there was no possibility for China to obtain from Russia the arms and equipment needed for the liberation of Taiwan. And if Kim Il Sung's campaign failed, China would have to take a stand. In the meantime, plans had to be made.

Kim Il Sung had convinced both Stalin and Mao that the war in Korea would be short. Kim counted on the uprising of some 200,000 members of the South Korean Workers' Party and on the guerrilla movement in the southern part of the country to supplement the attack of the NKPA. With all three, he believed the war would be over in two or three weeks.

Thirteen days of watchful waiting for Mao and the Chinese passed. The Workers' Party didn't rise. On 30 June, President Truman announced authorization for the use of American ground forces in Korea. U.S. troops began trickling into Korea as early as 1 July. More ominously for the Chinese and North Koreans, the news carried stories of troops preparing to rush to Korea from other parts of the Pacific. There would be no quick victory. It was time to prepare.

At Mao's direction, Zhou Enlai called a meeting of the Central Military Commission on 7 July. Present were Zhu Deh, commander-in-chief of the army; Acting Chief of Staff Nie Rongzhen; Lin Biao; and others. Zhou told those present that Mao believed that troops should be assembled along the border. "In case we needed to enter the war we should be prepared."[6]

There was no shortage of manpower in the Chinese Army. China's military manpower assets were huge, although primitive. The People's Liberation Army (referred to as the CCF or Chinese Communist Forces in U.S. reports) was the largest in the world, with 5,238,000 men under arms in 253 divisions. Only about half of those divisions, however, could be considered combat-effective.

The PLA came under the direction of the Central Military Commission, made up of senior leaders of the Communist Party. Major elements of the army were organized as follows:[7]

Commander in Chief	General Zhu Deh	
Acting Chief of Staff	General Nie Rongzhen	
First Field Army	General Peng Dehuai	34 divisions
Second Field Army	General Lin Po Cheng	49 divisions
Third Field Army	General Chen Yi	72 divisions
Fourth Field Army	General Lin Biao	59 divisions

Unaware of Kim's timing for the Korean venture, the Chinese Army was poorly deployed to be of any assistance. The First Field Army was in northwest China, carrying out the pacification of Xinjiang. The Second Field Army was in western China, preparing to advance into Tibet. The Third Field Army, on the east China coast to the north and south of Shanghai, had the mission of preparing for the seizure of Taiwan. The Fourth Field Army, along the south China coast, had the additional missions of seizing Hainan Island and clearing out the remaining pockets of Nationalist resistance in south China. Both the Third and the Fourth Field Armies were also charged with coastal defense. The Chinese still feared that a rampant United States might attempt to seize one or two coastal cities in an attempt to restore the Nationalist government.

Lin Biao's Fourth Field Army had been recruited mostly in Manchuria, had fought most of the civil war there, but had moved south during the war. In the early spring of 1950, a few elements of the Fourth Army returned to Manchuria. Included was the 42d

Army, which took up station at Qiqihar, Heilongjiang Province, in northern Manchuria. But, when the war broke out, there were only five divisions, including the three in the 42d Army, and local troops, about 170,000 men in total, in Manchuria to cover the Korean border.[8]

The PLA had formed a central reserve force in the late winter of 1949 by taking the 13th Army Group[9]—consisting of the six divisions of the 38th and 39th Armies—from the Fourth Field Army and moving it to an area on the railroad south of Zhengzhou in Henan Province. The army group was also given an agricultural mission and put to work farming. In May 1950, the 40th Army, weary from the recently completed conquest of Hainan Island, was added to the strategic reserve.[10]

Also in the spring of 1950, the 9th Army Group, made up of the 20th, 26th, and 27th Armies, was pulled back from the coast and deployed around Shanghai as a reserve for the Third Field Army and Taiwan invasion force. The 9th Army Group had captured Shanghai from the Nationalists and surprised the citizens of that cosmopolitan city with decorous behavior. Its commander, Gen. Song Shilun, was a seasoned and politically reliable commander. As a very young man, he had commanded a regiment through the Long March.[11]

The Central Military Commission (CMC) decided to order the central reserve, the 13th Army Group, north to Manchuria. At the same time, the 42d Army, then in northern Manchuria, would be moved closer to the border. Combined, they would form the Northeast Frontier Force (NEFF). The assigned mission would be to "defend the borders of the northeast, and prepare to support the war operations of the Korean People's Army, if necessary."[12] Altogether, the NEFF was to consist of four armies with a total of twelve divisions, three artillery divisions, one AAA (antiaircraft artillery) regiment, and one engineer regiment, a total of some 255,000 men. All units were to be in position within twenty-five days.[13]

Command Problems in the Northeast Frontier Force

Two different command problems faced the formation of the NEFF. The then-commander of the 13th Army Group was not considered entirely suitable for the proposed mission. General Deng Hua, who commanded the 15th Army Group, was thought to be more suitable. Consequently, it was decided to swap headquarters. Deng, with his staff, would move to Andong, establish headquarters, take command of the troops, and be redesignated as the 13th Army Group.[14]

Overall command of the NEFF also was a problem. The NEFF was to be a separate headquarters, with forces added as needed. The unanimous choice of the CMC was Su Yu, then the deputy commander of the Third Field Army and the principal planner for the invasion of Taiwan. But Su Yu was ill at the time. The second choice was Xiao Jingguang, the navy's commander. He too was unavailable, deeply involved in expansion of the Chinese Navy. As a stopgap measure, the units of the NEFF were placed directly under the command of Gao Gang, head of the Northeast Military Region and Mao's proconsul in Manchuria.[15]

The other major recommendation of the CMC was to begin mobilizing the minds of the military. The recommendation was made to commence political mobilization under the slogan, "Defending national security." The general political department of the army was to work out a directive with concrete plans.

The Chinese rail system, worn and neglected from twenty years of war, struggled to move the troops. It came close to total breakdown. Consideration was given to halting all civilian traffic in order to move the troops, but intelligence warned against drawing undue attention to troop movement into Manchuria. Mao was reported to have talked of taking three weeks to move the armies into Korea. His railroad adviser told him it would be more like three months, which was in fact close to the mark.[16]

By the end of July, the three divisions of the 42d Army had moved down from Heilongjiang and had deployed in the vicinity of Tonghua. The three armies from central China had reached Manchuria and taken up positions with the 40th Army at Andong, together with the headquarters of the 13th Army Group, the 39th Army at Liaoyang and Haiche, and the 38th Army at Fengcheng. All four commenced training and preparations for action.[17]

North Korea Is Stalled

By 4 August, all United Nations Command (UNC) forces had been driven back to a line along the Naktong River but were holding. The

North Korean offensive had been brought to a halt. Kim's estimate of two to three weeks to conclude the war had stretched to nearly six weeks without a decision. UNC strength was building. To Mao Zedong, it appeared that the war might become "protracted." General Nie Rongzhen reported to a conference that the North Korean Army had suffered 40 percent casualties.[18] It was time to consider alternatives.

If North Korea succeeded, with or without Chinese help, and UNC forces were driven from Korea, it would take considerable time and effort to mount an operation to return to the peninsula. Further, the United Nations would be presented with a fait accompli. Any return of United Nations forces could be more forcefully and accurately labeled as aggression. If North Korea failed and UNC forces advanced northward, the Chinese feared they would be threatened. As Zhou Enlai put it, "If the U.S. prevails over Korea it will be swollen with arrogance and endanger the peace [in the Far East]."[19]

Mao concluded that if the UNC succeeded, "We must therefore come to Korea's aid and intervene in the name of a volunteer army, although we will select the best timing to do so." To emphasize that this was not a final decision, he continued: "In any case we shall get fully prepared so that we won't be caught by surprise and rush into war unprepared."[20]

After a meeting of the Revolutionary Council on 5 August, Mao sent the following telegram to Gao Gang: "All troops of the Northeast Frontier Force have now been concentrated. It seems unlikely that any operational tasks will be assigned to these troops in August, however, they should be prepared for war operations in early September. Comrade Gao Gang . . . call a meeting of all the army and division cadres in mid-August to outline the goals, significance and general directions of the war operations. It is required that all the troops must complete preparations within this month and be ready for orders to carry out war operations. The troops must maintain high morale and be well prepared. Questions raised by officers and soldiers regarding the war must be answered. . . . "[21]

Trouble in the NEFF

At the headquarters of the 13th Army Group in Andong, the staff was busy coping with the problems of readiness. Most of the major subordinate units were in place and had commenced training, but some were still straggling in via the heavily taxed railroads. The troops and their equipment were in no condition to fight. Much of the 13th Army Group had been employed in farming tasks, in addition to their reserve mission. Equipment was rusty and in poor condition due to disuse. Army draft animals were worn down from farm work. The troops themselves were tired. Training had deteriorated. Perhaps most telling, troop morale was depressed. Having finished so many years of war, the troops were reluctant to leave the farms and prepare to fight again.[22]

To carry out Mao Zedong's orders, Gao Gang convened a meeting of the senior officers of the NEFF on 13 August. Gao talked about political mobilization of the troops. Deng Hua talked about the problems in fighting Americans and the tactics to be used. Both earnestly asserted that the PLA could successfully fight the Americans. Subordinate commanders were not so sure and voiced their concerns. They were worried by the lack of transportation and antitank artillery. There was a shortage of medicine and doctors. Training and proficiency were at a low level.[23]

Xiao Jingguang, who had attended the meeting as the representative of the Central Military Commission, hurried back to Beijing to report on the condition of the NEFF. After receiving the report, Mao extended the deadline and ordered everything wrapped up and ready by 30 September.[24]

Can We Fight Americans?
As the possibility of having to fight the Americans increased, Chinese leaders began to worry about their ability to do so. Could the relatively primitive Chinese Army fight the modern American Army? What if the Americans used the atomic bomb? Grave misgivings were uttered by some of the senior generals, including Lin Biao. Fighting in Korea was another problem. The PLA had never fought outside of China. Mao had asked his ambassador to Korea to report on problems that would be encountered by the Chinese armies moving into Korea. The diplomat reported that the biggest problems would be inadequate transportation and lack of Korean- and English-language interpreters. The railroads were insecure and the highways

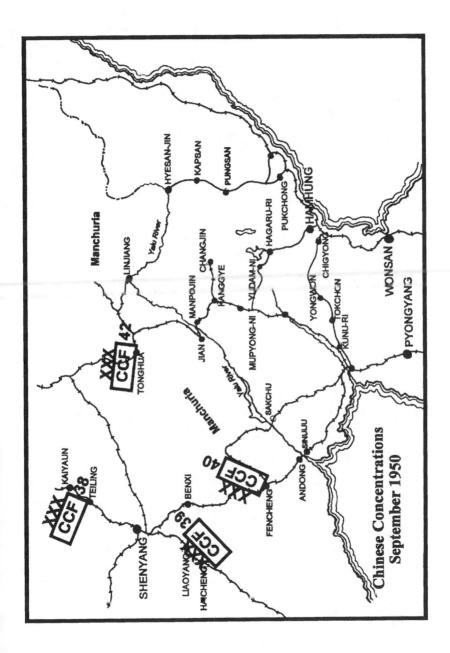

Chinese Concentrations
September 1950

were in poor shape and quite narrow. Unlike with operations in China, sufficient local supplies could not be obtained, and it was unlikely that enough could be captured from the enemy.[25]

PRC leaders were concerned that the United States might widen the war with air raids on coastal cities, perhaps followed by an amphibious attack using Nationalist forces from Taiwan. A northward thrust from the French in Viet Nam was another potential threat. The Chinese were well aware of American amphibious capability and General MacArthur's World War II experience in amphibious operations.

Despite the misgivings of his senior generals, Mao was still inclined to intervene. Eventually he developed a lengthy rationale that concluded that success against the Americans was possible. Mao conceded that U.S. forces enjoyed absolute superiority on the sea and in the air. They had better equipment and superior firepower and mobility. But there were crucial weaknesses. The most vital was lack of political motivation. He argued that U.S. forces were politically unmotivated because "they are invading other people's country, fighting an unjust war, and thus encountering opposition from not only the Americans but other peace-loving peoples around the world." More important, he believed, ". . . our troops have a stronger political consciousness and higher combat spirit."[26]

From the military point of view, he argued that U.S. troops were inferior in terms of combat effectiveness because, ". . . although they have excellent modern equipment, their officers and soldiers are not adept in night battles, close combat, and bayonet charges." By contrast, the PRC troops "have had rich experience over the past ten years in fighting an enemy with modern equipment . . . and are good at close combat, night battles, mountain assaults, and bayonet charges."[27]

Tactically, U.S. forces were not flexible, because "American soldiers always confine themselves to the bounds of military codes and regulations, and their tactics are dull and mechanical." On the other hand, the PRC forces were "good at maneuvering, flexibility and mobility and, in particular, good at surrounding and attacking [the] enemy's flanks by taking tortuous courses, as well as dispersing and concealing forces."[28]

American soldiers were not capable of enduring hardship: "They are afraid of dying and rely on firepower . . . on the contrary our soldiers are brave and willing to sacrifice life and blood and capable of bearing hardship and heavy burdens"—attributes that should remedy the disadvantages of inferior firepower. Finally, the U.S. forces had greater logistical problems. The United States was "carrying on a war across the ocean and has to ship most of the necessities from the American continent even if it can use supply bases in Japan. Therefore its supply lines are much longer, eventually making it difficult for them to reinforce manpower and supplies." The Chinese would be close to the rear bases and "backed by their fatherland." The organization of supplies would also be much easier because "We have less trucks and artillery, we won't consume that much gasoline and ammunition."[29]

Chinese Concerns Are Heightened

As planning progressed, PRC leaders, already furious over the interdiction of Taiwan, were made more suspicious when they learned of Chiang Kai-shek's offer of 30,000 troops for Korea. Suspicions were further heightened when General MacArthur took time out from direction of the war to make a highly publicized inspection trip to Taiwan.

The Joint Chiefs had decided to send a survey team to Taiwan to see just what shape the island was in. General MacArthur decided to go himself. In allied capitals, there was considerable consternation at this decision. Was something being planned with the Nationalists? In Washington, the concern was that MacArthur's presence was focusing too much attention on Taiwan. Chiang Kai-shek ratcheted up the tension a few more notches with an announcement that the meeting had taken place at a "most difficult time" for his cause, but that "the foundation had been laid for a joint defense of Taiwan and for Sino-American military cooperation." He looked forward to cooperation with "our old comrade in arms, General MacArthur," who was admired "for the determination with which he has carried on the common struggle against totalitarianism in Asia and for the depth of his understanding of the menace of Communism." MacArthur threw more fuel on the fire with his statement, on his return to Tokyo, praising Chiang for his "indomitable determination to resist Communist domination."[30]

Yet more fuel was added on 26 August with the release of a letter MacArthur had written to the national encampment of the Veterans of Foreign Wars (VFW). MacArthur had been invited to attend and speak, which he was unable to do. Instead, he sent a letter stating his view on the importance of Taiwan. He called it, as he had earlier, "an unsinkable aircraft carrier and submarine tender" that must not be allowed to fall into hostile hands. With Taiwan, United States air power could dominate every Asian port from Vladivostok to Singapore. To the Chinese, this was a threat that fed their paranoia and suggested a change in U.S. thinking. Then MacArthur added this gratuitous criticism:[31]

> Nothing could be more fallacious than the threadbare argument by those who advocate appeasement and defeatism in the Pacific that if we defend Taiwan we alienate continental Asia. Those who speak thus do not understand the Orient. They do not grasp that it is in the pattern of the Oriental psychology to respect and to follow aggressive, resolute and dynamic leadership—to quickly turn from a leadership characterized by timidity or vacillation—and they under-estimate the Oriental mentality. Nothing in the last five years has so inspired the Far East as the American determination to preserve the bulwarks of our Pacific Ocean strategic position from future encroachment, for few of its people fail accurately to appraise the safeguard such determination brings to their free institutions.

MacArthur was ordered to withdraw the message, but it had surely heightened PRC fears of hostile American action. Nor were the Chinese Communists the only paranoid ones. MacArthur had his own suspicions. According to Maj. Gen. Courtney Whitney—MacArthur's military secretary, close confidant, and later biographer—the general saw the order to withdraw his letter as the first clear illustration of the devious workings of the Washington-London team who wanted to hand over Taiwan to the Communists.

There were more alarming signals. On 17 August, the U.S. ambassador to the United Nations, Warren Austin, made a speech suggesting that Korea should be unified and the North Korean Army should be destroyed. This was the first hint that the United States seriously considered going north of the thirty-eighth parallel. On 1 September, the United States vetoed a USSR proposal at the United Nations for a cease-fire in Korea to be followed by a political settlement.

In late August, Secretary of the Navy Francis P. Matthews made a speech suggesting that the United States should start a war to compel cooperation for peace. Less than a week later, the commandant of the Air War College, Gen. Orvil Anderson, delivered a lecture in which he claimed that America was already at war and that he could "break up Russia's five A-bomb nests in a week."[32] President Truman attempted to allay Chinese fears in a public statement: "We do not want the fighting in Korea to spread into a general war: It will not spread unless Communist imperialism draws other armies and governments into the fight. . . . We hope in particular that the people of China will not be misled or forced into fighting against the United Nations and against the American people who have always been and still are their friends."[33]

Rambunctiously, Syngman Rhee added his own contribution to Chinese fears on 10 September when he stated that the advance northward must not stop until the Reds were driven entirely out of Korea. At the end of September, Ambassador Warren Austin, in connection with the UN resolution authorizing the advance across the thirty-eighth parallel, argued that opportunities for new acts of aggression should be removed. The North Koreans should not be permitted to take refuge behind an imaginary line. He declared the line along the thirty-eighth parallel an artificial barrier that had no basis for existence in either law or reason.

On 28 September, the British high commissioner to India had told Jawaharlal Nehru that it was not the present intention for UN forces to go beyond the fortieth parallel, approximately the line of the narrow neck of Korea, and that the idea was that the occupation forces of North Korea as far as possible would be composed of South Koreans.[34] Subsequent statements by Zhou Enlai indicate this information was passed on to the Chinese. So, by 1 October, the Chinese were aware that the UN Command planned to cross the thirty-eighth parallel in pursuit of the North Korean Army and was only waiting for UN authorization to do so. In November, Zhou wrote in the Communist Party newspaper: "Our intelligence [was] that the [Americans] planned first to cross the 38th Parallel without provoking China and then to direct their spearhead at China. We saw through that trick. . . . Nehru told me that the UN forces would stop 40 miles short of the Yalu River after crossing the 38th Parallel. . . . If we did nothing, the aggressive enemy would surely continue its advance up to the Yalu River and would devise a second scheme [against China]."[35]

In the week prior to 9 October, *Newsweek* published its feature article on the planned UNC advance to the "MacArthur Line."

Training

Mao's arguments on the ability to fight Americans was incorporated into the political training of the NEFF. Political training, which the Chinese Communists considered as important or more so than tactical training, also emphasized the theme of defending China. Training in the 42d Army was typical. Intensive political motivation began after arriving at concentration areas. The troops were told that U.S. forces were marching toward the Yalu River and planned to invade Manchuria. They could expect to encounter South Korean, Japanese, Chinese Nationalist, and American forces. Any PLA members who surrendered would be immediately decapitated.

The 42d Army had a large number of former Guomindang soldiers from the 50th Nationalist Army who had been incorporated wholesale into the PLA. Many of those had been trained by an American military advisory force late in World War II. Those with such experience were selected to lecture on U.S. tactics.

In the 13th Army Group, much thought was devoted to the tactical problem of facing up to superior U.S. firepower and equipment. The Chinese realized that U.S. firepower was so heavy that frontal attacks would not be effective. That could be countered by surprise, by night attacks, and by quickly closing with the enemy. U.S. troops feared being cut off from their line of communication and withdrawal. Envelopment and cutting lines of communication would be effective. These were traditional PLA tactics. Unit commanders were directed to concentrate on them in their training.

By the latter part of August, it was understood at all levels that Chinese troops would have to enter the war sooner or later. Just when, where, and how they should intervene was the subject of a study prepared by the 13th Army Group and forwarded to Beijing. The conclusion was that the sooner Chinese forces entered the war, the better. They should help the North Korean Army maintain the initiative before a U.S. counteroffensive could reach the point where northeast China was under threat. The study assumed that a portion of the U.S. forces would hold the Pusan perimeter while additional forces made an amphibious counterattack in the rear. In that event, the most propitious time for Chinese entry would be when the U.S. counteroffensive had crossed the thirty-eighth parallel. This would put the Chinese forces in a favorable position militarily. It would also be politically advantageous. The report was forwarded to Beijing, where, it appears, it coincided with thinking within the Central Military Commission.[36]

New Decisions

On 23 August, Zhou Enlai assigned Lei Yingfu of the general staff to analyze the possibilities of U.S. action. Based on reports that several Marine divisions were being transported to Japan, Lei thought that the UNC counteroffensive would come by sea at one of six ports. He believed Inchon would be MacArthur's most likely choice.[37] All railroads joining North and South Korea funnel through Seoul, just twenty-five miles inland from Inchon. Except for the serious hydrographic problems, it would be the natural choice of any planner.

On 25 July, elements of the 2d Marine Division were ordered to the U.S. west coast to join the 1st Marine Division. On 27 July, the 7th Infantry Division was alerted to prepare for movement to Korea. On 2 August, the 1st Provisional Marine Brigade reached Korea. By 12 August, MacArthur had decided on Inchon as the target for a landing and established a separate planning group for the operation on 15 August. By 10 August, the 1st Marine Division had been brought to war strength, less one regiment, and had sailed from the west coast. On 24 August, X Corps was activated as the force to command the Inchon landing.

Unquestionably, the Chinese were aware of some of this activity, as evidenced by the report of several Marine divisions being transported to Japan. Not knowing that all three Marine units were, or would become, part of one division, they undoubtedly considered it a formidable force. It is interesting to note that the Chinese identified the commander of the 1st Marine Division as H. M. Smith, the well-known World War II Marine general, rather than Maj. Gen. Oliver P. Smith.

The source of their information might have been the notorious British espionage agents Kim Philby and Guy Burgess, both of whom were then in Washington, D.C., or other sources in Japan. MacArthur's State Department adviser, William Sebald, reported that before the landing it was almost an open secret in Tokyo that Inchon was the target.[38] Lei Yingfu's prescience in selecting Inchon most probably was based on more accurate information than the Chinese accounts are willing to reveal. It appears that the Chinese were unaware of the timing for the landing, because the subsequent orders to the PLA's 9th and 19th Army Groups indicated a leisurely schedule. Whatever the source of the Chinese information, Kim Il Sung was notified of the conclusion but appeared to ignore it.

Zhou Enlai called a meeting of the Central Military Commission on 26 August and outlined the situation: "China should get ready for a reversal of the war. . . . we should prepare for the worst and prepare quickly."[39] An estimate of 200,000 casualties in the first six months of the war was presented. There was the possibility of having to deal with three or even four more U.S. divisions. More troops would be needed. Mao telegraphed to Peng Dehuai, vice chairman of the CMC and vice commander of the army: "To cope with the current situation, we must now assemble 12 corps [armies] for emergency use. The decision, however, can be made at the end of September when we will invite you to Beijing for face-to-face discussions."[40]

To provide the additional forces, the 9th and 19th Army Groups were alerted. The 9th Army Group was ordered to move inland to embarkation points on the Tianjin–Pukou (near Nanjing) Railway. Those formations were then to move in October to positions along the railroad in Shandong Province, to Qufu and Feicheng, and commence training. They would then move to Manchuria or into Korea as the situation dictated. The 19th Army Group, then in western China, was also alerted to take positions along the Longhai Railroad.[41] The 19th Army Group would be readied for employment in the spring. Once the 13th Army Group entered Korea, the Manchurian side of the border area would be left undefended. To provide for this, the 50th Army was ordered northward from Hubei on 6 September to become part of the Northeast Frontier Force.[42]

Inchon and the Decision to Fight
The historical evidence seems to indicate that the timing of the Inchon landing came as a surprise to the Chinese. Nie Rongzhen tells of Mao's agonizing over the decision to intervene in the war. Within days of the landing, two emissaries from North Korea reached Andong and appealed for help from the 13th Army Group. Deng Hua sent their request on to Beijing. Stalin urged the Chinese to step in, promised arms and air support, and even extended the promise that the Soviet Union would come in if the Chinese were threatened with defeat.[43]

Looming over the final decision was the mushroom cloud of atomic war. Fear of the bomb had spread through the PLA and much of China. In the 13th Army Group, the Yalu River bridges were called the "gates of hell." Debate raged among the senior officers of the PLA. Mao steadfastly maintained that the Chinese could face atomic war and survive. His conclusion was based on both tactical and strategic considerations.

If atomic weapons were employed strategically, there were special considerations. The Chinese were aware of the limited U.S. stock of atomic weapons. There were no prime targets. Chinese industry was limited and scattered. To Mao's way of thinking, the war was a people's war. The outcome would be decided by men, not weapons. The Soviet Union had extensive interests in Manchuria, such as the railroad. The use of atomic weapons there would provoke the Soviets and possibly bring them in. In any case, the United States would hesitate to use atomic weapons for fear of retaliation from the new Soviet atomic arsenal. The Chinese would be protected by the Soviet nuclear umbrella.[44]

On the tactical level, methods could be devised to minimize the damage. In mobile warfare with the troops dispersed, there would be no good targets. Forces could concentrate quickly for a decisive effort then disperse quickly. Forces could take cover in field fortifications, which would limit the impact. The mountainous terrain was not suitable for an atomic drop; much of the blast would be shielded by the terrain. In the expected pattern of action, Chinese and U.S. units would be intermixed in a "jigsaw pattern."[45]

The U.S. nuclear arsenal was the linchpin of American strategic planning. The status of that arsenal was generally believed, at the time, to be one of the most closely guarded American secrets. Actually, the stockpile was in pitiful condition. In April 1947, David Lilienthal, then head of the Atomic Energy Commission (AEC) and the man responsible for production and custody of the bombs, inspected the stockpile and found no assembled bombs and no assembly teams trained. By June, thirteen bombs had been assembled, with no more than thirty by March 1948. Production in 1948 was limited to two bombs per month. A string of spies had passed onto the Soviets the most crucial secrets of the nuclear program. Further, for four years, until September 1949, the month the Soviets detonated their own bomb, Donald Maclean—who, along with Philby and Burgess, was one of the most notorious Soviet spies of the Cold War—had been the British liaison with the AEC. It was admitted later that Maclean knew the requirements for uranium and the status of its supply for the atomic-energy program. That knowledge would be highly useful for Soviet strategic planners. The Chinese, through the good offices of their Soviet allies, would have been acutely aware of the limited American stock of atomic weapons. Mao could be confident that the U.S. use of such weapons would be limited.

Chinese Warnings
In the weeks leading up to the formal decision to enter the war, the Chinese had sent a series of steadily escalating warnings. As early as 16 August, *World Culture,* the CCP organ, had claimed that American action in Korea was a threat to Chinese security and that the problem of Korea could not be settled without the participation of its closest neighbor, China. More ominously, the article had stated: ". . . North Korea's enemy is our enemy. North Korea's defense is our

defense. North Korea's victory is our victory."[46] A few days later, Zhou Enlai sent a telegram to the UN with essentially that same message. On 25 August, Zhou responded to MacArthur's letter to the VFW regarding Taiwan. In a telegram to the UN, he called U.S. support of Chiang a criminal act of armed aggression and vowed to liberate all Oriental territory from the tentacles of the U.S. aggressors.

Beginning in late September, after the Inchon landing and while the Chinese decision to enter the war began to take firm shape, the tempo of belligerent Chinese statements increased. On 22 September, a Foreign Ministry spokesman answered MacArthur's August complaint that the Chinese had returned ethnic Korean members of the PLA to North Korea to augment the NKPA. The spokesman admitted the charge and claimed that China would always stand by the side of the Korean people. Two days later, Zhou sent another telegram to the UN complaining of U.S. bombing of Chinese territory. Although his telegram to the UN was reasonably mild, the extension of his remarks in the Chinese publication *Renmin Ribao* was more militant. He said, "The flames of war being extended by the United States are burning more fiercely." If the UN General Assembly should continue to bow to the demands of the United States and ignore these crimes, he added, ". . . it would not escape a share in the responsibility for lighting up the war-flames in the Far East."[47]

On 30 September, Zhou Enlai made a report to the Chinese People's Government Council. His speech, broadcast the following day, was a long litany of complaints against the United States. The warning came in an oblique statement near the end: "The Chinese people absolutely will not tolerate foreign aggression, nor will they supinely tolerate seeing their neighbors being savagely invaded by the imperialists."[48]

As UNC forces were mopping up in Seoul and preparing to move north, Kim Il Sung made a personal and urgent plea for help. Mao convened the Politburo on 2 October to review Kim's request and announced to the conference that the questions were who would command and when troops should be sent. There was no question of whether or not to send troops. Mao stated his arguments about atomic warfare. He admitted that the Communists might lose the coming struggle. If they did, they would again withdraw into the interior, as they had done before the Japanese and the GMD, and would rebuild for future generations. He did not think the ROK forces, whom the Chinese always referred to as "puppet" troops, would fight hard or well. With the Americans, it was a matter of breaking their will: "The key lies in the number of Americans we can kill." In a prophetic bit of insight, he believed that heavy American casualties would make people wonder if it was worth it, forcing Washington to end the war on terms favorable to the Chinese.[49] The meeting continued for several days, but Mao had made up his mind. That same day, he telegraphed Stalin that the Chinese had decided to send troops to fight under the name of volunteers.

Mao made it clear to Stalin that the initial stage would be defensive. Only when his troops were equipped with Soviet weapons would he undertake offensive action in cooperation with the Korean comrades. In addition to the initial force of twelve divisions, another force of twenty-four divisions, the 9th and 19th Army Groups, was being readied for deployment as the second and third waves in the spring and summer of the following year—if the situation required and if adequate supplies and equipment were forthcoming.[50]

Further Discussions

Many members of the Politburo and many senior PLA officers opposed entry into the war. Zhou Enlai, Ren Bishi, Chen Yi, and Lin Biao all argued against it. They argued that China had a huge deficit and there was a need to recuperate after the years of the civil war. Land reform needed to be carried out. There were still areas of China to be pacified and cleared of bandits. They argued that the PLA was unequipped to fight a modern war. It had no tanks or artillery. Despite Mao's arguments, scare stories were sweeping the country on the menace of the atom bomb.[51]

Only Nie Rongzhen, Peng Dehuai, and Mao were in favor of intervention. Mao asked Lin Biao to take command of the troops entering Korea. Lin was one of the most successful of the Chinese generals. He declined, saying he was ill. He cited the shortcomings of the Chinese Army, noting, "We have a certainty of success in defeating the Nationalist troops. The United States is highly modern-

ized. In addition, it possesses the atomic bomb. I have no certainty
of success [in fighting the U.S. Army]. The central leadership should
consider this issue with great care."[52] Nie Rongzhen said he had never
seen Lin so frightened of anything.[53] Instead of Lin, Peng Dehuai was
appointed to command.

Although the war was subsequently entitled "The Anti-U.S.–Aid-
Korea War," defense of the Manchurian border was a major consideration. The Chinese did not fear ROK troops on their border. Given
their poor opinion of men they referred to as "puppet" troops, they
probably doubted their ability to reach the border. But U.S. troops
on the border would be a continuing threat. In discussing the need
for intervention with the members of the Politburo, Mao pointed out
the threat to Manchuria if U.S. troops were on the border. The Chinese border with Korea—a tortuous line some 650 miles long—
would be very difficult to defend. Mao emphasized that the burden
of stationing a large number of troops at the northeastern border
for defense was unacceptable. "We would have to wait there year after year, unsure of when the enemy will attack us."[54]

The Chinese Commander
The decision had been made. General Peng Dehuai had been appointed to command the intervention force. The pace of Chinese
preparations accelerated.

At the time of the Chinese entry into Korea, the United States believed that Lin Biao was in command of the Chinese forces. This belief persisted for most of the war and, for some histories, many years
afterward. The assumption that he was in command was probably
because the armies initially engaged were from the Fourth Field
Army, Lin's command. Lin was the best known of the Chinese generals. His campaigns in Manchuria had been brilliant. He had the
reputation of having never lost a battle. He was a clever and worthy
opponent, one who was capable of devising the daring maneuvers
that drove the UN out of North Korea.

Peng Dehuai, the man who actually did command, was far less well
known.[55] He played out his role in the Chinese Civil War in a remote
part of China with few spectacular successes and with little public attention. It is worth a small diversion to put a human face on this mys-

terious general who came to our attention only when he appeared to sign the armistice agreement.

At the time of his appointment, Peng was fifty-three years old, had served the Red Army for twenty-two years, and was the vice chairman of the Central Military Commission and commander of the First Field Army. Prior to being called to Beijing, he was in the northwest engaged in a campaign to complete Communist pacification of the provinces of Shaanxi, Ningxia, Gansu, and Xinjiang, a huge territory that stretched for nearly 2,000 miles across that sparse area.

In the fine distinctions the Communists made about desirable proletarian origins, Peng classed himself as being of lower/middle peasant origins, one step above the lowest of the twelve classes. During the great Cultural Revolution, Red Guards classified him as being of "rich peasant" origin, by definition untrustworthy. Later, when he was rehabilitated, the government officially classified him as "poor peasant." The disputed classifications seem to have depended on the weight given to the fact that his father owned a bean-curd shop.

Details of Peng's early years are vague and contradictory. He was born in the village of Shikksiang, Hunan Province, not far from the provincial capital of Changsha and also not far from Mao Zedong's birthplace. He attended school for three years, then left for reasons unknown and spent several years in odd jobs at various places, returning home in 1913. That year there was a bad drought in Hunan. In Shikksiang there was a demonstration, which Peng joined. He took part in breaking into a grain merchant's storehouse and distributed grain to the demonstrators. Finding he was wanted by the police, he departed again. Until the age of seventeen, he worked at various jobs, including construction, until he enlisted as a second-class private in the "Hunan Army." This was in 1915.

Many of the young officers in warlord armies were increasingly influenced by nationalist feelings and with the aims of Sun Yat-sen and the Guomindang. Peng's first platoon commander had taken part in the 1911 rebellion, hated corrupt officials and landlords, and influenced Peng to become more interested in politics and the national revolution.

For the next six years, Peng soldiered on, gradually being promoted through the enlisted ranks until 1921, when he was promoted to second lieutenant and became a platoon commander. The following year, hc took the examination and entered the Hunan Provincial Military Academy. He returned to his unit and took part in a number of campaigns, rising in rank to major and finally to colonel in February 1928. In the meantime, his interest in politics, and particularly in Communism, had increased. In the summer of 1928, his regiment was sent to Pingjiang, northwest of Changsha, to chase down some Communist rebels.

The Guomindang was introducing commissars into the National Revolutionary Army. Many of them were Communists. The agitators found a promising target in Peng, who remembered the hardship of his youth. Peng was permitted to join the Party some time early in 1928. Under Peng's leadership, his regiment revolted on 22 July, arrested and executed the county magistrate and some 100 landlords, and declared the establishment of the Hunan Provincial Soviet Government. He announced his unit as the 5th Corps of the Chinese Workers' and Peasants' Army.

Peng's "5th Corps" was quickly driven out by GMD forces. He retreated to the mountains of Jinggangshan, joined Mao Zedong (who had established the Central Soviet Area there), and commenced his thirty-year association with the Communist Party.

Peng fought for six years in defense of the Central Soviet Area. He was wounded twice in the "extermination" campaigns conducted by the GMD Army. By 1933, he was commanding the 3d Army Corps, First Front Army. In October 1934, this corps marched out of Jiangxi as the advance guard on the Long March.

After the Communists reached North Shaanxi, Peng's corps merged with the 15th Army Corps to form a new First Front Army with Peng as commander and Mao as political commissar. In 1937, when the Communists joined with the Guomindang in a common front against the Japanese, the Red Army was reorganized as the 8th Route Army, with Zhu Deh as commander and Peng as deputy. In 1940, Peng launched the "Hundred Regiments Campaign," an offensive against the Japanese that made considerable progress. Ultimately, Peng's forces were driven back, sustaining serious losses, in a Japanese counteroffensive called the "Three All" campaign: "Kill all—Burn all—Destroy all."

When the Japanese surrender occurred, Peng was assigned to the Northwest Military Field Army, with the initial mission of accepting the surrender of Japanese in northwestern China and Inner Mongolia. Then, with the outbreak of the Chinese Civil War, he continued in command of this remote region. The campaigns in that huge region were both more difficult and less critical than those conducted in Manchuria and other areas. Peng's performance was mixed. He lost nearly as many battles as he won. In the end, he did succeed in destroying the GMD armies in the area and was making substantial progress in pacification when he was called on to assume command in Korea.

Peng remains a somewhat ambiguous figure. He probably was never a deep student of or believer in all the complexities of international Communism. His great desire was to improve the living conditions of the rural masses. It was this which brought him into conflict with Mao after the Korean War and led to his eventual fall. As a military commander, he was a competent tactician and a good organizer but generally considered to be only an average strategist. But he was persistent and determined.

Peng disagreed with Mao on a number of subjects. Early on, in the Central Soviet Area, he tried to emphasize organized mobile tactics, troops well trained in the technical aspects of military operations, whereas Mao emphasized guerrilla operations and the primacy of political will. It was the classic debate of the moral versus the material factor in war. During the Anti-Japanese War, he disagreed with Mao on military policy. Mao wanted to operate very cautiously, saving the strength of the Red Army for the coming battle with the Guomindang. Peng felt that an all-out effort against the Japanese was morally warranted. Eventually, however, he came around to Mao's thinking.

Not long before his appointment to command in Korea, Peng had completed a report on the modernization of the Red Army. The report emphasized professionalism, good equipment, and subordination of the commissars and the political instructors to the commanders of each unit. Mao disagreed strongly with this emphasis on the materiel and technical aspects. It was a subject that has arisen time and time again in the Chinese armed forces.

Despite these differences, Peng was a strong and loyal supporter of Mao from the very early days. In November 1930, an "Action Committee" made up of members of the local Communist Party expressed opposition to some of Mao's policies. There was fear they were subversives, sympathetic to Chiang Kai-shek. Some of the leading members were arrested and jailed by Zhu Deh's troops. Then, some 400 members of the Red 20th Corps mutinied and freed the prisoners. With the help of Peng Dehuai, the rebellion was suppressed and 4,000 were executed in reprisal. As a result, Peng was appointed deputy commander of the Red troops. He threw his support behind Mao on a number of other critical occasions.

Otto Braun, the Soviet representative and military adviser in the Central Soviet Area, described the Peng–Mao relationship this way: "The most remarkable figure among the corps commanders was Peng Dehuai. Since he had joined the Red Army with his troops in 1928, he supported Mao in whom he saw the charismatic leader of the revolutionary armed force. Yet this does not mean that he agreed to everything. As active politically as militarily, he never minced his words when he thought that criticism was necessary."

Although Peng was well known for the concern he showed for the well-being of his troops, he nevertheless was extravagant in their use in battle. One of the criticisms of his conduct of the war in Korea was his heavy dependence on the "short attack"—a tactic he is said to have invented. This simply consisted of repeated assaults by small groups at the same point in an enemy line until the line gave way. In the West, this was sometimes described as the "human wave," or the "horde." It was a prolific use of men, but one that exploited the one great advantage the Chinese had—a huge supply of manpower.

Personally, Peng's image was that of a modest man of simple wants and tastes who lived a rather spartan existence. He liked to project himself as a basic man of the soil, at one with the Chinese peasant. P. P. Vladimirov, a Soviet adviser to the PLA who did not think very highly of other PLA leaders, described Peng as follows: "Peng Dehuai is well versed in military affairs and is popular in the army. He dresses simply. . . . The most significant trait of his character is modesty. He has a deep, coarse voice, his movements are slow. This man has a rare sense of personal dignity."

In his role as vice chairman of the Central Military Commission, Peng was in touch with overall military planning. In the days prior to the UN thrust into North Korea, he had been in contact with a Soviet liaison group developing joint plans for defense of the USSR and Chinese border and had consulted with other PLA leaders in Beijing concerning the problems of defense of northeastern China.

The decision was made and a commander was selected. Mao sent a telegram to Kim Il Sung informing him of the decision. Zhou Enlai was to go to Moscow to obtain Soviet assistance. Lin Biao would go with him. The name of the Northeast Frontier Force was changed to the Chinese People's Volunteers (CPV). Peng was issued orders to be in readiness to move into Korea, and he flew to Shenyang to take charge.

Notes

1. Zhang, *Mao's Military Romanticism,* 56.
2. Quotcd in Goncharov et al.,*Uncertain Partners,* 157.
3. Ibid., 158.
4. Jian, *China's Road to the Korean War,* 129.
5. Zhang, *Mao's Military Romanticism,* 71–72.
6. Jian, *China's Road to the Korean War,* 136.
7. Allen Whiting, *China Crosses the Yalu: The Decision to Enter the Korean War* (Palo Alto, Calif.: Stanford University Press, 1968), 90.
8. Goncharov et al., *Uncertain Partners,* 159–61.
9. The Chinese designation of military units does not translate precisely into English. The conventions adopted during the Korean War are followed here. CCF armies were numbered with arabic numerals and consisted of three or four divisions, corresponding generally to a U.S. corps. The sizes of CCF divisions varied considerably, but those employed in Korea generally had about 10,000 men. CCF army groups were numbered with arabic numerals and consisted of two or more armies, corresponding generally to a U.S. field army. CCF field armies were made up of two or more army groups and corresponded in size to a U.S. army group. The numerical designation of CCF field armies was generally spelled out.
10. Goncharov et al., 153n.
11. Zhang, *Mao's Military Romanticism,* 48; William W. Whitson, ed., *The Chinese High Command* (New York: Praeger, 1973).
12. Jian, *China's Road to the Korean War,* 137.
13. Goncharov et al., *Uncertain Partners,* 162–63.
14. Chinese Academy of Military Science, *The War History of the Chinese People's Volunteers in the War to Resist U.S. Aggression and Aid Korea* (Beijing: Military Science Press, 1988). Unpublished partial translation in possession of the author (hereafter cited as *Chinese People's Volunteers*).
15. Goncharov et al., *Uncertain Partners,* 159–61.
16. Russell Spurr, *Enter the Dragon; China's Undeclared War Against the U.S. in Korea, 1950–51* (New York: Henry Holt, 1988), 59–60.
17. Goncharov et al., *Uncertain Partners,* 162–63.
18. Ibid., 62–66.

19. Zhang, *Mao's Military Romanticism*, 64.

20. Ibid., 56–57.

21. Xiaobing Li, Wang Xi, and Chen Jian, trans., "Mao's Dispatch of Chinese Troops to Korea: Forty-Six Telegrams, July–October 1950." *Chinese Historians* 5, no. 1 (spring 1992), hereafter cited as 46 Telegrams.

22. Zhang, *Mao's Military Romanticism*, 60.

23. Ibid., 62.

24. Goncharov et al., *Uncertain Partners*, Doc. 59, 272.

25. Ibid., 173.

26. Zhang, *Mao's Military Romanticism*, 76–77.

27. Ibid.

28. Ibid.

29. Ibid.

30. Rees, *The Limited War*, 73.

31. MacArthur letter 20 August 1950 to VFW.

32. *HJCS*, 260.

33. Quoted in Whiting, *China Crosses the Yalu*, 98.

34. Telegram Henderson (India) to Sec State, *FRUS*, 808–9.

35. Goncharov et al., *Uncertain Partners*, 193–94.

36. Jian, *China's Road to the Korean War*, 151–52.

37. Ibid., 171.

38. Sebald, *With MacArthur in Japan*, 182.

39. Jian, *China's Road to the Korean War*, 150.

40. Goncharov et al., *Uncertain Partners*, Doc. 60, 272.

41. *Chinese People's Volunteers*.

42. Ibid.

43. Goncharov et al., *Uncertain Partners*, 174.

44. Ibid., 165–66.

45. Ibid.

46. Quoted in Whiting, *China Crosses the Yalu*, 70.

47. Zhang, *Mao's Military Romanticism*, 77.

48. Nie Rongzhen, *Inside the Red Star*, 635.

49. Goncharov et al., *Uncertain Partners*, 182.

50. Ibid., Doc. 63, 276.

51. Ibid., 180–81.

52. Ibid., 167.

53. Nie Rongzhen, *Inside the Red Star,* 636. In 1974, Lin Biao fell from grace when he led an abortive coup against Mao; he died in the crash of the airplane in which he was attempting to escape.

54. Zhang, *Mao's Military Romanticism,* 82.

55. The material in this section is taken from Jurgen Domes, *Peng Te-huai: The Man and the Image* (Palo Alto, Calif.: Stanford University Press, 1985), and Whitson, *The Chinese High Command.*

5
The Chinese Threat

We know what we are in for, but at all costs American aggression has to be stopped. The Americans can bomb us, they can destroy our industries, but they cannot defeat us on land.
—General Nie Rongzhen

Will the Chinese Intervene?
The possibility of Chinese intervention was of concern from the very opening of the Korean War. U.S. military authorities believed that the entire Communist bloc was a monolithic organization closely controlled from the Kremlin, although diplomatic experts were less certain. If the forces of any Communist country were involved, the USSR was likely behind it. With the decision to pursue the North Korean Army across the thirty-eighth parallel and enter what had been Communist territory, the concern about intervention increased.

Two important provisions of MacArthur's new instructions were to submit all plans for approval and to make a special effort to determine ". . . whether there is a Chinese Communist or Soviet threat to the attainment of your objective." Standard military doctrine of the time would have made this question "an essential element of information" that would focus the intelligence efforts of all subordinate units on the collection and evaluation of any information indicating Soviet or Chinese intervention. General J. Lawton Collins, then Army chief of staff, estimated that 90 percent of the intelligence received came from the Far Eastern Command (FEC). That made it even more urgent that Far Eastern intelligence agencies focus on any evidence of Chinese intervention or intention to intervene.

Sources of political intelligence, which might provide advance warning of Chinese intention to intervene, were limited. Without diplomatic relations with the People's Republic of China (PRC), the United States had to rely on information supplied by a small corps of friendly diplomats in Beijing. Considerable political and military information came from the Republic of China (ROC) government on Taiwan, which retained some useful connections on the mainland. But information from the ROC had to be handled with caution. The ROC had a vested interest in fomenting friction with the Communists. The Communist takeover on the mainland had eliminated many of the U.S. sources of information. Because there was regular movement of people back and forth between Hong Kong and mainland China, much information, quite often contradictory, came through the listening post in Hong Kong.

For several weeks after the outbreak of the war, the Chinese were silent. Then, on 16 August 1950, the article in *World Culture* (see chapter 4), saying that American action in Korea was threatening the security of China, provided a clue to Chinese thinking. Another clue was Zhou Enlai's cable to the UN saying the question of Korea could not be settled without the participation of China. Beijing's announcement on 22 September that China would always stand on the side of the Korean people was a further clue. These were the first of several warnings against any advance beyond the thirty-eighth parallel.

On 23 September, a report from the ROC minister of defense, partially confirmed by other sources, said that the Chinese Communists were preparing to send 250,000 troops in North Korean uniforms to fight in Korea. An intriguing footnote to this report pointed out that because winter was approaching, the Chinese would need quilted cotton uniforms, which would have to be made by hand. Consequently, the conclusion was that it would be some time before the Chinese troops could deploy.[1]

Other reports were more reassuring. Also on 23 September the U.S. consul general in Hong Kong forwarded a report from a source, believed to be reliable, saying Zhou Enlai had stated the Chinese would not get involved in the Korean War or fight outside China unless attacked. The reasons were the desire to avoid any action that would prejudice China's entry into the UN, and the desire to focus all efforts on reconstruction. But China would provide token support in the form of food and medicine. This was confirmed by a second report that China had given 100,000 first-aid parcels and 500 tons of food to North Korea.[2] The consul general also noted fewer articles in the New China News Agency (Xinhua) on Korea or U.S. "aggression" against Manchuria, lending credence to the belief that China would not intervene. Two days later, another source reported a similar statement from Zhu Deh, PLA commander, saying that China would not send troops into Korea but that the Chinese people were sympathetic with the Korean people and would give them other forms of aid.[3] These reports seemed reassuring. They were quickly seized upon as reinforcement for what seemed the logical conclusion that it was too late for the Chinese to intervene.

The Panikkar Reports

The most direct and positive intelligence on the Chinese intention to enter the war was a series of reports by Kavalam M. Panikkar, Indian ambassador to Beijing. Throughout the summer, Jawaharlal Nehru, the Indian prime minister, had attempted to bring hostilities to a halt. He had kept in close touch with the Chinese through Panikkar, trying to convince them that the UN forces were no threat to China and that they had no need to become involved. Panikkar became a regular conduit to and from the Chinese.

On 20 September, Panikkar met with Zhou Enlai to deliver a message from Nehru. Incidental to his talk with Zhou, Panikkar reported that Zhou had displayed "no interest [in Korea] beyond [an] expression of sympathy." Zhou had intimated the PRC would take action only ". . . if a world war starts as a result of UN forces passing beyond the 38th parallel and the Soviet Union deciding directly to intervene." Panikkar felt that China by herself would not interfere. He also reported his additional belief, based on firsthand observations, that, on balance, "there is no evidence of military preparations in Manchuria."[4]

Two days later, the U.S. State Department asked India to inform the Chinese that it would be in their best interest not to interfere in Korea, and that China's territorial integrity would be respected. After delivering the message, Panikkar reported that Chinese direct participation in the Korean War appeared "beyond the range of possibility."[5]

Dramatically different information emerged on 25 September. Panikkar had invited Gen. Nie Rongzhen, acting chief of staff of the

PLA, to dinner. The resulting conversation is best told in Panikkar's own words:

> Nie told me in a quiet and unexcited manner that the Chinese did not intend to sit back with folded hands and let the Americans come up to the border. This was the first indication I had that the Chinese proposed to intervene. . . . I was taken aback a little by this statement, all the more impressive because it was said in a quiet and pleasant tone, as if he were telling me that he intended to go shooting the next day. I asked him if he realized in full the implications of such an action. . . . He replied, "We know what we are in for, but at all costs American aggression has to be stopped. The Americans can bomb us, they can destroy our industries, but they cannot defeat us on land." I tried to impress on him how destructive a war with America would be . . . put China back by half a century. . . . He only laughed, "We have calculated all that. They may even drop atom bombs on us. What then? They may kill a few million people. Without sacrifice a nation's independence cannot be upheld." He gave some calculations of the effectiveness of atom bombs and said, "After all, China lives on farms. What can atom bombs do there? Yes, our economic development will be put back. We may have to wait for it."[6]

Panikkar made a full report to his government, which passed it on to the British, who passed it on to the United States. Panikkar emphasized Nie's bitterness at the PRC's being denied a seat in the United Nations and at an accidental UN air attack on Andong.

The United States first heard of Panikkar's conversation with Nie when the councillor of the British Embassy in Washington arrived at the State Department with copies of two telegrams from Panikkar. The State Department was not permitted to make copies of either. The first outlined Nie's conversation and in particular his complaint of the accidental bombing of Chinese territory. Panikkar also quoted a conversation with the Polish ambassador, assumed to have more reliable information, that the Chinese would not endure further provocation and would not "sit idly by with folded hands" in the face of it. In the second telegram, Panikkar changed the conclusion he had drawn from his previous conversation with Zhou on 20 September. At that time, Zhou had said that, ". . . since the UN had no obligations to China, China had no obligations to the UN." Based on that, and Nie's conversation, Panikkar concluded that China had decided on a more aggressive policy and might intervene directly in Korea.[7]

The U.S. delegation to the United Nations was attempting to obtain a resolution authorizing UN forces to cross the thirty-eighth parallel to destroy the NKPA. India, a strong and influential member of the neutralist bloc in the United Nations, doubted the wisdom of this. Evaluation of this and subsequent reports from Panikkar was muddied by the belief that the messages coming from China were intended to coerce India into opposing the proposed UN resolution.

At the UN, the British said that they did not take too seriously Panikkar's fears; they believed him to be a volatile and unreliable reporter. The report of his conversation with Nie was a complete about-face from his previous accounts. On 28 September, the British weighed in with a lengthy estimate, reviewing the evidence to date and concluding that Chinese intervention in Korea would be contrary to their interests and not likely to occur.[8] However, this estimate reported that, contrary to what had come from the U.S. consul general in Hong Kong, there was a significant increase in violent Chinese propaganda against the United States.

Within the State Department, Panikkar's report was viewed with skepticism. Secretary of State Dean Acheson agreed that Panikkar was an unreliable reporter. Further, Panikkar was considered to be a left-leaning Communist sympathizer. The report was dismissed as Chinese bluster.[9] Nearly all statements or demands made by the Communists since taking power had been truculent and strident. Amid all the bluster, it was difficult to tell what was genuine.

On 29 September, Adm. Alan G. Kirk, the U.S. ambassador in Moscow, forwarded a report received from a Dutch source that the Chinese were thinking of intervention. Kirk added that Panikkar's report stressing the possibility of Chinese intervention was based on the Chinese belief that the United States would carry the war on into Manchuria and China in order to facilitate the return of Chiang Kai-shek. Kirk discounted both reports, arguing that the optimum time for Chinese intervention had passed. Kirk added that he believed the Chinese were making a strong effort to bluff the UN out of crossing the thirty-eighth parallel. Nevertheless, Kirk advised caution.[10]

Further forceful evidence of Chinese concern came soon afterward in a speech by Zhou Enlai on 1 October, the first anniversary of the People's Republic of China. In honor of the day, Zhou spoke to the Central People's Government Council, saying, ". . . the Chinese people will absolutely not tolerate foreign aggression in Korea, nor will they supinely tolerate seeing their neighbors being savagely invaded by imperialists." That same day, South Korean troops crossed the thirty-eighth parallel and Kim Il Sung again begged for assistance from China.[11]

Zhou's speech was closely studied, but in Hong Kong, the consul general, after receiving a full copy of the speech, interpreted it to mean that China would support North Korea diplomatically and with some materiel, not with troops.[12]

The most forceful and plainly stated warning came from Kavalam Panikkar in Beijing on 3 October. He was roused from his bed at 12:30 A.M. and was asked to meet with Zhou Enlai at his official residence. As Panikkar later reported:

> Zhou thanked Pandit Nehru for what he had been doing in the cause of peace, and said no country's need for peace was greater than that of China, but there were occasions when peace could only be defended by determination to resist aggression. If the Americans crossed the 38th Parallel China would be forced to intervene in Korea. Otherwise he was most anxious for a peaceful settlement, and generally accepted Pandit Nehru's approach to the question. I asked him whether he already had news of the Americans having crossed the border. He replied in the affirmative, but added that he did not know where they had crossed. I asked him whether China intended to intervene if only the South Koreans crossed the parallel. He was emphatic: "The South Koreans did not matter but American intrusion into North Korea would encounter Chinese resistance."[13]

Panikkar was asked to report that to his government. By this time, Mao had already informed the Soviets of his decision to enter the war.

Panikkar's report of his conversation with Zhou was received by the United States via the British in a brief telegram at 5:35 A.M. on 3 October. It was immediately disseminated to all concerned embassies and to the Department of Defense for transmission to MacArthur. It was included in the daily selection of important telegrams sent to the president. However, opinion within the State Department again was mixed. At a morning meeting with the deputy secretary, the majority, nervous at the report, seemed to regard it as more bluff, pending further information.[14] The majority in the Far Eastern Department were not so sure. Acheson said the warning was not to be disregarded but was ". . . not an authoritative statement of policy."[15] Deputy Secretary James E. Webb thought the statement was indirect and obscure. Webb noted that Zhou Enlai had communicated directly with the UN on a number of matters. He concluded that because Zhou had not gone directly to the UN with this concern, his statements might be designed to dissuade India and intimidate other nations from firm support of the UN action in Korea.[16]

In New Delhi, U.S. ambassador Loy Henderson talked to the Indian Foreign Office about the Panikkar reports. Initially he was not given the full text. Some of Zhou Enlai's remarks about the Americans were so derogatory that there was concern they would further widen the breach the Indian government was trying to close. Eventually Henderson saw the full telegram. In his report, Panikkar passed on the Chinese argument that the Korean War was a civil war, within Korea. Invasion of the South by the North was not foreign aggression. However, if the United States insisted on calling it foreign aggression, then it would also be foreign aggression if U.S. troops crossed the border into North Korea.[17]

The Burmese ambassador to Beijing knew the Chinese well. He reported to his government, which passed it on to the American ambassador, that he shared Panikkar's apprehensions concerning Chinese intentions. He felt that the suddenness of Zhou's warning, given late at night, coupled with what he observed to be feverish activity and unusual security measures adopted in Beijing before and after the warning, together with the reports of half a million Chinese Communist troops assembled near the Korean border, all lent weight to the message. In passing on the message, the Burmese foreign minister noted that he thought his ambassador's fears were exaggerated.[18]

The Dutch considered Panikkar to be either a fellow traveler or highly sympathetic to the Chinese regime, but they believed his report was essentially correct. When it was pointed out to Zhou that events in the UN General Assembly seemed to indicate more favorable concern, Zhou had insisted that China had to defend itself against "further aggression" by the United States, and that crossing the thirty-eighth parallel would be considered as such. Nie Rongzhen's conversation included the statement that if no resistance were offered now, China would be forever under American control. Panikkar had apparently pointed out to the Dutch ambassador that U.S. retention of Secretary of the Navy Francis B. Matthews was an indication that the United States was determined on a war-like course.[19] Matthews's speech advocating a "preventive war" for peace had been noted in Beijing.

Reaction from Hong Kong to Panikkar's report was mixed. The prevailing opinion among informed Chinese was that the PRC would not intervene, but that if Panikkar was actually told the Chinese would send troops if U.S. forces crossed the thirty-eighth parallel, the Chinese must intend to carry out the threat. But the actual language used might have conveyed the threat indirectly so that it would not have to be backed up if their bluff were called. It did not seem that there would be any advantage to the PRC to leave the issue in doubt, then intervene. Issuing a public warning would be much more effective. The U.S. consul general in Hong Kong again reported that there did not seem to be any indication of psychological preparation, such as an increase in hostile propaganda, as there had been on other occasions.[20]

Not all thought it bluster. In London, Charles Ringwalt, one of the "China hands," read Panikkar's report and advised that it was probably true.[21] Edmund Clubb, in the Far Eastern section of the State Department, had warned that the Chinese could not be expected to stay out of the war in certain circumstances, that if the United States crossed the thirty-eighth parallel, the Chinese would almost certainly react. On 30 September, after hearing of Nie Rongzhen's statement, Clubb warned that the threat might be real, that the Chinese might not wait until the Manchurian border was reached but might fight outside China.[22] On 4 October, Clubb submitted an extensive evaluation of the situation. He considered it serious for the same reasons mentioned by the Burmese ambassador—that is, it was made just after midnight, indicating urgency, and it was made prior to the U.S. crossing the thirty-eighth parallel. He concluded that an advance into North Korea should be made with the assumption that Chinese Communists might in fact intervene with armed force, and that if they did, the USSR might likewise intervene, and that in such a case, hostilities might not be limited to Korea.[23]

On 7 October, the New China News Agency (Xinhua) quoted a Beijing paper as saying the Korean War had entered a new stage. "This will be a drawn-out war of attrition." The Hong Kong consul general interpreted that to mean Korea would not receive open, large-scale, military support from China.

Hong Kong had reported no increase in a propaganda campaign, usually a reliable indicator of Chinese intentions. But such a campaign began three days later, on 10 October, with a broadcast on Beijing Radio by a Ministry of Foreign Affairs spokesman reiterating Zhou's message: "The American War of invasion of Korea has been a serious menace to the security of China from its very start. . . . The Chinese people cannot stand idly by with regard to such a serious situation created by the invasion of Korea by the U.S. and its accomplice countries and to the dangerous trend toward extending the war. . . . The Chinese people firmly advocate a peaceful solution to the Korea problem and are firmly opposed to the extension of the Korean War by America and its accomplice countries. And they are even more firm in holding that aggressors must be answerable for all consequences resulting from their frantic acts in extending aggression."[24]

This marked the beginning of an internal crackdown and an escalating propaganda campaign that, initially, went unnoticed. But on 17 October, the Netherlands chargé d'affaires in Beijing reported increased attacks on the United States, charging aggression in Korea, imperialism, and other offenses. The chargé said that he considered the new attacks significant because they followed the 10 October warning by Zhou Enlai.[25]

With conflicting information on the possibility of Chinese intervention, and UNC forces preparing to cross the thirty-eighth parallel, President Truman prodded the Joint Chiefs of Staff. MacArthur's existing instructions told him what action to take if Chinese forces were employed openly or covertly south of the thirty-eighth parallel. What instructions should MacArthur follow if Chinese forces were employed covertly *north* of the thirty-eighth parallel? Additional instructions were issued to MacArthur: "Hereafter in the event of open or covert employment anywhere in Korea of major Chinese Communist units, without prior announcement, you should continue the action as long as, in your judgment, action by forces now under your control offers a reasonable chance of success. In any case you will obtain authorization from Washington prior to taking any military action against objectives in Chinese territory."[26]

New Estimates by the CIA

Faced with contradictory information, and preparing to meet with General MacArthur, President Truman asked the CIA to make a complete reassessment of Chinese and Soviet intentions. Delivered on 12 October, the report stated that, lacking requisite air and naval support, the Chinese were capable of intervening effectively but not necessarily decisively. Despite troop movements to Manchuria, there were no convincing indications of Chinese Communist intentions to resort to full-scale intervention in Korea. It concluded that intervention was possible, but barring a Soviet decision for global war, it was not probable in 1950 because:

1. The Chinese feared the consequences of war with the United States.

2. Anti-Communist forces would be encouraged and the very existence of the regime would be endangered.

3. The Chinese Communists would hesitate to endanger their chance for a seat in the United Nations.

4. They would suffer heavy losses without USSR air and naval support.

5. Acceptance of Soviet aid would make them more dependent on the USSR and on Soviet control of Manchuria.

6. The most favorable time for intervention was past.[27]

The president, the National Security Council, the Joint Chiefs of Staff, and the State Department all concurred in this estimate.[28]

Concerned that the war in Korea might break out into a full-scale global war, the CIA also produced an estimate on the likelihood of war with the Soviet Union. The estimate believed that "Soviet leaders will not consider that their prospective losses in Korea warrant direct military intervention. . . ." The report stated that the USSR would intervene only if they had concluded from the worldwide situation, not just Korea, that it was in their interest to precipitate a global war. The estimate did point out that the Soviet Union might precipitate global war when they believed their strength, versus U.S. strength, was at its greatest. Ominously, according to the estimate, that condition already existed and would continue until 1954, by which time NATO forces would be built up to the point where they could withstand the initial shock of a surprise Soviet attack. The sobering conclusion was that the risk of general war existed.[29]

An ominous report from Moscow arrived while MacArthur was at Wake Island. A reliable source in Moscow said that Moscow was preparing a surprise for American troops when they approached the northern border.[30] This was followed by a report from the Dutch chargé in Beijing, who said that the Chinese reaction to the Truman–MacArthur meeting on Wake Island was to assume it was the final conference leading to U.S. aggression against China. The report was based on information from knowledgeable people assumed to reflect that attitude of Chinese Communist officials.[31]

At the Far Eastern Command
General Charles Willoughby (assistant chief of staff G-2, Far Eastern Command, and General MacArthur's intelligence officer) has been

accused by historians of major errors in the weeks leading up to the
Chinese offensive of 25 November 1950, which drove the UNC forces
back below the thirty-eighth parallel and brought the UN effort in
the Korean War to the brink of disaster. Most have selectively quoted
portions of his reports that seem to indicate one view or another. Another suggested that at the insistence of MacArthur, Willoughby
downplayed the possibilities of Chinese intervention after the start
of the "end the war" offensive. One officer in X Corps accused him
of outright fabrications and suggested he should have gone to jail.[32]
Willoughby was one of MacArthur's closest confidants and had been
with him since the days of Corregidor. He had joined MacArthur's
staff in Manila prior to the start of World War II and had served with
him through Bataan and Corregidor and in Australia. He took
pride in having produced a Daily Intelligence Summary (DIS) for
MacArthur for more than eight years.

Because, as General Collins reported, 90 percent of the intelligence available in Washington originated with the Far Eastern Command in Tokyo, it is worthwhile to consider how it was obtained and
processed.

The DIS was a lengthy document that could run, with special studies and maps, to forty or more pages. It covered not only Korea but
also Japan, China/Manchuria, and Southeast Asia, as well as regularly listing world "intelligence highlights." The section on Korea was
divided into subsections that listed the enemy situation, including
air and naval actions, and the G-2's estimate, including enemy capabilities and a discussion of those capabilities. There followed a
"miscellaneous" section that would include order-of-battle information, prisoner-of-war interrogation, captured documents, aerial
photo interpretation, and special studies of various kinds. As the war
progressed, the sections on China and Manchuria contained much
information bearing on the situation in Korea.

Spot reports were forwarded to the Department of the Army as
important information was received. Each evening, the essential portions of the DIS were transmitted to the Department of the Army by
"telecon," an interactive teletype conversation. Printed copies of the
summary were sent to Washington by courier, arriving in approximately three days.

Willoughby depended heavily, but by no means exclusively, on reports from units in the field, which would include information from front-line units, prisoners of war, and examination of captured documents. Of considerable value but sometimes of questionable authenticity were reports from the Chinese Nationalist Ministry of Defense, forwarded through the military attaché in Taipei. The U.S. Consulate in Hong Kong was a valuable source of information and forwarded copies of its reports directly to Tokyo.

In the summer of 1949, Willoughby had established the Korean Liaison Office (KLO) with the mission of penetrating North Korean governmental, military, and industrial organizations.[33] KLO agents occasionally provided some useful information but were not especially successful. The Far Eastern Command Survey Group was the cover name for men who apparently were agents controlled directly by Willoughby. These were probably the remnants of the Navy "External Survey" group established in Manchuria after the close of World War II and operating out of the consulate there. The activities of this group were the cause of the arrest, detention, and trial of Consul Angus Ward and his expulsion, along with the other American members of the consulate, in September 1949.

Communication intelligence played a vital role earlier in the war. The ability of the Eighth Army and the Far Eastern Command to read the North Korea traffic had been an important factor in the Eighth Army's ability to meet North Korean attacks along the Naktong River. During the fall of 1950, the FEC made several urgent requests for augmentation of Army Security Agency (ASA) units. In early December, plans were complete to increase the size of ASA units in the Far East from 1,070 to 2,524—to provide assets for the Far Eastern Command and to be part of a worldwide expansion of communication intelligence efforts. There were two fixed Army Security Agency intercept groups in the Far East, one in the Philippines and one in Tokyo. In addition, three mobile units—located on Okinawa; at Kyoto; and at Chitose, Hokkaido—were performing fixed-station-type missions. These were to be replaced by fixed-station units of about 700 officers and men, releasing the mobile units for production of theater intelligence. In addition, traffic intercepted by the fixed stations, which would operate under Washington's control, would be available for use in production of theater intelligence.[34]

Communication intelligence was also obtained through reciprocal arrangements with the British monitoring station and Hong Kong.

Augmentation of the communication intelligence agencies in the Far East at the time of the Chinese offensive would seem to indicate that they were obtaining some useful results. Much of the order of battle information on the Chinese buildup in Manchuria had to have come from communication intercept. Had it been obtained from agents or other sources, those sources should have been able to report the movement into Korea, movement that was not reported by any source.

Information received through other diplomatic sources was forwarded by the State Department, as was intelligence received by other U.S. agencies. MacArthur did complain later that some information known in Washington was not made available to him. Selected diplomatic intelligence received at that time has subsequently been published in the series *Foreign Relations of the United States*. Comparison of the material in the DIS with those diplomatic messages that should have had a classification no higher than secret indicates there were pertinent items that, for some reason, were not repeated in the DIS, thus giving substance to MacArthur's claim. Panikkar's initial report of his conversation with Gen. Nie Rongzhen on 25 September is one of these.

Most of the critical intelligence, but by no means all of it, was contained in the DIS. The DIS was classified secret, so information with a higher classification, or with other special restrictions, such as signal intelligence or information that would disclose the identity of a sensitive source, would not appear in the DIS. But Willoughby's conclusions and his determination of enemy capabilities might have been based on such information provided it didn't reveal a source.

At the risk of being accused of being selective after the fact, it is worthwhile to go through the summaries for the period during the buildup to the first Chinese contact on 25 October, and then for the period from the first contact to the major Chinese counteroffensive commencing on 25 November.

Buildup to the First Chinese Contact on 25 October

Only 116,000 regular Chinese Communist troops were initially believed to be in Manchuria when the war commenced. During the early days, there was some increase in forces there, but it was explained, initially, as no more than the return of some Fourth CCF Army troops to Manchuria, where they originated, after their campaigns in the south during the Chinese Civil War.[35]

That first report on 9 September stated that part of Lin Biao's Fourth Field Army, including the 40th Army and one unidentified army, with one artillery unit, was transferred from Hankou to Manchuria. The G-2 tentatively located the 40th Army in Shenyang (Mukden). The following day, another report from the Chinese Nationalist Ministry of Defense stated that three more CCF armies had been moved from northwest China to Manchuria.

Further information on Chinese northward movement trickled in. Four of Lin Biao's armies were to have moved north between 15 July and 12 August, with the majority located in the Shenyang–Andong area, providing some confirmation of earlier reports. By 21 September, there were believed to be 244,000 regular CCF ground troops in Manchuria, formed in nine armies totaling thirty-five divisions. It was considered possible that there were an additional eight armies with twenty-four divisions, potentially 396,000 troops.[36]

During the latter part of September, the FEC had the same conflicting reports received in Washington: The Chinese Communists would enter the war; the Chinese Communists wouldn't enter the war. Zhou Enlai was reported to have told a conference of bankers and businessmen that China would support North Korea with all means short of armed intervention, but that China would fight if the North Koreans were pushed back to the Manchurian border. On the other hand, there were reports that Zhou did not want to do anything that would jeopardize China's admission to the United Nations.

Other reports indicated that China considered a UNC approach to the Manchurian border as a serious threat and would fight. There was increased war propaganda in China. The Nationalist Ministry of Defense claimed that some Chinese Communist Forces had entered North Korea by 24 September. The decision to fight was believed to have been made at a Cominform conference on 14 August. China was to supply between 200,000 and 250,000 troops, with the USSR providing two-thirds of the arms and equipment and Czechoslovakia the remainder. The mysterious Lin Biao was to command the Chinese troops.[37]

Zhou Enlai's startling radio broadcast and his subsequent warning to Panikkar were reviewed in the DIS for 4 October. Included was a defiant statement by Kim Il Sung congratulating the PRC on its first anniversary and lauding it as a model for the North Koreans. Willoughby commented: "Even though the above utterances are a form of propaganda they cannot be fully ignored since they emanate from presumably responsible leaders in the Chinese and North Korean government. The enemy retains a potential for reinforcement by the CCF."[38]

The following day, the DIS contained a lengthy review of the potential for Chinese reinforcement—and reinforcement, for the first time, was listed as capability number 1. Willoughby discussed the pre-war support given by both the Chinese and the Soviets—the Soviets in the form of materiel, the Chinese in the form of several CCF divisions composed primarily of ethnic Koreans. He noted the enormous increase in railroad and vehicular traffic from Manchuria since the start of the war. He commented on what was assumed to be the obvious understanding between the Chinese Communist and North Korean governments, with the tacit approval of the Soviets. With the collapse of North Korean resistance, the immediate problem was the attitude of Communist China and the Soviet Union. The question now: Would either one or both intervene openly or surreptitiously to help North Korea?

It is accepted that Russia would find it both convenient and economical to stay out of the conflict and let the idle millions of Communist China perform the task as part of the master plan to drain United States resources into the geographical rat holes of the Orient. The interest of all intelligence agencies consequently is focused on the Yalu River and the movements of the elusive Lin Biao. A build-up of Chinese forces along the Korea–Manchurian border has been reported in many channels, and while exaggerations and canards are always evident, the potential of massing at Antung [Andong] and other Manchurian crossings appears conclusive. This mass involves a possible 9/18 divisions organized in 3/6 armies [out] of the total strength of 36 divisions and 9 armies now carried in all of Manchuria. . . . Recent reports take on a sinister connotation: Formosa sources, sometimes colored, but possibly the only serious information channel from within China, flatly stated the release or transfer of nine divisions to North Korea organized from 111th to 118th divisions of the 12th Army Group.[39]

A supplement to the DIS lists 244,000 regular ground forces in Manchuria organized in thirty-eight divisions and nine armies; it assumes armies have a strength of about 26,000 and divisions about 7,000. An additional 152,000 men were believed to be in Manchuria in eight armies and twenty-four divisions.

On 6 and 7 October, reinforcement by Soviet satellite China/ Manchuria dropped to second place and on 8 October dropped further to third place, where it remained until 14 October. The DIS for 9 October carried a report that a senior officer of the Fourth Field Army informed subordinates that 90,000 men of the Fourth Field Army were ordered to enter the Korean War on the North Korean side if U.S. troops crossed the thirty-eighth parallel. The statement was supposed to have been made at Andong on 20 September. The force was divided into three armies, two of which were located in the Andong area and the other at Sinuiju. Even though "reinforcement" had dropped to third place, Willoughby commented ominously: "Cursory interest in this capability would be extremely unwise. Recent daily reports merely add to the substantiation of evidence set forth in detailed discussion of this capability in DIS 2948 of 5 Oct."[40]

More Reports—Pro and Con

In the next week, more conflicting information was received. Reports from Hong Kong passed on more belligerent statements from the Chinese, but the reporters were of the opinion that the Chinese Communists would not intervene. Reports, usually originating on Taiwan, asserted they *would* intervene, and said on several different occasions that some Communist troops had already crossed into North Korea, although Willoughby carried this information as unconfirmed. On 9 October, the northward movement of portions of Gen. Song Shilun's 9th Army Group was reported. One source believed that the Chinese Communist might give overt aid to North Korea for the following reasons: (1) Chinese Communists were indebted to North Korea for aid and assistance received from the Korean Volunteer Army in the Chinese Communists' Manchurian campaign; (2) UN occupation of North Korea would be a threat to Chinese Communist territory; (3) An order could come from the USSR directing the Chinese to participate in the war.

The DIS reported that the question of Chinese Communist entrance into the Korean War was the subject of heated debate at a conference in Beijing during September. Mao Zedong and Liu Shaoqi were reported to be opposed to active participation, while Zhou Enlai, Zhu Deh, and Li Lisan insisted on intervention. The final decision allegedly called for Chinese Communist intervention if UN forces crossed the thirty-eighth parallel.[41]

The possibility of a buffer zone to protect the hydroelectric facilities in North Korea and along the Yalu River was mentioned for the first time on 22 October.

Focus on the North Korean Army

During most of October, while keeping watch on the Chinese, the DIS focused on the North Korean People's Army (NKPA). On 6 October, it was expected the NKPA would make a stand in the old fortifications along the thirty-eighth parallel. In the coming days, the capture of prisoners from several different units in the same area gave mounting evidence of serious deterioration in the North Korean Army.

The collapse of the North Korean Army was dramatically underscored when troops of I ROK Corps secured Wonsan against negligible resistance on 11 October. Wonsan was an important supply, transportation, and training center and was expected to be the eastern anchor of the defense line from Pyongyang eastward. To Willoughby, this news indicated that North Korean losses were much greater than expected, that they simply did not have enough troops to cover the line and had focused on defending Pyongyang instead. It also indicated that North Korean forces were avoiding encirclement and escaping north. Willoughby opined: "This open failure of the enemy to rebuild his forces suggests that the CCF and Soviets, in spite of their continued interest, and some blatant public statements, have decided against further expensive investment in support of a lost cause."[42] Still, until the unexpected fall of Pyongyang, Willoughby expected the North Koreans to continue a defensive line anchored on that city.

Beginning at the end of September, the DIS had listed intervention by the Chinese as the last of six enemy capabilities. On 5 October, as the ability of the NKPA to resist declined, the possibility of Chinese intervention became the most serious threat and was listed in first place until 24 October. In that last half of October, the possibility of reinforcement by Chinese troops was forcefully discussed in extended comments carried in the DIS on 5, 9, 14, 20, and 22 October. The DIS of 14 October included an especially lengthy discussion of the reinforcement capability. This may have been in preparation for General MacArthur's meeting with President Truman the following day on Wake Island. Willoughby stated: "Recent declarations by CCF leaders, threatening to enter NK if American forces were to cross the 38th Parallel, are probably in the category of diplomatic blackmail. The decision, if any, is beyond the purview of collective intelligence: It is a decision for war on the highest level; that is, the Kremlin and Peiping. However, the numerical and troop potential in Manchuria is a fait-accompli. A total of 24 divisions are disposed along the Yalu River at crossing points. In this general deployment, the group in the vicinity of Andong is the most immediately available Manchurian force, astride a suitable road net for deployment southward."

The comment about the decision for war being a decision at the highest level was aimed squarely at one of the major controversies raised later by MacArthur. He forcefully argued many times that the responsibility for determining any decision of the Chinese to go to war was a responsibility of the central government, that only the central government had the intelligence capabilities to obtain such information. In short, unless that central government informed him the Chinese were coming in, he was at liberty to consider they would not. It is hard to justify this view. The other view, about as fundamental a principle as there is in warfare, is that every commander is responsible for securing the information needed to provide for the security of his own command.

In reading through Willoughby's intelligence summaries for the period it is impossible not to conclude that he is in the position, known to all staff officers, of trying, diplomatically and cautiously, to tell the boss something the boss does not want to hear.

While MacArthur was discoursing with the president and his staff at Wake Island, Adm. Arleigh Burke, chief of staff at COMNAVFE, and his intelligence staff had reviewed the intelligence reports and concluded that the Chinese were already in Korea. Burke argued with Willoughby. As a precaution, Burke decided to hold one in five ships that came in with supplies so that there would be ships ready in the event of a need for evacuation.

On the day MacArthur returned from Wake Island, Kim Il Sung broadcast a message saying North Korea would "fight to the death." There would be no capitulation.[43] The following day, 17 October, seeing the Wonsan landing stalled by mines and the remaining North Korean forces slipping away from him, MacArthur issued UNC Operation Order No. 4.

The order stated that, should Pyongyang be secured by the Eighth Army before the need arose for attack westward by X Corps, the Eighth Army, on his order, would advance in a new zone on the western side of the peninsula to a new stop line: Sonchon–Chongsan-jangsi–Koin-dong–Pyongwon. On the east side of the peninsula, X Corps, remaining under direct control of the Far Eastern Command, would advance to the previously designated line: Toksil-li–Pungsan–Songjin. Restrictions on the use of non-ROK ground forces north of the original line were lifted, but only ROK forces would operate north of the new stop line. The 3d Infantry Division, then in Japan, would assemble in the Wonsan area.[44] The 3d Division, hastily filled out from a near-skeleton force, had been sent as a defense force for Japan.

Advancing in the west, the 1st Cavalry Division broke through resistance at Sariwon on 17 October and reached Pyongyang in a dead heat with the 1st ROK Division on 19 October. On 20 October, General MacArthur ordered the 187th Airborne RCT to drop at Sunchon and Sukchon in an attempt to trap withdrawing North Korean forces and civil officials. Like the amphibious jaws at Wonsan, the airborne jaws snapped shut on an empty trap. Minor rear-guard elements caught in the net put up a short but vicious fight. On the east, the "Ramblin' ROKs" of I ROK Corps secured Hamhung and prepared to advance north and northeast.

The most concrete information on the coming Chinese intervention was contained in a series of messages received from Hong Kong and Taiwan during the early morning hours of 19 October. At an emergency meeting in Beijing the previous week, Communist China had decided to participate in the Korean War. More than 400,000 troops were at the Yalu border, alerted to cross on 18 or 20 October. The information came from C. L. Chen, president of the Central Air Transport Corporation. He was passing on information from one of his representatives who had been in Beijing at the time. Chen was known to be "pink" but had been a reliable source. The report, however, was considered with skepticism both in Washington and in Tokyo. The Chinese Nationalists had a vested interest in promoting tension between the United States and Communist China.[45]

In a "speculative estimate" given the chief of staff at 1 A.M. on 20 October and distributed to the staff and to COMNAVFE, Willoughby commented: "The language of these radios . . . reaffirm [sic] the accuracy of the general information. Reference [sic] to troop movements, however, are exaggerated. Radios speak of 400,000 in the area when Manchuria OB [order of battle] does not show more than 250,000 and of that number less than half in deployment, along the Yalu River. While the general opinions discount the actual intervention by the CCF at this time as being tactically unsound since the Chinese would run into aggressive UNC Divs in full deployment and under very strong air cover, this may be wishful thinking. There is plenty of cannon fodder in the Chinese Manchurian armies to be expended as a gesture of communist solidarity. As the date of Oct 20th is positively stated, we should know within the next 48 hours."[46]

In his discussion in the DIS, Willoughby stated that the Chinese strength in Manchuria was an accomplished fact and there was no question of their ability to cross the river. The decision, he stated, again, ". . . is not within the purview of local intelligence: it will be based on the high-level readiness of the Kremlin to go to war through utilizing the CCF in Manchuria. . . ." He reported that the UN Command had taken precautionary measures in conducting daily air reconnaissance flights over all avenues of approach from the Yalu River. No positive movement had been sighted. But large-scale truck movements had been observed.[47]

In the early morning hours of 19 October, with Pyongyang about to fall and alerted by Chen's report of the imminent possibility of Chinese intervention, MacArthur ordered UN Operation Order No. 4 executed. His order stated: ". . . Desired that maximum effort be made by all units. . ." and ". . . prepared for continued rapid advance to the border of North Korea."[48]

The Joint Chiefs of Staff were provided with information copies of his order. MacArthur was, technically, exceeding his authority by ordering advance beyond the stop line previously approved by the JCS. In addition, he was signaling his intention to overrule the policy guidance to use only ROK troops close to the border. The Joint Chiefs either overlooked this warning or ignored it. They raised no objection at that time.

"Organized resistance on any large scale has ceased to be an enemy capability," was the word from Willoughby on 21 October. He added that there were no signs of enemy surrender.[49] The following day, he again emphasized that reinforcement by Chinese Communist Forces was the first capability, and he followed it up with another lengthy review that included a report from Chinese Nationalist sources alleging there were fifteen Chinese armies in Manchuria.[50]

In the remaining days of October, there were further reports that elements of the Fourth Field Army, as well as elements of Song Shilun's 9th Army Group, part of the Third Field Army, were moving northward. There was speculation over the importance of the hydroelectric facilities in North Korea and along the Yalu. Coupled with this were reports that a buffer state was being created in the central part of North Korea along the Yalu, and that its boundaries coincided approximately with that of Chagang Province, the most remote and mountainous area in Korea. In the following weeks, con-cern about the establishment of a "Chagang Redoubt" arose fre-quently both at the Far Eastern Command and in X Corps.

By 24 October, General Willoughby estimated that CCF strength in Manchuria had risen to 316,000 men in twelve armies and forty-four divisions, identified and accepted. Another six armies and eighteen divisions, with 147,000 men, were reported to be in Manchuria but not confirmed—potentially a total of 463,000 men.

Advance to the Border

On 24 October, General MacArthur lifted all restraints: "Restrictions . . . [in his previous message] are lifted. Restraining line for UN Ground Forces, other than ROK, established initially in view of pos-sible enemy capitulation. You are authorized to use any and all ground forces of your commands as necessary to secure all of North Korea. . . . The line prescribed in [his previous message] to be con-sidered only as an initial objective. Commanders are enjoined to drive forward with all speed and with the full utilization of all forces."[51]

This time, on receipt of a copy of this order, the Joint Chiefs re-sponded, stating their objection diplomatically: "While the Joint Chiefs of Staff realize that you undoubtedly had sound reasons for issuing these instructions they would like to be informed of them, as your action is a matter of some concern here."[52]

The following day, MacArthur replied that the change in plans was a matter of military necessity: "Not only are the ROK forces not of sufficient strength to initially accomplish the security of North Ko-rea, but the reactions of their commanders are at times so emotional that it was deemed essential that initial use be made of more sea-soned and stabilized commanders." He went on to argue that there was no conflict with his instructions of 27 September, because they had stated that use of ROK forces north of the stop line was only a matter of policy. He added that his instructions were subject to mod-ification, and were in fact modified by General Marshall's letter, which stated: "We want you to feel unhampered tactically and strate-gically to proceed north of the 38th Parallel." MacArthur said he was fully aware of the purpose and intent of this instruction and was taking every possible precaution. However, he suggested ominously that "tactical hazards" might result from any other action than that which he had directed. He concluded with the statement that the entire subject had been covered at the Wake Island conference.[53]

Although MacArthur had definitely overstepped his authority in ordering the drive to the border when his approved plan called for a halt, none of the Joint Chiefs, then or later, were willing to call it a disobedience of orders. At the Senate hearings, General Marshall stated that MacArthur didn't violate a single order as to military operations. Later in the hearings, General Collins hesitantly mentioned that MacArthur had possibly not followed policy in sending non-ROK troops into the border provinces. He said: "What . . . General MacArthur did was not to follow a matter of policy which had been clearly delineated to him in a directive 27 September. . . . Giving our field commanders plenty of leeway . . . we felt it incumbent upon them to follow our broad policies and that if they felt impelled to vary from them to consult us." At that point, Collins backed off from calling it a directive or an order.[54]

On receipt of MacArthur's reply, the Joint Chiefs let the matter stand. It was too late anyway. By the time MacArthur's message was received in Washington, it was accompanied by reports of the capture of the first Chinese Communist prisoner. The armies had collided.

Reflection
In hindsight, it is clear that much of the conflicting information received during September and early October reflected the conflicting opinions that were being debated within the Communist government. The various internal factions had discussed their views with others outside the Politburo. An example of this is a report forwarded by the consul general in Hong Kong. A reliable informant said the Chinese observation group in Korea recommended against open military intervention because: (1) The Chinese would be unable to cope with UN air power; (2) UN artillery would be superior; (3) Even if the USSR supplied air support, a UN air attack would disrupt transportation in China and make supply very difficult. The report went on to say that the Chinese already had two divisions in Ko-

rea. If any of them were captured, they would claim to be part of the North Korean Army. The Chinese Communists believed UN forces would not retaliate against China in the absence of intervention by troops that were openly a part of the regular Chinese Army. However, they had no intention of sending in more Chinese troops.[55] As noted in chapter 4, the Chinese observers did report serious difficulties operating in Korea, but they were overruled by Mao.

Although it is speculative, it is almost certain that Zhou Enlai's message to Panikkar and the subsequent announcements of Chinese intentions to intervene if U.S. forces crossed the thirty-eighth parallel were directed squarely at MacArthur's authorization ". . . to conduct military operations . . . north of the 38th Parallel in Korea, *providing that at the time of such operation there has been no entry into North Korea by major Soviet or Chinese Communist forces, no announcement of intended entry, nor a threat to counter our operations militarily in North Korea* [emphasis added]."

Both Kim Philby and Guy Burgess, the noted British spies, were attached to the British Embassy in Washington at the time and were positioned to have access to instructions to MacArthur and possibly also to pertinent decisions of the National Security Council. They had the means to pass on that information to their Soviet masters, who unquestionably shared such information, possibly on a selective basis, with the Chinese.

The real mystery here is the failure of all authorities at the national level, particularly the Joint Chiefs, to recognize the Chinese announcement as a direct response to their own instructions to MacArthur and to act upon that realization. On the record, the only two persons in government who seemed to take Zhou's statement seriously were Clubb and Ringwalt, both very well acquainted with the Chinese Communists but both viewed with some suspicion. Neither they nor anyone else put two and two together.

This oversight or failure reflects the collective view of the State Department, the CIA, and the JCS that the Chinese alone could not make a decisive difference in the Korean War. This is implied in the instructions to MacArthur telling him to assume the defense if major Soviet forces were encountered but to continue the action if Chinese forces were encountered. It was an attitude that played a major part in the decisions of the next few weeks. This viewpoint was explicitly stated by Maj. Gen. Charles L. Bolte, Department of the Army G-3, in a memorandum to the chief of staff: "It is not envisaged that the Chinese Communists can succeed in driving presently committed UNC forces from Korea, unless materielly assisted by Soviet ground and air power." He believed that MacArthur had sufficient strength to hold any line in North Korea, "in light of circumstances now prevailing."[56]

Clubb, Ringwalt, John Davies, John Carter Vincent, and some of the U.S. Army officers who had been with the Dixie Mission or had worked with General Marshall in attempting to arrange a truce in the Chinese Civil War were among the few with sufficient firsthand knowledge of the Chinese Communists to evaluate their statements intelligently. Unfortunately, there were many more Americans who had experience before and during the war with the Nationalists and the demoralized and corrupt warlord society that prevailed. They had an entirely different, and far less favorable, view of the Chinese as soldiers. It is unfortunate that most of the senior officers and State Department officials who were attempting to evaluate the incoming material based their conclusions on their experience with, or observation of, the Nationalists.

The intelligence noted above can only be a sampling of that available at the time. None of it was conclusive. But there was enough to warrant the assumption, as Clubb had recommended, that Chinese Communists might in fact intervene with armed forces. The assumptions stated in FEC Operation Plan 9-50, MacArthur's plan for destruction of the North Korean Army, was "(1) Neither the Soviets nor the Chinese Communists will undertake any open military operations in North Korea or any open or major covert operation in ROK, and (2) The US–Soviet international relations will remain basically as they exist today."

The assumed conditions on which the plan was based had changed. The plan didn't. At the very least, there was sufficient information to dictate caution in the advance northward.

Notes

1. Telegram Wilkinson (Hong Kong) to Sec State 22 Sept. 50, *FRUS*, 765.

2. Ibid.

3. Telegram Wilkinson (Hong Kong) to Sec State 25 Sept. 50, *FRUS*, 768.

4. Goncharov et al., *Uncertain Partners*, 170.

5. *HJCS*, 259.

6. Kavalam M. Panikkar, *In Two Chinas: Memoirs of a Diplomat* (London: Allen and Unwin, 1955), 108.

7. Memorandum of conversation Merchant with Graves 27 Sept. 50, *FRUS*, 793.

8. Telegram Rusk to Webb 28 Sept. 50, *FRUS*, 797.

9. Joseph C. Goulden, *Korea: The Untold Story of the War* (New York: McGraw-Hill, 1982), 281.

10. Telegram Kirk (Moscow) to Sec State 29 Sept. 50, *FRUS*, 821–22.

11. Goncharov et al., *Uncertain Partners*, 175–76.

12. Telegram Wilkinson (Hong Kong) to State 2 Oct. 50, *FRUS*, 852.

13. Panikkar, *In Two Chinas*, 110.

14. Memorandum Merchant to Rusk 3 Oct. 50, *FRUS*, 848.

15. Acheson, *Present at the Creation*, 452.

16. Memorandum of meeting with Sec State 4 Oct. 50, *FRUS*, 875.

17. Telegram Henderson (New Delhi) to Sec State 4 Oct. 50, *FRUS*, 869.

18. Telegram Key (Burma) to Sec State 14 Oct. 50, *FRUS*, 944.

19. Telegram Chapin (Netherlands) to Sec State, *FRUS*, 858–59.

20. Telegram Wilkinson (Hong Kong) to Sec State 7 Oct. 50, *FRUS*, 912.

21. E. J. Kahn, *The China Hands: American Foreign Service Officers and What Befell Them* (New York: Viking, 1975), 226.

22. Memorandum Clubb to Rusk 27 Sept. 50, *FRUS*, 851.

23. Memorandum Clubb to Rusk 4 Oct. 50, *FRUS*, 864–66.

24. Whiting, *China Crosses the Yalu*, 94.

25. Telegram Chapin (Netherlands) to Sec State 17 Oct. 50, *FRUS*, 974.

26. JCS msg to CINCFE 9 Oct. 50, *FRUS*, 915.

27. Memorandum from CIA, "Threat of Full Chinese Intervention," 12 Oct. 50, *FRUS*, 933.

28. Blair, *The Forgotten War*, 338.

29. Memorandum from CIA, ". . . Regarding Possible Soviet Decision to Precipitate Global War," *FRUS*, 936–37.

30. Appleman, *South to the Naktong*, 759.

31. Telegram Chapin (Netherlands) to Sec State 17 Oct. 50, *FRUS*, 974.

32. Blair, *The Forgotten War*, 337 (quoting interview with Lt . Col. Chiles, X Corps G-3).

33. Report by Lt. Col. Leonard J. Abbot to Willoughby 18 May 1951.

34. Army Security Agency Pacific (ASAPAC) letter 9 Nov. 50 to Commander in Chief, Far East (CINCFE); DEPTAR (Department of the Army) msg W97801, 2 Dec. 50, to CINCFE.

35. *Command Report November 1950*. Far Eastern Command, 2.

36. Far Eastern Command Daily Intelligence Summary (FEC DIS) 2934, 12 Sept. 50.

37. FEC DIS 2943, 30 Sept. 50.

38. FEC DIS 2947, 4 Oct. 50.

39. FEC DIS 2948, 5 Oct. 50.

40. FEC DIS 2952, 9 Oct. 50.

41. FEC DIS 2954, 11 Oct. 50.

42. FEC DIS 2957, 14 Oct. 50.

43. FEC DIS 2959, 16 Oct. 50.

44. FEC Operation Order No. 4, 17 Oct. 50.

45. Callum A. MacDonald, *Korea: The War Before Vietnam* (New York: Macmillan, 1987), 62.

46. Special Report by Willoughby to Chief of Staff FEC 20 Oct. 50.

47. FEC DIS 2963, 20 Oct. 50.

48. CINCUNC msg CX 66705, 19 Oct. 50, to Eighth Army, X Corps, and others.

49. FEC DIS 2964, 21 Oct. 50.

50. FEC DIS 2965, 22 Oct. 50.

51. CINCUNC msg CX 67291, 24 Oct. 50, to UNC forces.

52. JCS msg 904933, 24 Oct. 50, to CINCFE.

53. CINCFE msg C-67397 to DEPTAR.

54. *Military Situation in the Far East: Hearings before the Committee on Armed Services and the Committee on Foreign Relations, United States Senate, Eighty-second Congress, First Session.* 5 vols. (Washington, D.C.: Government Printing Office, 1951), 393 and 1299 (hereafter cited as *Military Situation in the Far East*).

55. Telegram Wilkinson (Hong Kong) to Sec State 27 Oct. 50, *FRUS*, 1003.

56. Schnabel, *Policy and Direction*, 267.

6
Into the North Korean Wilderness

Snow is not neutral.
—Frunze Military Academy maxim

When Gen. Douglas MacArthur issued his "run for the border" directive on 24 October 1950, Gen. Charles Willoughby's picture of "aggressive UNC divisions racing forward in full deployment and under very strong air cover" was not quite realistic. Already battle-weary, worn thin, and widely spread in the rush northward from the Pusan perimeter, they were about to outrun their badly frayed logistics tether.

Allied air attacks had cut the Korean rail lines in many places, including the all-important bridge across the Taedong River into Pyongyang. The port of Chinampo, serving Pyongyang, and its approaches were heavily mined. A major effort by transports of the Fifth Air Force was able to deliver 1,000 tons a day into forward airfields—700 for the Eighth Army, 300 for the Air Force units.[1] As a result, the Eighth Army could only support the further advance to the Chongchon River and beyond by a much-reduced force consisting of II ROK Corps with three divisions and I Corps with only the 24th Infantry Division, the 1st ROK Division, and the Commonwealth Brigade. The 2d Division, with nearly half its vehicles deadlined for lack of spare parts or gasoline, and the 1st Cavalry Division remained in the Pyongyang area, with the 25th Division farther south. In the east, the 1st Marine Division had only begun landing at Wonsan. The 7th Division was still at sea, portions of it actually still in Pusan.

In addition to logistics shortages, there were shortages in personnel. The fighting on the Naktong River and the advance northward had taken their toll. When General MacArthur reviewed an honor guard company of the 8th Cavalry on his visit to Pyongyang, he asked anyone who had been with the company since it arrived in Korea to take one pace forward. Three men stepped forward. A platoon leader in the 8th Cavalry later reported that his platoon had only two rifle squads instead of the normal three.

The Terrain

Much of North Korea has been described as a trackless wilderness. It did have tracks, but often little else. Had it not been for timber, minerals, and hydroelectric potential—all of which fed the Korean industrial machine—it might have been a wilderness. The geography, topography, and climate in North Korea presented problems that, at times, could be as difficult to overcome as the enemy. The Asian continent begins to cool in late September. In the days to come, the weather inflicted nearly as much damage, nearly as many casualties, although fewer fatalities, on both sides as did the actions of their opponents. Weather and terrain dominated the action well beyond their normal importance. A review of how weather and terrain affected the opposing forces provides some useful insights into the Chinese strategy, the actions of both armies, and the outcome of the fighting.

Like much of Korea, that part of it north of the narrow waist of the peninsula—that is, north of the line from Anju to Hamhung—is a mass of mountains, but they are higher and steeper than those to the south. One early traveler described the mountainous interior of Korea as resembling a "sea in a heavy gale."

Splitting this sea of mountains and separating northeastern Korea from its northwest sector is the Nangnim Range, a broad range of mountains reaching heights of up to 8,000 feet.[2] This central range varies in width from thirty to fifty miles. During the coming fighting, it was not crossed or penetrated by United Nations Command (UNC) forces of any significant size. A Far Eastern Command (FEC) terrain study issued to all units at the commencement of operations in North Korea labeled it BARRIER AREA—UNSUITED TO LARGE-SCALE MILITARY OPERATIONS.[3] As will be seen, Chinese forces did maneuver through this area.

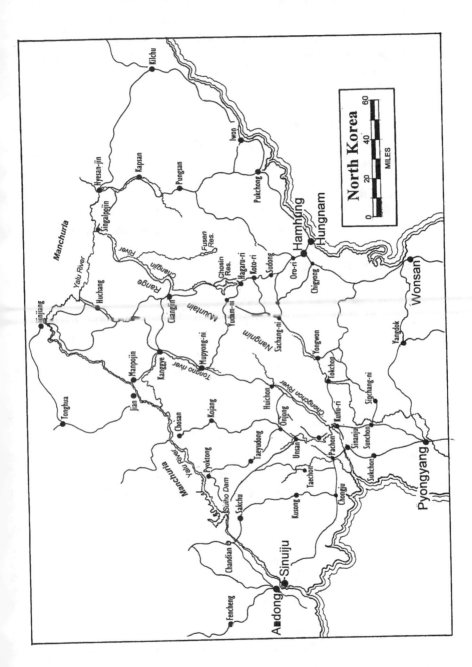

Although no UN forces crossed the Nangnim Range north of the Hamhung–Anju line, there are three potentially usable routes through the mountains. From north to south they are:

- Changjin Town to Kanggye
- Yudam-ni to Mupyong-ni
- Majon-dong or Chigyong to Huksu-ri to Yongwon to Tok-chon

Northeast Korea
A narrow and often rugged coastal strip borders most of northeast Korea as far as the Soviet border. A single-track railroad and a usable highway run along the coast.

Inland from the coast, the Hamyong Range forms an escarpment separating the interior from the coast. Between this range and the border is a basin called the Kaema Uplands. The western border of the uplands is the Nangnim Range. The Kaema Uplands is a basin in name only. It is an area further split by a number of mountains, ridges, spurs, and narrow valleys. The rivers in this area drain northward to the Yalu River rather than southward to the sea.

Four major routes, leading north to the Manchurian border, run through northeast Korea. There is a fifth route in the far northeast to Hoeryong and Vladivostok, but that route played no part in the coming action. From east to west, they are:

- Kilchu along a road and railroad to Hyesan-jin
- Pukchong north along a road through Pungsan and Kapsan to Hyesan-jin
- Oro-ri to the Fusen Reservoir, then north to Singalpojin on the Yalu River. There was no road to the Fusen Reservoir, but there was a narrow-gauge railroad. From the reservoir northward, there was a road.
- Oro-ri to the Chosin Reservoir, then north to Changjin

This last route was the main supply route for the forces operating around the Chosin Reservoir. From the relatively flat plains around Hamhung, the road and a narrow-gauge railroad run north to Chinhung-ni. Then, in a relatively short space, the road climbs nearly 4,000 feet over the Funchillin Pass, where it reaches the Kaema Uplands near the village of Koto-ri, close to the headwaters of the Changjin River. From there, it runs northward through a relatively broad valley to the Chosin Reservoir and on north to the town of Changjin. There it splits, with one route running westward to Kanggye. The other branch continues somewhat more tortuously north to Huchang and the Yalu River, then down the river to Linjiang on the Chinese side of the Yalu.

From Chinhung-ni northward through the pass, the road was one way. At the time of this campaign, the railroad terminated about halfway up the east side of the Chosin Reservoir but was operable only as far as the town of Chinhung-ni.

Northwest Korea
West of the Nangnim Range, the mountains drop off to the corridor formed by the Chongchon and Tongno Rivers. A road and a railroad follow this corridor up the Chongchon, through a low pass, then down the Tongno Valley to Kanggye, then west to the Yalu at Manpojin.

To the northwest, between this corridor and the Yalu River, are the Chokyuryong–Kangnam Mountains, with heights of 3,000 to 5,000 feet. A number of smaller corridors run northwest through this area to the Yalu River. The principal ones are:

- A road and railroad line from Taechon to Kusong to Sakchu
- A road from Unsan to Pyoktong
- A road from Onjong through Kojang-dong to Chosan
- A relatively broad coastal plain borders the area on the west. Along the coast runs a fairly good road, plus a double-track railroad.

The Border Barrier
The Chinese border with Korea is a tortuous line some 650 miles long. For much of its length, the border is formed by the valley of the Yalu River and, further on, the Tumen River Valley. With the ex-

ception of the lower valley around Andong, the valley is steep and narrow. Near Sakchu is the giant Suiho dam, with its reservoir extending northeast for some sixty miles, backing up water into lateral valleys. The terrain along the Yalu is such that there are only four major crossing sites with either road or railroad bridges for a force of any significant size, and a number of lesser sites crossed by ferries. East of Linjiang, the terrain on the Chinese side of the border is a roadless mountain wilderness for about 125 miles. At the headwaters of the Yalu, the border climbs up over the twin mountain peaks of Paektu San to the headwaters of the Tumen River, then follows that course to the sea. In this area, the location of the border itself is indeterminate. Only in the extreme northeast of Korea does the border again reach an area where there are usable communication routes crossing the border.

Twelve highway and railroad bridges crossed the Yalu and Tumen Rivers from Manchuria and Russia into Korea. The most important were the rail and highway bridges at Sinuiju and Andong; a double-track railroad bridge near Sakchu; a footbridge and a rail bridge at Manpojin; and a highway bridge at Linjiang.

The Chagang Redoubt
As the North Korean defense collapsed, General Willoughby relayed a report that a province, possibly a buffer state, had been created in the central area of North Korea along the Yalu River. Although information was not available as to exact delineation of this province, it was believed to conform generally to the boundary of the old Chagang Province. This was in the heart of the Kaema Uplands, the area in which Kim Il Sung and other guerrillas had clashed with the Japanese occupiers for many years. Willoughby thought it was also possible that arrangements could have been made between North Korea and the Communist Chinese Forces (CCF) or the Soviets for the acquisition of this territory. With these factors in mind, and with Chinese Communist Forces readily available, he considered it possible that a narrow sector of North Korea, extending from the Rashin area on the east coast along the entire Manchurian border to the Sinuiju area on the west coast, might be occupied by the CCF to serve as a buffer area. As pursuit progressed, it appeared that on both the east

and the west coasts, North Korean remnants were withdrawing inland, away from the coasts, toward this central location.[4]

Weather

In the Kaema Uplands, including the area around the Chosin Reservoir, the combination of being cut off from the sea to the west and
the southeast and being open toward the north has an astonishingly
strong effect. Not only is it the most remote and isolated part of Korea; it also is the coldest. Temperatures here routinely are twenty to
thirty degrees colder than in the western part of the country. The
coldest recorded temperature in Korea, prior to 1950, occurred at
Hagaru-ri at −43.6°C (which works out to −46°F). On average, ice begins to form on the reservoir on 23 September. Residents in the area
could expect between 16 and 20 weeks each year when the mean
temperature would not rise above freezing.

The impact of these frigid temperatures is magnified by the windchill created by the strong north winds that prevail throughout the
area. Whatever problems the terrain provided were vastly compounded by the severe weather. The winter of 1950—when temperatures dropped as low as −30°F—was reputed to have been one
of the harshest winters in recent years. The cold drastically reduced
combat efficiency.

The effect on individual men was probably the most critical. It was
awkward and tiring to move in heavy clothing. Men would perspire,
then become chilled when they halted. As long as UNC forces had
the initiative, they could take time to halt and practice preventive
measures. Once the Chinese had the initiative and UNC forces had
to conform to their movements, the men had no time to rest,
change socks, warm themselves, and do other housekeeping tasks
needed to maintain combat efficiency. The state of training with regard to cold can be compared to the state of disciplinary and tactical training. If you have time, you can do it right. If the situation does
not provide time—because either of the enemy situation or the lack
of understanding of commanders—casualties increase. Simply getting enough to eat was a problem when there was little time or opportunity to heat the frozen rations.

Frostbite and exposure were constant threats. Wounded men were more prone to shock because of the cold. Casualties from cold out-numbered the casualties from enemy action by almost three to one. At times, the cold was so intense and the fatigue so debilitating that men, American and Chinese alike, might sit or lie down along the road or trail to rest and freeze to death.

A partial listing of the effect of the cold on equipment will help explain some of the problems encountered. Construction was seri-ously hampered. Road work had to deal with frozen ground, as did the construction of the Hagaru Airport. The simple act of digging a foxhole was difficult, and in some conditions impossible. Radio bat-teries lost power quickly in the cold, impairing communication. Sometimes the life of the batteries could be extended by warming them, but there was always a shortage of batteries. Engines were hard to start. Brakes froze. Diesel engines could hardly be started at all, so they were seldom shut down. Artillery fire was slowed because the guns took so long to return to battery. Mortar base plates fractured due to the constant pounding against the hard, frozen ground. Small arms malfunctioned when the accumulated carbon in machine guns, Browning automatic rifles (BARs), and rifles froze.

An earthy illustration of how one problem was handled will pro-vide additional insight. The light machine gun would sometimes freeze up when the carbon around the front barrel bearing froze, making it difficult to load. One method of solving this problem, not taught in infantry training, was to urinate on the barrel. That usu-ally would warm it up enough to free the barrel and permit a few bursts to be fired—but the smell was awful.

The saying goes that winter is neutral. Perhaps so. But winter will favor the side best trained and equipped for it.

Population
Compared to South Korea, North Korea was sparsely settled. In 1950, the North's population density was about 190 people per square mile, roughly the same as in California or Illinois today. As in Cali-fornia, the greatest part of that population was concentrated in the lowland valleys and along the narrow coastal strip. In the central mountain mass of North Korea, villages were few, small, and poor. The hardy farmers scratched out a thin living from the few level ar-eas suitable for cultivation.

The Koreans, a stubborn and independent race, had little affection for Communism, not caring a bit more for it than they had for the Japanese. They liked the Chinese even less. Mao Zedong has said that a guerrilla among the population must be as a fish in water. That didn't work in Korea. The result was that UNC forces found the villages to be excellent sources of information on enemy activity. Reports of the villagers and refugees were quite often timely and accurate as to locations. There was, however, a problem with estimating number. "Many, many" seemed to be the most prevalent measure. Consequently, in higher headquarters, there was often skepticism of reports originating with civilians. Nevertheless, the active cooperation of a majority of the civilian population was a very considerable military asset, although not exploited to the degree it might have been.

Conversely, the civilian population in North Korea and the meager resources of the land did not provide the Chinese armies with the support upon which they relied in China. There was little opportunity for living off the land. Even so, the Chinese did requisition grain from the limited resources of some of the villages. Those grain requisitions, depriving many villages of their winter food supply, contributed to a huge refugee problem.

The principal assets of the mountainous region of North Korea were mineral resources, timber, and hydroelectric power. The Japanese had developed extensive mining operations and there was a substantial network of dams, power stations, and transmission lines. The Chinese industries in Manchuria were major users and heavily dependent on these facilities. This gave them considerable strategic importance. Because it was believed that damage or disruption of the power supply to China would be extremely provocative, considerable care was taken initially by American forces not to damage it.

Key Terrain Features
In 1950, in North Korea, the principal means of transportation were railroads and oxcarts. Few paved roads existed and most of those were in the southern part of the country. Nearly all other roads were dirt, scarcely of all-weather construction, and mostly single lane. A good many were barely traversable by military vehicles. Fortunately, most of them held up reasonably well in the freezing weather.

Given these conditions and the difficult terrain, the all-important road net, always crucial, assumed exceptional importance to modern mechanized forces. Sustained cross-country movement of major forces was simply not possible. Although the primitive road network could support modest forces for a limited period of time, the only way sufficient tonnage could be moved to meet the needs of sustained combat for a major modern military force would be via the railroads. This made the railroads of extraordinary operational and strategic importance.

The few "trafficable" road junctions, and the villages that usually developed around them, became key terrain features. Not only did they control movement, they also became centers of information. The movement of local people through the area made them, in effect, an early warning system.

Tactical Effect of the Terrain
The effect of the terrain on mobility cut both ways. Movement of major UNC forces was tied to the roads. The speed of advance was regulated by the speed with which supplies could be moved over the primitive roads. The upside was that with adequate supplies, UNC forces were capable of sustained combat. The Chinese, on the other hand, carrying lighter equipment and less dependent upon a large volume of supplies, were not confined to the roads and were able to use mountain trails and footpaths for the movement of large forces. The downside for the Chinese was their lack of sustained combat power due to inadequate logistical support. Chinese local mobility was an advantage, tactically. But operationally, UNC wheels could outrun Chinese feet.

The precipitous terrain posed other serious tactical problems. With slopes as steep as 45 degrees, troop movement was slow, exhausting, and, in many cases, impossible except in the draws or along the narrow ridges. In the attack, men might have to assault up these slopes at a crawl or on hands and knees. On the narrow ridgelines, it was difficult to deploy on more than a squad front, if that.

Although rations and ammunition could be moved quickly by truck to the vicinity of the front lines, getting them from the road to the positions on the hills was often agonizingly difficult and slow, as was the evacuation of wounded. Early in the operations in North Korea, X Corps asked about the availability of mules. They were not available. Soldiers, Marines, or Korean packers were substituted.

The narrow valleys limited room for deployment on the valley floors and limited places for supporting installations to be emplaced. The mountain ridges limited the range of high-frequency and UHF radios and often masked the fires of supporting artillery.

Given the wide frontages, it was never possible to secure all the dominating high ground, so opposing forces always had observation over friendly installations. For the most part, this was not as critical as it might otherwise have been, because the Chinese seldom had the artillery to exploit that advantage.

The overall effect was to make it very difficult to concentrate the power of a modern military force, which depended on a good road net. It was nearly always necessary to attack on a narrow front. Providing mutual support to adjacent units was limited by the mountains—obstacles that separated them as effectively as long distances might otherwise have done.

Strategic and Operational Problems
The tactical problems imposed by the terrain and the weather were immense and challenging. The operational and strategic problems were totally unique, compounded by both the geography of the area and the situation. Once past the peninsula's narrow neck, the war shifted to the mainland. In the mountains, UNC forces were fighting on the mainland, with unlimited boundaries on either side, and advancing through primitive areas of the mainland—the place where all military leaders, including General MacArthur, had said they would never be. In essence, the UNC had blundered onto the Asian mainland.

The first problem was that of advancing right up to the border of China—with her huge military resources, threatening posture, and uncertain intentions. As UNC forces advanced past the Anju–Hamhung line, their axes of advance diverged—advancing west, northwest, north, and northeast. Not only would the forces in the west be separated from those in the east by the Nangnim Range; each of those major forces would continue to diverge, increasing the distance between formations, increasing the loss of mutual support, and increasing exposed flanks and lines of communication. Each mile of advance past the Chongchon–Hamhung line would make them more vulnerable.

As UNC forces approached the border, another unique problem would come into play. Unable to operate across the border, UNC aircraft would have an increasingly smaller zone in which to provide support, gradually decreasing the effectiveness of air interdiction. At the border, UNC forces would have no air support. A similar situation would occur with regard to artillery support, then heavy infantry weapons, until UNC forces would arrive at the border reduced to using small arms.

At the border, the problems changed. Control of the four essential crossing sites was the key to control of North Korea. With the limited road network, no serious operation could be launched or sustained from Manchuria without control of at least one of these sites and the railroad they served. The problem would become somewhat more difficult once the Yalu froze. Forces could then cross at a variety of points but would still need control of a railroad crossing for a major operation.

MacArthur's strategic concept for the advance northward is not disclosed in any of the presently available material. However, much of it can be inferred from subsequent actions. There were essentially two choices. The first choice was to advance and seize the four major crossing points, halting the escape of any substantial North Korean forces and preventing the entrance of substantial Chinese forces. With those sites under control, UNC forces could then conduct a systematic campaign to mop up remaining centers of North Korean resistance. This concept would temporarily bypass such centers that could, potentially, be reinforced to a limited extent from China, prolonging the war and leaving China with an excuse to intervene on some scale.

The alternative would be for UNC forces to advance rapidly to the Yalu River on a broad front, cleaning out and destroying North Korean remnants en route. This would clear the country. If it could be done before substantial Chinese forces entered the country, this would eliminate any excuse the Chinese might have for intervening to support a neighbor. The Yalu River would be a clearly defined international border. Crossing it would be a clear act of aggression. Success in this plan depended on the ability of UNC forces to reach the Yalu River in strength before substantial Chinese forces could be moved across. In the heady days before the appearance of the Chinese, commanders at all levels believed they were in the exploitation phase of action, pursuing a beaten enemy.

The plan for rapid movement to the Yalu on a broad front found support on a higher level. In November, Gen. Charles Bolte continued to argue that the advance north of the thirty-eighth parallel was based on the assumption that all of Korea would be cleared of Communist forces so that an attack from Manchuria would be recognized as an open act of aggression. Possibly reflecting MacArthur's view, Bolte felt there would be a better chance of localizing the war by driving all Communist forces from North Korea. As he stated: ". . . A show of strength might well discourage further aggression where weakness would encourage it."⁵

Notes

1. *History of the Korean Conflict,* Part 2, Vol. 1, "GHQ Support and Participation, 25 June 50–30 Apr. 51" (Tokyo: Far Eastern Command, n.d.), 37 (hereafter cited as *History of the Korean Conflict*).

2. The Nangnim Range is basically a northward extension of the Taebaek Range, which runs nearly the entire length of the Korean Peninsula.

3. *Terrain Study No. 6: Northern Korea* (Tokyo: Far Eastern Command, n.d.).

4. FEC DIS 2965, 22 Oct. 50.

5. Memorandum G-3 DA for C/S USA 21 Nov. 50, quoted in Schnabel, *Policy and Direction.*

7
Across the Yalu

Initial Objective

The Chinese objective was outlined by Mao in a telegram of 2 October 1950 to Stalin, informing him of the decision to enter the Korean War.[1] The long-term objective was to defeat the UN forces and drive them out of Korea. For the present, the Chinese planned to fight north of the thirty-eighth parallel, prepared to confront any forces that crossed the parallel. The initial effort would be primarily defensive. Twelve divisions under the name "volunteers" would enter Korea starting on 15 October.

In the spring, when reequipped with modern weapons and trained in their use, they would launch a counteroffensive to drive out the foreign forces. Mao emphasized the need for materiel support from the Soviet Union. He told Stalin, ". . . we do not now have any certainty of success in annihilating a single American corps in one blow. Since we have made the decision to fight the Americans we certainly must be prepared to deal with a situation in which the U.S. headquarters will employ one American corps against our troops."[2] Mao told Stalin a four-to-one superiority in manpower would be needed to do this. Further, he estimated that a one-and-one-half-to-one or a two-to-one superiority in firepower would be needed. He assumed that the Soviets would provide air cover, something also previously agreed to.

Mao told Stalin of his arrangements to send an additional twenty-four divisions to positions from which they could be moved to Korea as the second and third groups of troops to be sent to aid Korea in the spring and summer, as the situation required.

The Soviets Renege
As advance Chinese units were on the way into Korea, the Soviets began to back away from their agreement to provide materiel and air support.

Zhou Enlai and Lin Biao had flown to Moscow to brief the Soviets on the Chinese plans and arrange for assistance. They met Stalin at his Black Sea villa, where there was considerable diplomatic bluffing and maneuvering. Stalin finally agreed that Russia could send materiel but not troops or air support, although some air support might be sent once Chinese troops were established in Korea. Zhou returned to Moscow on 12 October. He was shocked when Molotov told him the decision had been changed. Russia would not supply materiel. Zhou immediately notified Beijing.[3]

Mao quickly called a halt to all movement. The 9th and 19th Army groups had been ordered to move on 11 October; they were halted the next day. A telegram went out to Gen. Peng Dehuai to halt movement and fly to Beijing for an emergency meeting of the Politburo. For the next two days, the Chinese agonized over their decision to intervene. All of the original arguments about intervention were reviewed. Finally, Mao prevailed upon the group to go ahead regardless.[4] From April 1949, when the victorious PLA had crossed the Yangtze and driven south to complete the conquest of China, Mao had believed that armed conflict with the United States was inevitable. He never believed the U.S. pledge not to assist Taiwan, and he was furious when the promise was broken by the Seventh Fleet. His deep suspicion of the United States would not let him believe the Americans would stop at the Yalu River. Paranoia carried the day. With or without air and materiel support, China would enter the war.

The decision was communicated to Moscow. In turn, the Soviets relented. They would supply arms and equipment, but, for now, no air cover. Major commands were notified and movement resumed. Peng returned to Shenyang and pressed on with preparations.

Four crucial days had been lost. Republic of Korea forces on the east coast had secured Wonsan and begun their advance to Hamhung. The old defense line along the thirty-eighth parallel had been penetrated. I Corps had secured Kumchon and was preparing to advance on Pyongyang.

Plan for Defense in the Mountains

The basic Chinese plan was to hold a redoubt in the central mountain mass north of the Wonsan–Pyongyang line and west of the main north–south line of the Nangnim Range.[5] The plan that Peng developed would hold a line generally from the Changjin area southward along the central range and the Myohyang Mountains to Huichon, then westward along the foothills of the Chokyuryong Mountains to Kusong. (This was not essentially different from the Chagang-do Redoubt area reported by Gen. Charles Willoughby.) This would protect the three most important Yalu River crossings—Changdian, Jian, and Linjiang—with the crossing Jian to Manpojin–Kanggye being the most important axis of support. The coastal areas, vulnerable to air and naval attack, would be given up. Peng emphasized that not too much could be expected in the initial action. His thinking reflected genuine concern over the ability of the Chinese Army to fight a modern mechanized army, and the belief that defending in the mountains would eliminate some of the advantage of the UN forces.[6]

The Chinese plan, devised by Mao and Peng, was based on several assumptions. The principal assumption was that the North Korean Army would vigorously defend Pyongyang, holding off UN forces long enough for the "volunteers" to cross into Korea, march to their assigned positions, deploy, and commence building field fortifications. Additionally, all of Mao's initial plans and pronouncements imply that he was well aware of the planned UN stop line and the fact that only ROK forces would be used north of that line.[7] There is every reason to believe that knowledge of this UN plan was a major factor in the Chinese decision to go ahead with intervention with or without Soviet air cover.

Chinese planning was shaped also by the information available on UN dispositions and movements. Mao's concept was that UN forces were advancing in two separate columns. Chinese intelligence, on 14 October, reported that the western column made up of the U.S. 1st (Cavalry), 2d, and 24th Divisions, plus the Commonwealth Brigade and the 1st ROK Division, were at Kumchon preparing to attack Pyongyang. The eastern column, the ROK Capital Division and the 3d Division, was at Wonsan, while the three divisions of II

ROK Corps (the 6th, 7th, and 8th), moving up through central Korea, were advancing toward the Wonsan area to be resupplied by sea. The 1st Marine Division was in Seoul, with the U.S. 7th and 25th Divisions farther south.[8]

Informing Zhou Enlai of the Chinese decision to go ahead, Mao gave more detail on the Chinese plans. "In the first phase, we can establish a base in the large mountain area to the north of the Wonsan–Pyongyang line and thus encourage the Korean people." He told Zhou, ". . . we can probably force the U.S. and puppet troops to think twice before continuing to advance northward and to protect the areas north of the Pyongyang–Wonsan front, at least the mountainous areas, from being occupied by the enemy. Thus, our army does not have to engage in fighting and can gain time to become well equipped and trained."[9] He even considered the possibility that the United States would not attack and that half of the troops could be sent back to China for training, ready to return if a big war should break out.[10]

As the situation developed and radical changes began to take place, differences between Mao's tactical concepts and those of Peng began to emerge. Peng, aware that the Chinese Army was not well prepared for the kind of war it was about to enter, and well aware of the difficulties of moving his armies into Korea, emphasized the necessity of establishing a strong defensive position before undertaking any aggressive action. To implement this strategic plan, Peng Dehuai planned to construct two or three defensive fronts in the area north of the Pyongyang–Wonsan Railroad and south of the Tokchon–Yongwon Road.

Mao, seeing that the UNC forces were advancing in widely separated columns beyond supporting distance of each other, repeatedly emphasized the possibility of taking advantage of this division of UN forces between east and west to destroy one or more divisions of the ROK Army (ROKA). In his study of the early wars of the Red Army around the Central Soviet Area, he concluded that the first principle of success was "The first battle must be won."[11] To ensure this success, he believed that the available Chinese forces could hold off any enemy forces advancing from Pyongyang while the remainder dealt with the South Koreans.

The Chinese entry into Korea was to begin on 19 October. Mao estimated it would take seven days for the advance army to reach Tokchon. With two days of rest, they could arrive in the area south of the Tokchon–Yongwon Road on 28 October and begin work on defensive positions. It would take ten days for the full 260,000 men of the "volunteer" force to cross into Korea, but Mao wanted to be prepared for a successful campaign in November when the enemy began an attack on the Tokchon region. Optimistically, Mao stated: "It will take time for U.S. troops to reach Pyongyang and more time to attack Tokchon. It will be difficult for ROK troops in Wonsan to attack on their own if U.S. troops don't attack. This leaves time for the entry of our troops and for construction and organization of defense works."[12]

Peng Dehuai's Activities

Late in the afternoon of 8 October, Peng flew to Shenyang to take command of the Northeast Frontier Force, now renamed the Chinese People's Volunteers (CPV). The following day, he convened a meeting of the army commanders. Peng had brought with him only his personal aide from the First Field Army. The staff and the subordinate commanders were all new to him. He had concerns about working with unfamiliar people. The other officers, in turn, had concerns about working with Peng. He had a reputation as a very strict disciplinarian. After sizing up each other, Peng and his Army commanders decided they could work together very well.[13]

Gao Gang, who was turning over command to Peng, briefed the assembled officers on the Politburo's discussions and decisions.

For the first time, Peng learned the strength of the UNC forces he was facing. Based on the estimates of the 13th Army Group officers, the first-line force was believed to be 130,000 strong, with the total force in Korea reaching nearly 400,000. The officers pressed Peng to request that the 9th Army be sent forward earlier than spring, and that another army be assigned to guard the rear as they advanced into Korea. Peng immediately asked that the 9th and 19th Army Groups be activated ahead of time and be ready for deployment.[14]

The Central Military Commission's original plan for deployment in Korea was to send six divisions initially. The other six divisions would remain in Manchuria until Soviet equipment arrived. But the senior officers of the 13th Army Group were concerned. Air attacks might destroy the bridges at Andong, leaving the advance units isolated. Peng agreed and immediately recommended that the plan be changed. All should cross at one time. Mao approved.[15]

Peng had planned to go to Tokchon on 11 October to meet with Kim Il Sung and discuss cooperation. Instead, he received an urgent telephone call to fly at once to Beijing for consultation. The Soviets had reneged on their commitment for support. For the next three days, Peng remained in Beijing while Mao and the Politburo again agonized over the decision to enter the war.[16]

In his initial meeting with the Chinese Army commanders, Peng had learned that Lin Biao was not the only one concerned about the difficulties of fighting well-equipped American forces. There was apprehension throughout the CCF. To counter this, Peng prepared a speech while he was in Beijing. Returning to Andong on 16 October, he assembled the senior officers of the army. The speech had much of the standard Communist invective about lackeys, running dogs, imperialist aggression, world conquest, and so on. But it also had some very interesting points. His assessment: "Our enemies in Korea consist of seven U.S. divisions . . . seven puppet [ROK] divisions that have some combat capability; one British brigade; and a few troops from other vassal countries. . . . the puppet troops are mainly deployed on the eastern coast. Three divisions have already occupied Wonsan. . . . The enemy troops on the west are attacking Kumchon. . . . If they continue launching offensives, the enemy forces will be dispersed. In addition, they will need to hold back some forces to deal with guerilla forces. The enemy can release [only] three U.S. divisions and three puppet divisions for the northward advance. We can resist such forces."[17]

Peng justified entry into the war on the basis of helping a fraternal nation. But he noted that there had been strong arguments pro and con, and he enumerated them. He admitted that China and the Chinese Army were not prepared, but he insisted that the "imperialist bloc" was not prepared either. Oddly, based on information supplied by Beijing, he gave as an estimate of U.S. forces in existence twenty-one divisions, seventeen of them combat-ready. He repeated the estimate that only three U.S. and three ROKA divisions could be spared for action in North Korea. Peng pointed out the belief that the U.S. forces were afraid of close combat, in contrast to the Chinese Communist Forces (CCF), which excelled in such action. The United States was vulnerable because of a long supply line, he claimed, in contrast to the short supply line of the Chinese.

Tactics were discussed. Because Korea was a peninsula, the fluid and mobile tactics that had worked so well in China could not be applied. A combination of positional and mobile warfare would be needed. Defense would have to be in depth. Positions would not be held to the last. It was important to defend territory but also important to annihilate the enemy's strength.

Peng wound up with an exhortation to the troops to respect the Korean people, not to criticize the shortcomings of the Korean Communist Party, and to maintain the discipline prescribed in the Three Main Rules and the Eight Points of Attention.

Apprehension was not so easily overcome. On 17 October, Deng Hua and Hong Xuezhi, commander and first deputy of the 13th Army, raised the question anew. In a cable to Peng in Beijing, where he had gone to make a last-minute report, they repeated concerns about equipment: "We can carry out the original order as scheduled, provided the delivery of new equipment is guaranteed within two or three months [the introduction of the air force is especially important]. Otherwise a postponement of the departure schedule deserves attention." Peng rejected the request.[18]

Deployment Begins

To carry out the Chinese plan, Peng decided to have the 42d Army and then the 38th Army, in that order, cross at Jian. The 42d Army could cover Changjin while the 38th Army would turn south down the Chongchon Valley to Huichon. The 40th Army would cross at Andong–Sinuiju and at Changdian, with the 39th Army following behind.

Logistic preparations under the direction of Gao Gang of the Northeast Military Region had begun on 11 October. Service troops began moving munitions and equipment in advance to supply depots in North Korea. By the time the Chinese troops entered Korea, substantial supplies had been delivered, but at a cost of 200 trucks, nearly one-half of the trucks available.[19]

In addition to moving supplies into Korea, each of the armies organized an advance party made up of one battalion from each division, formed them into composite "units," and sent them forward from one to three days in advance of the main body as a covering force. General Anthony Farrar-Hockley, basing his comments partly on information collected while held as a prisoner of war, states that each CCF division sent over advance parties and that routes were well marked, report centers were established along the routes, and field kitchens and supply points were established. He quotes Gen. William F. Dean (captured earlier in the war), who observed Chinese troops twenty miles north of Huichon on 13 October.[20] To cap it all, and to preserve the initial fiction that the Chinese were volunteers, each army was redesignated with a code—the 38th Army being the "54th Unit," the 39th Army being the "55th Unit," and so on. The advance parties and the "unit" designations were the basis for very serious initial confusion within UNC intelligence agencies during the coming month.

The 124th Division, 42d CCF Army, had the longest distance to go of any unit. Peng ordered it to commence crossing ahead of time at Jian on 16 October. The main body of the forces prepared to march in accordance with Mao's order to Peng on 18 October. "We are determined to move on schedule four corps and three artillery divisions . . . to commence operations. Tomorrow evening, the 19th, the first units will start crossing the Yalu between Andong and Jian. To keep the operation absolutely secret, the troops should start crossing the river every day at dusk and stop at 4:00 A.M. By 5:00 A.M., the troops should have taken cover, and you should keep a close watch on this. To gain experience you should plan for two or three divisions to cross the river on the first night . . . and for more or less the same number of troops to cross the river on the second night. Thereafter, handle the matter at your own discretion."[21]

At Andong, trains carried the 119th and 120th Divisions of the 40th Army across the Yalu River to Sinuiju. From there, they started on foot for Tokchon. The 118th Division of the 40th Army crossed from Changdian to Sakchu and moved off toward Onjong. The 39th Army crossed at Andong and Changdian behind the 40th Army and headed toward the Onjong–Unsan area. To the north, the remainder of the 42d Army crossed the river at Jian and Linjiang. The 124th and 126th Divisions marched southward toward the Chosin Reservoir. The 125th Division remained on the west side of the Nangnim Range to cover passes through the mountains. Behind the 42d Army came the 38th Army.

By the following morning (20 October), elements of five divisions had entered Korea, but deployment was slow. At Andong, the 116th Division of the 39th Army was delayed for two days by a jam-up on the railroads.[22] At Jian, movement was even slower. By 25 October, only two divisions of the 38th Army had been able to cross the river and start down the Chongchon Valley. The 114th Division still waited at Jian.

The Changed Situation
On the morning of 19 October, Pak Il-yu was sent by Kim Il Sung to Andong to request immediate assistance. Pak reported that the North Korean defense was disintegrating. Leaving Deng Hua, commander of the 13th Army Group, to supervise movement of the troops, Peng headed across in a Jeep, followed by a radio van. Peng proceeded to Taeyudong, just north of Bukjin, where he set up his headquarters in an old mine shaft.[23] The following morning, he met with Kim Il Sung to brief him on the Chinese efforts and to learn his situation. Kim reported that all he had left were two infantry divisions, one tank division, a workers' regiment, and a tank regiment.[24] The speed of the UNC advance had been surprising. Kim intimated that the Chinese would have to assume responsibility for the entire battlefield. Any idea of defending along the Wonsan–Pyongyang line was now out of the question.

At Andong, Deng, in Peng's absence, called a hasty meeting of the army commanders, briefed them on the new situation, and outlined the possibilities:

1. The enemy forces may reach our gathering areas before we get there;
2. The enemy force may engage us shortly after we arrive but before we can consolidate our defense positions; or
3. The enemy forces may run up against us on our way.

Deng believed that the only option now was to move as fast as possible into defensible areas to stall the enemy advance and cover the withdrawal of the North Korean forces.[25]

For the next two days, a communication and coordination problem developed between Peng, at Taeyudong, and Deng, at Andong. Both could contact Beijing by radio, or wire, but they had difficulty reaching each other.

In Beijing, Mao thought he saw an opportunity. The ROK Capital and 3d Divisions had reached Hamhung and Oro-ri. Various "bits and pieces" of information indicated that the 6th, 7th, and 8th ROK divisions were to change direction and advance toward Tokchon. Still anticipating ROK forces only north of the Anju–Hamhung line, Mao believed the ultimate objective of these five ROK divisions was the line from Sinuiju to Kanggye.[26] Reports stated the 1st Marine Division was to land at Chinampo to assist in the capture of Pyongyang.

Mao's estimate shows that the mountainous interior, the "barrier area" cited in the Far Eastern Command (FEC) area study, was not considered a significant obstacle in the minds of the Chinese. Mao assumed that the ROK divisions on the east coast could advance through this area with little difficulty.

Early on the morning of 21 October, Mao pointed out the possibilities in a telegram to Peng. The UNC forces had not detected the entry of the Chinese. Given the exposed position of the three divisions of the ROK II Corps, it would be possible to wipe out three ROK divisions, win a first victory, and stabilize the war situation.[27]

Mao proposed a fanciful plan that would require the 40th Army, now proceeding toward Tokchon, to reach the Tokchon–Yongwon area by 23 October and pass around the right flank of II ROK Corps. The 39th Army, arriving from the northeast, and the 38th Army marching down the Chongchon Valley from the north, would engage the ROKA in the front while the 40th Army would attack from the rear. One division of the 42d Army would be sent to the area of Changjin to block any approach from that direction, while the remainder of the 42d Army would move southward to cut the railroad between Wonsan and Pyongyang to prevent reinforcements from reaching II ROK Corps from that direction.[28]

In Korea, Peng Dehuai was concentrating on defense—the original and still primary mission. On 21 October, he reported to Mao the bleak situation of the collapsing NKPA and stated that it was now extremely important to control the central mountain passes, particularly Myohyang-san and Sinchang-dong. Defensive positions should be constructed there so the UNC forces in the west could be isolated from those in the east.[29] Myohyang-san is a 1,500-meter mountain about twelve miles south of Huichon, almost midway between Huichon and Tokchon. It is the terminus of Myohyang Ridge, a southwesterly trending offshoot of the Nangnim Range separating the east coast from the west. Sinchang is thirty miles southeast of the Yalu crossing at Sakchu. Each would form one anchor of a defensive arc oriented on Kanggye.

The next morning, Mao countered with another plan. Although he agreed with the overall plan for defense, he was still focused on offensive action to destroy II ROK Corps. Reporting that ROK forces were expected to cross the Chongchon and advance toward Taechon and Huichon, he ordered Chinese forces to remain twenty kilometers away from the regions north of Chongju, Paekchon, and Kunuri. These were areas favorable for a Chinese ambush, so he wanted the oncoming ROKs to continue into these areas. If the presence of Chinese were discovered, he was concerned that the ROKs would halt or even turn back.[30]

At some time on 22 or 23 October, the picture changed drastically when Mao learned of the plan to land the 1st Marine Division and the 7th Infantry Division at Wonsan on the east coast. He sent an urgent message to Chen Yi, commanding the Third Field Army, to have Song Shilun, commander of the 9th Army Group's twelve divisions, report to Beijing and to have Song's army group complete training and have one army ready to move to the northeast.[31] To the Northwest Military Region, home of the 19th Army Group, Mao reported: "The war situation is critical. The headquarters of the 19th Army Group and two of its main armies must complete all preparations for departure and be ready to depart . . . 24 November."[32]

On 23 October, Mao and Peng arrived at their plan for the initial action. The 40th Army would take up positions in the Onjong–Unsan area. The 39th Army, which had crossed behind the 40th, would concentrate in the Unsan–Taechon area. The 38th Army, not yet all across at Jian, would drive down the Chongchon Valley, move to the southeast of Huichon, and attempt to encircle the rear of the ROK forces advancing up the valley. Mao warned all units to remain well back in the hills and let the ROK forces advance deep into the valleys.[33] On the east, one division of the 42d Army would defend the Changjin area. The two remaining divisions would assemble on the east side of the Nangnim Range as an army group reserve.

Mao emphasized that the situation depended on whether or not the CPV could take advantage of the enemy's unawareness of the Chinese entry to destroy two or three ROK divisions. If the Chinese achieved a major victory, the United States would have to reconsider its strategy. He went on to outline additional possibilities. If the ROK divisions were not destroyed, they might be reinforced, forcing the Chinese to draw back and making it difficult to defend their mountain position. On the other hand, if they were destroyed, the Chinese might then take on a U.S. division. It might even be possible to force the U.S. command to ask for a cease-fire.

Reinforcements

In September, China's 9th Army Group, stationed to the north and the south of Shanghai, had moved inland to embarkation points on the railroad. In response to Peng's request to have them activated and ready for employment, the group had been ordered to move north to the areas around Taian and Qufu in Shandong Province. The move had been halted on 12 October while the decision to intervene was again reviewed. On 14 October, orders were given to resume movement, and some units reached Qufu while others remained in the south. About the same time, the 50th Army had been moved north and was guarding installations in Manchuria.

Now, on 23 October, Peng asked for more troops. He wanted the entire 9th Army Group as reinforcement. In addition, he wanted another army to guard his rear as the 39th and 40th Armies moved eastward to confront the ROK forces. In response, advance elements of the 66th Army moved off toward Sinuiju, followed by the remainder of the divisions. Movement of the 9th Army Group toward Korea commenced.[34] In the next two weeks, the size of the Chinese People's Volunteers would increase from twelve to thirty divisions.

At the same time, Mao and the Central Military Commission, concerned about the problem of coordination between the CPV and the 13th Army Group, ordered the two headquarters combined. The 13th Army Group headquarters was disbanded and consolidated with the headquarters of the CPV. Deng Hua, former commander of the 13th Army Group, was named deputy commander, as were Pak Il-yu, the Korean liaison, and Hong Xuezhi and Han Xianchu, formerly deputy commanders of the 13th Army Group. Xie Fang was named chief of staff and Du Ping director of the political department. Deng Hua was ordered to proceed immediately by car to Peng Dehuai's headquarters.

Notes

1. Goncharov et al., *Uncertain Partners*, Doc. 63, 275–76.

2. Ibid. There is a slight difference in translation between this version of the telegram and that appearing in 46 Telegrams, No. 10. The latter uses the term *army* ambiguously, indicating either a three-division organization or a larger formation, whereas the *Uncertain Partners* version calls three divisions a corps, as in U.S. usage. Assuming the *Uncertain Partners* version is correct might imply that Mao was aware that, initially, U.S. forces employed above the thirty-eighth parallel would consist only of one corps (I Corps). There is further evidence this might have been the basis for the Chinese decision in Deng's speech to senior officers of the 13th Army Group on 16 October wherein he gives the estimate, "The enemy can release [only] three U.S. divisions and three puppet divisions for the northward advance."—Goncharov et al., *Uncertain Partners*, Doc. 77, 286.

3. Ibid., 192–95.

4. Ibid., 193.

5. Ibid., 282.

6. Zhang, *Mao's Military Romanticism*, 99.

7. Goncharov et al., *Uncertain Partners*, Doc. 76, 284.

8. 46 Telegrams, No. 21, 14 Oct. 50.

9. Goncharov et al., *Uncertain Partners*, Doc. 75, 283.

10. Ibid., Doc. 76, 283 (Telegram Mao to Zhou Enlai 14 Oct. 1950).

11. Ibid., 196, and Mao Zedong, "Problems of Strategy in China's Revolutionary War," in *Selected Military Writings of Mao Zedong* (Beijing: Foreign Language Press, 1963), 75–144.

12. Goncharov et al., *Uncertain Partners*, Doc. 76, 284 (Telegram Mao to Zhou).

13. Zhang, *Mao's Military Romanticism*, 89.

14. *Biographies of PLA Generals* (Beijing: Liberation Army Publishing House, 1984–89). Unpublished partial translation in author's possession (hereafter cited as *Biographies of PLA Generals*).

15. Ibid.

16. Goncharov et al., *Uncertain Partners*, 193.

17. Ibid., Doc. 77, 284–89.

18. Ibid., 197.

19. Ibid., 187.

20. Anthony Farrar-Hockley, "Reminiscence of Chinese People's Volunteers in Korea." *The China Quarterly* 98, (June 1984).

21. Goncharov et al., *Uncertain Partners*, Doc. 82, 290.

22. Spurr, *Enter the Dragon,* 120.

23. Zhang, *Mao's Military Romanticism,* 95.

24. John Toland, *In Mortal Combat: Korea, 1950–1953* (New York: William Morrow, 1991), 249.

25. Zhang, *Mao's Military Romanticism,* 94.

26. 46 Telegrams, No. 28, 21 Oct. 50.

27. Zhang, *Mao's Military Romanticism,* 95.

28. Ibid.

29. Ibid., 96.

30. Ibid.

31. 46 Telegrams, No. 40, 23 Oct. 50.

32. 46 Telegrams, No. 35, 22 Oct. 50.

33. Zhang, *Mao's Military Romanticism,* 99–100.

34. Ibid., 101.

8
The Armies Collide

Well, there are a lot of Mexicans in Texas, aren't there?
—Gen. Walton Walker,
on finding Chinese prisoners in North Korea

24 October

Spurred on by President Syngman Rhee, II ROK Corps was rushing forward with all speed toward the Yalu River and the Manchurian border. The 6th ROK Division, leading, had advanced through central Korea, bypassed Pyongyang, passed through Kunu-ri on the south bank of the Chongchon River on 23 October, and turned northward toward Huichon, reaching there about midnight. The following day, one battalion of the 6th ROK Division's 7th Regiment marched northward along a primitive trail toward Kojang. That evening, the remainder of the 7th ROK Regiment mounted up on trucks, drove through Onjong, and joined with the cross-country battalion. Unknown to them, or to their next higher command, the ROK regiment had slipped through a gap between the 38th CCF Army advancing down the Chongchon Valley and the 40th CCF Army moving southeastward toward Kujang-dong.

The 8th ROK Division, following the 6th, pushed northward from Sunchon and reached Tokchon an hour before midnight on 23 October. The next day, it closed on Kujang-dong, on the river, and turned north behind the 6th ROK Division. Behind the two came the 7th ROK Division, approaching Kunu-ri by the evening of 24 October.

To the west, the 27th Commonwealth Brigade, attached to and leading the advance of the 24th Infantry Division, had reached the Chongchon River at Sinanju on 23 October. Crossing in assault boats, the brigade turned left, crossed the Taeryong near Pakchon, and started west.

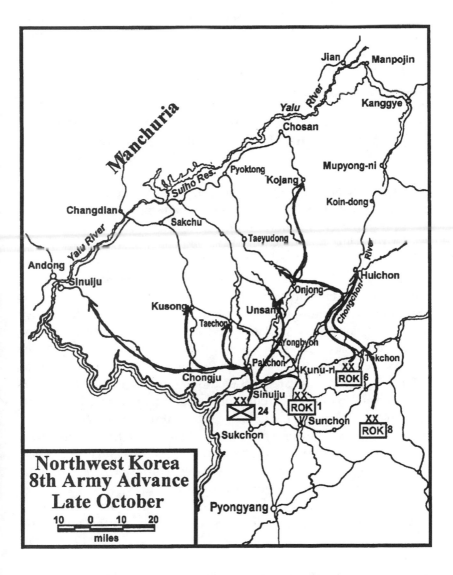

**Northwest Korea
8th Army Advance
Late October**

10 0 10 20
miles

The 1st ROK Division also was across the Chongchon on the right side of the 24th Division and, supported by tanks, advanced to the vicinity of Yongbyon.

All along the front, resistance was negligible but the bag of prisoners was impressive. A total of 1,167 North Koreans were collected on 24 October.

That evening, the Eighth Army Periodic Intelligence Report (PIR), prepared by Lt. Col. James C. "Clint" Tarkenton, Eighth Army G-2, gave an optimistic estimate: "Considering the relative impotency of the remaining North Korean Force, it may be expected that friendly movement to the Manchuria border will be rapid." Then, with a token note of caution, Tarkenton added: "This could be a critical period for possible intervention by Chinese Communist Forces. . . ." They could, he noted, move "security units across the Yalu to protect industrial installations. They could move substantial forces south of the Yalu to protect the border. Or they could intervene with major forces to aid the North Koreans." He then tempered this warning: ". . . the fact that these forces have not previously intervened, coupled with the apparent lack of commensurate returns for intervention at this late date, make it appear unlikely that overt commitment of Chinese Communist forces will occur at this time."[1] The following morning, Gen. Walton Walker issued a news bulletin saying, "Everything is going just fine."[2]

Advance parties of the Chinese People's Volunteers had begun moving into Korea as early as 8 October. On 20 October, the main forces began to move. Traveling only at night and adhering to very strict march discipline, the Chinese forces were able to maintain absolute secrecy as they entered Korea. But the severe security measures, together with the congestion on the railroads and at the crossing sites, slowed movement and created confusion. Deployment began to fall behind the optimistic time schedule.[3]

Peng Dehuai had turned over supervision of the deployment to his chief of staff and proceeded ahead to confer with the North Koreans. En route, he lost contact with his radio van. By 23 October, when he established his headquarters in a former gold mine[4] in the village of Taeyudong, about 20 miles northwest of Onjong on the road to Pyoktong, he was having difficulty reestablishing control of the advancing troops. Conflicting objectives further complicated his problems.[5]

Learning of the very rapid advance of the UNC troops, he realized that his first task was to secure the crossing sites at Changdian–Sakchu, Jian–Manpojin, and Linjiang and provide sufficient room for the remaining units to cross and deploy. Then he proposed to establish a defensive line: Kusong–Taechon–Kujang-dong–Tokchon–Yongwon –Oro-ri. North Korean forces had prepared field fortifications along this line north of Unsan and Oro-ri, and probably at other points. The Chinese armies could build up behind this line during the winter for the planned offensive in the spring. Once this line was secure, he could then exploit whatever opportunities presented themselves. He was prepared to attack the three advancing ROK divisions if there was any chance of success. But the leadership should not expect too much from it.[6]

Mao, bubbling over with optimism, thought he saw an opportunity to attack the three ROK divisions, which were now leading the advance of the Eighth Army. His fantasy was to hurry the 38th Army southward to a position southeast of Huichon, cut off the two ROK divisions, which were then moving toward Huichon, and then attack with the other two armies and destroy them.[7]

By late evening of 24 October, the Chinese were situated as follows:

The *40th Army* was across the Yalu with all three of its divisions. The 118th Division was in position north of Onjong and the 120th Division was west of Onjong on the hills between the Taeryong and Samtan Rivers. The 119th Division was still en route.

The *38th Army* was strung out along the route from Jian to Kang-gye and down the Chongchon Valley. The 114th Division was still at Jian, the 112th Division was in the vicinity of Mupyong-ni, and the 113th Division was about thirty miles north of Huichon.

The *39th Army* was across the Yalu in the vicinity of Kusong but moving slowly. The 116th Division had been delayed for two days by a jam-up at the bridge and snarls on the trains.

The *42d Army*, with the mission of flank protection for the forces west of the mountains, was to guard against the advance of ROK forces toward Chosin. The 124th Division was around Koto-ri and had advanced one regiment south to Chinhung-ni. The 125th Division had taken up a position at Yongnim-dong, west of the main mountain divide, about halfway between Yudam-ni and Mupyong-ni on the upper reaches of the Chongchon. The 126th Division and Army Headquarters were at Changjin, with one regiment of the 126th Division around the Fusen Reservoir.

The *50th and 66th Armies* were just starting to cross. The 50th was to cross all three of its divisions. Initially, the 66th sent across only one division, the 196th, holding the others in reserve.

Peng was concerned. ROK troops at Huichon had advanced beyond his planned defensive line, while the slow movement of the 38th Army made it unlikely they would be able to march undetected around the right flank of the ROKs. But, at this point, the presence of the Chinese troops was unsuspected.

25 October

On 25 October, the 7th ROK Regiment, having slipped unopposed through the gap between two advancing Chinese armies, reached Kojang. The regiment halted at Kojang for the night but sent a patrol, which reached the Yalu River at Chosan—the first UNC unit to reach the Yalu and the only one to do so on the Eighth Army front.[8]

In the morning, the 3d Battalion, in advance of the rest of the 2d ROK Regiment, moved in trucks through Onjong and turned north on the Onjong–Pukchin Highway, headed for Pyoktong on the Yalu River. Their route would take them right through Taeyudong and Peng's command post. At his Taeyudong headquarters early on the morning of 25 October, Peng learned the 2d ROK Regiment was advancing along the road toward his command post. Reluctantly, he gave permission for the 118th and 120th Divisions to attack, knowing that this would reveal the Chinese presence. At various times and places, the remnants of North Korean units had been used as a screen behind which the Chinese could deploy. None seemed to be available on the Pukchin Road. The threat to CPV headquarters had to be eliminated.[9]

About ten miles north of Onjong, the advancing ROK forces were halted by Chinese fire. By 10 A.M., the Chinese commenced an attack that split the column into three sections, overran it, and captured 230 of the 750 men in the battalion. The remainder fled on foot. The 2d Battalion, moving to their assistance, was strongly attacked and driven back into the town of Onjong.

Farther west, the 15th ROK Regiment, leading the 1st ROK Division, reached Unsan, crossed through the town, and headed northeast across the Samtan River. At the bridge, at about 11 A.M., they were halted by mortar fire. Following the 15th ROK Regiment, the 12th ROK Regiment turned west up the Samtan River and was similarly halted. There was heavy fighting for the remainder of the day.

About noon, the 15th ROK Division captured Shien Chang-san, the first Chinese prisoner of the Korean War. Shien was hustled back to I Corps, where arrangements were made to fly him to Pyongyang for interrogation at Eighth Army Headquarters. At I Corps, the prisoner claimed to be from the 3d Battalion, 60th Regiment. His battalion began crossing the Yalu on 19 October. He revealed that 10,000 Chinese were establishing strong defensive positions from Unsan southwest to the coast, with another 10,000 in a defensive line covering Huichon–Kanggye.[10]

At Eighth Army HQ, he told his interrogators that the 40th CCF Army was composed of three branch units (brigades or understrength divisions, of about 6,000 troops), with one artillery regiment and three infantry regiments. The regiments were about 2,000 men each. Half of the troops were not armed. Two other branch units of the 40th Army were on either flank.[11] Interrogation by the 164th Military Intelligence Service Detachments reported him as saying he belonged to the 3d "Branch Unit" of the 3d Division, creating further confusion. There was skepticism when he stated he had been told that 600,000 Chinese would be sent to Korea because the U.S. Army was about to invade China. Shien had been inducted into the Chinese Nationalist Army in 1947, had deserted, had been reinducted, had been captured by the Communists in 1949, then indoctrinated for four months and inducted into the PLA.[12] He was almost certainly a deserter from the CCF, having chosen the opportune moment that morning.

A second prisoner was captured that day by the 2d ROK Regiment in the vicinity of Onjong. He claimed to be a member of the 56th "Army Unit," with a size of approximately 1,000, and had crossed the Yalu on 12 October.[13]

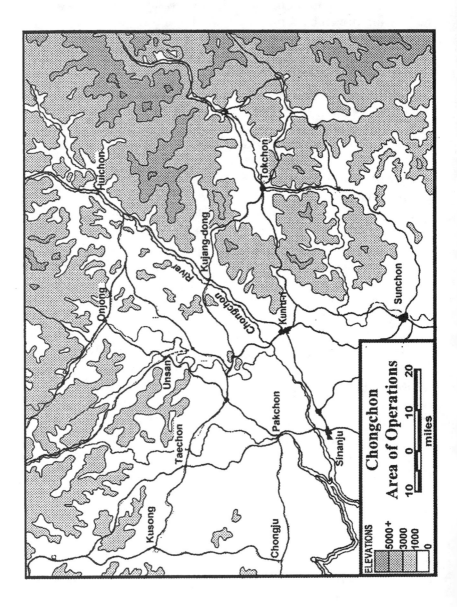

Chongchon
Area of Operations

miles

ELEVATIONS
5000+
3000
1000
0

Then began one of the most interesting cases of massive military denial in history. The possibility of Chinese reinforcement—which all had discussed and professed to believe—was about to come true. It was difficult to accept. Military commanders and their intelligence agencies at all levels began a month-long scramble to create reasons why the appearance of the Chinese was only a minor obstacle. The confusion about the organization of the Chinese, whether they were in task units or regular organizations of the PLA, led to the disastrous underestimate of the Chinese strength and to the failure to understand their purpose in intervening, or even to understand that they had intervened.

The Eighth Army Periodic Intelligence Report for that evening did not even mention the capture of the two Chinese prisoners, but it did mention the capability of the enemy to reinforce with Chinese Communist and/or Soviet forces. When informed of the capture of Chinese prisoners as the forces approached the border, Gen. Walton Walker is reported to have said, "Well, there are a lot of Mexicans in Texas, aren't there?"[14]

In Beijing, Mao was disappointed. This first, minor contact would disclose the Chinese presence. Nevertheless, he urged Peng to make every effort to surround one or two units, which would then lure reinforcements that could be ambushed and destroyed. Peng answered back, somewhat peevishly, in a telegram to Mao the evening of 25 October, saying that it is very difficult to surround and attack two or three entire divisions, and that it would be difficult to conceal entry of the CCF troops. Accordingly, he told Mao, he had decided to allow the troops in the units of army or division to take on the enemy's one regiment and two battalions, an operation already under way. The goal was to wipe out one or two divisions of the enemy and stabilize the situation.[15]

26 October

The Chinese forces chasing the remnants of the 2d ROK Regiment toward Onjong had surrounded the town by midnight and commenced to attack. By early morning, what was left of the ROK regiment was overrun. A substantial number escaped on foot, but all vehicles and the artillery were captured, along with many prisoners. In the fighting, the 2d ROK Regiment reported that it was under attack by a reinforced regiment consisting of a large number of Chinese.

At Unsan, the 12th ROK Regiment held under a Chinese attack, but the 15th ROK Regiment had to give ground. The 11th ROK Regiment, then in division reserve south of town, was moved up to reinforce the 12th. But during the day, the road behind the division was cut. The 11th ROK Regiment then was turned around and attacked south to open the road. Heavy resistance forced it back almost into the town. The division was now cut off.

27 October

At Huichon, apparently unaware of the advancing 38th CCF Army, Maj. Gen. Yu Jai Hung, II ROK Corps commander, organized a rescue force made up of two battalions of the 19th ROK Regiment and two battalions from the 10th ROK Regiment to advance from Huichon and retrieve vehicles at Onjong.

By 27 October, Peng, after considerable difficulty, had reestablished contact with his forces and was beginning to cope with the rapidly changing situation. He was attempting to work out a plan while at the same time deal with Mao's "suggestions" coming long distance from Beijing. Mao learned that the 24th Division had crossed the Chongchon and was advancing along the coast. He directed that the 39th Army, on the right of the CPV, should not engage the U.S. troops. Mao wanted Peng to focus on the 1st, 6th, and 8th ROK Divisions on the right of the Eighth Army.[16]

The 8th ROK Division and the remaining 10th Regiment of the 6th ROK Division were still at Huichon. Those units, along with the isolated 7th ROK Regiment at Kojang, seemed to be the most exposed elements and offered the best opportunity for a quick success. Peng assigned the 118th Division of the 40th Army and the 148th Division of the 50th Army, now arriving from the north, to take out the 7th ROK Regiment. The two remaining divisions of the 40th Army would assemble southeast of Huichon, while the three divisions of the 38th Army, with the 125th Division in reserve, would attack southward against the ROK forces at Huichon. The available units of the 39th Army would man previously constructed defensive positions north of Unsan, prepared to attack when the Huichon battle ended.[17]

Mao then learned of the departure of the 6th and 8th ROK Division units from Huichon. He ordered Peng to change his plan. Rather than strike at the small remaining units at Huichon, Peng decided that the next best opportunity was to surround but not attack the 7th ROK Regiment at Kojang. He hoped that their plight would draw rescue forces, which then could be engaged and overwhelmed. To carry out this plan, the 40th Army's two divisions in the Onjong area were to hold off advancing forces while the 38th and 39th Armies redeployed to intercept rescue forces. Mao agreed, saying he hoped the 7th ROK Regiment would ". . . cry for help . . . so loudly that the ROK 1st, 6th, and 8th Divisions will have to rescue it and then we will have a battle to fight."[18]

At Unsan, Maj. Gen. Paik Sun Yup, 1st ROK Division commander, who had been absent on another mission on 25 and 26 October, returned, went forward, inspected the bodies of the CCF dead, and interrogated some new prisoners. Paik had served with the Japanese Army in Manchuria and was well acquainted with the Chinese Communists. He recognized them and told Gen. Frank W. Milburn, I Corps commander, that there were "many, many more" in the hills, at least one division.

Resupplied by an air drop, the 11th ROK Regiment was able to reopen the road. The 12th and 15th ROK Regiments renewed their attack but made only slight gains against the Chinese, who were now occupying previously prepared positions.

A third Chinese prisoner, Lee Shin-lin, captured by the 15th ROK Regiment, claimed to belong to the 360th Regiment, 120th Division, 40th CCF Army. He said that the other two regiments of the 120th Division, the 358th and the 359th, were present; that the other two divisions of the 40th Army were present; and that his army had a strength of about 30,000. Lee had been drafted into the Chinese Nationalist Army in 1939, had been captured by the PLA in April 1950, and had been inducted into the PLA. He was a deserter; he had heard that there were Chinese Nationalist forces in Korea, and he wanted to rejoin them.[19]

The three Chinese prisoners captured by 27 October were not the only captives. During the same three-day period, 331 other prisoners had been taken in the Eighth Army zone. But the small number of Chinese and their conflicting answers were a puzzle. Colonel Tarkenton speculated that an unknown number of Chinese had been incorporated into North Korean units to assist in defense of the border area. But he admitted that because of the circumstances, no firm conclusions could be drawn. He continued to believe that the evidence did not indicate open intervention on the part of Chinese Communist Forces.[20]

General Headquarters (GHQ) in Tokyo was reacting slowly to the new information. On 26 October, the DIS reported the resistance at Unsan but not the capture of Chinese prisoners. Still in an optimistic vein, General Willoughby stated: "The enemy is no longer in a position to offer organized resistance to the advance of UN forces to the Korean–Manchurian border. . . . The present position of UN forces seems to leave the enemy with only one alternative regarding his main forces—retreat across the border."

The next day, the DIS carried the information from the interrogation of Shien Chang-san and the report that the 2d ROK Regiment believed it was opposed by a regiment consisting of a large number of Chinese. It then stated that those reports were based on prisoner interrogations, were unconfirmed, and therefore were unaccepted. As he had for the previous three days, Willoughby believed the first capability was the conduct of guerrilla warfare, with reinforcement in second place.[21]

28 October

Despite the uncertain picture of the battlefield, General Walker took some precautionary steps. The 1st Cavalry Division, then at Pyongyang, was ordered to move forward at best speed, prepared to pass through the 1st ROK Division and continue the attack northward. The 27th Commonwealth Brigade, slated to be relieved by the 21st Infantry, would not go into reserve but rather would take up position in the vicinity of Pakchon to protect the rear of the 24th Division as it continued northwest. The 7th ROK Division, then in reserve at Kunu-ri, would move up the Chongchon River to Kujang-dong to reinforce the battered 6th and 8th ROK Divisions.

At Kojang, the isolated 7th ROK Regiment had been ordered to withdraw to the south on 26 October, but, out of fuel and ammunition, it had been unable to move. Resupplied by air on 28 October, it commenced moving but was halted by a Chinese roadblock twenty miles south of town.

The appearance of the Chinese sobered the euphoric ROK command. The four ROK battalions from Huichon, instead of rushing forward to rescue the trapped 7th ROK Regiment, had cautiously advanced toward Onjong. By late afternoon, they had reached the hills overlooking the town. Peng was disappointed that the bait offered by the surrounded 7th ROK Regiment was not snapped up. Learning of the cautious ROK move, he ordered an immediate attack by all organizations. The 119th and 120th Divisions of the 40th Army would attack and destroy the four ROK battalions at Onjong. The 115th Division would hold off the 1st ROK Division at Unsan. The 118th Division of the 40th Army, together with the 148th Division of the newly arriving 50th Army, would surround and destroy the 7th ROK Regiment. The 38th Army, slowly approaching Huichon, would continue to drive down the river valley in an effort to cut off UNC forces north of the river.[22]

At Kojang, afraid the 7th ROK Regiment would escape, the 118th Division commander decided not to wait for the arrival of the 148th Division. Late that afternoon he attacked. By midnight, the battle was over. The regiment had been overrun and destroyed. Only 875 of 3,552 escaped. The remainder were killed or captured.[23] At Onjong, the two CCF divisions rolled over the four ROK battalions. By daylight, the 40th CCF Army began to turn southwest and advance down the Chongchon Valley.

Like everyone else, General Willoughby was having difficulty adjusting to the idea that the very threat he had emphasized for the previous month might actually be developing. He again noted the forty-four divisions in Manchuria, pointed out that twenty-nine of them were along the river where they were immediately available, and assessed their capabilities. He discussed the Chinese logistic capabilities, the qualities and training of the Chinese soldier, and the problems of fighting without air cover, concluding: "From a tactical viewpoint, with victorious UN divisions in full deployment, it would appear that the auspicious time for such intervention had long since passed; it is difficult to believe that such a move, if planned, would have been postponed to a time when the remnant NK forces have been reduced to a low point of effectiveness."[24] A possible rationale for the Chinese appearance was face. Perhaps a small number of troops, 2,000 to 4,000, had been sent as a token from the CCF since their threatening announcement about intervention.

29 October

By the morning of 29 October, only one battalion of the 6th ROK Division remained intact. The 8th ROK Division was somewhat better off, with one battalion of the 10th ROK Regiment, together with the 16th and 21st Regiments. Those remnants began withdrawing down the Chongchon Valley ahead of the advancing 38th CCF Army. Walker took further steps to bolster the crumbling right flank of the army. The 8th ROK Division was ordered to take up a defensive position on the line Yongbyon to Kujang-dong. The 7th ROK Division would move forward and extend the line from Kujang-dong to Tokchon.

In the I Corps zone, the 8th Cavalry arrived that evening and went into an assembly area at Yongsan. The 1st ROK Division, now resupplied, resumed the attack in bitter fighting against determined resistance with little gain. Forced to move in the daylight, the Chinese set forest fires in the hills so the smoke would help conceal their movements from UNC aircraft. On the far left flank, the 24th Division continued the advance.

At Huichon, the advance of the 38th CCF Army was delayed. North Korean forces fleeing up the valley blocked the road and slowed the advance. UNC air attacks hit the 38th Army command post and knocked out communication for several hours. Then the army commander, unable to determine if the troops opposing him were ROKs or Americans (who were not yet to be attacked), hesitated. Not until night began to fall did the 38th Army commence its advance.[25]

By 29 October, ten Chinese prisoners had been captured in the Eighth Army area. Three identified themselves as belonging to a "branch unit" of the 56th Army Unit. Four identified themselves as belonging to either the 119th or the 120th Division of the 40th CCF Army. Three had yet to be interrogated. It was ultimately determined that these latter three, captured by the 5th RCT, were from the 117th and 115th Divisions of the 39th CCF Army.

In these and future interrogations, there was difficulty. There were few Chinese-speaking language personnel. Interpreters had been recruited from a variety of local sources. Some of the available Chinese speakers did not speak English well. Those who did speak both Chinese and English reasonably well had difficulty understanding Chinese military terms and their English equivalents. And there were problems because of the many unfamiliar dialects spoken in the Chinese Army.

Colonel Tarkenton now believed there were indications that the enemy had been reinforced by complete Chinese units. He estimated the Chinese strength at the equivalent of two regiments. They might be committed in piecemeal fashion to secure the approaches to the border. They might be the beginning of open intervention on the part of Chinese forces to defeat UN forces in Korea. There was not yet sufficient evidence to support either conclusion. In Tokyo, General Willoughby accepted the Eighth Army conclusion that thus far there had been no indication of open intervention on the part of Chinese Communist Forces.[26]

30 October

In five days of fighting, Peng Dehuai and his CCF had nibbled away at the ROK Army, had halted the UNC offensive, and had reached the general line he had planned to hold. But he had not inflicted the dramatic blow he had hoped for. Mao, however, was elated. In a telegram on 30 October, he congratulated Peng on eliminating four battalions of puppets and on his present deployment. The Chinese Army had a clear picture of the enemy—his numbers, position, combat effectiveness, and morale. With some satisfaction, he told Peng the enemy knew only vaguely that the Chinese Army had 40,000 to 60,000 men. The full strength of the Chinese Army was not yet known. He urged Peng to totally annihilate the enemy's frontal forces. The 38th Army and one division of the 42d Army could surely cut off the enemy retreat, ". . . and other armies and divisions can bravely thrust deep into the side and rear of each enemy unit, penetrating and slicing up the enemy forces to destroy them piece by piece."[27]

Encouraged, Peng determined to press on with the following plan:

The *39th and 40th Armies* would make a frontal attack to hold I Corps in position.

The *38th Army* would continue the advance down the Chongchon Valley to cut off UNC troops north of the river.

The *125th Division* would make a very deep envelopment through Tokchon and Pukchang-ni toward Sunchon.

The *66th Army,* now arriving, would take positions to hold off the advance of the 24th Infantry Division along the coast.

His aim would be to deal with the remnants of the 6th and 8th ROK Divisions, then face the 1st ROK Division and the 1st Cavalry Division.[28]

As the day wore on, smoke from the many forest fires gradually lessened visibility through the valley, helping to conceal the Chinese as they moved into position for their renewed attack.

31 October

A hungry and frightened but articulate deserter, Tshu Tsei-chiang, the eleventh Chinese prisoner to be captured, seems to have provided the information that convinced Tarkenton to accept the Chinese forces as token task units from each army rather than the entire army.

Tshu was twenty years old, had been in the PLA for two years, and was one of the small number of prisoners who had been recruited directly into the PLA without previous service. He was assigned as a messenger but deserted because he said he had never been in combat and was afraid of being killed. He said he was from the 2d Battalion, 56th Unit, Chinese Peace Preservation Army. The 56th Unit was made up of a battalion from each of the 118th, 119th, and 120th Divisions of the 40th CCF Army. He claimed that the 40th Army remained in Manchuria while this token force entered Korea on 20 October. He had heard that the 55th Unit, with a strength of about 2,000, composed of troops from the 115th, 116th, and 117th Divisions from the 39th CCF Army, had crossed into Korea about 21 October and was in the vicinity of Taechon. He believed there was also another 54th Unit made up of troops from the 38th CCF Army.[29]

Here was the clearest explanation yet of the Chinese organization.

Based on this, it appears that Tarkenton concluded that two previous prisoners who reported belonging to the 360th Regiment of the 120th Division were really from the 56th Unit, and that the elements of the 39th Army deployed on their right were really the 55th Unit, and that elements reported to be from the 38th Army were really the 54th Unit, although this latter was not confirmed. Thus Tarkenton concluded: "It now appears likely that the enemy forces in front of the II ROK Corps have been bolstered by at least one and possibly two composite Chinese regiments. As stated, these units are tentatively identified as the 55th Unit and the 56th Unit."[30]

Looking back, and knowing that later in the war the Chinese ordered selected Communist Party members to surrender in order to carry instructions to their prisoners of war, and given Tshu's background, to the extent the records show, it seems reasonably certain that he was a ringer, a deliberate plant. But Tarkenton stuck with the "unit" theory for the next three weeks.

There were more guesses about the presence of the Chinese. They might be there to maintain a "stronghold" area in the northern section, which could be relatively easy to defend and which would serve as a base of operations for future guerrilla activity. Alternatively, their purpose might be to delay friendly forces from advancing northward until the NKPA could be reorganized. The Communist leaders in China could disclaim responsibility and assert that these troops were from Korean forces trained in China, or were volunteers for this duty. Again Tarkenton stoutly maintained that aside from the identification of the two regiment-size units, "There have been no indications of open intervention by Chinese Communist Forces."[31]

Down at the headquarters of I Corps, Col. Percy W. Thompson, the G-2, had a different interpretation. Thompson reviewed the reports on all CCF prisoners captured to date. Then he looked at the damage inflicted by the Chinese attack. He estimated that at least two CCF divisions had reinforced the NKPA in the Huichon–Onjong area.[32]

In Tokyo, General Willoughby referred to the collapse of II ROK Corps as a "setback" but noted that this setback, together with stiffened resistance, indicated the entrance of fresh troops. They could be reorganized NKPA units, or new NK units previously unlocated, or they might signify the commitment of Chinese Communist Forces.

He thought the reports of the strength and number of CCF units were probably exaggerated. Most reports had come from ROK units. There was general skepticism over the reliability of reports from the ROKs. Not yet ready to commit himself, Willoughby temporized: ". . . greater credence must be given to the foregoing reports in light of prisoner identification of Chinese Communist units in combat area of Korea and the fact that these identifications correspond generally to unit designations previously reported."[33]

At Unsan, the 8th Cavalry, skeptical of Colonel Thompson's reports of Chinese, had moved up and begun the relief of the 12th ROK Regiment, which would then go into reserve. The 5th Cavalry moved up to Ipsok, southwest of Unsan, to keep the main supply route open. By this time, the 1st ROK Division, and the 8th Cavalry, formed a huge bulge in the Eighth Army line, open on both flanks. In the west, the 21st Infantry had passed through Chongju and was moving forward on the road to Chongo-dong. The 5th Infantry had reached Kusong and was meeting heavy resistance.

1 November

The situation on the right flank of the Army had become serious. At noon on 1 November, General Walker informed General Milburn of the situation and ordered him to take command of II ROK Corps. The ROK Corps commander reported that his only available forces were three battalions at Kunu-ri. He had lost contact with the others. A scratch force was organized by I Corps to move to Kunu-ri to hold that vital position. The 8th ROK Division had been penetrated. The 12th ROK Regiment was moved east to help plug that hole. General Hobart R. Gay, 1st Cavalry Division commander, aware of the situation, requested permission to pull the 8th Cavalry back from what was now an exposed position and to consolidate his division. His request was disapproved.

The 39th CCF Army, assigned to attack from the north, arrived at the following plan for Unsan: The 115th Division would attack the 15th ROK Regiment east of the Samtan River. The 116th Division would attack the 8th Cavalry. The 117th Division would move around

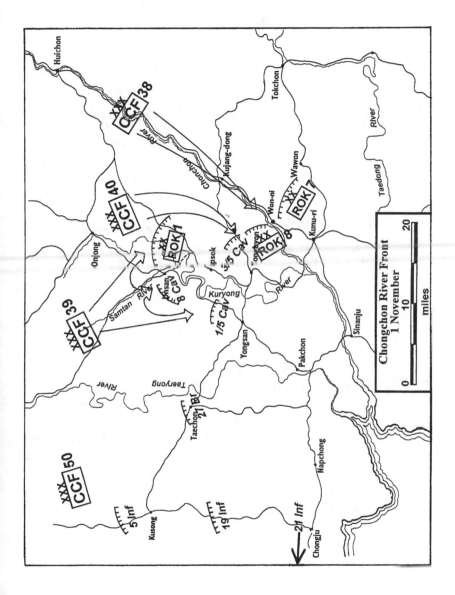

Chongchon River Front
1 November

the flank and cut the road leading from the west.[34] Heavy fighting continued throughout the day. By nightfall, the 116th Division had begun the attack against the 8th Cavalry.

The extent of the II ROK Corps collapse, and the threat to the right flank of the Army, was clear by eight o'clock that evening. In coordination with General Walker, General Milburn ordered I Corps to go over to the defensive. The 24th Infantry Division was to withdraw to a bridgehead north of the Chongchon covered by the 27th Brigade. The 19th Infantry and the 27th Brigade would hold the bridgehead while the 21st Infantry went into reserve. The 5th Infantry was to move to the right flank of the Army at Kunu-ri to back up the ROKs.

The 1st Cavalry Division was to withdraw. The 8th Cavalry at Unsan was being heavily pressed by the Chinese and threatened with roadblocks to its rear. The 5th Cavalry and the 7th Cavalry (less the latter's 3d Battalion) would mount an attack to open the road for the 8th Cavalry to withdraw. The 3d Battalion, 7th Cavalry, would go to Kunu-ri with the 5th Infantry.

The 9th and 38th Infantry of the 9th Infantry Division were ordered north to take up positions south of Kunu-ri to protect the Army's right flank. The 23d Infantry would join them as soon as possible.

At Unsan, the 15th ROK Regiment had begun to give way under the Chinese attack. The three battalions of the 8th Cavalry were now in serious trouble. Around eleven o'clock that night, the commander of the 8th Cavalry received the order to withdraw. But by that time, the road south had been cut and the 1st and 2d Battalions had been badly disorganized. By daylight, the majority of men from those two battalions had gotten out by infiltrating through the hills alone or in small groups. The 3d Battalion was trapped.

That evening, Tarkenton accepted Colonel Thompson's estimate that the enemy strength in the Huichon–Onjong area was two divisions but included only two Chinese units of regiment size. The attack against the II ROK Corps was attributed to reorganized NKPA units with only token support from the Chinese.[35]

2 November
Repeated attacks by all three battalions of the 5th Cavalry, reinforced

by two battalions of the 7th Cavalry in an attempt to break through to the surrounded 3d Battalion, 8th Cavalry, succeeded only in generating heavy casualties. The Chinese defense held. By noon, the effort was given up and the 1st Cavalry Division was ordered to withdraw, leaving the 3d Battalion to the Chinese.

Seventeen Chinese prisoners were now in Eighth Army hands. Assessing interrogation reports, Tarkenton believed there were two units composed of portions of each division in an army. The strength of those units had been variously reported as 3,000, 5,000, or 9,000. Follow-up interrogation indicated the possibility they were composed of three subunits of 3,000 men each. This would make the identified 55th and 56th Units approximately 9,000 men, or division strength. Tarkenton believed it was a force of division strength that had struck the 1st Cavalry Division and the 1st ROK Division, possibly one of the two Chinese units.[36]

Still reluctant to state a firm conclusion regarding the presence of Chinese forces, Willoughby reported: "Recent captures of . . . Chinese . . . and information obtained from their interrogation together with the increased resistance being encountered by advancing United Nations forces removes the problem of Chinese intervention from the realm of the academic and turns it into a serious proximate threat." Although he admitted that the reason for committing Chinese forces formed as units was unknown, he elaborated on his "token" theory, saving face: "One theory based on acknowledgment of Chinese subtlety and their traditional obsession with saving 'face' is that by this type of action China after a fashion can have her cake and eat it too. By labeling these troops as volunteer outfits and claiming that no recognized organizations of the CCF are in Korea, China can claim to the world that no formal intervention has occurred."[37]

He theorized that the Chinese may have selected former Nationalists who would represent no appreciable loss, but by furnishing troops they could claim credit from the North Koreans for trying to help in their hour of need. He also reported on a broadcast from Sinuiju Radio stating that a volunteer corps had been formed for the protection of the hydroelectric zone, because ". . . that zone has a great effect on industries in the People's Republic of China." Defense of the hydro zone was immediately seized upon at all levels as another theory for limited intervention by the Chinese.

Withdrawal to the Chongchon Bridgeheads

Milburn, with Walker's approval, ordered a general withdrawal to the Chongchon bridgehead line. On the left flank of the army, the 24th Division moved back to the river in orderly bounds. Attempts by the 66th CCF Army to break through the 27th Commonwealth Brigade at Pakchon failed. By 4 November, the 27th Brigade and the 19th Infantry held the bridgehead on the left, with the 21st Infantry in reserve south of the river.

On the right, on a hill above Kunu-ri, the Chinese attack broke the 3d ROK Regiment of the 7th ROK Division. The 8th ROK Regiment was committed. By the evening of 3 November, the ROK forces held. The 5th Infantry, with the 3d Battalion, 7th Cavalry, attached, was driven back a thousand yards but managed to hold.

By 5 November, all units had withdrawn across the river or into the bridgeheads. Chinese attacks on the bridgeheads caused some serious losses, but the bridgeheads held. The following day, air observers could see long lines of Chinese withdrawing back into the hills. The Chinese offensive had ended. Limited Eighth Army attacks northward on 7 November met little resistance.

When the 38th CCF Army had reached Won-ni, about seven miles northeast of Kunu-ri, on 2 November, Mao repeatedly urged the army to press on to Kunu-ri and Anju. If they could reach there, they could halt the forward movement of the 9th Division and cut off forces north of the river. Peng urged his armies forward, but they made slow progress against heavy air and artillery attacks. On 4 November, Mao ordered Peng to fight on. He visualized a breakthrough, even an attack on Pyongyang.[38]

But by 4 November, the Chinese were exhausted. They were running out of food and ammunition. Eighth Army defense had halted the Chinese short of Kunu-ri. At 3 P.M. on 4 November, Peng reported to Mao that the counteroffensive in North Korea was over, and he followed it up with a detailed report on the condition of the CPV. Mao accepted the report. On 5 November, all offensive action was broken off.[39]

The following day, forward Chinese elements began to withdraw northward. Commanders and troops were dumbfounded as aerial observers reported long lines of Chinese moving back into the hills.

At I Corps, Col. Percy Thompson reviewed the situation. Possibly spurred by the Eighth Army's estimate that one division had driven back the 1st ROK and 1st Cavalry Divisions and overrun a portion of the 8th Cavalry Regiment, he totaled up the potential strength of all CCF units that had been mentioned in prisoner interrogations. Thompson estimated there might be as many as twelve divisions in four armies, meaning 108,000 troops. That assumed that all divisions were present in each of the 38th, 39th, 40th, and 66th Armies. To Thompson, there were three possibilities: (1) The organizations identified were actual organizations of the CCF Army under Chinese command openly employed with the mission of stopping UN forces short of the border or driving them from Korea; (2) CCF troops were lent to the North Koreans to form the nucleus of a revitalized defense and were employed offensively to give all NKPA units time to reorganize; (3) CCF units in Manchuria were cadred to form units to be used in Korea, possibly under joint control or mixed with North Korean troops. In that case, the total size would be 27,000.[40]

The report of a prisoner from a totally new army, the 197th Division of the 66th Army, was mentioned only in passing in the Eighth Army's PIR for that day. With a total of twenty-seven Chinese prisoners, Tarkenton settled on the tentative estimate of three division-size units, the 54th, 55th, and 56th. He did note that recent prisoners no longer referred to special task units. He speculated that the task units might have been advance forces, but then he apparently rejected that idea and continued to evaluate the Chinese organizations as task "units" in succeeding days.[41]

The evidence was growing thinner that the Chinese forces were only portions of each division represented. A re-interrogation report by the 164th MIS Detachment on 8 November reported on nineteen Chinese prisoners. Twelve of them reported belonging to a division in the 40th Army, six of them the 39th Army, and one the 66th Army. Only six mentioned belonging to some "unit": three from the 56th Unit, two from the 55th Unit, and one from some unknown unit.[42] Review of twenty-three prisoner reports found in the Eighth Army War Diaries for the period 25 October through 6 November finds that only eight of those interrogated mentioned membership in a task unit.

The Chinese withdrawal on 7 November was mystifying. Tarkenton, again focused on the possibility of defending the borders or the hydro zone, speculated that the Chinese would hold the high ground north of the Chongchon River and provide a secure base from which the North Koreans could attack southward. It was, he said, ". . . one way in which the Chinese could secure the power facilities of North Korea, continue to tie down UN forces and still not declare 'all out' intervention."[43] Other possibilities for the withdrawal were the need for reorganization and resupply, a shift eastward to remain in the mountainous areas where the Chinese troops would be at their best advantage, or preparation for a main effort to the south and west toward Sunchon to flank UNC forces along the Chongchon.

On the Road to Chosin
On 21 October, Gen. Edward Almond had chafed impatiently at the delay the Wonsan minefield was causing in the landing of the 1st Marine Division and the 7th Infantry Division. But an upbeat view of the future emanated from X Corps CP. The ROK Capital Division was through Hamhung and turning northeastward along the coast. The 26th ROK Regiment of the 3d ROK Division was starting north from Hamhung toward the Chosin Reservoir. X Corps optimistically reported that enemy troops were moving directly north, expected to assemble in the vicinity of Changjin Town. Lesser forces were retreating up through Kapsan, and an unknown number were withdrawing along the coast road. X Corps expected these fragments to make a final stand somewhere, but, ". . . once overcome can do no more than flee to Manchuria or resort to guerilla tactics." Remaining enemy strength was believed to be no more that 24,000, including youths recently recruited.[44]

Almond had planned to use the 1st Marine Division to occupy three zones. The 1st Marines would occupy the Kojo–Majon-ni area south and southwest of Wonsan. The 5th Marines would secure the Wonsan area and up to the Yonpo Airport. The 7th Marines would relieve the 3d ROK Division north of Hamhung and secure the power installations of the Chosin and Fusen Reservoirs, both of which were within the stop line ordered on 20 October. It appeared to be strictly an occupation mission.

That all changed with General MacArthur's "go for the border" order of 24 October. The new plan was to send the entire 1st Marine Division northward as soon as it was relieved by the 3d Infantry Division now beginning to move from Japan. A landing site for the 7th Infantry Division had been found at Iwon, up the coast from Hamhung. The 7th Division would land there and advance north. I ROK Corps would continue along the coast.

But reports filtering in from the 26th ROK Regiment injected a jarring note in this optimism. Advancing north near Chinhung-ni on 25 October, they had encountered some brisk resistance and captured two prisoners who turned out to be Chinese. The prisoners said there were some 5,000 more in the hills nearby. Three days later, the regiment encountered some really determined resistance, then a Chinese counterattack, and came up with sixteen Chinese prisoners.

Communications with the ROK units were sometimes sluggish, making their way up through the division and II ROK Corps. Apparently X Corps did not know of the Chinese contact until sometime on 27 or 28 October. Then it reported only that two prisoners had been taken. The prisoners' units were not known, but they claimed to come from different battalions. They had entered Korea in the previous week, they said, at Sinuiju and Manpojin. Both said their officers had told them that other units would follow, although they had seen none.[45] By 29 October, it was learned the prisoners were from the 370th Regiment of the 124th CCF Division. The 371st and 372d Regiments had remained at Changjin while the 370th had advanced southward and collided with the 26th ROK Regiment. The latest sixteen prisoners were all from the regimental mortar company, were former members of the Chinese Nationalist Army, and were most certainly deserters.

To Lt. Col. William W. Quinn, the X Corps G-2, encountering the 124th CCF Division would certainly make a difference in enemy capability, if true. He stated that identification and location of the 124th Division at Changjin was not confirmed and not accepted, at this time. He admitted it could be the first definite evidence of large-scale CCF intervention as integral units in the war, and it would greatly augment the enemy's ability to defend. It could even give the enemy the capability of resuming the offensive. Quinn qualified his estimate by speculating that the Chinese prisoners may have been sent as replacements and fillers rather than as members of CCF units. It was also possible that entire groups of reinforcements may have been employed together, giving rise to the erroneous impression that CCF units were engaged.[46]

General Almond, his assistant G-2, Lt. Col. Robert R. Glass, and Lt. Col. Frank T. Mildren, from his G-3 section, went up to Hamhung with Gen. Kim Paik Yup, I ROK Corps commander, to have a personal look at the prisoners in the II ROK Corps prisoner-of-war (PW) compound.

The Chinese were wearing the standard quilted-cotton winter uniform of the CCF. They were, as were most CCF troops in the field or any other troops for that matter, a scruffy-looking lot. Through an interpreter, Almond interrogated each of them out of hearing of the others. Then he tried to give them some close-order drill through the interpreter. They didn't drill too well. Almond declared them to be "not intelligent" and ridiculed their appearance, referring to them as a bunch of Chinese laundrymen.

Almond had been a senior staff member of the Far Eastern Command since 1946. As such, he had seen, at second hand, the deterioration and venality of the Nationalist forces as the Chinese Civil War progressed to its unhappy end. This unquestionably had contributed to his belief in the conventional view that the Chinese were poor fighters. His evaluation of the CCF prisoners could not help but be strongly influenced by that experience, together with his racial bias.

Still, his G-2 noted that they were healthy and well fed. The prisoners were former Nationalists who had surrendered the previous year. They said about three-fourths of the troops in the 124th Division were veterans of the 50th Nationalist Army. They were willing to talk freely about their division's activities and movements. Although not impressed with the Chinese, Almond knew that he had in front of him more than a few Chinese "volunteer" soldiers. They were part of a major unit of the regular Chinese Army. Almond reported his findings to his own command at once and sent a personal message to General MacArthur.[47]

Willoughby, however, was not quite as impressed. When Almond informed him he had captured Chinese soldiers, Willoughby responded, "I don't believe you." Almond told him to come and look for himself. Willoughby did. He agreed they were Chinese but dismissed them as possibly "stragglers" or "volunteers" of no real consequence.[48]

Under pressure from the Chinese, the ROKs had withdrawn to the vicinity of Majon-dong. The Chinese then withdrew northward, permitting the ROKs to advance again as far as Sudong by 1 November. In the running fight, the ROKs had picked up one additional Chinese prisoner, this one claiming to be from the 372d CCF Regiment. X Corps strongly suspected the presence of the entire 124th CCF Division but did not fully accept it yet.[49]

The prisoner from the 372d Regiment was probably a straggler. The 124th Division's mission was defense of the Funchillin Pass leading to Koto-ri, called the Hwangcho Pass by the Chinese. General Yi, 124th Division commander, was doing just what Peng had advocated, combining mobile and positional warfare, by launching preemptive attacks while prepared to fall back to the previously prepared field fortifications defending the pass. By this time, the 371st CCF Regiment had been moved forward and deployed on the west side of the road, while the 370th took up positions on the east side, both waiting for the next development. The 372d was in reserve somewhere near the foot of the pass.

The 7th Marines of the 1st Marine Division had, on 1 November, moved into positions behind the 26th ROK Regiment, prepared to move through and attack north. On 2 November, the regiment passed through and began an advance in a column of battalions, the 1st Battalion leading, followed by the 2d. Colonel Homer L. Litzenberg, the regimental commander, aware of the Chinese presence and realizing his regiment was exposed, isolated, and beyond supporting distance of other friendly units, adopted the tactic of a "moving perimeter," with all units closed up within supporting distance of each other and with the supporting artillery protected by the reserve battalion. Litzenberg was under no illusion that the Chinese were a mere token force. He had briefed all his regimental officers on the presence of the Chinese and stated that it might well be the start of World War III.

The Marines moved cautiously forward against sporadic resistance throughout the day. The advance was slowed by the necessity of controlling as much of the high ground as possible on either side of the road. By nightfall, the advance was halted and the troops dug in for the night. They had covered about half a mile.

Near midnight, the Chinese launched a counterattack. As the night progressed, additional enemy units were committed. Some companies and platoons were forced to give ground. In other cases, Chinese units worked around the flanks and headed for the road and the supporting units in the valley. By morning, large numbers of Chinese were in the valley and across the road, cutting it behind the two advance battalions. With daylight and improved observation capability, supporting weapons and local counterattacks began cleaning up the penetrations. By dusk, the roadblock had been cleared and all positions had been restored. A lesson had been learned. If the defenders sat tight and held their position, roadblocks could be cleared.

On 4 November, the advance was resumed, again facing sporadic resistance. On 5 November, the 3d Battalion was passed through to take the lead. At the point north of Chinhung-ni where the road makes a sharp turn to the east and begins the climb to the pass, the 3d Battalion met very strong resistance. All forward progress was halted for the day. The battalion faced Chinese in well-prepared positions, an extensive trench network, and weapons emplacements with overhead cover. Marine artillery and air provided liberal support for the advance. Another attempt to envelop the defenders the following day also failed. That night, supporting 155mm howitzers, 4.2 mortars, and 105s fired a steady stream of interdicting fire on selected targets. On 7 November, patrols advancing warily found the Chinese gone.

By the afternoon of 6 November, the two front-line regiments of the 124th CCF Division felt pressed to hold their positions. That evening, the 372d Regiment, moving south to reinforce, encountered the interdiction fires. A prisoner later reported the 372d Regiment did not reach the front line but retreated in a disorderly fashion. Half the men in the prisoner's company were killed.[50] The 124th CCF Division was withdrawn with very heavy casualties and began movement to the west.

Mao believed that the X Corps forces were advancing toward the line Jian–Linjiang. On 1 November, he ordered Gen. Song Shilun's 9th CCF Army Group—composed of the 20th, 26th, and 27th Armies—to head northward. Song's goal was to deploy in northeast Korea and seek opportunities ". . . to eliminate four enemy divisions one by one: the South Korean Capital Division, the Third Divisions, the American Seventh Division, and the Marine First Division."[51] Advance elements were beginning to arrive and take up positions around and north of the Chosin Reservoir. The 1st Marine Division was to be drawn in more deeply.

The 17th Infantry of the 7th Infantry Division had commenced landing at Iwon on 29 October and immediately began to move inland. On 31 October, it reached Pungsan, which had been secured by the 1st ROK Regiment. After beating off an attack by what was estimated as a regiment of North Koreans, the 17th continued to advance another twelve miles to reach the Ungi River by 4 November; there it halted.

Weather on the exposed Iwon beaches slowed landing. The 31st Infantry was not able to complete landing until 4 November. It then was moved forward to take up positions on the left flank of the 17th Infantry in the area around the Fusen Reservoir. The 32d Infantry landed on 4 November, moved southwest along the coast, then went inland to a valley southeast of the Fusen Reservoir, about 30 miles northeast of Oro-ri. In the I ROK Corps sector, the ROKs, after a hard-fought battle, had secured Kilchu on 5 November and pressed on along the coast. Neither the 7th Infantry Division nor ROK forces encountered any Chinese troops during these movements.

Beginning with the advance from Sudong on 4 November, there were increasing indications of a buildup in the Chosin Reservoir area and to the north. The very stubborn resistance to the advance of the 7th Marines, particularly on 5 and 6 November—compared to the apparent lack of strong resistance to the 7th Division and the collapse of the defense at Kilchu—told Colonel Quinn that the enemy was making his principal defensive effort along the road to Changjin New or reconstituted NKPA units that had been identified in several areas were evidence of the enemy's ability to reassemble and reequip remnants of units that had fought in the south. They also demonstrated the determination of the NKPA command to maintain and build up forces.[52]

During the advance toward Chosin, several PWs reported either the arrival or the anticipated arrival of the 125th and 126th CCF Divisions in the area. Then, on 7 November, a wounded prisoner captured by a 5th Marines patrol near the south end of the Fusen Reservoir claimed to be from the 126th CCF Division. He further claimed that China was going to send twenty-four divisions to fight in Korea. This report was not considered conclusive. In fact, it was considered a wild fantasy. But air reconnaissance reports of the movement of vehicles and personnel southward into the Chosin area were considered significant. The conclusion was: "The evident enemy buildup which is taking place in this locality indicates not only a significant increase in the enemy's capability to delay and defend, but possibly preparations for the resumption of offensive operations. Unconfirmed reports suggest the presence of other CCF units in the X Corps zone, or the anticipation of their arrival in the near future. If such is confirmed, the enemy's capability to initiate an attack will assume serious proportions."[53]

Two days later, with the sudden withdrawal of the Chinese from ahead of the 7th Marines, Quinn pointed out that the enemy buildup in the Huichon–Yongwon area on the right flank of the Eighth Army posed a threat to the exposed left flank of X Corps. The Chinese were capable of moving forces across the very difficult intervening terrain.[54]

Time to Think It Over
The damage inflicted on the 5th and 8th Cavalries was reported by Willoughby on 3 November with little comment. Some days later, on a visit to X Corps, he offered an opinion. When asked about what had happened to the 8th Cavalry, he replied that the regiment had failed to put out adequate security, had been overrun by a small, violent surprise attack, and had scattered during the hours of darkness.[55] That view would reconcile with his estimate on 3 November that there were no more than 30,000 CCF troops in Korea and that three regiment-size task units of 3,000 each, plus the 124th CCF Division of 7,500, had been identified, but no more than 12,000—in-

cluding two, possibly three, of the task units plus one regiment of the 124th Division—were in contact.[56]

His estimate that day focused on the vastly improved defensive capability of the enemy—enhanced by the addition of Chinese units, the very difficult terrain, and the oncoming winter. That increased capability would enable the enemy to delay the final occupation of North Korea and could gain time for further CCF reinforcement.

To Willoughby, however, the puzzling factor was the vast CCF strength in Manchuria. It was possible that eight additional armies had been added in recent weeks to the twelve already there. Why would it be necessary to add more strength there if the Chinese planned to continue operations in Korea only on a limited basis?

Over the next four days, Willoughby's estimates changed moderately. By 8 November, he estimated there were as many as 33,700 CCF troops in Korea, that they were composed of three units—the 54th, 55th, and 56th, each at division strength of 9,000—plus the 124th CCF Division. He reemphasized the ability of the CCF to reinforce with ease, moving south under cover of night via back roads. This was a capability that, ". . . if fully exercised, could present a serious threat to UN forces now fighting in Korea."

A disconcerting note was injected on 6 November. A joint communiqué broadcast on Beijing Radio by the CCP and various other parties claimed that the advance of the UNC forces toward the Manchurian border was a direct threat to the safety of China. Willoughby reported it: "A Declaration of War?" He commented: ". . . thus far the Chinese Communists have issued no commentary that can be identified as official that is an indication of an overt declaration of war. . . . Each of the preceding broadcasts . . . has sounded like bombast and boasting. The above does not."[57]

The viewpoint of the Far Eastern Command at this time is reflected in this introduction to the history of operations in Korea:

> Early in November it became evident that allegedly "token" forces were the possible vanguard of complete divisions and armies to appear in the near future. In mid-November the enemy suddenly ceased his offensive, broke contact with UN forces and withdrew to positions farther north. . . . The lull in

enemy fighting along most of the front and the complete loss of contact in some sectors was considered as an indication that the CCF were effecting a withdrawal across the Korean–Manchurian frontier. Indications of continuing heavy troop movements into northeast China and Manchuria supported the possibility that Communist China intended to defend the vital reservoirs and power installations along the Yalu River.[58]

It is apparent that MacArthur and his staff were convinced that the Chinese intended to intervene, but they were unconvinced that they had done so and were uncertain of their intentions. Were they limited to protection of the hydro zone? Were they intent on holding a redoubt area in the mountains? Were they planning to recapture the area north of the thirty-eighth parallel? Or were they planning to drive UNC forces out of Korea altogether?

One puzzle was the disparity in the strength of CCF units across the border in Manchuria compared to that believed to be the strength of those forces already committed. Another puzzle was the disparity between the estimated size of the Chinese forces and the damage done to the Eighth Army. In the east, one Marine regimental combat team had defeated and driven back a Chinese division reinforced with some North Korean remnants. In the west, the Eighth Army had estimated the Chinese force to be no more than three CCF divisions with the assistance of some reconstituted North Korean units. But it had driven back two U.S. divisions and four ROK divisions. An estimated Chinese division had driven back both the 1st Cavalry Division and the 1st ROK Division, had overrun one battalion of the 8th Cavalry, and had inflicted punishing damage on the rest of the regiment. This did not make sense. Strangely, this disparity was never commented on. Equally puzzling was the commitment of task-force "units" in the Eighth Army area but a full, regularly organized division, with possibly two more, in the X Corps area.

One of the casualties of the divided command in Korea was the ability to look at the operations on that peninsula as a single campaign, rather than two separate operations. X Corps intelligence reports occasionally considered the impact of enemy activity in the Eighth Army area. The Eighth Army intelligence reports never mentioned enemy information in the X Corps area. General Willoughby, whose responsibility it was to present an overall view, never seemed to do so. It was almost as if each was fighting a totally separate war.

Notes

Where not otherwise noted, the movements of the Eighth Army and subordinate units are as described in Appleman, *South to the Naktong, North to the Yalu.*

1. Eighth Army Periodic Intelligence Report (8A PIR) 104, 24 Oct. 50.

2. Appleman, *South to the Naktong,* 671.

3. Spurr, *Enter the Dragon,* 120; Zhang, *Mao's Military Romanticism,* 95.

4. Zhang, *Mao's Military Romanticism,* 96.

5. Ibid., 101.

6. Ibid., 99.

7. Ibid.

8. Information on movements of Eighth Army units is based on that given in Appleman, *South to the Naktong, North to the Yalu,* except as otherwise noted.

9. Zhang, *Mao's Military Romanticism,* 101.

10. I Corps PIR 40 252100, Oct. 50.

11. Eighth Army Situation Report (8A SitRep) 248 262200, Oct. 50.

12. Eighth Army (8A) War Diary 25 Oct. 50: PW Interrogation Report 164th Military Intelligence Service Detachment (MIS Det.).

13. 8A SitRep 253 1530, 28 Nov. 50.

14. Max Hastings, *The Korean War* (New York: Simon and Schuster, 1987), 130.

15. Zhang, *Mao's Military Romanticism,* 102.

16. Ibid.

17. Ibid., 103.

18. Li Xiaobing and Glenn Tracy (trans.), "Mao Telegrams During the Korean War: October–December 1950," *Chinese Historians* 5, no. 2 (fall 1992), hereafter cited as Mao Telegrams.

19 . 8A War Diary 28 Oct. 50: PW Interrogation Report 165th MIS Det.

20. 8A PIR 107, 27 Oct. 50.

21 . FEC DIS 2970, 27 Oct. 50.

22. Zhang, *Mao's Military Romanticism*, 104.

23. Appleman, *South to the Naktong*, 675.

24. FEC DIS 2971, 28 Oct. 50.

25. Zhang, *Mao's Military Romanticism*, 104.

26. 8A PIR 110, 30 Oct. 50.

27. Mao Telegrams, No. 6, 30 Oct. 50.

28. Zhang, *Mao's Military Romanticism*, 104–5.

29. 8A War Diary 31 Oct. 50: PW Interrogation Report 164th MIS Det.

30. 8A PIR 111, 31 Oct. 50.

31. Ibid.

32. I Corps PIR 46, 31 Oct. 50.

33. FEC DIS 2974, 31 Oct. 50.

34. Spurr, *Enter the Dragon*, 140.

35. 8A PIR 112, 1 Nov. 50.

36. 8A PIR 113, 2 Nov. 50.

37. FEC DIS 2976, 2 Nov. 50.

38. Zhang, *Mao's Military Romanticism*, 105.

39. Ibid., 105–6.

40. I Corps PIR 59, 5 Nov. 50.

41. 8A PIR 59, 5 Nov. 50.

42. 8A PIR 119, 8 Nov. 50: PW Interrogation Report 164th MIS Det., correction sheet.

43. 8A PIR 118 072400, Nov. 50.

44. X Corps msg 211839I, Oct. 50.

45. X Corps PIR 32, 28 Oct. 50.

46. X Corps PIR 33, 29 Oct. 50.

47. Shelby L. Stanton, *America's Tenth Legion: X Corps in Korea, 1950* (Novato, Calif.: Presidio Press, 1989), 161.

48. Blair, *The Forgotten War*, 337.

49. X Corps PIR 35, 31 Oct. 50.

50. X Corps PIR 46, 8 Nov. 50: PW Interrogation Report, 163d MIS Det.

51. Mao Telegrams, No. 7, 31 Oct. 50.

52. X Corps PIR 40, 5 Nov. 50.

53. X Corps PIR 41, 6 Nov. 50.

54. X Corps PIR 43, 8 Nov. 50.

55. Appleman, *South to the Naktong,* 764.

56. FEC DIS 2977, 3 Nov. 50.

57. FEC DIS 2980, 6 Nov. 50.

58. *Command Report: November 1950.* GHQ (Far East Command/United Nations Command, n.d.), chapter I.3.

9
Time to Reconsider

*It is unlikely the CCF would venture into Korea in a limited
manner and would subject themselves to being instantly
bloodied and thrown out by the force which they themselves
have characterized as a "paper tiger."*
—O. Edmund Clubb,
Director, Office of Chinese Affairs, U.S. State Department

After two weeks of heavy fighting, the sight of long lines of Chinese
drawing back into the hills left commanders and staffs at all levels
scrambling to make some sense of the situation. Those who had
boldly predicted the Chinese would not enter the war were at some
pains to find an explanation for the Chinese presence.

The appearance of the Chinese had drastically increased the risk
of igniting worldwide war. Overriding nearly all other considerations
was U.S. determination to avoid actions that would ignite general
war, to avoid becoming bogged down in an extended war in Korea,
and to maintain the unified support of other UN members. U.S. decision makers recognized that although the United States and the
UN had much to gain in the Korean action, both also had a great
deal to lose.

Some intelligence received through State Department channels
indicated a major effort by the Chinese was either under way or in
preparation. Despite this, and despite some changes in the national
estimates, nearly all decisions were based on the fundamental conclusion that although the Chinese retained the capability of intervening on a major scale, the current Chinese strength in Korea was
limited; that significant intervention would require heavy reinforcement from formations in Manchuria; and that such reinforcement would take time, would be observed, and would expose the reinforcing forces to air attack.

It has been suggested that General Willoughby had a powerful influence on and shaped the thinking of both the X Corps and the

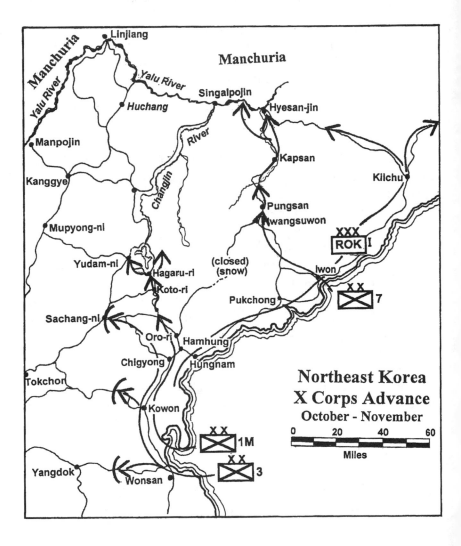

Northeast Korea
X Corps Advance
October - November

Eighth Army G-2s, particularly that of Colonel Tarkenton, who had been a junior member of the Far Eastern Command (FEC) intelligence section when Willoughby recommended him for the post of Eighth Army G-2. There is some suspicion that Willoughby deliberately chose the most innocuous evaluation of enemy information in order to play down the impact of the Chinese intervention. Unfortunately, Willoughby's book, *MacArthur: 1941–1950*, published in 1954, does little to shed any light on intelligence functioning at the time of the Chinese intervention.

It might appear that Willoughby accepted Tarkenton's estimates at face value. He did not. He was skeptical. For confirmation, he sent an order-of-battle team to Eighth Army Headquarters to review the evidence from prisoner-of-war (PW) interrogation. Despite the questionable evidence of Chinese order of battle, despite the presence of full division-size units in eastern Korea, and despite the improbability of a small Chinese force's having virtually destroyed II ROK Corps and decimated an American regiment, Willoughby accepted the lower estimate. He must have had other very convincing information. That would have to have been information from communication intelligence confirming the limited strength of the Chinese in Korea.

That same raw communication intelligence would have been available in Washington. It apparently was convincing. The estimates of both the Department of the Army and the CIA essentially concurred with the estimates by Tarkenton and Willoughby.

The view in Far Eastern Command Headquarters on 30 October was that the Chinese were volunteers incorporated into North Korean People's Army (NKPA) units to assist in the defense of border areas. Apparently accepting this view and considering the Chinese presence a minor matter, General MacArthur wrote a personal letter to President Truman that day, reporting: ". . . Operations in Korea are proceeding according to plan and as we draw close to the Manchurian border enemy resistance has somewhat stiffened, I do not think this represents a strong defense in depth such as would materially retard the achievement of our border objective. It is my current estimate that the next week or so should see us fairly well established in the border area, after which it shall be my purpose, as I outlined during the Wake Island conference, to withdraw American troops as rapidly as possible—this to the end that we may save our men from the rigors of winter climate at that northern latitude, and the Korean people from the undue impact of American troops upon the peaceful settlement of their internal affairs. . . . "[1]

To fulfill that optimistic expectation, the 1st Marine Division, with the farthest distance to go, would have to advance close to thirty miles per day for nearly 200 miles over primitive roads through some of the most difficult terrain in Korea. And winter was coming on.

On 3 November, the Joint Chiefs of Staff (JCS) asked MacArthur for an "interim appreciation" of the situation. A source had reported that the Chinese had decided to intervene in August but delayed to provide time to evacuate some heavy industries and to allow the Chinese Army to prepare. The strength in Manchuria had increased from twelve to twenty armies, nearly double. This seemed unnecessary if the Chinese planned only on limited operations in Korea. Still, only 30,000 Chinese were believed to be in Korea, of which only one division of 7,500 and two, possibly three, regiment-size task forces were in contact with United Nations Command (UNC) troops.[2] Reluctant to place too great a significance on the appearance of the Chinese, MacArthur outlined four different possible explanations:

1. That the Chinese Communist government proposes to intervene with its full military forces, openly proclaiming such course.

2. That it will covertly render military assistance but will, so far as possible, conceal the fact for diplomatic reasons.

3. That it is permitting and abetting a flow of more or less voluntary personnel across the border to strengthen and assist the North Korean remnant in their struggle to retain a nominal foothold in Korea.

4. That the Chinese believed that ROK troops would be used in the extreme northern reach of Korea, that they would be inadequate for the job, and Chinese troops had been sent to help the North Koreans retain a foothold.

MacArthur admitted that large-scale CCF intervention was a "distinct possibility," but there were many fundamental logical reasons against it. He believed that rather than open intervention, Beijing would render covert assistance to the NKPA, providing "voluntary personnel" to retain a nominal foothold in North Korea and salvage something from the wreckage. He went on to say that a final appraisal should await more facts.[3]

In paragraph 4, there was a subtle rebuke to the JCS for their original instructions excluding non-Korean troops from the border provinces. It implied that the Chinese, knowing of this limitation, were encouraged to move forces into Korea to hold enclaves that would provide a legitimate springboard for future offensives. It is certainly true that the Chinese believed, initially, that they would probably encounter only ROK troops on their initial entry.

Based on the above analysis, and believing that the Chinese troops present in Korea were only the advance elements of what could be a much larger force, MacArthur's next step was to do what he had told the conferees at Wake Island he would do—use his airpower to interdict the flow of reinforcements. On 1 November, he alerted the Far Eastern Air Force (FEAF) to prepare, and on 5 November, he ordered them to execute. From the Yalu southward, with the exception of the hydroelectric facilities, the FEAF was to "destroy every means of communication and every installation, factory, city and village." Lieutenant General George E. Stratemeyer, commanding the Far Eastern Air Force, was ordered to destroy the Korean ends of all international bridges on the Manchurian border. Flight crews were to be flown to exhaustion. The battlefield was to be isolated.[4]

That same afternoon, MacArthur, concerned that the Eighth Army had withdrawn from what the intelligence reports indicated was a relatively modest force, ordered Maj. Gen. Doyle O. Hickey, acting chief of staff for the Far Eastern Command, to call the Eighth Army chief of staff and demand an explanation. The following day, Gen. Walton Walker forwarded a lengthy memorandum. Walker reported that the advance of the Eighth Army north of Pyongyang was based on calculated logistical risk, with resupply barely sufficient for one reinforced U.S. division and four ROK divisions meeting only light opposition. The surprise attack by "fresh, well organized and well trained units, some of which were Chinese Communist Forces, . . . [led] to a complete collapse of ROK II Corps. . . ."

Walker went on to state that contributing factors were the intense, psychological fear of Chinese intervention and previous complacency and overconfidence in all ROKA ranks. He emphasized the threat to the Eighth Army main supply route (MSR) by the ROKA collapse and stated that intense effort was being made to reorganize and stabilize the ROKs.[5] Walker withheld mentioning the exceptional fragmentation of forces that resulted from the order to go for the Yalu "with all possible speed."

Walker is believed to have thought the Chinese forces were greater than those estimated by his G-2. By failing to point out this possibility, Walker made his own contribution to acceptance of the underestimate that contributed to the coming disaster.

The reluctance of U.S. commanders to realize the Chinese were present in full force has some interesting causes.

First and foremost was the great faith in the ability of the Air Force to identify and to attack large bodies of oncoming troops. Most officers simply did not believe it possible for any substantial numbers to enter Korea without being seen and attacked by aircraft. At Wake Island, MacArthur had told President Truman, ". . . there will be the greatest slaughter . . . ," and he believed it. That attitude was prevalent at all levels.

Knowing little about the workings of the Chinese Communist Army, intelligence officers were skeptical that private soldiers would be so well informed on the size and objective of the total force. They did not realize that this was an important and fundamental part of the political training of the Chinese soldier. Many thought the statements of PWs were gross exaggerations. They were discounted, or drastically reduced.

Through 30 October, no U.S. troops had made contact with the Chinese. All reports had come from ROK forces, and there was considerable skepticism of reports from non-U.S. forces, the ROKs in particular. During the operations in South Korea, reports from civilians, and sometimes from the military, gave exaggerated numbers. General Paik was not the only one to use the phrase ". . . many, many. . . ." It was a common response to questions about the size of enemy forces. "Many, many" became a humorous catchphrase among the American forces and was used as a flippant answer to any question of size.

There was an element of wishful thinking in many of these early estimates. Tired troops on the edge of total victory simply did not want to believe that the Chinese were coming in now, commencing a totally new war. The wishful thinking was not limited to the troops. The "volunteer" theory helped.

The "volunteer" name was a clever contribution to Chinese efforts at misleading the UN Command. It did have a basis in past experience. During the Chinese Civil War, there had been many Koreans in the People's Liberation Army who actually were volunteers. The reverse could be true. The Chinese had furnished more than two divisions of volunteers to the NKPA prior to the start of the war. The Chinese troops now being encountered could be genuine volunteers.

Underlying it all was a very poor opinion—especially among those who had served in the Far East—of the Chinese as soldiers. Chinese generals had the image of incompetent and venal nepotists who smoked opium, carried parasols, padded the payrolls, and won their battles with "silver bullets." The reputation of the peasant soldier fared no better than that of his commanders. The Chinese were deficient in the martial qualities elsewhere deemed virtues. The collapse of the Chinese Nationalist armies in the Chinese Civil War contributed to this reputation. The defeat of the Nationalists was believed due more to their own internal weakness and corruption than to any superior qualities of the Red Army. Nor had the Chinese people, in the past, held soldiers in high esteem. The saying went that one would not use good iron to make a nail or good men to make soldiers.

Thus, with the situation stabilized, the Chinese halted, and an intensive air campaign in preparation, MacArthur issued a communiqué on 6 November explaining what had happened:

> The Korean War was brought to a practical end with the closing of the trap on enemy elements north of Pyongyang and seizure of the east coastal area, resulting in raising the number of enemy prisoners of war in our hands to well over 135,000, which, with other losses amounting to over 200,000, brought total casualties to 335,000, representing a fair estimate of North

Korean total military strength. The defeat of the North Koreans and the destruction of their armies was thereby decisive. In the face of this victory of United Nations arms the Communists committed one of the most offensive acts of international lawlessness of historic record by moving without any notice of belligerency elements of alien Communist force across the Yalu River into North Korea and massing a great concentration of possible reinforcing divisions with adequate supply behind the privileged sanctuary of the adjacent Manchurian border. A possible trap was thereby surreptitiously laid calculated to encompass the destruction of the United Nations Forces engaged in restoring order and the process of civil government in the North Korean border area. This potential danger was avoided with minimum losses only by the timely detection and skillful maneuvering of the United Nations commander responsible for that sector, who with great perspicacity and skill completely reversed the movement of his forces in order to achieve the greater integration of tactical power necessitated by the new situation and avert any possibility of great military reverse. The present situation therefore is this. While the North Korean forces with which we were initially engaged have been destroyed or rendered impotent for military action, a new and fresh army faces us backed up by a possibility of large alien reserves and adequate supply within easy reach to the enemy but beyond the limits of our present sphere of military action.

Whether and to what extent these reserves will be moved forward to reinforce units now committed remains to be seen and is a matter of the gravest international significance. Our present mission is limited to the destruction of those forces now arrayed against us in North Korea with a view to achieving the United Nations' objective to bring units and peace to the Korean nation and people.[6]

The communiqué contains the germ of an explanation for MacArthur's order to advance to the border. If the communiqué reflects his view, the war had been won. Ordering the advance to the border was merely extending the occupation, temporarily, to all of Korea—which he thought he was obligated to do by the civil-affairs directive he had received.

Exchanges Between Washington and Tokyo

Alerted in roundabout fashion to MacArthur's bombing plan, and concerned that bombing the Yalu bridges might spill over into Chinese territory in Manchuria, the JCS, after hurried consultation with the president, instructed MacArthur, late on 5 November, to postpone all bombing of targets within five miles of the Manchurian border. They also said they urgently needed his estimate of the situation and the reason for ordering bombing of the Yalu bridges. Of serious concern was the U.S. commitment not to take action affecting Manchuria without consultation with the British.[7]

The request for an estimate of the situation was the second the JCS had made. MacArthur's torrid reply the following day was in total contrast to his reasoned appraisal of 4 November:

> Men and materiel in large force are pouring across all bridges over the Yalu from Manchuria. This movement not only jeopardizes but threatens the ultimate destruction of the forces under my command. The actual movement across the river can be accomplished under cover of darkness and the distance between the river and our lines is so short that the forces can be deployed against our troops without being seriously subjected to air interdiction. The only way to stop this reinforcement of the enemy is the destruction of these bridges and the subjection of all installations in the north area supporting the enemy advance to the maximum of our air destruction. Every hour that this is postponed will be paid for dearly in American and other United Nations blood. The main crossing at Sinuiju was to be hit within the next few hours and the mission is actually already being mounted. Under the gravest protest that I can make, I am suspending this strike and carrying out your instructions. What I have ordered is entirely within the scope of the rules of war and the resolutions and directions which I have received from the United Nations and constitutes no slightest

act of belligerency against Chinese territory, in spite of the outrageous international lawlessness emanating therefrom. I cannot overemphasize the disastrous effect, both physical and psychological, that will result from the restrictions which you are
imposing. I trust that the matter be immediately brought to the
attention of the President as I believe your instructions may well
result in a calamity of major proportion for which I cannot accept the responsibility without his personal and direct understanding of the situation. Time is so essential that I request immediate reconsideration of your decision pending which
complete compliance will of course be given your order.[8]

The vehemence of this reply was startling and puzzling to the JCS.
That same day, MacArthur's G-2 had reported to the Department of
the Army that Chinese strength in Korea was estimated to be 34,000.
After consultation with President Truman, the Joint Chiefs had no
option but to approve MacArthur's plan, with some severe restrictions.

The Joint Chiefs pointed out that this very startling reply was at
considerable variance with his estimate of 4 November. They asked
for further information and, in a modest rebuke, reminded him: "It
is essential that we be kept informed of important changes in situation as they occur and that your estimate as requested in our [mes-
sage of 3 November] be submitted as soon as possible."

In response, on 7 November, MacArthur adopted a brief but mea-
sured tone: ". . . Since my C 8285 [message,] intelligence reports have
confirmed the estimate contained in 2, 3, and 4 thereof, which I stated
to be the most likely condition at that time. The military facts in substantiation were reported in the daily telecons and radio reports. . . ."

The referenced paragraphs indicated MacArthur's estimate that
the intervention was covert, that it was composed of volunteers aug-
menting the North Korean forces, that it was done to permit the
North Koreans to keep a toehold, that it had been done only because
of the Chinese belief that only ROK forces would be used in the
northernmost reaches and that they would be inadequate for the job,
and, especially, that the Chinese did not intend to intervene in full
military force. MacArthur went on:

... unquestionably CCF forces have been and are being utilized against our forces; that while the exact strength is impossible to accurately determine, it is sufficient to have seized the initiative in the west sector and to have materially slowed the offensive in the east section. The principle seems thoroughly established that such forces will be used and augmented at will, probably without any formal declaration of hostilities. If this augmentation continues, it can well reach a point rendering our resumption of advance impossible and even force a movement in retrograde.

An effort will be made in the west sector in due course of time, possibly within ten days, to again assume the initiative provided the flow of enemy reinforcement can be checked. Only through such an offensive effort can any accurate measure be taken of enemy strength.

I deem it essential to execute the bombing of the targets under discussion as the only resource left to me to prevent a potential buildup of enemy strength to a point threatening the safety of the command. This interdiction of enemy lines of advance without Korea is so plainly defensive that it is hard to conceive that it would cause an increase in the volume of local intervention or, of itself, provoke a general war.[9]

This message established what became the most favored evaluation of the Chinese intervention—a limited effort designed to help the North Koreans maintain a foothold. The Chinese forces were only advance units entering Korea for this limited purpose, but there was a potential for serious reinforcement. Such reinforcement would take time and would be vulnerable to air interdiction. The sentence stating that offensive action was necessary to take the measure of enemy strength also contained the germ of what was later to become MacArthur's claim that resumption of the advance was merely a "reconnaissance in force."

The estimate was also brief to the point of brusqueness, bordering on impudence. The Joint Chiefs, or any other senior in similar circumstances, would have been entitled to a more detailed analysis of the situation, including the significant information on which

MacArthur's conclusions were based. An estimate of the situation, as taught in all service schools, includes much more than MacArthur's brief paragraph. MacArthur and his staff were certainly capable of providing such details. Instead, he left it to the JCS to sort through the voluminous daily reports for whatever information they felt might support his conclusion. The terse reply was a symptom of the increasing tension between Washington and the field commander.

The same day this estimate was sent, General MacArthur also made a strong plea for replacements. In the weeks prior to the Chinese entry, when it had seemed the war was winding down, plans had been made to cut back on personnel, even though FEC organizations had been, in many cases, seriously below strength. Now, with the Chinese threat, replacements were needed. MacArthur demanded that the flow of replacement be resumed immediately. He offered, as an alternative, a choice of either a stalemate or the prospect of losing all that had been thus far gained in Korea.[10]

In a third message that day, MacArthur presented another major problem that required the attention of the Joint Chiefs. Hostile aircraft had appeared along the Yalu by 1 November. Clashes had increased. Using hit-and-run tactics, the MiG-15s, presumed to be operated by Chinese pilots, could make a quick pass at UNC aircraft and then duck back into protected territory north of the Yalu River. Giving the Joint Chiefs more to think about, on 7 November he reported this situation, stating: "The present restriction on my area of operation provides a complete sanctuary for hostile air immediately upon their crossing the Manchuria–North Korea border. . . . The effect of this abnormal condition upon the morale and combat efficiency of both air and ground troops is major. Unless corrective measures are promptly taken, this factor can assume decisive proportions. Request instructions for dealing with this new and threatening development."[11]

The Joint Chiefs were sympathetic to the cause, but it became a serious problem with America's allies. The "sanctuary" problem became another source of controversy between MacArthur and Washington then and later.

To reassure MacArthur, ease the tension, and give him some perspective on the tenuous political situation, Gen. George Marshall sent off a personal message:

> This is a very personal and informal message to you from me. I have just talked to the President in Independence, Missouri. Though absent from Washington he has been kept almost hourly aware of the latest developments as reported by you. The discussions and decisions here are heavily weighted with the extremely delicate situation we have before the Security Council of the United Nations, whose meeting tomorrow may have fateful consequences.
>
> We all realize your difficulty in fighting a desperate battle in a mountainous region under winter conditions and with a multinational force in all stages of preparedness. I also understand, I think, the difficulty involved in conducting such a battle under necessarily limited conditions and the necessity of keeping the distant headquarters, in Washington, informed of developments and decisions. However, this appears to be unavoidable—but I want you to know that I understand your problem. Everyone here, Defense, State and the President, is intensely desirous of supporting you in the most effective manner within our means. At the same time, we are faced with an extremely grave international problem which could so easily lead to a world disaster.
>
> Incidentally, for my personal information, do you feel that the hydroelectric and reservoir situation is probably the dominant consideration in this apparently last-minute move by the Chinese Communists incited by the Soviets to protect their interests in Vladivostok, Dairen and Port Arthur?[12]

Rising to the occasion, MacArthur responded, professed an understanding of the delicacy of the situation, and added:

> I do not believe that the hydroelectric system is the dominant consideration animating the Communist intervention in Korea, although it might well be contributory to such action. It is unquestionably being utilized as an argument to conceal

the aggressive belligerency of the Chinese Communists. This view is supported by the fact that their activities in Korea throughout have been offensive—never defensive. . . . Moreover, from technical information available here, there appears to be a tendency to greatly overemphasize the industrial importance of the hydroelectric system which actually, following Soviet post-war looting, is clearly of insufficient consequences to become provocative of major war.

The motivating influences are far more fundamental than might be represented by immediate material considerations. In order to understand them one must examine the changes in Chinese character and culture over the past fifty years. Up until fifty years ago, China was de-compartmented into groups divided against each other. Their war-making tendency was almost non-existent. Not until the turn of the century, under the regime of Chang So-lin [Zhang Zuolin], did China's nationalist urge begin. This was further and more successfully developed, under the leadership of Chiang Kai-shek, but has been brought to its greatest fruition under the present regime, to the point that it has now taken on the character of a united nationalism of increasingly dominant aggressive tendencies.

Through these past fifty years the Chinese people have thus become militarized in their concepts and in their ideals. They now make first class soldiers and are gradually developing competent staffs and commanders. This has produced a new and dominant power in Asia which for its own purposes has allied with Soviet Russia, but which in its own concepts and methods has become aggressively imperialistic, with a lust for expansion and increased power normal to this type of imperialism.

There is little of the ideological concept either one way or the other in the Chinese makeup. The standard of living is so low and the capital accumulation has been so thoroughly dissipated by war that the masses are desperate and avid to follow any leadership which seems to promise alleviation of local stringencies. I have from the beginning believed that the Chinese Communists' support of the North Koreans was the dominant

one. Their interests at present are parallel to those of the Soviets, but I believe that the aggressiveness now displayed, not
only in Korea but in Indo-China, and Tibet and pointing toward the south, reflects predominantly the same lust for the expansion of power which has animated every would-be con-
queror since the beginning of time.[13]

MacArthur biographer Courtney Whitney reports that MacArthur
was disappointed that this message did not elicit a response. In Washington, Marshall's staff thought this answer seemed high-flown and
patronizing and resented what it termed this "idiot treatment" of the
secretary of defense. After all, Marshall had spent considerable time
in China in recent years, had more recent experience with China
than MacArthur had, and had observed and dealt with the Communists firsthand, which MacArthur had not. It was one more man-
ifestation of long standing tension between these two, the highest
ranking American soldiers of the age.[14]

The interesting aspect of this exchange is how badly flawed was
MacArthur's view of the Chinese and contemporary Chinese history.
Notwithstanding this, MacArthur's view of the independence of the
Chinese Communists was closer to the mark than that of the Army's
G-2 or the CIA.

The air campaign began in an effort to isolate the battlefield.
Available material provides little information on the degree to which
advice from the Air Force commanders supported this effort. But
what neither MacArthur nor the Air Force commanders knew was
that the claim about men and materiel pouring across the border
was essentially correct. Commencing on 5 November, the 9th CCF
Army Group—150,000 men under the command of Gen. Song
Shilun—arrived from the Shanghai area. They began crossing into
Korea and taking up positions east of the Nangnim Range, with their
principal target being the leading element of X Corps, the 1st Marine Division.

The Joint Chiefs and the Department of Defense
As the evidence of Chinese presence grew, the Joint Chiefs, their intelligence advisers, and the CIA struggled to evaluate the Chinese

actions. The first report of a Chinese prisoner was given the lowest evaluation. But by 1 November, the CIA informed Truman that between "15,000 and 20,000 Chinese Communist troops organized in task force units are operating in North Korea while the parent units remain in Manchuria." The report stated that the main motivation seemed to be establishment of a limited *cordon sanitaire* south of the Manchurian border to protect the Manchurian border and to ensure the continued availability of power from the Suiho hydroelectric system.[15]

American military authorities believed strongly in a monolithic, worldwide Communist bloc tightly controlled from the Kremlin. The initial North Korean attack in June raised the possibility of a major Communist offensive. Entry of the Chinese increased the possibility that world war would break out. After all, the Chinese were mere surrogates of the Soviets. But, even given all this, the Chinese actions were puzzling. Why had they waited so long? What were their intentions? All the vital decisions of the coming weeks stumbled and fell over one mystifying question: With such large numbers across the river in Manchuria, why were there so few in Korea?

Attempts to make the current facts fit with existing preconceptions produced some interesting theories. Defense of the hydropower zone became a favorite. The "face-saving" theory was also popular. General Lawton Collins told the Army Policy Council that it might just be a face-saving effort. He did not think the Chinese would cross the river in sufficient numbers to risk a serious beating by MacArthur's forces. But he did admit they could be a serious threat.[16]

In an attempt to marshal all available information, the Department of the Army G-2 compiled an estimate on 6 November. He estimated a Chinese strength of 30,000 to 40,000 in Korea with up to 700,000 men in Manchuria, including 350,000 ground troops that could be crossed into Korea as reinforcements. The Chinese were capable of halting the UNC offensive and driving it back to defensive positions farther south. He warned that each side could reinforce until major forces were involved, potentially leading to loss of control and the outbreak of general war.[17]

As early as 31 October, General Bradley had expressed puzzlement over the pattern of Chinese participation. Organized units were present, but only in small numbers. General MacArthur's instructions did not seem to fit this halfway situation.[18] The Joint Chiefs had an emergency conference on the evening of 6 November to deal with General MacArthur's bombing plans. After taking action on that, they spent several hours discussing the changed situation. With the sobering estimate of the Army's G-2 and MacArthur's alarming message in hand, they considered the worst possible case—massive Chinese intervention. They concluded this was a genuine possibility. If so, the best course would be to pull back to the narrow waist of Korea and initiate diplomatic attempts at a cease-fire. The Eighth Army and X Corps should be consolidated and the gap between them eliminated. Consensus was reached on this course late in the evening, but the members were tired and left without arriving at a formal recommendation.[19]

The following day, the Far Eastern Command reported the startling news that the Chinese and North Korean troops, in a "surprise maneuver," had broken contact, had withdrawn and disappeared. General Bradley noted that this report ". . . tended to foster the conclusion that the Chinese had only intervened in moderate numbers and that these few had suffered such a bloody nose that they may have lost the taste for battle."[20]

In preparation for a meeting of the National Security Council on 9 November, the Joint Chiefs were asked to evaluate the military significance of the Chinese intervention. News of the Chinese withdrawal had changed some minds. Based on a review of the situation as reported by MacArthur, General Bradley decided that the consensus to pull back, reached Monday night, was premature: "The actual physical threat to Eighth Army and X Corps has been substantially diminished or, on the evidence presented, had not been that great in the first place. There seemed to be more than a reasonable chance of success. It should not be abandoned by 'timidity' in Washington. We had to back the man on the scene."[21]

The joint staff in Washington, however, was more cautious. They did not advocate a pullback to the waist, but they had deep reservations about the coming offensive. Their recommendation was that MacArthur should hold in place, avoid the risk of further Chinese intervention, and ask the State Department to seek a cease-fire. MacArthur was informed that the eventuality anticipated in his 27 September instruction—entry into North Korea by major Chinese forces—appeared to have arrived. The mission of the Far Eastern Command—destruction of the North Korean armed force—might have to be reexamined. His view was sought.[22]

In another lengthy and strongly worded reply, MacArthur vehemently denied the necessity, pointing out that the present situation was fully covered by his instructions, and he quoted them. He went on:

> In my opinion it would be fatal to weaken the fundamental and basic policy of the United Nations to destroy all resisting armed forces in Korea and bring that country into a unified and free nation. I believe that with my air power . . . I can deny reinforcements coming across the Yalu in sufficient strength to prevent the destruction of those forces now arrayed against me in North Korea.
>
> I plan to launch my attack for this purpose on or about 15 November with the mission of driving to the border and securing all of North Korea. Any program short of this would completely destroy the morale of my forces and the psychological consequences would be inestimable. It would condemn us to an indefinite retention of our military forces along difficult defense lines in North Korea and would unquestionably arouse such resentment among the South Koreans that their forces would collapse and might even turn against us. It would therefore necessitate immediately a large increment in foreign troops. That the Chinese Communists, after having achieved complete success in establishing themselves in North Korea, would abide by any delimitation upon further expansion southward would represent wishful thinking.

Having learned of a British proposal to create a buffer zone along the border, MacArthur devoted three paragraphs to denouncing the idea, saying the "British desire to appease the Chinese Communists by giving them a strip of Northern Korea finds its historical prece-

dent in the action taken at Munich." It would be, he said, ". . . a tribute to aggression which encourages that very international lawlessness which it is the fundamental duty of the United Nations to curb."
Then, growing even more impassioned:

> To give up any portion of North Korea to the aggression of
> the Chinese Communists would be the greatest defeat of the
> free world in recent times. Indeed to yield to so immoral a
> proposition would bankrupt our leadership and influence in
> Asia and render untenable our position both politically and
> militarily. We would follow closely in the footsteps of the British
> who by the appeasement of recognition [of Red China] lost all
> the respect of all the rest of Asia without gaining that of the Chi-
> nese segment. It would not curb deterioration of the present
> situation into the possibility of general war but would impose
> upon us the disadvantage of having inevitably to fight such a
> war, if it occurs, bereft of the support of countless Asiatics who
> now believe in us and are eager to fight with us.

He recommended that Washington press for a UN resolution condemning Chinese aggression and demanding they withdraw behind
their borders "on pain of military sanctions." But, if the UN failed
to do so, "I recommend with all the earnestness that I possess that
there be no weakening at this crucial moment and that we press on
to complete victory which I believe can be achieved if our determination and indomitable will do not desert us."[23]

Although the Joint Chiefs apparently did not subscribe to Mac-
Arthur's colorful analogy, they did reconsider their inclination to
draw back. The intensive air effort promised to slow or halt the
flow of reinforcements. There seemed to be a reasonable chance of
success.[24]

The CIA's National Intelligence Estimate also offered some hope.
To a substantial extent, it followed MacArthur's appraisal and that
of the Army's G-2. The principal objective of the Chinese was ". . . to
halt the UNC advance and maintain a Communist regime in being
on Korean soil." The CIA estimated between 30,000 to 40,000 Chinese in Korea and pointed out the huge forces assembled in

Manchuria. It was estimated that as many as 350,000 could be deployed in Korea in thirty to sixty days. Such troop strength could halt any further advance and possibly force withdrawal of UNC forces to defensive positions farther south.[25]

The estimated time needed to reinforce had a strong influence on subsequent decisions. Given the modest Chinese strength, the CCF would have to reinforce to attain decisive results. Such reinforcement in the face of the extended air campaign would require time. Consequently, the situation would develop at a pace that would permit reassessment as necessary.

Relying on the assumption that "well-organized, well-led and well-equipped Chinese Communist units, *probably as large as divisions* [emphasis added], were entering Korea," and unable to determine just what the Chinese objectives were, the JCS postulated three possibilities: Protection of the hydroelectric facilities along the Yalu, tying down the United States in an undeclared war at little cost to themselves, or driving the United Nations out of Korea entirely.

Achieving a unified Korea was a firm but not unconditional objective. The defense of Europe was more important. With that as a background, the options were: Force the action to a conclusion, defend along a line short of the border, or withdraw to the narrow neck. Withdrawal was considered politically unacceptable at the time. Defending in present positions might be a temporary expedient pending clarification of the military and political situation. Forcing the action to a conclusion might require additional augmentation that was not now available.

After discussing these options in detail, the Joint Chiefs then temporized. They recommended a fourth option, which they had not discussed: "Pending further clarification of the military objectives of the Chinese Communists and the extent of their political commitments, the missions assigned to CINCUNC should be kept under review but should not be changed."[26]

State Department

O. Edmund Clubb, then director of the Office of Chinese Affairs in the State Department, initially took a much more serious view of the appearance of the Chinese. In memoranda on 1 and 4 November, he suggested that the intervention was direct (even though modest efforts had been made to conceal it), that it was intentional and well planned, that it was intended to be in considerable force, and that it was intended to achieve some real measure of victory. Clubb said it was ". . . unlikely the CCF would venture into Korea in a limited manner and would subject themselves to being instantly bloodied and thrown out by the force which they themselves have characterized as a 'paper tiger.'"

Clubb listed six possible objectives. Nothing in the Chinese propaganda had mentioned the power plants; the estimated scale of their intervention indicated more than a desire to protect a local area. As for the *cordon sanitaire,* it would accomplish no worthwhile political objective for the Chinese. He concluded that the minimum Chinese Communist objective must be considered to be either the restoration of the status quo ante 25 June in North Korea or the expulsion of UNC forces from the entire Korean Peninsula.[27]

Additional weight was lent to Clubb's analysis by a report from Assistant Secretary of State for Public Affairs Edward Barrett, who reported:

> Having appeared unduly disturbed over the Chinese in North Korea subject for several days, I'll now risk seeming really alarmist. Solely on the basis of the very unusual Chinese Communist propaganda campaign of recent days, it seems to us that:
>
> 1. At the very least the Chinese are building up to very large numbers (perhaps a hundred thousand or so) "volunteers" in Korea, with the probable purpose of keeping us bogged down in Korea for many months.
>
> 2. At the most they are building up to open employment of hundreds of thousands of Chinese troops in Korea with a full expectation that this will mean general war between the Chinese and ourselves (for which they are preparing their own people psychologically).
>
> On the basis of propaganda alone, it would appear that they are not planning to limit their participation to anything like as small a force as the presently reported 18,000 "volunteers."[28]

• • •

Reports from the consul general in Hong Kong on 3 November reinforced this view, stating that there had been a sharp increase in articles on Korea and a more bellicose tone toward the United States. The line followed was that the United States was bent on world conquest and that aggression against Korea would be followed by invasion of Manchuria. An article in the *People's Daily* emphasized the weakness of U.S. ground forces and stated that Communist strategy would be to annihilate U.S. manpower through fierce, long-drawn-out guerrilla warfare. There were reports of large troop movements toward Korea; schools in Shenyang were being moved from towns into surrounding villages.[29]

By 9 November, Wilkinson reported that the Communist press was no longer talking of a "long-term war of attrition," but rather of "turning tide of war, annihilating and repulsing the 'invading troops.'"[30]

Information from Taipei on 6 November, substantiated by an impressive array of facts, justified the view that all-out action by the Communists in Korea could be expected. The report cautioned that even with allowances made for wishful thinking among the Chinese military, the information was credible.[31]

By 7 November, possibly after receipt of news of the Chinese withdrawal, Clubb had moderated his view, saying, "GHQ . . . numbers the Chinese Communist troops at some three or four divisions. If that estimate is correct as of this date, the UN position is serious only in potentiality, not in actuality at this moment." He urged efforts to seek detente. Clubb believed that ". . . in the presence of three new divisions and a very handful of enemy planes, there would seem to be time to stabilize and await further developments. . . ." He advised that the battle for Korea be continued on the basis of General MacArthur's standing orders, but that there should be a temporary abandonment of "all-out offensive" in favor of more wary tactics, with perhaps withdrawals as necessary: "This should be a period for some slowing up of military operations to permit political estimates and discussions with our allies, to the end that, in our haste to win a battle, we shall not lose the war."[32]

John Paton Davies, another "China hand" now in the State Department's policy-planning staff, weighed in with a lengthy memorandum on the situation: "Quite aside from their ideological antipathy to us, the Chinese Communists view us with morbid distrust and hatred. This is the product of five years of intensely bitter civil war in which they regarded us as allies of their enemies, culminating in the galling frustration of our action this summer with regard to Formosa [Taiwan]." He believed the PRC had accepted the risk of U.S. retaliation and made preparations for that. Davies pointed out that ". . . in international affairs Mao and company are bigots," and he suggested they were being manipulated by the Kremlin. Davies recommended seeking a diplomatic solution. But he said that to avoid the appearance of weakness that a diplomatic solution might give, we should, at the same time, initiate a very public and very substantial increase in military power to serve as a warning.[33]

National Security Council
The National Security Council met on Thursday, 9 November, with Secretary of State Dean Acheson presiding. President Truman was absent. The congressional elections two days earlier had narrowed the Democratic majority in both houses of Congress.

General Bradley presented the conclusions of the Joint Chiefs of Staff. He reported that MacArthur was still out of contact with the enemy and that two days of aerial reconnaissance had revealed nothing. Questioned by Acheson, General Bradley indicated that the UNC forces could hold approximately along their current line, but he was uncertain how much pressure they could withstand if MacArthur was not permitted to bomb the Manchurian airfields—an act that both agreed would require UN approval. Bradley also doubted that bombing the Yalu bridges would, as MacArthur had asserted, measurably impede the flow of Chinese Communist troops into Korea. Acheson wanted to explore the possibilities of a buffer zone and asked if a line farther south would be easier to defend. Bradley agreed that a defensive line would become stronger as it moved southward, but he stated the belief that a withdrawal from the existing position would have a severe impact on the morale of ROK forces.

CIA Director Walter Bedell Smith stood firm on his agency's estimate that the Soviets did not want to involve their own troops in a general war and that they might like to see the United States and the

PRC at war. Acheson pointed out that the United States did not have a commitment to conquer all of Korea. Smith thought that either standing pat or drawing back would have serious political consequences, while going forward would be difficult.

Marshall was deeply concerned but reluctant to change UNC objectives. The wide dispersion of UNC forces in northeastern Korea worried him. They were vulnerable. The UNC forces were 20 percent understrength, with South Koreans used as fillers. He also pointed out that winter weather had made the Yalu River meaningless as a military obstacle.

The meeting concluded by adopting the JCS recommendation. As an interim measure, MacArthur should be permitted to continue the action as long as there appeared to be a reasonable chance of success. This tacitly assumed the situation would develop at a rate that would permit timely reevaluation as necessary. By default, MacArthur's plan to renew the offensive was approved. The NSC also decided to continue political and diplomatic action in the United Nations and elsewhere to demand withdrawal of Chinese forces from Korea as well as to intensify efforts to find out exactly what the Chinese objective was. The council recommended that preparations be made on the basis that the risk of global war had increased.[34]

The sticking point was obvious. Had the UNC forces halted at the line previously chosen by MacArthur—approved by the Joint Chiefs of Staff and published to the world via *Newsweek*—there would have been few objections. But, having advanced beyond that line and been halted by the Chinese attack, the United Nations, and particularly the United States, was not willing to risk the loss of prestige, built up at considerable cost, of having to withdraw under pressure from a primitive military force held in such low esteem.

At the United Nations
On 5 November, MacArthur had forwarded a special report to the United Nations on the Chinese intervention. It was presented to the UN on 6 November and scheduled for debate two days later. Over objections of the Soviet representative, the Security Council decided to discuss the report, but it did agree, at Soviet insistence, to invite a representative of the People's Republic of China to attend and participate.

On 10 November, a draft resolution—sponsored by Cuba, Ecuador, France, Norway, the United Kingdom, and the United States, but prepared principally at the U.S. State Department—was introduced. The resolution, noting that the special report of the UNC commander had reported Chinese Communist military units were deployed in Korea, called on all states and authorities to refrain from assisting North Korea and for the immediate withdrawal of any such forces assisting North Korea. The resolution further affirmed the UN's intention not to remain in Korea any longer than necessary. Last, the resolution reiterated that it was the policy of the UN to protect legitimate Chinese and Korean interests in the frontier zone and to hold the Chinese frontier with Korea "inviolate."[35]

The Chinese declined the invitation to discuss MacArthur's report but did accept an invitation, extended two months earlier, to attend and discuss alleged U.S. "aggression" against Taiwan. This refusal, and acceptance, plus news of Chinese withdrawal, seemed to convince some Security Council members that no immediate action was necessary. If the Chinese delegation was coming, discussion could wait until their arrival. Perhaps all problems could be settled at that time. This viewpoint was buttressed by a message from Ambassador Kavalam Panikkar, via the Indian government. The Chinese delegation left Beijing on 15 November and was due in New York on 19 November. Panikkar reported the belief that the delegation had wide power to discuss Korea—provided the whole question of Korea was taken up, not just MacArthur's report. Encouraged by these developments, UN ambassador Warren Austin sent a message to General MacArthur suggesting that the mere introduction of the resolution alone seemed to have had the desired effect of reassuring the Chinese.

At the same time, both President Truman and Secretary of State Acheson took other steps to reassure the Chinese. At a conference on foreign affairs, Acheson used the opportunity to issue a public statement, saying, ". . . everything in the world should be done and is being done to make them understand their proper interest will be taken care of." President Truman also issued a statement the following day that was read to the Security Council. The Chinese did not seem impressed. The day after Truman's statement, Beijing Radio ridiculed his comments.

Believing a settlement was possible was reassuring. The Chinese effort might be limited after all. But the Chinese delegation dawdled and did not arrive until 27 November. By that time, the Chinese offensive had begun. The Chinese decision to accept the UN invitation, coupled with the delegation's delay in arriving, was simply a diplomatic ruse to help cover their preparations for a general offensive. Panikkar was used as a cat's-paw to delude the UN by hinting that the Chinese were interested in settling the Korea question by negotiations.

The Manchurian Sanctuary
Finding a way to deal with the hostile aircraft and their use of the Manchurian sanctuary was equally difficult. The CIA argued that because the USSR and China had accepted the risk of general war by sending troops into Korea, attacking the Manchurian airfields would not increase that risk; neither China nor the USSR would make its decision for general war based on a local provocation. The contrary argument was that Manchuria was a trap. The airfields were bait that would entice the United States to take action that Communists could use as a pretext for general war. Attacking the Manchurian airfields might allow the Chinese to call into action the provisions of the Sino-Soviet Treaty.

"Hot pursuit" was discussed as an alternative to attacking the airfields. Under this doctrine, recognized in international law, UNC aircraft would be permitted to follow hostile aircraft for six to eight miles inside Manchuria. Before bringing up the question at the UN, Acheson had diplomatic representatives float this proposal among nations supporting the UN effort. The response was overwhelmingly negative. UN members supporting the action in Korea were nervous enough as forces approached the Manchurian border. The idea of hot pursuit made them even more fearful that some incident would escalate the war. There was the genuine possibility that other UN members might dissociate themselves with any action across the Manchurian frontier, destroying the UN solidarity so necessary to the action. The French, knowing of MacArthur's reputation for independence, were particularly concerned—and especially concerned about what MacArthur would do.[36]

In the midst of the discussion of "hot pursuit" and the UN resolution, the British proposed a "fresh approach" to the problem. The British had recognized Red China and sent a minister. They had also contributed troops to the UNC effort, placing them in an awkward position. The British plan stated that because the great bulk of the North Korean armed forces had been destroyed, the threat to South Korea had been eliminated. The military campaign thus should be regarded as complete. Economic and political rehabilitation should begin. The area north of the line from Hamhung westward to Chongju would be declared a demilitarized area, a temporary measure pending unification of the country.

In discussing the military aspects, the British pointed out that the waistline was shorter and more easily defended, and that guerrilla action was possible but would be a problem in any case. More to the point, they believed there was considerable doubt that MacArthur had the force to fight his way to the border and maintain himself there without being able to strike at targets in Manchuria. And they pointed out the problem of a narrowing zone for air support and other supporting weapons as the border was approached. This was a more realistic military appraisal than, it appears, had been made in either Washington or Tokyo.

The State Department favored the idea of a demilitarized or buffer zone. Acheson had brought up a similar idea at the 9 November meeting of the National Security Council. Nevertheless, he convinced the British to withhold this proposed resolution until the six-power UN resolution calling for Chinese withdrawal could be acted on. Like other UNC action, the proposal became moot with the Chinese attack.

The Last-Chance Meeting
Additional information from international sources continued to arrive in Washington. On 13 November, the Swedish ambassador to China reported large-scale movement of troops toward Korea. On 15 November, the Far Eastern Command received a report of the conference in Beijing on 17 October when Chinese officials allegedly had decided to go to war. On further consideration in the light of new material, Willoughby commented, "This information may be evaluated as probably true."[37]

The Netherlands Embassy in Beijing reported on 17 November

that Chinese intervention in Korea was motivated by fear of aggression against Manchuria. If UNC forces halted fifty miles south of the Yalu River, the Netherlands believed there would be no further intervention. The Burmese Embassy reported evidence that the Chinese were planning a new and larger intervention. The CIA appraised these reports skeptically and concluded that China's operations in Korea "will probably continue to be defensive in nature."[38] Within the State Department, the newer information was viewed with increasing concern. Efforts revived to bring about a review of MacArthur's mission.

General James H. Burns, Marshall's assistant for foreign military affairs and military assistance, and his principal liaison with the State Department, was concerned with what seemed to be misunderstanding between Washington and Tokyo. In a memo to Marshall, he pointed out that the differences of opinion between Washington and Tokyo were between means and ends, not the ends themselves. Complete victory was desirable, but at what price? It was obvious that General MacArthur estimated a lower cost than the Joint Chiefs of Staff. Burns suggested that JCS members, accompanied by State and Defense officials, go to Tokyo, meet with MacArthur, and seek a meeting of minds. Marshall doubted the wisdom of transferring discussion to Tokyo and distracting MacArthur at that moment, but he asked Burns to sound out the State Department. Rusk and Jessup indicated they were opposed to such a meeting at that time, although they recognized that U.S. objectives needed reexamination. They said they would consider it further, but no further discussion took place.[39] Burns reported his lack of success to General Marshall and repeated his concerns: "Many people feel, and I am one of them, that if we continue to pursue our present military objectives in Korea we are running a serious risk of becoming involved in the world war we are trying to avoid."[40]

Burns's efforts were not fruitless. Within the State Department, concern had grown and efforts commenced to obtain a further review of the situation. On 17 November, the State Department's intelligence organization produced a recommended revision of the national intelligence estimate. This paper concluded that the Chinese would continue their present holding operation until overall preparations were completed and until the prospects for securing U.S with-drawal through intimidation and diplomatic maneuvers had been exhausted. Then, however, there would be increasing intervention, possibly to the point of large-scale military operations.[41]

With this as a basis, a working group headed by Ambassador Jessup agreed on recommendations for what has come to be called "The Last-Chance Meeting." The group's working paper suggested that it was not necessary to occupy all of North Korea to achieve the UNC objective. Agreeing with the British, the paper suggested that the unoccupied part of North Korea would be no different from those other parts of Korea where guerrilla activity was still a problem. The group continued to believe that, for the present, the main Chinese motivation was establishment of a *cordon sanitaire* south of the Yalu.

In a diplomatic expression of concern over MacArthur's understanding of his mission, the paper stated: ". . . the CINCUNC should be in possession of the clearest indication of the mission with which he is charged." After paying lip service to the three options of the JCS, the group reiterated the British concern over the military capability of reaching the border. It emphatically recommended a halt short of the border and establishment of a demilitarized zone.[42]

Within the military, there was a different opinion. General Charles Bolte recommended strongly against any change in MacArthur's mission. He had no doubt about the ability of the UNC to fight its way to the border and hold there. He pointed out that the decision to cross the thirty-eighth parallel was based on the consideration that all of Korea should be cleared of Communist forces and that an attack from Manchuria would be recognized as an open act of military aggression. The UNC would actually have a better chance of localizing the conflict by driving out all Communist forces. A show of strength might well discourage further aggression, whereas weakness would encourage it.[43]

The following day, 21 November, the secretaries of state and defense, with their principal civilian assistants and the Joint Chiefs, met with presidential adviser Averell Harriman to fully review the situation once more.

Both Marshall and Acheson expressed concern about the gap be-

tween X Corps and the Eighth Army and the disposition of X Corps.
Acheson further pointed out that MacArthur seemed to have confused his military directive (the destruction of the North Korean
armed forces) with his civil affairs directive intended to follow military success. With some concern, they agreed that MacArthur's attack should proceed, but that once it reached the Yalu, serious consideration should be given to drawing back.[44]

There was extended discussion of a demilitarized zone—how
deep it should be, when it should be announced, and how it
should be administered. General Collins pointed out a line along
the high ground south of the Yalu, which he thought would make
a sound defensive line. Marshall stressed the desirability of making proposals while the UNC forces were advancing, or after UNC
forces had reached the border. There was a brief discussion of what
would happen if the attack bogged down, but no conclusions were
reached.

Harriman, Acheson, and Marshall withdrew while the others remained to continue discussion, but no firm conclusions emerged.
Again, implicit in this discussion, like others, was the assumption that
the attack would succeed, but if increasing resistance was met, the
situation would develop progressively, allowing time for subsequent
review.[45]

Acheson later said the dispositions of the Eighth Army and X
Corps were "startling," and he expressed what he called a layman's
concern to Generals Marshall and Bradley. They pointed out that
they could not, from 7,000 miles away, direct MacArthur's dispositions. "Though no one could explain them, and General MacArthur
would not, no one would restrain them."[46]

As a result of the "last-chance meeting" and, apparently, a follow-
up meeting, General Collins sent a message to MacArthur outlining
the possible requirement for a buffer zone and asking his opinion
on holding a line short of the river. With his offensive under way and
announced to the world, MacArthur replied on 24 November:

> The concern underlying the search for the means to confine
> the spread of the Korea conflict is fully understood and shared
> here, but it is believed that the suggested approach would not

only fail to achieve the desired result but would be provocative of the very consequences we seek to avert.

In the first place from a military standpoint my personal reconnaissance of the Yalu River line yesterday demonstrated conclusively that it would be utterly impossible for us to stop upon commanding terrain south of the river as suggested and there be in a position to hold under effective control its lines of approach to North Korea. The terrain ranging from the lowlands in the west to the rugged central and eastern sectors is not adaptable to such a system of defense were we, for any reason, to sacrifice the natural defense features of the river line itself, features to be found in no other natural defense line in all of Korea. Nor would it be either militarily or politically defensible to yield this natural protective barrier safeguarding the territorial integrity of Korea.

Moreover any failure on our part to prosecute the military campaign through to the achievement of its public and oft repeated objective of destroying all enemy forces south of Korea's northern boundary as essential to the restoration of unity and peace to all of Korea would be fraught with the most disastrous consequences. It would be regarded by the Korean people as a betrayal of their sovereign and territorial integrity and of the solemn undertaking the United Nations entered into in their behalf, and by the Chinese and all the other peoples of Asia as weakness reflected from the appeasement of Communist aggression. As pointed out in my message C-68572 of 9 November, such action as tribute to international lawlessness and aggression would but encourage further international lawlessness and aggression. Furthermore, the political tension existing between the two countries requires that the international boundary be closed to reduce to a minimum lawless border incidents including bandit raids and smuggling and such action could not be effected if there existed a border zone beyond our immediate control.

Study of the Soviet and Beijing propaganda line discloses little to suggest any major concern over the potentiality of United Nations control of the southern banks of the Yalu River. Even what has been said concerning the hydroelectric facilities in North Korea is for the most part a product of British–American speculation, finding little reflection in any Soviet or Chinese utterances. Indeed, our information on these facilities and the disposition abroad of their power output fails to confirm that dependence upon this source of power is a major factor in the basic causes giving rise to the Chinese aggressive moves in Korea. Thus despite the fact that these hydro-electric facilities at Changjin brought under control of the X Corps had been closed down completely for a full month prior to the arrival of our forces with much of the vital machinery and other equip removed and dispersed and are not yet restored to operation, no suggestion of complaint has emanated from Soviet or Chinese sources over the deprivation of power consequent thereto. In view of these factual considerations one is brought to the conclusion that the issue of hydro-electric power rests upon the most tenuous grounds.

The entry of Chinese Communists into the Korea conflict was a risk we knowingly took at the time we committed our forces. Had they entered at the time we were beleaguered behind our Pusan perimeter beachhead, the hazard would have been far more grave than it is now that we hold the initiative and have a much smaller area within which to interdict their hostile moves. Our forces are committed to seize the entire border area, and indeed in the east have already occupied a sector of the Yalu River with no noticeable political or military Soviet or Chinese reactions. We have repeatedly and publicly made it unmistakably clear that we entertain no aggressive designs whatsoever against any part of Chinese or Soviet territory. It is my plan just as soon as we are able to consolidate positions along the Yalu River to replace as far as possible American Forces with those of the Republic of Korea and publicly announce orders effecting: (1) The return of American Forces to Japan; (2) The parole of all prisoners of war to their homes; (3) The leaving of the unification of Korea and the restoration of the civil processes of government to the people, with the advice and assistance of the United Nations authorities.

I believe that the prompt implementation of this plan as soon as our military objectives have been reached will effectively appeal to reason in the Chinese mind. If it will not, then the resulting situation is not one which might be influenced by bringing to a halt our military measures short of present commitments. By resolutely meeting those commitments and accomplishing our military mission as so often publicly delineated lies best—indeed only—in the hope that Soviet and Chinese aggressive designs may be checked before these countries are committed to a course from which for political reasons they cannot withdraw.[47]

In retrospect, Acheson called this "the last clear chance. . . . all the dangers from dispersal of our own forces and intervention by the Chinese were manifest. We were all deeply apprehensive. We were frank with one another, but not quite frank enough. I was unwilling to urge on the President a military course that his military advisers would not propose. They would not propose it because it ran counter to American military tradition of the proper powers of the theater commander. . . . So they hesitated, wavered, and the chance was lost. While everyone acted correctly, no one, I suspect, was ever quite satisfied with himself afterward."[48]

Although there was serious doubt about the conduct of the war, no realistic effort was made to alter MacArthur's plans. As Truman later said, you pick your man and back him. Later it was explained that the Joint Chiefs were reluctant to override MacArthur because of the American tradition of giving the theater commander broad latitude in the accomplishment of his mission. But there were few times in recent American history when higher political considerations were such a powerful consideration in the conduct of operations in the field.

In Tokyo

While Washington was debating, the bombing campaign was proceeding and MacArthur was preparing to resume the offensive. Solid results were expected of the bombing campaign. On 14 November, MacArthur told William Sebald, his political adviser, that his immediate objective was to destroy the Yalu bridges and isolate the area between the present battle line and the border. The Far Eastern Air Force was to destroy the built-up areas between his forces and the border so that the Communist forces could not live off the country. If his forces could reach the border before the Yalu froze, the Korean campaign would be at an end. If not, and reinforcements continued, there was no alternative but to bomb Manchuria. The "fat would be in the fire then": the USSR would certainly come in.[49]

In contrast to the Joint Chiefs and the CIA, MacArthur thought the Chinese were acting on their own initiative, that the USSR approved but remained in the background. The aggression in North Korea, Tibet, and Indo-China was motivated by Chinese imperialistic aspirations. He believed that if the drive to the border succeeded, the war would be over. The Chinese would have demonstrated their desire to help their neighbor and their ability to conduct a modern war, and they would be satisfied. They had not intervened earlier because they were confident that the North Koreans could defeat the UNC forces without help. When they learned otherwise, it had taken them some time to shift forces northward.[50]

Three days later, MacArthur expressed similar ideas in a conversation with Ambassador John Muccio. He put his personal estimate of Chinese forces at 30,000 men. He told Muccio that any more than that would have required large troop movements that would have been detected by air. He predicted that he could clear the remaining areas held by Communist troops within ten days.[51]

Afterward, General MacArthur complained that he wasn't given intelligence that the Chinese were coming in, that it was a responsibility of the highest political levels to do that. General Bradley also complained that they had no positive intelligence that the Chinese were going to enter the war.

However much this might have been a failure of national intelligence, it really amounted to a failure of combat intelligence in the field. The evidence was convincing and credible that the Chinese forces were not just the small advance element of a larger force but instead fully formed units. The intelligence analysts at both the Eighth Army and the Far Eastern Command were competent professionals. Only other information more convincing and credible could cause them to accept the enemy merely as advance forces. Communication intelligence could have provided that evidence. It is significant that Col. Percy Thompson at I Corps, who probably would not have had access to the communication intelligence, believed the Chinese to be in much greater strength.

The relatively small size of the Chinese force, as reported by the Eighth Army and the Far Eastern Command, skewed all other estimates. Analysts were perplexed at the small size and by the Chinese motives in entering the war so late. Had they been equipped to look at the situation from the Chinese point of view, as Edmund Clubb and John Davies in the State Department did, different conclusions might have been reached. While commanders at all levels were wondering if the Chinese were really coming in, the answer was right there in the Eighth Army. They were already in—in force—with more on the way.

Notes

1. MacArthur letter to Truman 30 Oct. 50.
2. FEC DIS 2977, 3 Nov. 50.
3. *HJCS,* 289.
4. CINCUNC msg CX68247 to CG Far Eastern Air Force (FEAF) 4 Nov. 50, quoted in Schnabel, *Policy and Direction,* 241.
5. Schnabel, *Policy and Direction,* 235–36.
6. *History of the Korean Conflict,* 16.
7. *HJCS,* 292.
8. Bevin Alexander, *Korea: The First War We Lost* (New York: Hippocrene Books, 1986), 290.
9. FEC msg C-68465 to DEPTAR 7 Nov. 50, quoted in Schnabel, *Policy and Direction,* 245.
10. CINCFE msg CX 68436, 7 Nov. 50, to JCS, quoted in *History of the Korean Conflict,* 5.
11. CINCFE msg CX 68411, 7 Nov. 50, to JCS, quoted in *History of the Korean Conflict,* 20.
12. *HJCS,* 297; MacArthur, *Reminiscences,* 370. Portions quoted in the MacArthur memoirs leave out the part about the grave international situation and the possibility of disaster.
13. MacArthur, *Reminiscences,* 371.
14. Doris M. Condit, *History of the Secretary of Defense.* Vol. 2, *The Test of War: 1950–1953* (Washington, D.C.: Office of the Secretary of Defense, 1988), 76.
15. Memorandum CIA to the president, "Chinese Communist Intervention," 1 Nov. 50, *FRUS,* 1025.
16. Schnabel, *Policy and Direction,* 234.
17. Intelligence Estimate 6 Nov. 50, G-2 DA, quoted in Schnabel, *Policy and Direction,* 245.
18. *HJCS,* 289.
19. Bradley, *A General's Life,* 588; *HJCS,* 295 n15.
20. Ibid., 590.
21. Ibid.
22. JCS msg 96060 to CINCFE 8 Nov. 50, quoted in Schnabel, *Policy and Direction,* 250.

23. CINCFE msg C-68572, 9 Nov. 50 in *FRUS*, 1107.

24. Bradley, *A General's Life*, 590.

25. National Intelligence Estimate 8 Nov. 50, *FRUS*, 1101ff.

26. Memorandum JCS to Sec Def 9 Nov. 50, *FRUS*, 1117.

27. Memoranda Clubb to Rusk, 1 Nov. and 4 Nov. 50, *FRUS*, 1023, 1039.

28. Memorandum Barrett to Rusk 3 Nov. 50, *FRUS*, 1030.

29. Telegram Wilkinson (Hong Kong) to Sec State, *FRUS*, 1034.

30. Telegram Wilkinson (Hong Kong) to Sec State, *FRUS*, 1128.

31. Telegram Rankin (Taipei) to Sec State, *FRUS*, 1069.

32. Memorandum Clubb to Rusk, *FRUS*, 1087.

33. Draft Memorandum by John Paton Davies, *FRUS*, 1078.

34. Researchers have found no formal minutes of this meeting, or none that have been declassified. This summary is based on Harry Truman, *Memoirs*. Vol. 2: *Years of Trial and Hope* (Garden City, N.Y.: Doubleday, 1956), 378–80; Bradley, *A General's Life*, 592–94; Condit, *History of the Secretary of Defense*, 78–80.

35. *Yearbook of the United Nations (195)*, 239.

36. Memorandum by Hayden Raynor, U.S. delegation to the UN, *FRUS*, 1219.

37. FEC DIS 2989, 15 Nov. 50.

38. *HJCS*, 312.

39. *HJCS*, 308–9.

40. Condit, *History of the Secretary of Defense*, 81.

41. Proposed National Intelligence Estimate, *FRUS*, 1188–90.

42. Memorandum Jessup to Sec State 20 Nov. 50, *FRUS*, 1193.

43. Schnabel, *Policy and Direction*, 267.

44. Jessup: Memorandum of conversation on the situation in Korea, *FRUS*, 1204–8; Acheson, *Present at the Creation*, 466–67.

45. Ibid., and Bradley, *A General's Life*, 596.

46. Acheson, *Present at the Creation*, 467.

47. CINCFE msg C-69808, 25 Nov. 50, *FRUS*, 1231–33.

48. Acheson, *Present at the Creation*, 468.

49. Sebald: Memorandum of Conversation with MacArthur 14 Nov. 50, *FRUS*, 1148–49.

50. Ibid.

51. Muccio: Memorandum of conversation with MacArthur 17 Nov. 50, 1175–176.

10
The Armies Prepare to Renew the Battle

Available evidence is not conclusive as to whether or not the Chinese
Communists are as yet committed to a full-scale offensive effort.
—CIA, National Intelligence Estimate, 24 November 1950

Results of Phase I

Without question, the Chinese success was as much a surprise to
them as it was to the UNC forces. In Korea's west, the Chinese were
approximately on the line they had planned initially to defend. They
had room for the deployment of follow-on forces. The principal
crossing sites at Sakchu and Jian were secure. The crossing site at
Jian–Manpojin was potentially threatened by the advance of X Corps
in the east, where the 1st Marine Division had penetrated the
planned defensive line. Still, the Chinese had a secure foothold that
could be defended.

More satisfying, they had been able to conceal the movement of
large forces. The very strict march discipline and other deception
measures had worked. The UN Command had no idea the Chinese
Communist Forces (CCF) in Korea approximated 180,000 men, with
more arriving by the day.

It must have been a considerable relief to them to find that UN
aircraft were observing the territorial integrity of Manchuria. The
movement of heavy industries inland from Shenyang and evacuation
of some of the schools, reported in the Far Eastern Command's Daily
Intelligence Summaries (DIS) and other sources, indicate their considerable concern about possible air attacks. India's Jawaharlal
Nehru made a serious attempt to reassure the Chinese that the
United States would respect the border. MacArthur later claimed the
Chinese would never have ventured into Korea had they believed
there could be UN air attacks on facilities in Manchuria. He believed

someone had told them. In any case, they must certainly have been relieved—and even more relieved to learn that absolute respect for the border was a subject of debate in the United Nations. Perhaps most encouraging of all, the feared American military machine had been roughly handled and pushed back. Shortly after breaking off action on 6 November, the headquarters of the Chinese People's Volunteers produced a lengthy report of lessons learned and a discussion of American tactics. Most telling was their estimate of the fatal weaknesses of the American soldier. It was published in various forms and circulated throughout the Chinese Army. The following comes from a document captured by the Eighth Army during the Phase II offensive:[1]

1. Their infantrymen are weak, afraid to die, and haven't the courage to attack or defend. They depend on their planes, tanks and artillery. At the same time, they are afraid of our fire power. They will cringe when, if on the advance, they hear firing; they are afraid to advance further.

2. In setting up their defense, if they discover that we are close by, they will pull back.

3. They must have proper terrain and good weather to transport their great amount of equipment. They can operate rapidly along good highways and flat country, not in hilly country.

4. They specialize in day fighting. They are not familiar with night fighting or hand to hand combat. They are afraid of our big knives and grenades. Also afraid of our courageous attack, regular combat, and infiltration.

5. If defeated they have no orderly formation. Without the use of their mortars they become completely at a loss and (as in the operation) were killed off. They were in a daze and completely demoralized.

6. They are not good in fighting. At UNSAN, they were surrounded for several days yet they did nothing.

7. They are afraid when the rear is cut off. When transport comes to a standstill, the Infantry loses the will to fight.

8. They are afraid of our weapons and firing power. They will

take to the hills. Those surrounded by us will think we are well organized and equipped with weapons. They, in this case, will not fight but will surrender.

The most unkind comparison of all came in a message from the Central Military Commission to the 19th Army Group, giving that organization instructions on necessary preparations for entering Korea: "By comparison the American forces have lower combat effectiveness than some capable troops of Chiang Kai-shek's army."[2]

The Chinese were not the only ones who had a poor opinion of American infantrymen. Hanson Baldwin, a prominent military commentator, wrote a column quoting an experienced officer who criticized the Army's performance. He said the United States had a "cream puff" army, not an army of soldiers, "too much I and E [information and education] and not enough fundamentals." Baldwin said the same comment was repeated by officer after officer. That prompted a message from Maj. Gen. Floyd L. Parks, the Army's chief of information, to the Far Eastern Command, asking for specifics on what could be done to improve the information and education program. MacArthur was angered by such criticism. He fired off a rocket to Gen. Walton Walker stating that Baldwin's column reflected the embarrassment caused by the loose and unbridled comments coming from the Eighth Army.[3]

MacArthur had, earlier that day, sent Walker a message chastising him for statements by Eighth Army officers criticizing the divided command in Korea. MacArthur viewed such statements with "grave disfavor" and added: "I have from the beginning of the campaign disliked the loose and sometimes reckless talk which has been attributed to the elements of your command."[4]

Notwithstanding the embarrassment, there was genuine concern about the quality of the training and performance of the Army forces. Later in the month, Gen. Matthew Ridgway asked for information that could be presented to Congress, ". . . immediate information which can have an impact now rather than detailed studies." General Doyle Hickey replied: "The Korean Campaign has again demonstrated the inadequacies of our 'peacetime' training with particular respect to the mental and physical preparation of soldiers to meet the realities of combat. In the effort to make the Army attractive to volunteers, it has been necessary to subordinate protracted and strenuous combat training in order to make room in the forty-hour week for 'social subjects.' It must be obvious to the American public that the Army must be hardened to the actualities of combat."[5]

Chinese Situation at the End of Phase I

Mao Zedong had entered the war with the hope that he would initially have to face only ROK forces. He felt he could handle the ROK Army (ROKA) with a certainty of success. But there were still six U.S. divisions. On 23 or 24 October, Mao realized that U.S. forces were going to advance past the stop line and that X Corps would be landing at Wonsan. At the request of Peng Dehuai, and to deal with this new threat, he ordered the 9th Army Group forward from Shandong. On 31 October, the 9th Army Group, moving into Manchuria, was ordered to send the 27th Army forward into Korea in reserve—either to meet the still-uncertain situation on the Eighth Army front or to be employed against forces advancing up the eastern side of the mountains. The 27th Army would send two divisions to Jian, while one would remain temporarily to backstop the western forces.[6]

By 5 November, the situation on the western front had turned in the favor of the Chinese, but the advance of the 1st Marine Division on the eastern front had driven back the 124th CCF Division and posed a serious threat to the Changjin–Kanggye area. Mao decided the entire strength of the 9th Army Group was needed on the eastern front. The 20th Army was dispatched to Jian to move into Korea, while the 27th Army was sent north to Linjiang to secure that crossing and commence moving south to meet the advancing Marines.[7] General Song Shilun's mission was to find opportunities to eliminate all four divisions of the X Corps, luring the enemy in deep and destroying forces one after another. The tactics that had worked so well against similarly armed and equipped Chinese Nationalist forces were now aimed at U.S. forces.

In the west, Peng had drawn his forces back to the area north of the line Tokchon–Kujang-dong–Yongbyon–Taechon. That area would become his base for mobile offensive operations.[8]

Chinese Plan—Phase II

Peng met with his commanders on 8 November to begin planning for the next offensive. The second-phase objective of the CPV was to attack southward to reach the Pyongyang–Wonsan line. Prisoners captured in the east said there had been much talk among the troops about what great times they would have when they reached Wonsan.[9]

The chief of staff of the Chinese People's Volunteers, Gen. Xie Fang, made this evaluation: "Our troop strength in Korea has reached nine armies, 30 divisions, over 380,000 men, giving us a 1.7 advantage over the enemy frontline ground forces. We have over 150,000 men on the eastern front, the enemy 90,000, giving us a 1.66 advantage over him. We have 230,000 men on the western front, the enemy 130,000, giving us a 1.75 advantage over him. Our forces are superior on the eastern and western fronts."[10]

The Chinese were now confident they could deal with U.S. forces, but they were beginning to struggle with the tremendous logistics problems they faced. The Chinese command anticipated only modest gains in the next phase. About 11 November, Peng told his staff that the 13th Army Group, given the amount of surprise they would undoubtedly achieve, might be able to push the enemy back to Pyongwon (about halfway between the Chongchon estuary and Pyongyang). "We must content ourselves for the moment with establishing a line just beyond the 39th Parallel. We do not have the logistics to back up an advance much more."[11] In the spring, with Soviet materiel and airpower, and with the 19th Army Group, it might be a different story.

The plan developed was classic Chinese strategy—the defensive offensive, hit them while they are moving. Rather than take up the offensive and launch an attack to secure the position he desired, Peng would wait for the resumption of the UN attack, draw the forces northward into the mountainous areas south of the border, then destroy them.

In the east, the Chinese focused on destruction of the 1st Marine Division.[12] The Chinese were aware as early as 12 November that the advance of the division was being led by two regiments. Plans were made to draw the X Corps forces to the vicinity of the Changjin

(Chosin) Reservoir and Kujin-ni, then attack.[13] Mao expressed concern. In a telegram to Peng on 12 November, he stated: "It is said that the American Marine First Division has the highest combat effectiveness in the American armed forces. It seems not enough for our four divisions to surround and annihilate its two regiments. [You] should have one to two more divisions as a reserve force. The 26th Army of the Ninth Army Group should be stationed close to the front."[14]

Against the Eighth Army, Peng planned to use five armies. The 38th and 42d Armies would make the main effort, concentrating action against the ROK forces on the right flank of the Eighth Army. The ROKs were recognized as the most vulnerable units in the Eighth Army. At the same time, they held the most difficult terrain in the Eighth Army sector. Breaking through the ROK forces around Tokchon, the Chinese were to drive southwestward to cut off UNC forces north of the Chongchon River. In the October offensive, the 38th CCF Army had hesitated to push the attack at Huichon and lost the chance to drive down the river and isolate UN forces to the north. Peng had publicly upbraided Gen. Lian Xingchu, the 38th Army commander, for his hesitation. Lian was determined not to repeat the error.

The 40th Army was to defend in the Yongbyon–Unsan area and be prepared to join in a general offensive once the attack against II ROK Corps was under way. The 39th Army would hold back the Eighth Army forces in the Taechon area. The 66th Army would cover the coastal route.

Mao approved the general plan, adding his own original comments. Pleased that the huge number of Chinese forces had not been discovered, on 18 November Mao telegraphed to Peng that the enemy still believed the Chinese forces were approximately 60,000 to 70,000 men, "not an unchallengeable force."[15] Still, Peng's deputy, Deng Hua, worried about the very deliberate advance of the Eighth Army. The longer it took, the more likely that the Eighth Army would discover the huge Chinese concentration. Taking Deng's advice, Peng, around 16 November, ordered a halt to all further delaying operations and directed rapid withdrawal. He also arranged to release some American PWs. Both measures helped to convince UNC commanders that the Chinese were withdrawing to defensive positions farther north.

The Chinese Deploy

Mao had ordered Peng to build several roads reaching the Tokchon–Yongwon–Maengsan area. Using these roads, the 38th Army moved east and southeast to deploy against II ROK Corps. On the far left flank of the Chinese, the 42d Army, regrouping after their move from northeast Korea, began to deploy in the vicinity of Yongwon.

In the east, the first 9th Army Group formation to arrive along the Yalu was the 27th CCF Army under Gen. Peng Deqing. It had departed Shandong Province on 25 October, arrived at Liaodong on 29 October, remained there four days, moved to Jian and on to Linjiang at the very northernmost tip of Korea, crossed the river there, and moved southward. It appears that one division, either the 79th or the 80th, took up positions around Changpyong-ni (about nine miles north-northwest of the Chosin Reservoir), covering the routes northward from the reservoir. The 81st Division is believed to have taken up a position farther to the east, covering what the Chinese believed to be a route north from the Fusen Reservoir.[16]

The next 9th Army Group formation to arrive was the 20th Army. On 13 September, it had started northward from Shanghai to Shandong. It was reinforced with the 89th Division and commenced moving toward the Yalu on 6 November, reaching Jian on 10 November. It crossed there and moved on to Manpojin, where the troops boarded trains for Mupyong-ni, then marched eastward to Yudam-ni.

The 89th Division of the 20th Army reached Yudam-ni about 12 or 13 November. Part of the 89th Division moved southeast to Toktong Pass to take up delaying positions. Other portions moved southward, prepared to cover the road west through Sachang-ni.

Following next was the 60th Division, which turned southwest to Chang-ni, then turned east to cover the route west from Koto ri. The 58th CCF Division followed the same route as the 60th to Chang-ni, then turned east to the vicinity of Samdaepyong. It appears that, initially, these two divisions began to prepare defensive positions along the route through the mountains at this point.[17] Advance parties, assisted by local guides, showed the way.

The 59th Division was the fourth and last unit of the 20th Army to arrive in the area. It moved south and assembled in the area of Hansang-ni–Sojung-ni, just to the southwest of Yudam-ni.

The 124th Division, after withdrawing from the Funchillin Pass, had moved west from Koto-ri to Chang-ni, then south to the vicinity of Sachang-ni. The 126th Division had remained in the Chosin Reservoir area, withdrawing ahead of and observing the advance of the 1st Marine Division. About 17 November, it was relieved by arriving 20th Army troops, then moved south from Yudam-ni to the vicinity of Tokchon, where it joined the 125th Division of the 42d CCF Army.

The corridor from Yudam-ni to Sachang-ni, joining two of the lateral routes through the mountains, was part of the thirty-mile gap that separated X Corps and the Eighth Army. In deployment for the second offensive, at least six Chinese divisions moved freely through this corridor, or parts of it, two of them moving from east to west and four moving from west to east—ample evidence that, despite assertions to the contrary, the Chinese made effective use of this gap.

The last formation to arrive was the 26th Army under Gen. Zhang Renchu. It arrived at Linjiang about the middle of November. This army had been hastily moved forward, and the men were still wearing the summer uniforms they had worn while on the Taiwan coast. Efforts were made to provide them with some cold-weather clothing, but the men were not well outfitted. The bulk of the 26th Army remained close to Linjiang, where it could be more readily supported logistically. Two divisions of the 26th Army were moved southeast along the Yalu River to the point where it was joined by the Huchang River, with the mission of defending against any forces coming down the river from the vicinity of Hyesan-jin.

Eighth Army Situation
Immediately upon the Chinese withdrawal, the Eighth Army began a series of limited-objective advances to expand the bridgehead and to secure a new line of departure for a resumption of the offensive.

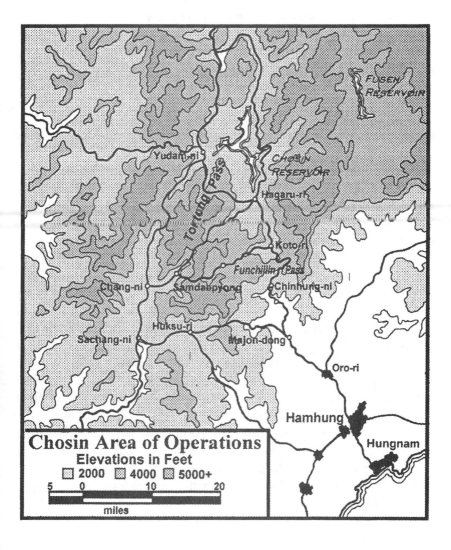

Chosin Area of Operations
Elevations in Feet
2000   4000   5000+
5   0   10   20
miles

In the meantime, urgent measures were being taken to improve the critical logistics situation.

The advance northward from Seoul to Pyongyang had been undertaken by only one U.S. division and four ROK divisions, because additional troops could not be supported logistically north of the Han River.[18] The port of Inchon was tied up for the first portion of the month with the outloading of the 1st Marine Division. The Eighth Army had to move its supplies all the way from Pusan. When Pyongyang was secured and the port of Chinampo was cleared, the port was found to be mined. All available minesweepers were engaged at Wonsan. The Eighth Army then asked for LSTs to land supplies at Chinampo. The shallow-draft LSTs could ride over the three-fathom-deep mines. But with the decision to land the 7th Division at Iwon, northeast of Hamhung, the division, already loaded in attack shipping, had to unload and reload on the only available LSTs for a possible opposed landing. None were available to support the Eighth Army.

To complicate things further, task-force ships involved in the Inchon landing had been bottom-loaded with a considerable quantity of supplies and equipment for the Eighth Army and the Fifth Air Force. Before off-loading of these ships could be completed, the ships were required for the Wonsan operation, sailing away with supplies needed by the Eighth Army. Consequently, both the ships and the supplies they contained were delayed several weeks.[19] The Fifth Air Force voluntarily agreed to divert the bulk of its share of available supplies to General Walker's forces. In addition, the Fifth Air Force arranged to fly in supplies for advance units north of Pyongyang, but in limited quantities.

The initial advance to the Chongchon River had hung on a slender logistic thread. Combat units had little more than one day of fire in their ammunition dumps. Tank crews were never sure there would be sufficient fuel on hand for the next day's advance. Strenuous efforts were made to improve the situation.

The oncoming winter created a need for cold-weather clothing. In the euphoric view of mid- to late October, the Far Eastern Command quartermaster had stated: "With the recent turn of events in Korea, it appears evident that the need for arctic items will not be necessary during the winter." According to that report, there was only sufficient stock on hand, and due in, to supply arctic clothing for one division.[20] An urgent call went out to the Department of the Army for action. Stocks of mountain sleeping bags and pile-lined parka overcoats were in critical supply in Korea. News reports appeared in the stateside press saying, ". . . along windswept fields there are more men in thin cotton garments than in woolens. . . ."[21] To counter this, on 15 November General MacArthur authorized issuance of a statement, saying, "United Nations troops of X Corps now fighting in the most advanced northern area of Korea, both Army and Marine, have been fully equipped with suitable cold weather clothing for current conditions. The same type of winter clothing was stock piled early in Korea in sufficient quantity to equip all UN units of Eighth Army."[22]

That information had not penetrated to X Corps, however. On 17 November, Gen. Edward Almond sent a message saying, "The 7th Infantry Division has urgent need for 250 squad tents complete and 400 stoves, tent, with oil burners. . . . Soldiers are freezing for lack of shelter."[23] In the 7th Infantry Division, the G-4 ran a daily tally of sleeping-bag shortages in his periodic logistic report. For 17 November, it showed: "Short items: 6,705 mountain sleeping bags for U.S. personnel, 6,855 mountain sleeping bags for ROK personnel."[24] The 7th Division had previously asked for mountain (down-filled) sleeping bags for ROK personnel but had been told there were not enough for U.S. troops.

X Corps Situation

In X Corps, the 1st Marine Division, taking advantage of the Chinese withdrawal, moved ahead to secure the formidable barrier of the Funchillin Pass. A one-way road cut into the side of steep mountains wound upward nearly 3,000 feet in a little more than three airline miles. The road was totally dominated by hills on either side and by the mass of Hill 1457, at the very top of the pass. A defender would have perfect observation over any approaching force. In the hands of a determined defender, the pass could be held for an extended period of time against a very large force. It was difficult to believe that the Chinese would give up such a strong position so readily. The

Chinese withdrawal from the Funchillin Pass fueled speculation that the Chinese intended only a token effort in Korea.

Elsewhere, X Corps units held their positions until the situation in the Eighth Army zone became clear.

On the right of X Corps, the 17th Infantry of the 7th Division had reached the Ungi River, north of Pungsan, and halted there on 4 November. The 31st Infantry had completed landing and was moving into the roadless area around the Fusen Reservoir on the left of the 17th Infantry. By 9 November, the last regiment of the 7th Division, the 32d Infantry, had completed landing and was moving into position in a valley southeast of the Fusen Reservoir.

The 3d Infantry Division, hastily organized in the United States, had been moved to Japan to provide a garrison force. It was ordered to Korea at the time MacArthur ordered the advance to the border. The first units began landing at Wonsan on 5 November, with the complete division ashore by 17 November. The 3d Division then relieved the remaining Marines in the Wonsan–Majon-dong area, allowing them to close up with the rest of the 1st Marine Division.

The UNC Plan
In his memoirs, General MacArthur gave his rationale for continuing the advance to the Yalu River border. He outlined three options—going forward, remaining in place, and withdrawing. He stated: "If I went forward there was the chance that China might not intervene [in force?] and the war would be over." Remaining in place did not seem a realistic possibility to him because of lack of good terrain for defense and the impossibility of establishing a defense in depth with the limited forces at hand, while the Chinese could continuously reinforce with fresh divisions. Withdrawal would be in contradiction to his orders and would end any chance to bring the war to a close.

MacArthur related that after reviewing his orders, he concluded that the best course was to go forward: "This would deny the enemy the selection of the time and place of his attack, and the accumulation of additional force from Manchuria. It would be simultaneously a mopping-up of the defeated North Korea forces and a reconnaissance in force to probe the intentions of the Chinese. If our forward movement should prematurely expose Chinese involvement, my troops would have the necessary freedom of action to escape its jaws."

He claimed that if he went forward and found the Chinese in force, he would break contact, then withdraw to lengthen the Chinese supply lines, increasing their logistic difficulties and exposure to air attack until some equilibrium was reached. He added: "In anticipation of such a situation, I directed Walker to prepare complete operational plans for disengagement and withdrawal from action in the event it developed that Red China was entering the Korean War in determined force."[25]

However, the authors of *History of the Joint Chiefs of Staff* reported being unable to find any evidence such orders were issued. General Almond stated later that he knew of no such plan.[26] Although MacArthur says that withdrawal would be in contradiction to his orders, he omits any mention of his discussions with the JCS about changing those orders.

Another view is put forward by Shelby Stanton in his book *America's Tenth Legion:* "MacArthur believed that the only way to strip away the artifice of Chinese intervention was to unify Korea quickly under American backed UN protection. He wanted the Yalu to be a clearly defined international border. To solidify UN mastery over the Yalu it was imperative to reach the Manchurian border on a broad front. He was convinced a rapid emplacement of allied forces along the northern border would terminate the Korean communist regime's claim to territorial legitimacy. This fait accompli would deprive China of any valid excuse to intervene in North Korea's behalf. Thus he believed that a quick push to the border offered the best chance to end the war and safeguard against Chinese action."[27]

Stanton does not give any specific documentation for this statement, but it does reflect a very similar concern that MacArthur had expressed earlier in the war should the situation be reversed and the North Koreans succeed in driving UN forces from Korea.

Eighth Army Plan

The Eighth Army's cautious forward movement to a line of departure for a renewed offensive met little resistance on the left flank. On the right, in the II ROK Corps sector, the enemy reacted with sharp local counterattacks until the middle of the month, then withdrew farther north, permitting the ROK forces to occupy Tokchon and its commanding height called Honey Comb Hill.

By 22 November, the cautious forward movement of the Eighth Army had brought it up to a line running generally from the mouth of the Chongchon River through Pakchon and Yongbyon to Kujangdong on the Chongchon. Across the river, the line extended north of Tokchon to Yongwon and Maengsan on the extreme right. From there, a gap of some thirty miles extended to the farthest-left unit of X Corps.

General Walker's plan was to advance with three corps abreast. I Corps would be on the right with the 24th Division and the 1st ROK Division on line. Initial objectives would be Chongju and Taechon. In the center, IX Corps would pass through the 1st Cavalry Division, which would then go into reserve. IX Corps would attack with the 25th Infantry Division on the left, advancing toward Unsan, and the 2d Infantry Division on the right, moving from the vicinity of Kujangdong northward toward Huichon. On the far right, II ROK Corps would advance alongside the 2d Division toward the town of Woncham, just north of Huichon, then continue the attack north along the Chongchon–Tongno corridor to Mupyong-ni and Kanggye.

The plan was for a controlled and closely coordinated advance to successive phase lines, no unit advancing beyond the designated phase line until ordered to do so. There were to be no further independent forward rushes by individual units, as there had been in October. Units would remain, initially, within mutual supporting distance. Unfortunately, the attack, as it advanced, would diverge, increasing the distances between units and making it impossible for them to be mutually supporting.

By 15 November, the planned date for resuming the advance, the logistics situation was still not able to provide the tonnage needed for a sustained effort. The attack was put off until 24 November.

X Corps Planning—Assistance to Eighth Army
The appearance of the Chinese raised concerns about the widely dispersed situation in X Corps. General Edwin Wright, Far Eastern Command G-3, worried about the deployment of the corps in small

units spread over 100 miles from south to north and nearly the same distance west to east. Disposed as it was, the corps was in no position to lend support to the Eighth Army, if needed, or even to provide mutual support to its own units.

General Wright's concern was echoed in Washington. At a meeting of the National Security Council, Secretary Marshall noted the wide dispersion of X Corps and commented on it. General Omar Bradley stated that this disposition had been made by MacArthur in order to carry out his directive to occupy the entire country and hold elections.[28] Bradley's statement seems to be evidence that there was some misunderstanding, by both MacArthur and Bradley, of just what MacArthur's instructions were at that particular time.[29] By 28 October, MacArthur had received his civil affairs instructions for the occupation of North Korea, but those instructions were not to become effective until hostile resistance had ceased.

Perhaps Marshall's concern about X Corps reached the Far Eastern Command and buttressed Wright's concern. On 10 November, he was able to persuade General MacArthur to let him alert General Almond to a possible change of mission. By that date, the advance elements of X Corps were more than forty miles ahead of the nearest Eighth Army forces. General MacArthur's directive, transmitted by personal letter from Wright, directed X Corps to become familiar with Eighth Army plans in order to be prepared for any possible change in the situation, and it suggested that X Corps plans be developed for a strong effort in coordination with resumption of the Eighth Army offensive—which, at that time, was anticipated to commence on 15 November.[30]

Reassured by the Chinese withdrawal, Almond had issued X Corps Operation Order No. 6 on 11 November. The X Corps mission was: "Destroy enemy in zone and advance to the Northern Border of Korea." The 1st Marine Division, 7th Infantry Division, and I ROK Corps all were ordered to advance and "destroy enemy in zone." The border in the 1st Marine Division's zone was more than eighty-five airline miles away (more than double that by road) through some of the most difficult and mountainous terrain in Korea. No intermediate objectives were given to either division, which meant that each was to advance without regard to the progress of

units on either flank. It was an order for all-out exploitation. However, as an apparent concession to the desires expressed in General
Wright's letter, both the 1st Marine Division and the 3d Infantry Division, just arriving, were directed to be prepared for offensive operations to the west on order.[31]

The 1st Marine Division and the 3d Infantry Division were widely
separated. To execute a coordinated, mutually supporting attack
would require lengthy redeployment of both divisions, a slow and
difficult task in that mountainous country with a very limited road
net—and especially so, given the shortage of trucks in X Corps.[32]
Simply directing them to be prepared to attack to the west didn't
quite fulfill the need for closer cooperation with the Eighth Army.
Widely dispersed as X Corps was, it would become more so as it advanced toward the border.

In Tokyo, Wright was not satisfied with the gesture in the X Corps
operation order. He directed the Joint Strategic Plans and Operations Group (JSPOG), which reported to him as G-3, to study the situation to see what assistance X Corps might offer to the Eighth Army
in addition to or in place of that already planned by X Corps.

The JSPOG study assumed that North Korean forces totaling
50,000 men in six divisions—two armored divisions and three
brigades—and 18,000 CCF troops from six armies faced the Eighth
Army. The CCF was given the capability of reinforcing at the rate of
three 8,000-man divisions per day. Opposite X Corps were assumed
to be elements of four North Korean brigades totaling 12,000 men
and one CCF division of 7,500 men, most of them concentrated in
the Chosin–Fusen Reservoir areas.[33] This considerably underassessed
the Chinese strength as given by General Willoughby, who estimated a total of 46,596 Chinese Communist troops and 69,111
North Koreans.[34] JSPOG noted that the critical aspect of the proposed Eighth Army operation was not the availability of troops but
supply shortages: "Assignment of additional troops would only mag-
nify the problem. . . ."

According to JSPOG, the advantages of the X Corps plan were:

   1. Momentum of forces continuing in the same direction
   would be retained.

2. North Korean forces would not have time to dig in and resist.

3. Logistics difficulties within X Corps would be minimized.

4. The route of the 1st Marine Division's advance would pose a threat of envelopment to the enemy.

The disadvantages that would result were:

1. Advance by X Corps would not immediately affect enemy forces facing Eighth Army.

2. The mass of forces would be moving away from the main strength of the enemy.

3. By continuing advance to the north, X Corps incurs the danger of becoming seriously overextended.

4. If progress of the right flank of Eighth Army was slower than X Corps, the left flank of X Corps would be exposed.

This last item was elaborated: "As the 1st Marines move toward Changjin they will tend to be extended. The left flank of the Marines will be on the mountainous ridge that divides the watersheds of the peninsula. It is generally impassable for heavy military traffic. However, prisoner reports show that the 124th CCF Division entered North Korea at Manpojin and is now in the Chosin Reservoir area. If the 1st Marine Division attacks north beyond this route well ahead of the Eighth Army it will be vulnerable to attacks on its flank and rear."[35]

JSPOG believed that with sound adherence to the principles of concentration and objective, the only course of action was to mount an attack to the northwest, which would threaten the rear of the enemy confronting the Eighth Army and cause him to withdraw. By halting the forward movement and reorienting toward the west, two divisions could be made available. Because the attack would probably be along a narrow front as a fight for the route of advance, concentration of forces for a coordinated attack would not be necessary. The attack could be launched with forces already in position.

But before any operations were feasible, it would be necessary to clear the reservoir area. Once this was done, an attack could be

mounted to the northwest to cut the enemy's Manpojin–Kanggye–Huichon main supply route (MSR). The JSPOG recommended
that no immediate change was necessary, but that X Corps should
be directed to commence planning for an attack to the northwest
to cut the enemy MSR.

General Hickey approved the study on 14 November and presented it to MacArthur. The following day, X Corps was directed by
message to ". . . develop as an alternate feature of your Operation
Order No. 6 plans for reorienting attack to westward upon reaching
vicinity Changjin in order to cut enemy MSR. . . . Alternate operation would be executed on order CINCUNC [Commander in Chief,
UN Command]. Submit plans and any pertinent recommendations
this headquarters."[36]

Coinciding with the deliberations of JSPOG, General Almond had
been giving further thought to the role of X Corps. The same day
the JSPOG study was complete, Almond sent a letter to General
Wright outlining his views:

> Dear Pinky,
>
> I have your letter of 10 November relaying the CinC's di-
> rective that the X Corps be made fully familiar with Eighth
> Army's plans in order to be prepared for any possible change
> in the situation, and suggesting that we develop X Corps plans
> for a strong effort in coordination with the resumption of
> Eighth Army's attack. Two members of my planning staff have
> just returned from Eighth Army with a draft copy of General
> Walker's Operations Plan No. 15, yet to be published in final
> form. They discussed Eighth Army's plan at some length with
> General Walker and certain members of his staff.
>
> As you may already know, the Eighth Army plan is for a very
> deliberate and thorough advance to objectives distant only an
> average of some 20 miles north of present front line positions.
>
> You will recall that during your recent visit with us at Won-
> san we presented X Corps capabilities of making an all out ef-
> fort, with not less than two U.S. Divisions, to the west in the
> event of an enemy breakthrough or envelopment of Eighth
> Army's right flank. We have devoted continued efforts in plan-

ning possible operations not only to further the CinC's overall objective of securing all of North Korea within our assigned zone as expeditiously as possible but also to assist Eighth Army's effort.

With the containment by Eighth Army of the Communist offensive in that area, coupled with the unchanged overall mission, it now appears to me to be inadvisable, at this stage of Eighth Army and X Corps operations, for X Corps forces to operate in any strength to the west. The principal reason for this conclusion is that the only two feasible vehicular routes to the Westward in X Corps Zone, short of Chosin Reservoir, are the Yonghung–Taepyong-ni and the Wonsan–Yangdok roads. Since both of these routes enter the Eighth Army Zone in rear of General Walker's present front lines, any advance in strength to the westward over them would appear to be a fruitless operation. Even contacting the Eighth Army right flank in the vicinity of Onyang-ni with more than foot troops would require a major engineer road-building effort in the mountains to the eastward thereof.

In view of the foregoing, I am convinced the X Corps can best support Eighth Army's effort by continuing its advance to the North, prepared to move westward if desirable, when X Corps elements are well north of Chosin Reservoir, and they will be prepared to trap and destroy any enemy forces engaging Eighth Army which depend upon a line of communication through Manpojin. North of Chosin Reservoir suitable lateral routes to the west appear to exist, but these routes would have to be verified when the area is reached.

Thus, X Corps Operations Order No. 6, 11 November 1950, directing aggressive advance in zone to the Northern border of Korea is in accordance with Part II CX 67291, and is, I believe, at present the most important contribution we can make to the overall operation in Korea. The success of this advance will result in the destruction of Chinese and North Korean forces in the reservoir area, which might otherwise be employed on the Eighth Army front, and will place X Corps units in a position to threaten or to cut enemy lines of communication in the Eighth Army Zone. As a corollary, X Corps will secure the important hydro-electric power installations in its zone and will be well along toward completing its ultimate mission prior to the advent of severe winter conditions.

I fully appreciate the CinC's desire for us to assist the Eighth Army in every possible way. I trust that my analysis of present X Corps capabilities explains our views there and hope that energetic execution of my Operations Order No. 6 will place the X Corps quickly in a position where it can be of direct assistance to the Eighth Army before the cold weather now upon us is much more severe.[37]

Inherent in the thrust of the letter is the unwillingness of General Almond to subordinate his advance to that of the Eighth Army. The second paragraph subtly suggests excessive caution on the part of the Eighth Army, while the remainder of the letter implies that the rapid advance of X Corps would do more to accomplish the desired objective of General MacArthur. And there is the belief that the Eighth Army has contained the Chinese and are quite capable of handling the matter. Strangely absent is any recognition that the entry of the Chinese has changed the situation in any significant way. Also missing is discussion of one other route through the mountain range, which became of some importance a short time later. That was the route from either Majon-dong or from Chigyong to Huksu-ri and Sachang-ni. There the roads would join at the upper reaches of the Taedong River, which led through a gap in the mountains to Nankpo-ri and thence to Tokchon, Yongwon, and Maengsan. Not long afterward, the 3d Infantry Division was able to push one regiment along this road as far as Sachang-ni.

The optimistic view of the X Corps potential for rapid advance was not reflected in the realistic appraisal of General Almond's staff. The corps engineer inspected the road through the Funchillin Pass to Hagaru-ri. He estimated that it would require six battalion-months of effort to improve it enough to support X Corps operations.[38] Available for the work were two engineer construction battalions and two engineer combat battalions, provided they could be relieved of all other work.

X Corps Advance

With the Eighth Army holding north of the Chongchon River and building up for a resumption of the offensive, X Corps moved ahead. By 14 November, the 7th Marines, leading the 1st Marine Division advance, had pushed on to Hagaru-ri at the south end of the Chosin Reservoir.

The following day, Gen. Oliver Smith expressed the same concern about his open left flank as had the JSPOG. Smith passed on his misgivings to Adm. Albert K. Morehouse, chief of staff of COMNAVFE, who had arrived on an inspection and liaison trip. The same day, in a letter to the commandant, Smith said he felt Almond's orders were wrong, and that he (Smith) was not going to press his troops forward rashly to possible destruction: ". . . we are the left flank division of the corps and our left flank is wide open. No 8th Army units are closer than eighty miles southwest." X Corps would assure him, "when it is convenient," that there are no Chinese on his flank: "If this were true, there could be nothing to prevent the Eighth Army from coming abreast of us. This they are not doing. Although the Chinese have withdrawn to the north, I have not pressed [Col. Homer] Litzenberg to make any rapid advance. I do not like the prospect of stringing out a Marine Division along a single mountain road for 120 air miles from Hamhung to the border. I now have two RCTs on this road, and when [Col. Lewis] Puller is relieved by the 3rd Infantry Division I will close him up behind." Smith had reason to be concerned. The road distance to the border was closer to 200 miles.[39]

When the 7th Marines reached Hagaru-ri, the 17th Infantry, leading the 7th Infantry Division advance, began to cross the Ungi River, about ten miles north of Pungsan on the road to Hyesan-jin.

Almond and Wright Offer Alternative Plans

General Almond's letter to General Wright crossed with the message of General MacArthur telling X Corps to ". . . develop as an alternate feature of your Operation Order No. 6 plans for reorienting attack to westward upon reaching vicinity Changjin in order to cut enemy MSR. . . ." The alternate plan would be executed on MacArthur's order. Plans were to be submitted to FEC. In a follow-up instruction, perhaps as a concession to Almond or the 7th Infantry Division, MacArthur directed that "minimum forces only" could advance to the Yalu.[40]

Obedient to the orders of the commander in chief, Almond's staff the following day drew up Operation Plan 8, draft 1. Under it, X Corps would seize Kanggye by a drive from Changjin. Almond rejected it. By advancing that far north, the MSR would become too extended. He ordered a new plan prepared based on an advance along the axis Hagaru–Mupyong-ni, ordered that an RCT of the 7th Division be assigned the mission of seizing Changjin to protect the right flank of the 1st Marine Division, ordered that the Hamhung–Hagaru route be developed as a corps MSR, and, finally, directed that the plan be based on the assumption that extreme minimum temperatures of −30 to −40°F would severely restrict both friendly and enemy operations.[41]

General Wright had not been convinced by the Almond letter. He proceeded to do some additional planning himself. On 17 November, he produced a lengthy memorandum for the chief of staff, setting forth an alternative disposition for X Corps that would, he believed, more effectively support the Eighth Army offensive, which was to be the main effort.

Wright reminded the chief of staff of his continuing concern about the possibility that an enemy force might drive down through the central mountainous area and execute an envelopment of either the right flank of the Eighth Army or the left flank of X Corps. To counter this possibility, he had recommended regrouping X Corps to secure the Hungnam area and establishing a force of division size or larger in the Wonsan area, prepared to attack to the west or northwest.

Now he pointed out that the enemy had consistently shifted forces toward the center in the Tokchon–Yongwon area and sideslipped forces westward from the Chosin area, making that the weakest position for friendly forces and enabling the enemy to strike in force in either direction. He pointed out that there was little enemy strength in front of the 7th Division and that there was little of strategic importance to be gained east of the line Hyesan-jin–Pukchong, or north of Kapsan.[42]

Wright proposed that X Corps be deployed with the 3d Infantry Division in the Wonsan–Kowon area. The 7th Infantry Division would break off its northward advance and be inserted between the 3d Division and the 1st Marine Division in the sector from Kowon northward. The 1st Marine Division would then extend eastward to cover a frontage stretching from Sobaek-san, about ten miles southwest of Yudam-ni, across the Chosin and Fusen Reservoirs to the vicinity of Hwangsuwon-ni, about ten miles southwest of Pungsan.[43]

General Willoughby concurred in this recommendation. In his comments on the memo, he pointed out that the meager-to-light resistance in the 7th Division's zone of action indicated the enemy was concentrating in the Huichon area. He also noted that while the road net in the area was poor, the Chinese had demonstrated the capability for mountain operations, were certainly not road-bound, and were aware of the weakness of II ROK Corps holding this rugged sector. This, coupled with the Chinese capability of reinforcing with one division each night, gave them the ability to launch an attack to the southeast or a flanking attack to the southwest against the Eighth Army. Willoughby went further in suggesting that redeployment was not enough, that the 7th Infantry Division should launch an attack to the northwest, which would bring the Division into the rear of the heaviest enemy resistance. Wright's plan would have split the Marine division, forcing it to operate on two separate MSRs well beyond supporting distance. It was a map-exercise fantasy.

In the next few days, the Wright and Almond plans competed for General MacArthur's approval. Very probably, three plans were under discussion—the Wright plan, X Corps Operation Plan 8, and General Almond's stated preference for continuing the attack to the north. Neither Almond nor the members of his staff wanted to change direction and attempt to cross the mountains. As Maj. Gen. Clark L. Ruffner, his chief of staff, put it: "The decision for X Corps to attack through the Chosin Reservoir westward to hook up with Eighth Army was made at GHQ–Tokyo. It was an insane plan. You couldn't take a picnic lunch in peacetime and go over that terrain in November and December."[44] There was the additional touchy personality consideration. As a result of his sometimes-highhanded treatment while acting as MacArthur's chief of staff, Almond had created considerable animosity between himself and General Walker. By now, X Corps was, in all but name, a five-division field army. The proposed attack westward would ultimately unite X Corps and the Eighth Army. Almond did not relish the idea of having to give up his coequal status to serve under the man he had previously antagonized.

UNC Appraisal of the Enemy

As the armies jockeyed for position, both preparing to renew their offensive, the initial questions persisted. How many Chinese were there, why were they there, and what was their stance? Willoughby's estimate of the Chinese strength grew almost daily.[45]

Date	Estimated CCF	Organizations
30 Oct.	16,500	3 regiment-size "units"
3 Nov.	34,500	3 division-size "units," 1 division
4 Nov.	30,700	
8 Nov.	51,600	8 divisions
9 Nov.	64,200	10 divisions
13 Nov.	76,800	12 divisions
16 Nov.	75,600	12 divisions
22 Nov.	70,935	12 divisions

Willoughby explained that the increase in estimated Chinese strength was due to reevaluation of initial information plus continued reinforcement by the Chinese. The very heavy day-by-day movement of vehicles from Manchuria southward convinced him that Chinese units initially were committed in piecemeal fashion but were being steadily reinforced.[46] Reevaluation indicated that the initial estimate of "unit" strength of between 3,000 and 9,000 was too low, and that each of the 54th, 55th, and 56th Units was in reality a complete CCF army with an estimated strength of 18,900.[47]

North Korean strength was estimated at only 9,400 on 9 November. Over the next two weeks, the estimate of North Korean strength increased to 82,779. One explanation for this was that the Chinese offensive had been launched to slow or halt the UNC drive, allowing the North Korean remnants to withdraw northward to reorganize and rebuild under the protection of the Chinese.

Soon there was a divergence of views on the strength of the Chinese. Colonel Tarkenton, on 18 November, prepared his estimate for the forthcoming Eighth Army offensive. He believed the 55th and 56th "Units" to be only 9,000-man division-size task forces of what might be a larger formation. His estimate of Chinese strength in the Eighth Army zone was two division-size "units" of 9,000 each, two divisions of 8,000 each, one division of 7,000, and another "unit" of 5,000 for a total of 48,000 CCF in his zone, plus another 48,741 in reconstituted North Korean formations.[48]

To reconcile this conflicting view, Willoughby diplomatically stated that although the estimate of 18,900 for "units" was based on limited interrogations, subsequent front-line unit commanders' estimates of opposing CCF enemy strength—based on his demonstrated offensive and defensive action—indicated that 9,000 and not 8,000 per army unit was possibly a more correct estimate. This led to the desirability of carrying an upper as well as a lower limit on CCF strength, which he did from that point onward.[49] (The figure given previously for the FEC estimate on 22 November is the upper limit.)

The question could have been settled by Liu Piao-wu. Liu, a company cultural officer from the 335th Regiment of the 112th CCF Division, was captured near Taechon on 9 November. Liu had served in the Chinese Nationalist Army (CNA) and had been captured and inducted into the PLA. Because he had attended three years of middle school—considerably more than most Chinese soldiers—he was given the post of cultural officer. He was well informed, cooperative, and persuasive, providing a wealth of detailed information on organization, training, tactics, and logistics—all of which, as it turned out, was true. Liu said that the redesignation of the 38th Army as the 54th Unit was done just before it entered Korea, with the specific purpose of confusing the Americans. He said that all three divisions of the 38th Army entered Korea on 20 November, and that each division had a strength of about 10,000 men, with a total for the army of 40,000.[50] That would have put the total Chinese forces opposing the Eighth Army at 240,000, just about what it was. Liu's story was not accepted.

The real Chinese objective was still a puzzle. The DIS carried many indications of possible large-scale Chinese intervention. There were reports that China was to commit 200,000 troops, with the Soviets contributing 250,000 more. Other sources believed the Chinese planned to go all out in Korea and step up efforts in Indo-China. ROC (Taiwan) sources reported that the PRC intended to "throw the book" at UNC forces in Korea. Even allowing for the Nationalist desire to see the United States and China in a full-scale war (which would permit them to return to the mainland), this information was impressive.[51] Sweden and Burma both provided evidence that the PRC was planning a new and larger effort. The buildup believed to be occurring in Manchuria was more than could be explained by any other purpose. Chinese propaganda was increasingly strident. The plan for aggression against China, according to the Chinese view, was developed back in February by U.S. generals who directed Korean forces to provoke the war, which would involve attacks on China from Korea, Taiwan, and Indo-China—all part of a plan for world conquest. The increased tempo of propaganda sounded very much like preparation for war, preparing the population to defend China and Manchuria. Mao, according to another report, believed that participation in the war would enhance Communist China's world stature.

All of this could be discounted as bluster, especially because it seemed so doubtful that the Chinese Communists, if intending to intervene in Korea, would wait this late in the war. Other sources reported the reasons for waiting. They were:

1. Chinese Communists assumed that the North Koreans would win and therefore were not prepared to intervene on short notice.

2. Waiting until the fighting reached the frontier region shortened lines of communication, making them more efficient and less vulnerable to air interdiction, and gave them time to deploy troops and replenish supplies depleted by help to North Korea.

3. In the frontier area, fullest advantage could be taken of world reaction to the threat against China.

4. It would be much easier to whip up support of public opinion if the immediate threat to the Manchurian border could be claimed—this despite the belief that the CCF leaders real-

ized the UN forces had no intention of crossing the Manchurian border.

As Willoughby put it, ". . . it seems incredible that the Chinese Communists have deluded themselves with their own propaganda and fear a U.S. attack on Manchuria.[52]

A much more acceptable interpretation was Chinese defense of the hydroelectric facilities. In his report for 9 November, Willoughby again pointed out the possibility that the enemy had been so determined in denial of the border to UN forces because of the importance of the Suiho dam and the power it supplied to Manchuria, Port Arthur, and Dairen (Dalian). He believed loss of the facilities at Suiho would seriously impact those areas.

Throughout the month, there were continuing reports of further buildup, particularly in the X Corps zone. On 10 November, Willoughby reported a threatening buildup of enemy forces in the Chosin–Fusen Reservoir area—a force capable of taking the offensive southward to cut off U.S. forces north and east of Hungnam. This was probably the 27th CCF Army moving into position. On 18 November, he repeated this warning, coupling it with a report of 8,000 to 10,000 enemy troops located just to the west of the X Corps MSR. That force—probably the 20th CCF Army, together with what was estimated to be the equivalent of four divisions in the Chosin–Fusen area—had considerable potential.[53]

The withdrawal from contact on 6 November lent weight to the belief in the Eighth Army that the Chinese were intent only on defending. The pattern of CCF resistance developed with light to little resistance on the left flank of the army, coupled with increasing resistance in the II ROK Corps zone. On 16 November, the Eighth Army reported a possible increase in enemy strength in the Tokchon area, but no indication of an impending general attack, although there were enough forces to support such an attack.[54] On 18 November, it appeared that enemy resistance in the eastern portion of the zone was decreasing, and the enemy was preparing to withdraw to the north.[55]

This pattern continued until about 20 November, when the Chinese, concerned that the deliberate UNC advance would reveal their concentrations, withdrew farther in the II ROK Corps zone. Willoughby thought the general withdrawal might indicate a high-level decision to defend from previously prepared positions, but he thought it too early to tell clearly. He did make the obligatory ob-servation—as had Tarkenton in Eighth Army and Quinn in X Corps—that such withdrawals were a Chinese tactic that, in the past, had preceded offensive action.

By 25 November, Willoughby reported there were some indica-tions pointing to a possible CCF withdrawal all the way to the Yalu, or even across into Manchuria. Unconfirmed reports gave possible reasons as heavy casualties and lack of the will to fight. The lull in the fighting, the loss of contact in some sectors, and the return of UN prisoners might well have indicated such an operation was un-der way.[56]

Since 5 November, Willoughby had listed "conduct offensive op-erations" as the enemy's first capability. On 25 November, as the Eighth Army offensive got under way, that dropped to second place, with "reinforcement" again as the first capability. On 26 November, he was bold enough to state: "It is now considered unlikely that the enemy will operate extensively on the flank of the Eighth Army," and that there was ". . . no evidence of new reinforcement other than the nine to twelve divisions already noted."

The Chinese strength in Korea by this time totaled thirty divisions in eight armies—more than 380,000 men. Based on those uncon-firmed reports—which may well have originated with the Central Mil-itary Commission of the PRC and been delivered by intercepted ra-dio messages—Willoughby believed the Chinese were suffering heavy casualties, had lost the will to fight, and might be withdrawing.

Accumulating Enemy Information in X Corps
X Corps produced a lengthy study of the Chagang-do Redoubt on 2 November. The basic X Corps assumption was that enemy forces would withdraw to the Chagang Redoubt for a final stand, or as a location from which they would withdraw into Manchuria. The ap-pearance of the Chinese—together with reports of an increasing buildup in the Chosin–Fusen area and to the north—was regarded principally as an increase in the enemy's defensive capabilities,

and secondarily as possible preparations for resumption of offensive operations.

As the Chinese withdrew from the Funchillin Pass and the 7th Marines advanced, reports of continued buildup both in the Chosin area and the Eighth Army area to the west focused attention on a possible enemy attack on the increasingly exposed X Corps flank and MSR. The possibility was discussed on 8 and 10 November, and again on 15 November, when reports were received of a convoy moving south from Yudam-ni to Chang-ni, and civilians reported Chinese forces in Sinha-ri, just 13 miles west of Koto-ri.

On 8 November, units of the 31st Infantry, twelve miles southeast of the Fusen Reservoir, had a running fight with an estimated battalion of Chinese, capturing several prisoners from the 376th Regiment of the 126th CCF Division. The Chinese withdrew. A week later, a patrol from the 3d Battalion of the 31st Infantry, now north of the Fusen Reservoir, encountered some 200 Chinese soldiers and drove them away after a brief firefight. In contrast to the fight the Chinese had put up at the Funchillin Pass, the desultory resistance to the 31st Infantry led the regimental commander and other officers to regard the Chinese with contempt.[57]

The next week provided only fragmentary information and fleeting glimpses of the Chinese. Colonel Quinn concluded: "The enemy's recent delaying operations are apparently concluded and he is once again withdrawing to the north." He opined that the enemy had suffered casualties, but the favorable terrain to which he was withdrawing would, to some extent, offset these losses: "With winter weather and good terrain he can present a stubborn defense."[58] The next day, it appeared at X Corps headquarters that the enemy was accelerating his withdrawal. The enemy forces were being compressed against the Manchurian border. His forces were in danger of being split by the drive to Hyesan-jin.[59]

The lull ended on 20 November. An agent reported the start of the CCF buildup in Samdaepyong, west of Koto-ri. Activity in Yudam-ni was reported by a civilian coming in through the lines with information that new troops had arrived to relieve CCF units in Yudam-ni, who then went north. The next day, there were reports of more troops moving through the town and going south. This was followed by an agent's report stating that enemy troops in the mountains between Yudam-ni and Huksu-ri were setting up defense lines.[60] On 21 November, a company patrol of the 1st Battalion, 7th Marines, had a brisk firefight with Chinese near the Toktong Pass. Air reconnaissance reported troops dug in on the high ground south of Yudam-ni.

Radically new information was obtained on 23 November, when the 1st Battalion, 7th Marines, captured two prisoners who turned out to be deserters from the 267th Regiment, 89th CCF Division, 20th Army. The PWs reported that there were three more divisions of their army in the general area. They said they had crossed the Yalu ten days earlier. This was an entirely new army and new army group, and it created additional confusion, because the 89th Division was not in the order of battle for the 20th Army but rather in the 30th Army. The prisoners also said that the 10th Army Group had entered Korea at the same time as the 9th Army Group.[61] Two days later, the 7th Marines captured six more prisoners.

Advancing toward Yudam-ni, the 1st Battalion, 7th Marines, estimated the town was defended by at least a battalion. An air observer reported what appeared to be another battalion located just north of Yudam-ni, where they had been dug in position in the snow since the previous night. All roads west of the reservoir gave the appearance of recent use. Civilians reported that many enemy were observed setting up defensive positions on the high ground about seven miles northwest of Yudam-ni.

More details were provided by civilians picked up on 22 November. They reported that a CCF officer had ordered their father to take an oxcart of grain from Muchon-ni to Yongji, about five miles northeast of Yudam-ni. A collecting point had been established at Yongji, and all civilians had been evacuated to make room for fresh CCF troops. CCF troops were moving south along the road from Changpyong-ni, about fifteen miles north of Yongji. That evening, the X Corps G-2 reported that the enemy apparently was preparing to make a defensive stand in his present positions, but that there was no evidence to indicate any considerable number of CCF units having crossed the border since the initial reinforcement.[62]

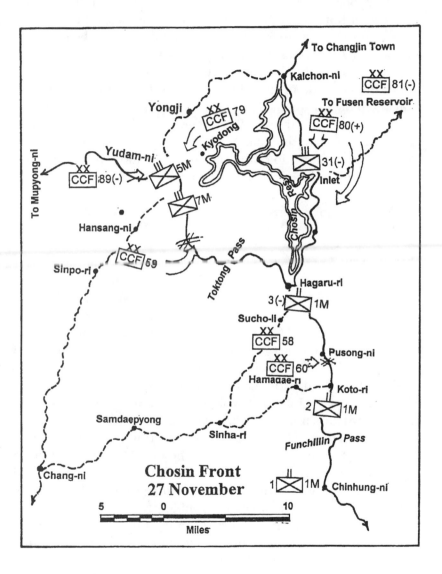

To Changjin Town

Kalchon-ni

CCF 81(-)

Yongji

CCF 79

To Fusen Reservoir

Kyodong

CCF 80(+)

To Mupyong-ni

Yudam-ni

5M

31(-)

CCF 89(-)

Inlet

7M

Chosin Res.

Hansang-ni

CCF 59

Sinpo-ri

Toktong Pass

Hagaru-ri

3 (-) 1M

Sucho-li

CCF 58

Pusong-ni

CCF 60

Koto-ri

Hamagae-ri

2 1M

Samdaepyong

Sinha-ri

Funchillin Pass

Chang-ni

**Chosin Front
27 November**

1 1M Chinhung-ni

5   0   10

Miles

By 24 November, civilians reported that the number of enemy at Samdaepyong had increased to 35,000. They were sending patrols east toward Koto-ri and the MSR. A seven-man patrol had entered Sinha-ri on 23 November and told the people there to be prepared to house 10,000 troops.[63] South of Yudam-ni, the 1st Battalion, 7th Marines, was in continuing contact with a Chinese force.

On the east side of the Chosin Reservoir, the 5th Marines, advancing to the north, first learned from civilians that some 400 Chinese had moved north from Sinhung-ni several days earlier. On 24 November, a 5th Marines patrol had a firefight with 100 to 150 Chinese at the northern tip of the reservoir. Two more patrol contacts were made in the vicinity of the Pungnyuri River. Then, at 3 A.M., an enemy raiding party attacked a 5th Marines roadblock in an apparent attempt to take a prisoner. Several Chinese were killed trying to drag away a wounded Marine.[64]

X Corps Changes Direction

Almond sent his revised plan for the attack west to MacArthur for review on 23 November. Competition between Wright and Almond ended on 24 November, when General MacArthur approved X Corps Operation Plan No. 8, draft 3, with a minor change of boundaries. In the same message, MacArthur ordered the plan executed at the earliest possible date. Almond could set his own D day.[65]

MacArthur's order to X Corps to execute was totally unexpected. The bulk of the 7th Infantry Division had been shifted well away from the westward direction of attack. General Almond has been criticized for ignoring the need to assist the Eighth Army and tacitly evading his orders. But the evidence seems to be that Almond had looked upon the westward attack only as a contingency plan to be executed if or when the Eighth Army got into serious trouble. He obviously did not think they were in serious trouble.

On receipt of MacArthur's order, Almond immediately issued a warning order to all units. By noon on 25 November, the 7th Infantry Division was to relieve the 5th Marines (now moving up the east side of the Chosin Reservoir) with no less than one infantry battalion. The battalion initially would be attached to the 1st Marine Division.

By 1 December, the 1st Marine Division was to complete an airfield already under construction at Hagaru-ri.[66]

That evening, X Corps Operation Order No. 7 was issued. X Corps was to attack at 8 A.M. on 27 November, sever the enemy lines of communication at Mupyong-ni, and destroy the enemy in the zone to the northern boundary of Korea along the Yalu River on the left and to the mouth of the Tumen River on the right. The 1st Marine Division was to attack at 8 A.M., seize Mupyong-ni, and advance to the Yalu River, destroying the enemy in its zone. The 7th Infantry Division was to attack northward from the Chosin Reservoir, advancing to the Yalu River and destroying the enemy in its zone, and to secure the Pungsan area. I ROK Corps was to continue the advance. The 3d Infantry Division had a series of assigned tasks, including protection of the Wonsan area as well as the left flank of X Corps. All units were given a series of admonitions, including: (1) All echelons of command exert utmost energy to surmount weather and terrain conditions; (2) Employ air and artillery support to maximum along axes of advance; (3) Rigidly enforce necessary measures to conserve food and fuel supplies; (4) Exploit to the maximum the superior capabilities of our troops and equipment.[67]

Accompanying the X Corps operation order, the intelligence estimate reported that the 126th CCF Division had sideslipped to the southwest, while the 124th CCF Division was not located. It noted the new identification, the 89th CCF Division. According to the estimate, the enemy capabilities were: (1) Delay with two divisions and create a stalemate; (2) Reinforce with additional divisions of the army, of which the 89th Division is a part, in order to improve defensive capability; (3) Limited-objective attacks against the MSR with the 126th Division and North Korean elements.[68]

MacArthur's order set Almond to scrambling for army units to dispatch to the Chosin Reservoir. He suggested to General Smith that he go ahead on his own while 7th Division units were moving. Smith declined to move until the 5th Marines could be relieved east of the reservoir and closed up with the 7th Marines at Yudam-ni. He planned to have the 5th Marines pass through and lead the attack.

The 7th Infantry Division staff, having been warned on 20 November of the possibility of reorienting their effort, had assumed there would be time to do so. They had planned for an orderly concentration of the regiments, then they would move them one by one. Instead, the force east of Chosin was assembled and moved forward in piecemeal fashion. Nothing in the X Corps operation order, or their own division operation order, said anything about providing flank protection for the 1st Marine Division. The order to the 7th Division, with no intermediate objectives, was an order for all-out advance without regard to adjacent units. A battalion of the 32d Infantry Regiment was rushed north to relieve the 5th Marines east of the reservoir so the Marines could be moved to Yudam-ni. The 7th Marines, moving one battalion toward Yudam-ni, now moved the remaining two battalions toward Yudam-ni to secure the town in preparation for the attack on 27 November.

As part of the plan, the rear boundary (between the 1st Marine Division and the 3d Infantry Division) was moved northward to a point just south of Hagaru-ri. This meant that the 3d Division needed to assume responsibility for the MSR as far as Hagaru. This would relieve the 1st Marines at Koto-ri and Chinhung-ni, allowing the entire regiment to close up on Hagaru-ri. There was no time to relieve the 1st Marines, other than to move portions of one battalion north to Hagaru-ri to relieve parts of the 7th Marines so they could move on to Yudam-ni.

"Home for Christmas" Begins
While X Corps units were scrambling to meet General Almond's deadline, the Eighth Army resumed the advance. General MacArthur had informed the Joint Chiefs of Staff on 18 November that the Eighth Army offensive would begin on 24 November. It would be aimed principally at enemy concentrations between Huichon and Kanggye. He reported: "The air attack of the last 10 days has been largely successful in isolating the battle area from added reinforcement and has greatly diminished the enemy flow of supply."[69]

With great fanfare, MacArthur flew to the Eighth Army on 24 November to watch the beginning of the attack. Based on a casual remark he made in the presence of reporters, it was dubbed the "Home for Christmas Offensive." That same day, MacArthur's headquarters in Tokyo released a unique communiqué:

> The United Nations massive compression envelopment in North Korea against the new Red Armies cooperating there is now approaching its decisive effort. The isolating component of the pincer, our Air Forces of all types, have for the past three weeks, in a sustained attack of model coordination and effectiveness, successfully interdicted enemy lines of support from the North so that further reinforcement therefrom has been sharply curtailed and essential supplies markedly limited. The eastern sector of the pincer [X Corps], with noteworthy and effective Naval support, has steadily advanced in a brilliant tactical movement and has now reached a commanding enveloping position, cutting in to the northern reaches of the enemy's geographical potential. This morning the western sector of the pincer moves forward in general assault in an effort to complete the compression and close the vise. If successful this should for all practical purposes end the war, restore peace and unity to Korea, enable the prompt withdrawal of United Nations military forces, and permit the complete assumption by the Korean people and nation of full sovereignty and international equality. It is that for which we fight. Douglas MacArthur.

Aside from the florid prose and the inflated description, the message gave the Chinese valuable intelligence. It told them, if they didn't know it before, that X Corps was changing direction and that their huge reinforcement had still not been detected.

MacArthur was not the only optimist. On 24 November, the CIA issued an estimate that, despite the obligatory qualifications, presented a favorable view. It said the Chinese would, at the same time, maintain Chinese–North Korean holding operations in North Korea, maintain or increase their military strength in Manchuria, and seek to obtain UN withdrawal from Korea by intimidation and diplomatic means. Failing that, there would be increasing intervention in Korea, although it was not believed the Chinese had the capability of driving UN forces from Korea. They were capable, however, of tying down UN forces and maintaining a North Korean state in being.

In support of those conclusions, the CIA estimate pointed out that the activities of Chinese troops in Korea up to that point did not demonstrate any plan for major operations, but the buildup in Manchuria and elsewhere was on a scale that would support major operations.

The estimate gave no indication of what the intimidation would consist of or what the diplomatic means might be, but it did point out that the Chinese delegation now on the way to the United Nations was believed to be willing to reach a diplomatic settlement that probably would require the withdrawal of foreign troops from Korea.[70]

The estimate echoed Willoughby's assumption that the Chinese forces in Korea were limited. They could be reinforced, but that would take some time.

Last-Minute Movements

In his memoirs, Hong Xuezhi, deputy commander of the Chinese People's Volunteers, said they had a basic perception of the enemy's plan of attack, but on 24 November they once again revised their scheduled operations plan. The 9th CCF Army Group plan was to take its main force and destroy two regiments of the 1st Marine Division. After that, they were to destroy the remaining units.[71] The 59th and 89th Divisions of the 20th CCF Army and the 79th Division of the 27th CCF Army would be concentrated against the forces expected at Yudam-ni. The 58th CCF Division would attack and seize Hagaru-ri, and the 60th CCF Division would cut the road between Hagaru and Koto-ri and isolate Koto-ri. The 80th Division of the 27th Army would attack the units on the east side of the reservoir. The 81st Division would move down the west side of the Fusen Reservoir, cutting what the Chinese believed were lateral communications between the 1st Marine Division and the 7th Infantry Division.[72]

Until 24 November, and MacArthur's pronouncement, the Chinese appear to have believed that the 1st Marine Division would continue northward past the Chosin Reservoir toward the border, and that the 7th Infantry Division, upon reaching the Yalu at Hyesan-jin, would then turn left and advance down the river toward Singalpo-jin and Linjiang. Their estimate appears to have been that the 7th Marines would occupy Yudam-ni and Hagaru-ri while the 5th Marines advanced to the north on the east side of the reservoir. Accordingly, the 20th CCF Army was deployed to operate on the left flank of the 1st Marine Division to threaten that flank and to screen the left flank of the Chinese armies west of the mountains; the 27th Army was poised to intercept the 5th Marines; and the 26th Army was deployed to the east as a reserve and to cover the advance of the 7th Infantry Division.

Peng Dehuai planned to launch his counteroffensive against the Eighth Army on 25 November. The 9th CCF Army Group would commence the same day. But substantial redeployment was needed for 9th Army Group forces. General Song Shilun reported that he could not launch his attack on 25 November, and he requested a two-day delay. It was approved.[13]

During the next two days, CCF units moved into new attack positions. The 79th Division moved southward to an attack position in the vicinity of Yongji, prepared to attack the 1st Marine Division units at Yudam-ni in conjunction with the 89th Division, while the 59th Division cut the road south of Yudam-ni. The 58th Division moved northeastward to attack positions in the vicinity of Sangpyong-ni, ready to attack and seize Hagaru-ri. The 60th Division moved westward to the vicinity of Sinha-ri, with the mission of cutting the road between Hagaru and Koto-ri in the vicinity of Pusong-ni. On the east side of the reservoir, the 80th CCF Division, with one regiment of the 81st attached, moved into position to destroy the units at Sin-hung-ni and Neidongjik.

Fragmentary bits of information on the Chinese trickled in. On 25 November, a civilian living in the mountains about five miles southwest of Yudam-ni reported he was forced to accompany a CCF patrol toward the Hagaru–Yudam-ni Road at a point north of Sin-hung-ni (near Toktong Pass). Harassing artillery fire forced this patrol to withdraw, and the men returned to a place near the civilian's home, where about 2,000 CCF troops were assembled. The patrol then proceeded to Sojung-ni, in the valley about four miles southwest of Yudam-ni, where all civilian buildings were found to be full of CCF troops. The civilian escaped and returned to his home in Hansang-ni, farther up the valley.[74]

The X Corps PIR for 25 November believed the enemy would defend generally along the line Changjin–Yudam-ni and Sachang-ni. There was further evidence of strong reinforcement of this area by CCF troops moving from the Chosin area down the valley to Sachang-ni, creating a serious threat to the left flank of X Corps.[75]

Despite the identification of the 89th CCF Division and the other information, the 1st Marine Division G-2 noted the seizure of Yudam-ni and commented: "Failure to conduct a more determined defense of the vital Yudam-ni area suggests a general weakness in the defensive capabilities of the enemy forces located to our immediate front. Apparently the recent enemy reinforcement of the Yudam-ni area was not in such strength as to permit more than a token delay against our continued advance. Undoubtedly the deterioration of defensive capabilities noted above is a direct result of his preoccupation with the western front. That preoccupation may well prove fatal. In light of the above it is believed that the enemy in his present strength is capable of conducting no more than a delaying action against our advance to Mupyong-ni."[76]

The PIR did carry a comment that the 20th CCF Army elements identified by the prisoners may have sideslipped to the southwest, where they would threaten the MSR. The PIR also reported that evening that information from the Eighth Army indicated enemy of unknown size was attacking across the front of the II ROK Corps. Tokchon was evacuated. The 2d and 25th Infantry Divisions were receiving counterattacks and withdrawing slightly. A later report from X Corps, which turned out to be erroneous, said that Tokchon had been recaptured.

The attack west toward Mupyong-ni went off on the morning of 27 November. That same morning, D Company, 7th Marines, moved out on a company combat patrol toward Kyodong-ni, north of Hill 1240, along the shore of the reservoir. Well short of their patrol objective, the company ran into heavy enemy fire and was withdrawn to take up defensive positions on Hill 1240. To the north, its companion company, E Company (2d Bn, 7th Marines), spent the day watching white-clad figures moving across the landscape.

To the south at Koto-ri, refugees from Hamadae-ri, approximately two miles west of Koto-ri, reported that there had been a buildup of about 4,000 to 5,000 North Korean and CCF troops in the areas two to three miles west of Hamadae-ri. A combat patrol from the 2d Battalion, 1st Marines, encountered enemy resistance just west of Koto-ri. Captured Chinese said they were part of an enemy division in that area.

The most ominous report came from three men captured by a patrol from the 1st Battalion, 7th Marines, a mile and a half southwest of Yudam-ni. They claimed to be from the 60th Division, 20th Corps, 9th Army Group, Third CCF Field Army. They had deserted from their unit on 21 November and surrendered to the patrol on 26 November. They said the 20th Army entered Korea on 11 November from Manchuria and arrived in Yudam-ni on 21 and 22 November. They said the 60th Division was the leading unit in the move southward, followed by the 59th and 58th Divisions, in that order. The 20th Army, when last seen, was heading west-southwest to a point at which it would swing south and position itself for an attack on the 1st Marine Division MSR. The 58th Division passed them moving south on 23 November. The attack of the 20th Army was to be in accordance with the following conditions: (1) Only to be conducted when two UN regiments have passed to the north of the 20th Army; (2) only to be conducted at night because that is the only time the mission can be accomplished with the number of troops and because of air attacks in the daytime.

The PWs further stated that there was an artillery regiment with the 20th Army consisting of horse-drawn, 122mm mountain guns. The mission of the 42d CCF Army (124th and 126th Divisions) was to contain the advance of UN units into the Chosin Reservoir area. They had no knowledge of the 89th Division.[77]

General Smith believed that Chinese strength in the reservoir area was considerable. General Almond doubted there were more than one or two CCF divisions, comprising 10,000 to 20,000 men, on the Chosin front.[78]

To recap, the Far Eastern Command estimated between 40,000 and 70,935 Chinese in Korea, plus 82,799 North Korean troops. X Corps estimated that the enemy was capable only of delay with two divisions. The 1st Marine Division estimated that the enemy was capable of defending with two divisions. In actuality, the Chinese had thirty divisions with a total of 380,000 men in Korea. In the X Corps zone, there were twelve divisions with 150,000 men.

That night, the 7th Marines ordered a full alert. As darkness settled in, elements of six of the twelve Chinese divisions moved forward from their assembly area to attack positions, with the mission of destroying the 1st Marine Division and elements of the 7th Infantry Division.

Notes

1. Based on handwritten notes, Headquarters 66th CCF Army, and published in X Corps Intelligence Bulletin dated 30 Dec. 50. A similar critique was forwarded by Mao to the 19th CCF Army Group: Mao Telegrams, No. 5, 30 Oct. 50.

2. Mao Telegrams, No. 26, 22 Nov. 50: to the 19th Army Group.

3. CINCUNC msg C-68324 to Walker, 5 Nov. 50, quoted in *History of the Korean Conflict*, 37. The anonymous author of this FEC history notes that there is no record of any similar message(s) having been directed to General Almond.

4. Ibid.

5. FEC C69898, 27 Nov. 50 to DEPTAR, Personal Hickey to Ridgway.

6. Mao Telegrams, No. 11, 2 Nov. 50.

7. Mao Telegrams, No. 19, 5 Nov. 50.

8. Mao Telegrams, No. 15, 5 Nov. 50.

9. O. P. Smith, *Aide-Memoire*, Marine Corps Historical Center, 1178.

10. Hong Xuezhi, *Recollections of the War to Resist U.S. Aggression and Aid Korea* (Beijing: PLA Publishing House, 1990). Unpublished partial translation in author's possession.

11. Spurr, *Enter the Dragon*, 169.

12. Zhang, *Mao's Military Romanticism*, 108.

13. Hong, *Recollections*, 69.

14. Mao Telegrams, No. 22, 13 Nov. 50.

15. Mao Telegrams, No. 24, 18 Nov. 50.

16. Marine air units reported artillery being emplaced in the vicinity of Changpyong-ni on 24 November and had reported other activity north of there: 1st Mar Div PIR 33, 24 Nov. 50.

17. Agent report, 1st Mar Div PIR 27, 20 Nov. 50.

18. Appleman, *South to the Naktong*, 638–40.

19. *History of the Korean Conflict*, 26.

20. Ibid., 7.

21. DEPTAR msg W96469 to FEC 15 Nov. 50.

22. Ibid., 9.

23. X Corps msg X 12561 to CG Eighth Army. By order of Gen-

eral MacArthur, the Eighth Army, although on a different coast, had been made responsible for logistic support of X Corps.

24. 7th Infantry Division Periodic Logistics Report 24 Nov. 50.

25. MacArthur, *Reminiscences*, 371–72.

26. *HJCS*, 329 n78: Lt. Gen. Edward M. Almond interview by Capt. Thomas G. Ferguson, 29 March 1975. Almond Papers, MHI.

27. Stanton, *America's Tenth Legion*, 168.

28. *HJCS*, 305.

29. Condit, *History of the Secretary of Defense*, 78.

30. *Command Report*, FEC, November 1950: Part I, 8.

31. X Corps Operation Order No. 6, 11 Nov. 50.

32. There was an acute shortage of trucks in X Corps. Two provisional truck companies, each with thirty-four trucks, were formed by taking trucks from corps units in fixed positions around Hungnam. *X Corps Command Report*, 50. To further augment truck transportation in Korea, trucks were taken from some service units in Japan and replaced by contracting out transportation with Japanese companies.

33. JSPOG Staff Study, "X Corps Assistance to Eighth Army 12 Nov 50," quoted in *History of the Korean Conflict*, 20–23.

34. FEC DIS 2985, 11 Nov. 50.

35. JSPOG Staff Study, op cit.

36. CINCUNC msg CX 69009 to X Corps 15 Nov. 50.

37. CG X Corps letter 14 Nov. 50 to General Wright.

38. *Special Report on Chosin Reservoir: 27 November to 10 December 1950*. X Corps. "Engineer Report," 54.

39. Lt. Gen. O. P. Smith to CMC 15 Nov. 50: Papers of Gen. O. P. Smith, Archives Branch, Marine Corps Research Center, Quantico, Virginia.

40. CINCUNC msg CX 69009 to X Corps, op. cit.

41. *Special Report*, X Corps, 9. The report states that one RCT of the 7th Division was to be assigned the mission of flank protection of the 1st Marine Division, but the order executing this plan makes no mention of that mission.

42. G-3 FEC Memo to Chief of Staff 17 Nov. 50.

43. Draft message FEC G-3 Top Secret file 722, 17 Nov. 50.

44. Eric Hammel, *Chosin: Heroic Ordeal of the Korean War* (New York: Vanguard Press, 1981), 9 (quoting letter from Ruffner).

45. This section is a summary of information contained in FEC DIS 2982 to 3000, 8–26 Nov. 1950.

46. FEC DIS 2988, 14 Nov. 50.

47. FEC DIS 2986, 12 Nov. 50.

48. Change 1 to Annex "A" Intelligence to Operation Plan No. 14, Eighth Army 18 Nov. 50. The detailed figures as given do not add up to 48,000, but we can apparently assume additional strength in miscellaneous Army units.

49. FEC DIS 2993, 18 Nov. 50.

50. Allied Translation and Interrogation Service (ATIS) Interrogation Report 2279, 17 Nov. 50.

51. Telegram Rankin (Taipei) to Sec State, *FRUS,* 1069–70.

52. FEC DIS 2989, 15 Nov. 50.

53. FEC DIS 2984, 10 Nov. 50, and DIS 2993, 18 Nov. 50.

54. 8A PIR 127, 16 Nov. 50.

55. 8A PIR 129, 18 Nov. 50.

56. FEC DIS 2999, 25 Nov. 50.

57. Blair, *The Forgotten War,* 390.

58. X Corps PIR 53, 18 Nov. 50.

59. X Corps PIR 54, 19 Nov. 50.

60. 1st Mar Div PIRs 28–29, 21–22 Nov. 50.

61. 1st Mar Div PIR 30, 23 Nov. 50.

62. X Corps PIR 57, 22 Nov. 50.

63. 1st Mar Div PIR 31, 24 Nov. 50.

64. 1st Mar Div Historical Diary, 25 Nov. 50.

65. CINCFE msg CX 69661, 23 Nov. 50, to X Corps. There was some belief at the time that the selection of General Almond's plan over that proposed by General Wright was influenced by the fact that General Almond was still the chief of staff of the Far Eastern Command. Almond, in his comments on the manuscript of *Policy and Direction,* calls this unfair (Almond letter to Gen. Hal Pattison, Office of the Chief of Military History, 20 February 1969, Almond Papers, MHI).

66. X Corps msg 241239I, Nov. 50, 7th Div G-3 Jnl No. 869.

67. X Corps Operation Order No. 7, 24 Nov. 50.

68. Appendix 1 to Annex A, Intelligence Estimate, X Corps Operation Order No. 7, 24 Nov. 50.

69. ClNCFE msg C 69211 to DEPTAR for JCS 18 Nov. 50, quoted in *HJCS*, 322.

70. National Intelligence Estimate 2/1, 24 Nov. 50, *FRUS*, 1220.

71. Hong, *Recollections*, 73.

72. *Chinese People's Volunteers.*

73. Hong, *Recollections*, 74

74. 1st Mar Div PIR 32, 25 Nov. 50.

75. X Corps PIR 60, 25 Nov. 50.

76. 1st Mar Div PIR 33, 26 Nov. 50.

77. 1st Mar Div PIR 34, 27 Nov. 50.

78. Blair, *The Forgotten War*, 423.

11
Defeat and Withdrawal of the Eighth Army

Our losses were devastating. The next day we could find only thirty-seven men of our battalion.

—Captain Harris Pope,
I Company, 9th Infantry, describing Kunu-ri

The Eighth Army Resumes the Offensive

On the morning of 24 November, the Eighth Army jumped off in the attack with four U.S. divisions, four ROK divisions, and two brigades, RCT-size units, in the second attempt to reach the Yalu River. Eighth Army intelligence estimated the enemy strength at 48,000 in six divisions. The actual enemy strength was close to 230,000 in eighteen divisions.

The Eighth Army—with modern communications, ample artillery support, tanks, and backed by adequate logistic support—was not significantly inferior in terms of combat power to the much more numerous but primitive Chinese. Still, there were problems and weaknesses. The 2d, 24th, and 25th Infantry Divisions were in relatively good shape, although understrength in the rifle companies. The 1st Cavalry Division, in army reserve, was still recovering from the serious damage done to it earlier in the month. The 7th Cavalry Regiment was in good shape, the 5th somewhat less so, but the 8th was still not back to form. Of the independent brigades, the 27th Commonwealth was in good condition, but the Turkish Brigade was an untested and unknown factor.

In II ROK Corps, in the rough terrain on the vital right flank, it was a different story. To begin with, the ROK divisions were smaller and had only one supporting artillery battalion rather than the four organic to the U.S. divisions. They had no armor and no corps artillery. Only the 8th ROK Division was in relatively good condition. The 7th ROK Division had lost heavily defending Kunu-

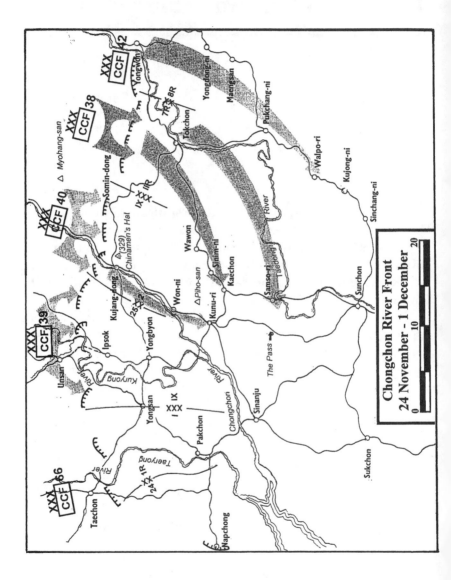

Chongchon River Front
24 November – 1 December

ri in the first Chinese attack. Raw new replacements filled much of its ranks. The 6th ROK Division had taken the heaviest hit of all. As the offensive opened, only the 21st ROK Regiment in that division was battle-worthy. The other regiments were still being reorganized.

Here's the lineup of the Army, from left to right. In the I Corps zone on the left, the 24th Division would advance west toward Chongju, then north. To its right, the 1st ROK Division would advance between the Taeryong and Kuryong Rivers toward Taechon. The 1st ROK Division was considered a very reliable unit. It had proved its mettle from the days along the Naktong. In the center of the line, IX Corps, with the 25th Division on the left and the 2d Division on the right, held a sector that ran from Kojang-dong to a point about five miles east of the Chongchon River. The 25th Division was to seize Unsan, while the 2d Division was to attack northward to seize Huichon. Myohyang-san (Hill 1226 in U.S. narratives) lay in the path of the 2d Division. Myohyang-san had been designated by Mao Zedong as one of the key positions guarding the Chinese deployment area in the Huichon–Kanggye sector.

On the far right, II ROK Corps was deployed with the 7th ROK Division on the left, extending to a point about six miles northeast of Tokchon. From there, the 8th ROK Division extended east to Yongwon, then bent southward to Maengsan. The 6th ROK Division, with just the 21st ROK Regiment present, was in reserve at Tokchon. The mission of II ROK Corps was the seizure of a town just to the north of Huichon. The zone of II ROK Corps, virtually devoid of roads, was the steepest and most broken in the Eighth Army zone. The village of Haengchen-dong, another point designated by Mao as a critical part in the defense of the Huichon–Kanggye area, lay within the II ROK Corps zone.

Along with the 1st Cavalry Division, the 27th Commonwealth Brigade and the Turkish Brigade made up the Eighth Army reserve.

General MacArthur flew in from Tokyo for the start of the offensive. On the return trip to Tokyo, he ordered his pilot to fly north and along the Yalu River for a personal reconnaissance. Arriving back in Tokyo, he issued an optimistic addition to his "massive compression communiqué," stating: "The giant UN pincer moved according to schedule today. The air forces, in full strength, completely interdicted the rear areas and air reconnaissance behind the enemy line, and along the entire length of the Yalu River border, showed little sign of hostile military activity. . . . Our losses were extraordinarily light. . . ."[1]

Afterward, he wrote that the tour of the front worried him, that the Eighth Army line was deplorably weak in numbers, and that the II ROK Corps was not yet in good shape. Nevertheless, the attack had gone forward.

The Chinese Counteroffensive Begins

For the first two days, all units moved cautiously forward without serious resistance, with three exceptions. On the right of I Corps, in the 1st ROK Division zone, the Chinese counterattacked the 11th ROK Regiment in strength on the first night. Pressure continued for the next two days, eventually forcing the ROKs back. In IX Corps sector, the 24th Infantry, advancing on the right of the 25th Division, moved north through a roadless area of broken hills, becoming separated and fragmented along the way and creating a vulnerable spot in the Eighth Army line. On the far right, II ROK Corps advanced well, except in the area northeast of Tokchon at the boundary of the 7th and 8th ROK Divisions. Here the Chinese defended stubbornly. On the extreme right flank of II ROK Corps, what appears to have been a Chinese reconnaissance force attacked the advance battalion of the 16th ROK Regiment east of Yongdong-ni and forced it back two miles.

Then, on the night of 25–26 November, the Chinese went over to the attack and struck in full force.

The crucial blows fell in the zone of II ROK Corps. Just after dark on 25 November, two divisions of the 38th CCF Army, reinforced with a division from the 41st Army, struck in two places. In the 7th ROK Division zone, they thrust deep between the 3d and 5th ROK Regiments. With all three regiments on line and without reserves, the ROK division was helpless to close the gap. Forced backward, the 3d ROK Regiment withdrew into the zone of the 38th Infantry on the right of the 2d Infantry Division.

Farther east, the 112th and 113th Divisions of the 38th CCF Army struck at the boundary between the 7th and 8th ROK Divisions. Within hours, the two Chinese divisions had penetrated between the two ROK divisions. Reinforcing units were moving through the gap. Both penetrations converged toward Tokchon.

On the far right, the 125th CCF Division soon drove the 21st ROK Regiment from Yongwon and headed south. The 124th and 126th CCF Divisions drove through Aechang, heading for Yongdong-ni and Maengsan in an attempt at a deep turning movement into the rear of the Eighth Army.

By morning, II ROK Corps was in chaos; by evening, it was in splinters. Attempts to seal off the penetrations failed. Chinese troops continued to filter through the rear areas of II ROK Corps, establishing blocks on the principal roads. The Chinese secured Tokchon early in the afternoon. American military advisory personnel were calling for air evacuation from their ROK units.

Second Infantry Division

In an attempt to present a continuous line, forces of the 2d Infantry Division were stretched to the limit. Units were thinly scattered across a broken and hostile landscape, with few reserves to back them up. Companies seldom were within supporting distance of each other. In some cases, even platoons within companies were not within supporting distance. Often out of radio or telephone contact with their parent battalions, unable to call for supporting fire from organic mortars or supporting artillery, the front-line rifle companies were deprived of their great advantage—the concentrated combat power of a balanced force of combined arms. Without that help, the companies were forced to fight the far more numerous Chinese on the basis of primitive equality—man for man, rifle for rifle, grenade for grenade.

On the night of 25 November, 2d Division units were casually disposed in whatever locations they had reached after the day's advance. The front line was a sieve. As night fell, Chinese units began moving boldly through the gaps between units, often without notice or opposition, in some cases turning to attack the front-line companies from the rear.

On the left of the 2d Division in the 9th Infantry sector, an entire regiment of Chinese moved at a trot down a dry creek bed, passing two isolated 9th Infantry companies. Without pause, the Chinese dropped off forces that cleared out the two companies, leaving only a few survivors of each to straggle into friendly territory to tell of their fate. The main force continued down the stream bed, crossed the Chongchon River, and drove through a portion of the supporting artillery, stopping only when unexpectedly confronted by a reserve battalion of the 23d Infantry. Following units crossed the river, attacked and overran the 2d Battalion, 9th Infantry CP, then occupied Hill 329, commonly called the "Chinaman's Hat," which then became a small Chinese redoubt in the middle of the 2d Division's zone. The "Hat" resisted all attempts to secure it for the next two days.

In the 38th Infantry sector on the right of the 2d Division, and adjoining the failing ROKs, the Chinese expunged A Company, which had been forward of the line on a long patrol, destroyed G Company, and overran L Company and the 3d Battalion CP. As dawn broke on 26 November, the 38th Infantry found troops of the 3d ROK Regiment, supposedly on their right, drifting back into their zone under pressure from the Chinese, bringing tales of the Chinese attack. Colonel George B. Peploe, the regimental commander, realized that not only was his right flank in danger; the right flank of the division and perhaps that of the entire Eighth Army was in jeopardy.

Farther West

The 25th Division attacked with the 35th Infantry on the left; Task Force (TF) Dolvin, a composite group of tanks and infantry, in the center; and the 24th Infantry on the right. The 27th Infantry was in reserve. The 24th Infantry, attacking through some very broken and confusing terrain with all three battalions on line, was halted by the Chinese and counterattacked. A portion of the 2d Battalion broke off, drifted eastward into the 2d Division sector, and joined the 2d Battalion, 9th Infantry, for the next few days.

The Chinese attack on Task Force Dolvin drove one company from its objective with very heavy losses. Infiltrators bypassed the front-line units and struck at the artillery, overrunning one battery before being driven off. By daylight, the task force had lost one hill but otherwise held the previous night's position. On the left of TF Dolvin, the 35th Infantry, west of the Kuryong River, spent a quiet night.

The 1st ROK Division had been under continuous attack by elements of the 66th CCF Army since the previous night. Becoming increasingly disorganized, the front-line units began to give way, exposing the flank of the 35th Infantry on its right.

The 50th CCF Army, deployed along the coast with the mission of protecting the approaches to Sinuiju, kept the 24th Division under observation but did not attack. The 24th Division spent a quiet night.

26 November

Instead of withdrawing at daylight, as was their usual practice, the Chinese in the II ROK Corps zone continued to press hard for exploitation. Yongwon had fallen. The 125th CCF Division was heading south toward Pukchang-ni. On the far right, the 124th and 126th CCF Divisions pressed on toward Songpyong and Maengsan.

In the 2d and 25th Division zones, the Chinese had drawn back at daylight. Without corps orders, local commanders took the initiative of assuming the defense and attempting to rectify their lines, bracing for further action. TF Dolvin, now commanded by the 25th Division's assistant commander, Brig. Gen. Vennard Wilson, drew back two miles and was reinforced with an engineer company, while the 2d Battalion, 27th Infantry, part of the division reserve, took positions to protect the artillery at Ipsok.

The 2d Division had taken the heaviest blow of U.S. units. Heavily battered the first night, the 9th Infantry was moved to the west of the Chongchon River and drawn back about a mile. Two battalions of the 23d Infantry were inserted into the line below the "Chinaman's Hat." In the 38th Infantry sector, some ground was regained. The regiment attempted to bend back the right-flank line facing to the east, but it lost two more companies in that attempt. Reorganized elements of the 3d ROK Regiment were moved into the line in an attempt to shore up the flank. General Laurence B. Keiser, commanding the 2d Division, recognizing the problem on the right flank, authorized Colonel Peploe to withdraw as necessary without further permission, in order to save his regiment.

With the collapse of II ROK Corps, the 2d Division became the effective right flank of the Eighth Army, threatened now by Chinese forces advancing southward down the Chongchon and westward from Tokchon. A breakthrough in the 2d Division sector would allow the Chinese to continue southwest down the Chongchon Valley and control the crossing points at Kunu-ri and Anju, isolating all forces north of the river. The 2d Division G-2 believed the Chinese capabilities were (1) Attack south in force against positions on the Chongchon River front; (2) Attack along the Tokchon–Kunu-ri axis to cut the division's main supply route and lines of communication.

The Chinese surprise was total and complete. The stunning reversal of the situation from optimistic attack to threatened destruction was so complete that comprehension lagged. Even though most division reserves had been committed, on 26 November it was not yet clear at corps and army level that a full-scale Chinese counteroffensive was under way and had the potential of enveloping the entire Army. In IX Corps and the 2d Infantry Division, it was believed that the attack of the previous night was a "local situation" that could be cleared up. Colonel Tarkenton, the Eighth Army G-2, upped his estimate of Chinese strength to 101,000, more than doubling his previous estimate. The Eighth Army reported: ". . . except for the vague situation on the east flank, the enemy reaction to EUSAK [Eighth U.S. Army in Korea] attack has been one of active defense with local counterattacks in strength." This was believed to be the most likely capability.[2]

Nevertheless, Gen. Walton Walker recognized the threat to his right flank. The road from Tokchon to Kunu-ri was one avenue of approach into the now-naked right flank of the Army. He ordered the Turkish Brigade, then at Kunu-ri, to advance east, to seize and defend Tokchon. By midnight, two Turkish battalions had been moved by motor shuttle to Wawon, prepared to advance from there.

The road south from Pukchang-ni to Sunchon was another route of approach, this one leading into the rear of the Army. Walker ordered the 1st Cavalry Division to be prepared to move to Sunchon to backstop the ROKs and block this avenue of approach. As a further precaution, he ordered the 27th Commonwealth Brigade from Pakchon to Kunu-ri as reserve for IX Corps.

The Night of 26–27 November

The Chinese attack continued after dark. It ground away at the 38th Infantry during the night of 26–27 November, with forces coming from the north and from the east. Action was focused around Somindong, the angle point of the 38th Infantry's defense. In a series of confusing engagements where ground was lost, regained, and lost again, the 38th Infantry was gradually forced back during the night and most of the following day.

The 23d Infantry was counterattacked and lost about 600 yards. The regimental command post was overrun. Across the river, the Chinese repulsed the much-reduced 2d Battalion, 9th Infantry, forcing it back across the river into the 23d Infantry's area. On its left, the remnants of the 3d Battalion were reinforced when two depleted companies of the 24th Infantry, forced eastward by Chinese attacks, joined up with the 3d Battalion, remaining with them for the next several days.

The situation in the 24th Infantry area became sufficiently confused to make it necessary for Gen. William B. Kean to order the remaining two battalions of his reserve, the 2d and 3d Battalions, 27th Infantry, up behind the 24th Infantry. It appeared that some time during the preceding day, one company had advanced too far and become trapped in Chinese territory. C Company, 24th Infantry, was ordered to assist. In moving toward the beleaguered company, C Company itself was surrounded by Chinese and surrendered as a unit.

Task Force Dolvin/Wilson was heavily attacked and took serious losses but was able, barely, to hold its position with support from the 2d Battalion, 27th Infantry, now a part of the TF. West of the Kuryong River, the 35th Infantry came under attack and now, with both flanks exposed, was ordered back to a new position three miles north of Yongsan-dong. Between the Kuryong and the Taeryong Rivers, the heaviest and most sustained attack continued against the 1st ROK

Division. There the 11th ROK Regiment finally gave way, withdrawing back through the 15th ROK Regiment, which, in turn, was forced back almost to Yongsan-dong.

On the extreme left flank, the 24th Division drew the 21st Infantry back from Chongju to Napchongjong. The 19th Infantry was ordered to take up a position near Pakchon as corps reserve, so it could, if needed, support the 1st ROK Division, which was being heavily pressed.

27 November
By the morning of 27 November, General Walker realized the extent of the II ROK Corps collapse. He took further steps. General John B. Coulter's IX Corps zone was extended to include all of the zone previously covered by II ROK Corps. To ease the load, the boundary between I and IX Corps was moved right to that between the 25th and 2d Divisions, with the 25th Division attached to I Corps. The 1st Cavalry Division was attached to IX Corps, with orders to move to Sunchon early on 28 November, then advance to Pukchang-ni. General Yu Jai Hung, II ROK Corps commander, was to provide one division, or its equivalent, to the 1st Cavalry Division. At that time, the 1st Cavalry Division was dispersed with the 8th Cavalry at Sinchang-ni on the road to Pukchang-ni, the 7th Cavalry was farther northeast at Kujong-ni, while the 5th Cavalry was at Kunu-ri.

In the western portion of the Eighth Army zone, the 25th Division and the 1st ROK Division continued to be hard-pressed by the 39th and 66th CCF Armies. Exposed by the withdrawal of the 1st ROK Division, the 35th Infantry was ordered back to a position just north of the vital road junction at Yongsan-dong. Task Force Dolvin/Wilson, badly mauled, was drawn back to Ipsok.

The most serious problem was faced by the 2d Division. Chinese forces were converging on it from the northwest and the north; other Chinese forces were driving in from the east through the gap in II ROK Corps. The pressure from three directions was bending back the 2d Division's line on both flanks. The 38th Infantry situation was critical. It had only one road, running east and west, by which it could withdraw or be resupplied. Twice the road had been blocked; twice it was reopened. Units were hurriedly committed to plug holes in the line. General Keiser decided that it was necessary to pull the entire division back to the vicinity of Kujang-dong, where it could be moved closer together. Orders were issued. By dark, the 38th Infantry was fighting its way westward to the Chongchon River Road.

The Turks had trucked eastward the previous night and reached Wawon about midnight. Reports came back of a rousing fight, with the Turks deciding the issue with the short swords they carried as sidearms. But by dawn, a Chinese-speaking U.S. Army officer arrived on the scene to find that the "Chinese" in fact had been withdrawing ROK forces. Hardly had this terrible blunder been resolved when the Turks, advancing eastward, collided with real Chinese. Details of the action are unknown, but it appears that the Chinese surrounded one Turk battalion, perhaps more. Some of the Turks were able to withdraw toward Sinnim-ni. Others managed to escape the trap and straggle westward and southward in the following days.

The 38th CCF Army, having secured Tokchon, moved on to the south. Parts of the army reached Pukchang-ni by the morning of 27 November. Two Chinese divisions advancing westward from Tokchon on the Kunu-ri Road had collided with the Turks and driven them back. At Pukchang-ni, the 113th CCF Division, spurred on by Gen. Peng Dehuai's public criticism of their laggard movement in the first CCF offensive, began a cross-country race toward Samso-ri, down the winding and roadless Taedong Valley, the side door into the Eighth Army's right flank.

About noon, the Eighth Army deputy chief of staff, Col. Eugene M. Landrum, telephoned a situation report to Gen. Doyle Hickey in Tokyo. The message, as dictated over the phone, said: "Indications are that enemy is no longer on defensive but is taking offensive action in strength. Main effort at the moment is against IX Corps (center) and II ROK Corps on our right. No important activity on our extreme west flank, but captured PWs indicate possibility of some strength in that area. We are consolidating positions of I Corps until situation clarifies. IX Corps is resisting strong attack but is under orders to resume the offensive. II ROK Corps on right has fallen back to general line east and west through Tokchon. Situation in that corps still fluid. IX Corps is employing Turks to attack Tokchon from the west to assist in stabilizing situation in II ROK Corps. 1st Cav Div being assembled east of Sunchon in rear of ROK as a precautionary measure."

Concluding, Landrum reported: ". . . the general feeling up there is not pessimistic. But it's a tight situation brought about primarily by lack of firmness on the part of our little friends."[3]

There is no tabulation of losses through 27 November. But a count of front-line rifle companies shows that at least nine (the equivalent rifle strength of one regiment) had either been totally lost or reduced to ineffectiveness and incorporated with other units. The heaviest losses were in the 2d Division.

The Night of 27–28 November

In the west, the 25th Division planned to withdraw to the vicinity of Yongbyon. To accomplish this, the 35th Infantry would have to move back through Yongsan-dong, then turn east across the Kuryong River. The remnants of Task Force Dolvin/Wilson drew back to a position where they could cover the crossing. But as the 35th Infantry started through Yongsan-dong, it found the Chinese there ahead of them. The Chinese had driven the adjoining 1st ROK Division south of the town in some disorder. Part of the 35th fought its way through the town, while one battalion managed to find a bypass to the north. In the 1st ROK Division sector, Gen. Paik Sun Yup came forward, helped reorganize the 11th and 15th ROK Regiments, and led them in a counterattack, which assisted the passage of the 35th Infantry. By late afternoon of 28 November, the 35th had reached Yongbyon and was preparing to move southward.

In the 2d Division sector, the remnants of the 9th Infantry had been attached to the 23d Infantry, which was ordered to hold north of the Tokchon–Somin-dong Road until the 38th Infantry had cleared. The 38th Infantry spent the remainder of the night and all of the next morning in a constant rear-guard action as it fought its way toward the valley road.

28 November

By morning, it was clear that the 2d Division was the pivotal unit and that it was in deep trouble. It would not be able to halt and reorganize at Kujang-dong. The Chinese were pressing closely on each backward step, leaving little time or opportunity to reorganize and prepare effective defensive positions. There were reports of large enemy forces heading southward on the Pukchang-ni–Sunchon Road and farther south. That force might sever the 2d Division's line of withdrawal.

At 10:50 A.M., General Walker ordered a general withdrawal by all units to the Chongchon bridgehead line, the line previously occupied at the conclusion of the Chinese first-phase attack. I Corps would occupy that portion of the bridgehead line from the mouth of the Chongchon River east through Pakchon then to Won-ni (Pugwon) on the Chongchon. IX Corps would be responsible for the zone from Won-ni eastward to the extreme limit of the Eighth Army zone at Taeul-li. As soon as it reached the bridgehead line, the 24th Division, minus the 5th RCT, would pull south of the Chongchon, then move to the Eighth Army's right flank at Sunchon. All units were instructed to prepare for resumption of the Eighth Army offensive at an early date.

General Hobart Gay already had two regiments of his 1st Cavalry Division at Sunchon. But one of these was the 8th Cavalry, still recovering from the battering incurred at Unsan. Before moving up the Sunchon–Pukchang-ni Road, Gay decided to await the arrival of the 5th Cavalry from Kunu-ri. Accordingly, the 2d Battalion, 5th Cavalry, leading off for the regiment, headed south on the Kaechon–Sunchon Road. Just north of Samso-ri, it encountered Chinese resistance. An all-day effort, assisted by one company of the 7th Cavalry coming up from the south, failed to dislodge the Chinese. Late in the afternoon, the 2d Battalion pulled back, loaded up on trucks, backtracked to Kunu-ri, and headed south on the Kunu-ri–Sunchon Road, following the other two battalions of the regiment. In the turmoil of the withdrawal to the bridgeheads, the significance of substantial Chinese forces at Samso-ri passed unnoticed. The advance units of the 113th CCF Division had reached Samso-ri just in time to halt the 2d Battalion, 5th Cavalry. The Chinese were knocking on the Eighth Army's unguarded side door.

By noon, the leading elements of the 38th Infantry reached the valley road at Kujang-dong and started south. Companies had by now been reduced to an average of two officers and forty men. The 23d

Infantry, then holding farther north, began to withdraw, leaving one battalion as rear guard.

Late in the afternoon, General Walker was summoned, along with General Almond, to a conference in Tokyo. Such details of the conference as exist are covered more completely in the following chapters. Initially, Walker offered the optimistic assessment that he could hold Pyongyang and establish a defense line north and east of the city. General MacArthur had a more realistic view. Before Walker left Tokyo, he was instructed to hold Pyongyang if he could but to withdraw if needed to keep the Chinese from enveloping the Eighth Army. Not until late in the afternoon of 29 November did Walker return to the Eighth Army command post at Pyongyang.

In the meantime, all 25th Division units had reached the bridgehead line and taken up positions. Task Force Dolvin/Wilson was dissolved, and the division was disposed with the 35th Infantry on the left, the 27th Infantry in the center, and the 24th Infantry on the right. The 1st ROK Division was holding south of Yongsan-dong, while the 24th Division moved into position on the bridgehead line, reaching there by nightfall. The following morning, the 1st ROK Division would then withdraw to the 24th Division's positions, relieving them and enabling the 24th Division to cross south of the river and move to Sunchon.

The Night of 28–29 November
The 2d Division plan for the rearward position was that the 23d Infantry would hold positions in the vicinity of Won-ni. The 38th Infantry would take up positions at Piho-san, a long ridge to the southeast of Won-ni and overlooking Kunu-ri. What was left of the Turkish Brigade would form on the right of the 38th Infantry, covering the Tokchon–Kunu-ri Road. A substantial number of stragglers from the Turkish Brigade had reached Kaechon and taken refuge in the town, while portions of the brigade continued to resist Chinese pressure, which had driven them back to Sinnim-ni at dusk on 28 November and was forcing them farther westward.

Shortly after midnight, the 23d Infantry had passed through 9th Infantry blocking positions at Won-ni and had taken up a position about two miles south of the town. The 9th Infantry blocking force faced heavy Chinese pressure and was forced back through the 23d Infantry. Colonel Peploe had taken the 38th Infantry into a temporary assembly area in an effort to sort out and reorganize the scrambled units prior to occupying the assigned positions on Piho-san Ridge. At daylight, with the 2d and 3d Battalions, 38th Infantry, moving to take up assigned positions, it was discovered that the Chinese had reached Piho-san first. The regiment was forced to take up a position on a lower ridge closer to town.

29 November

By the morning of 29 November, the situation on the left flank of the Eighth Army was under control. Except for portions of the 1st ROK Division now withdrawing toward the bridgehead line, all units had reached that line and were holding. The situation on the right, however, was deteriorating by the hour.

To the south along the Pukchang-ni–Sunchon Road, the Chinese were advancing. The 7th Cavalry had reached Kujang-ni and taken up positions there the night of 28 November. The next morning, the 6th ROK Division, withdrawing from Walpo-ri under pressure from the 125th CCF Division, fell back through the 7th Cavalry. The 7th Cavalry, then under Chinese pressure, withdrew farther south to Sinchang-ni.

The 2d Division area remained the most critical. In the Chongchon Valley, two battalions of the 23d Infantry were all that was holding back pressure from the 40th CCF Army. On the right of the 23d, the 38th Infantry, with the remnants of the 3d ROK Regiment still attached, attempted to hold their positions. All afternoon, the two front-line battalions of the 38th struggled to hold off the Chinese, who were attacking from the higher ground. Colonel Peploe was having difficulty getting anything more than two Turkish companies to cover his right flank.

In view of the situation, and with General Walker not yet back from Tokyo, the Eighth Army staff ordered abandonment of the bridgehead line and movement to a line below the river. I Corps was to occupy the lower bank of the Chongchon to a point just south of Kunu-ri. From there, IX Corps would defend a line that curved southeast, below Kunu-ri, to join that occupied by the 1st Cavalry Division from Sunchon through Sinchang-ni to Songchon.

An inkling of future trouble arose when a Turkish convoy bringing supplies north on the Sunchon–Kunu-ri Road reported being ambushed by a Chinese force. The 2d Division dispatched a military police patrol, the division's reconnaissance company, then an additional rifle company from the 38th Infantry—all without success in clearing what came to be called a fire block. The Chinese had not physically blocked the road but had kept it under fire for an undetermined distance. To the south, General Coulter had ordered his corps reserve, the 27th Commonwealth Brigade, to advance northward to clear the Chinese roadblock at Samso-ri, which had held up the 5th Cavalry the previous day. Before that effort could be launched, the order was changed to send a battalion north on the Sunchon–Kunu-ri Road to clear that block. The Middlesex Battalion advanced toward the "pass" near the south end of the road, came under fire, and halted for the night. Arrangements were made to coordinate an advance southward by the 2d Division the following day with a continuation of the attack northward by the Middlesex Battalion. The situation was confused when a platoon of tanks, ordered south, made it through the block without opposition and reported the road clear. At the 2d Division end, it was believed the block was only a short one.

Late that afternoon, General Walker returned from Tokyo. Shortly thereafter, he ordered the Army to withdraw to a new line generally from Sukchon east to Sunchon then to Songchon. I Corps would face north on the Sukchon–Sunchon segment; IX Corps would face northeast and east.

The Night of 29–30 November
In the I Corps area, the 24th Division, minus the 5th RCT, had cleared south of the river and was on the way to Sunchon. Moving along the diagonal road from Anju to Sunchon, the 19th Infantry, followed by the 21st Infantry, encountered a Chinese roadblock. Leaving a task force to deal with the roadblock, the two regiments shifted to an alternate route through Sukchon and reached their assembly area late on 29 November.

North of the Chongchon River, the 1st ROK Division and the 25th Division were commencing to move south. Portions of the 25th Division, the 24th Infantry, and portions of the 27th crossed the Chongchon at Kunu-ri, then moved southwest. The 5th RCT would cover the units crossing at Anju, follow across, blow up the bridges, then hold Anju until the remaining units moving over the Kunu-ri–Anju Road could clear.

The situation in the 2d Division zone was worsening. Both the 23d and the 38th Infantry were being heavily pressed by the Chinese. The 2d Division's problem was twofold. Problem one was to hold the Kunu-ri area long enough to keep units still north of the river from being cut off. The other was to pull the division together and concentrate it for further movement southward. All this was complicated by the fact that the Kunu-ri area did not lend itself well to defense. Hovering above all this was the problem of the roadblock to the south.

General Keiser's plan was for the 23d Infantry to withdraw from Won-ni, move south, and take up positions at the crossroads south of Kunu-ri, thus covering both the lateral road southwest to Anju and the Kunu-ri–Sunchon Road. The 38th Infantry would withdraw from the lower portions of Piho-san Ridge, move through Kunu-ri, and take up positions on the right of the 23d Infantry. The Turks would move south and take up positions east of the Kunu-ri–Sunchon Road.

The 23d Infantry moved back from Won-ni by bounds. The 1st Battalion took up positions two miles north of Kunu-ri. The 2d and 3d Battalions then moved south through Kunu-ri and took up positions south and west of the town at the road junction. One company and a platoon of tanks remained north of the town until early in the morning of 30 November so they could cover the withdrawal of the 38th Infantry.

Late in the afternoon, the crumbling Turks left the right flank of the 38th Infantry open. CCF units moved around the flank, cutting off the 2d and 3d Battalions. Unable to get his 1st Battalion forward through the stream of stragglers and refugees to reinforce the line, Colonel Peploe ordered the 2d and 3d Battalions back. The two front-line battalions had to fight and infiltrate through the encircling Chinese. By 4 A.M. on 30 November, the last 38th Infantry units cleared the Kaechon River bridge south of Kunu-ri and went into a temporary assembly area, where the intermixed units could be sorted out and reorganized.

Into the Gauntlet

The two critical points in the Eighth Army zone on the morning of 30 November were the Pukchang-ni–Sunchon Road and the 2d Division sector. The 7th Cavalry, defending two miles north of Sinchang, had been strongly attacked by the 125th CCF Division the night of 29 November. The Chinese had driven into the regiment, reached the artillery positions, and overrun the command posts of both front-line battalions. But by morning, the 7th Cavalry had counterattacked and regained its position. For the moment, the Chinese had been checked there.

The situation of the 2d Division was grim. There were very strong CCF formations advancing from the north and from the east. More ominously, Chinese forces moving down the Taedong Valley had established blocks on three of the four known roads available for withdrawal to the south. The 5th Cavalry had encountered the Chinese on the Kaechon–Sunchon Road on 28 November. On 29 November, the combined attacks of the Division Reconnaissance Company and C Company of the 38th Infantry had failed to dislodge the forces blocking the Kunu-ri–Sunchon Road. Also on 29 November, two smaller roadblocks had been encountered by the 19th Infantry in moving along the diagonal Anju–Sunchon Road.

The 2d Division may not have known of the blocks on the diagonal road. Nor did the division know just how deep the block was on the Kunu-ri–Sunchon Road. The significance of this series of three blocks across potential withdrawal routes of the 2d Division does not seem to have been recognized by 2d Division, IX Corps, or Eighth Army. The 113th CCF Division, having entered the unguarded side door, was prepared to inflict serious damage.

Knowing of the block on the Kunu-ri–Sunchon Road, General Keiser and his G-3 did discuss withdrawing west along the Kunu-ri–Anju Road, then south and east again to Sunchon. Late in the day, Gen. Frank Milburn, I Corps commander, offered the use of that route. Keiser accepted it for use by his advance party and his administrative vehicles, but he was reluctant to do so otherwise because of possible congestion. Later that evening, his G-3 sought and received permission to use that route, but only with the proviso that 2d Division vehicles would "work in as you can." Shortly thereafter, the division provost marshal reported erroneously that there was a Chinese block on that road. The question was settled for General Keiser when, at 1 A.M. on 30 November, he received a message from General Coulter to attack southward in the morning, moving his combat units over the Kunu-ri–Sunchon Road. Coulter had flown over the block that afternoon and didn't think it was that strong. The 27th Commonwealth Brigade would attack northward in the morning to assist in opening the road.

By 6 A.M., when the remnants of the 9th Infantry, now no more than two strong rifle companies, commenced their move south to open the fire block, the Chinese had at least two regiments of the 113th CCF Division deployed where they could cover six miles of the Sunchon Road by fire. By 9 A.M., the 9th Infantry was stalled. The 3d ROK Regiment was committed and achieved some minor gain, but they were stalled again by 11:30 A.M. Near noon, the Chinese were pressing hard on the 23d Infantry. With the assumption that the fire block was not deep, and with the Middlesex Battalion of the 17th Commonwealth Brigade at the other end, Keiser issued the order to advance. The 38th Infantry, mostly mounted on tanks, was to lead.

The first units came under heavy fire and sustained substantial losses, but they were able to make it through. They were shocked to find the fire block extending a much greater distance than believed. But, unable to communicate with the division to relay this information, succeeding units, unknowingly, entered the gauntlet. As units were forced to halt, if only momentarily, to clear damaged vehicles from the road, more vehicles were damaged by the merciless small-arms fire, soon thickened with mortar fire. The destruction of vehicles at halts escalated. Troops dismounting from halted vehicles and attempting to take cover in the ditches would lose their place. Without cover from the plunging fire, casualties increased. Disorganization spread. Units in the column became intermixed. Any semblance of command and control was lost. Fighter bombers from the Fifth Air Force made continuous bombing and strafing runs against the Chinese positions, with only temporary effect.

The worst place was "the pass" just north of the village of Yong-won. The road went through a cut some fifty feet deep, then made a sharp turn down a hill. By late afternoon, it was a mass of wrecked vehicles and wounded and dead soldiers. General Keiser came forward in an attempt to get the road cleared and the column moving. Forced by the confusion and disorganization to function more as a platoon leader than a division commander, he had little success.

Losses mounted with each successive unit. Still, those behind pressed urgently forward. As darkness came on and supporting aircraft departed, the Chinese defense strengthened and intensified, and the Chinese increased their efforts to block the road physically. Finally, some time after dark, all vehicular movement came to a halt. Remaining units, including the engineer battalion and most of the division artillery, were forced to abandon their vehicles and equipment and attempt to make their way to Sunchon on foot across country.

The Rear Guard

At the crossroads below Kunu-ri, the 23d Infantry's situation was becoming increasingly precarious. Front-line units could see very large Chinese forces building up. Apprehension increased as reports of heavy losses in the gauntlet came in over the division's command net. Several times during the afternoon, Col. Paul L. Freeman, Jr., the 23d's commander, attempted to get some instructions on when and under what conditions he could commence withdrawing. Finally deciding that he would need to withdraw over the Anju Road in order to save his command, he attempted to contact General Keiser for permission. In an uncertain conversation that had to be relayed by the 9th Infantry's Col. Charles C. Sloane, Freeman thought he had permission and began preparations.

Freeman did not want to take out the howitzers with the troops. One capsized gun would block the road. So, with the concurrence of the artillery commander, he planned to cover the withdrawal with a massive shoot of all remaining ammunition, destroy the guns, and withdraw. The shoot went off just before dark. In twenty minutes, 3,206 rounds were fired. Fearing a UN counterattack, Chinese troops were furiously digging in. The guns, paint blistered and barrels warped, were thermited; the troops loaded up and headed for Anju. The 5th RCT had remained to hold the road open for the 23d Infantry, which then, mingling with 25th Division traffic and halting now and then, proceeded to Sunchon.

At Sunchon, the 2d Division continued on through Pyongyang, assembling at Munsan, well to the south. It was considered combat-ineffective, having little more than the combat effectiveness of an RCT. The division had commenced the attack northward on 24 November with a strength of approximately 15,000, short of the 18,931 authorized strength. In seven days, it had lost 4,940 battle casualties. It was estimated that 3,000 of them occurred running the gauntlet through "the pass." The 9th Infantry had just 1,406 men, little more than a third of its authorized strength. Hardest hit of all was the engineer battalion, with barely a quarter of its authorized strength. The artillery had lost all but eight of the seventy-two tubes in the division.

In an effort to hold a continuous line, units were so widely dispersed that the concentrated power and mutual support of a modern force was lost. In a very real way, the soldiers of the Eighth Army were forced to face the huge numbers of Chinese on a man-for-man basis. Above all, it was a clear demonstration of the futility of attempting an advance to the border through the Korean mountains in winter weather with the limited and much-depleted forces at hand. No one can carefully study that battle without concluding that even had the Chinese, and the North Koreans, been no more numerous than the appalling underestimate given, the Eighth Army would still have been locked into a bitter, winter-long, terribly costly, and probably vain effort to reach the border. Any army that could not hold a line that was no more than seventy miles long could not be expected to be able to maintain itself on its portion of the 650-mile Yalu–Tumen frontier.

Notes

Unless otherwise noted, this chapter has been compiled from the following sources: Billy C. Mossman, *Ebb and Flow November 1950–July 1951*, U.S. Army in the Korean War Series (Washington, D.C.: Center of Military History, U.S. Army, 1990); Roy E. Appleman, *Disaster in Korea: The Chinese Confront MacArthur* (College Station: Texas A&M University Press, 1989); S. L. A. Marshall, *The River and the Gauntlet: Defeat of the Eighth Army by the Chinese Communist Forces, November 1950, in the Battle of the Chongchon River* (New York: William Morrow, 1953). In addition, the Eighth Army War Diary—containing the command report and summary, staff section journals, and various daily reports—has been consulted.

1. Appleman, *Disaster in Korea,* 59.
2. 8A War Diary, 26 Nov. 50.
3. Appleman, *Disaster in Korea,* 95.

12
The Chinese Offensive at Chosin

That's impossible. There aren't two Chinese Communist divisions in the whole of North Korea.
—Maj. Gen. Edward M. Almond
at noon on 28 November 1950

Positions for the Attack

Based on the information in their possession, the Chinese believed there was one Marine regiment at Yudam-ni and another either at Hagaru-ri or divided between Hagaru-ri and the east side of the Chosin Reservoir. The forces assigned to the destruction of the 7th Marines at Yudam-ni should have been more than sufficient to accomplish the Chinese objective of annihilation. Four battalions of the 89th CCF Division were to halt the drive westward. The 79th CCF Division was to attack from the north. The 59th Division was to cut the main supply route (MSR) to the rear. This seemed adequate enough, even given the Chinese inferiority in firepower and in supporting arms.

Two more divisions to deal with the Marine force at Hagaru-ri should also have been sufficient. The 60th CCF Division would cut the road south. The 58th Division would attack Hagaru-ri, with the 80th Division coming down the east side of the reservoir to assist. The Chinese based their plan on that estimate.

In the west along the Chongchon River, the Chinese had employed eighteen divisions against four U.S. divisions, four ROK divisions, and the British and Turkish Brigades—a ratio of a bit more than two-to-one. The Chinese forces there were disposed across the entire Eighth Army front, with the main effort against II ROK Corps. In the east, the Chinese had twelve divisions against three U.S. and two ROK divisions—a ratio of two-and-one-half-to-one. Further, the Chinese force had elements of eight of the twelve divisions concentrated against what they believed to be the 1st Marine Division. Clearly, the Chinese expected decisive results.

The Chinese estimate of the opposing forces was approximately correct on the night of 25 November, when the Chinese attack was supposed to begin in coordination with the attack on the Eighth Army. On that date, two battalions of the 7th Marines were approaching Yudam-ni. One battalion of the 7th Marines remained at Hagaru-ri. The 5th Marines, commanded by Lt. Col. Raymond L. Murray, were deployed east of the reservoir on 24 and 25 November. But last-minute movements of X Corps forces upset the Chinese plans.

General MacArthur's order to execute the plan for the attack westward sent General Almond and Maj. Gen. David G. Barr, 7th Division commander, scrambling for units to dispatch to the Chosin Reservoir. The first one grabbed was the 1st Battalion, 32d Infantry. That battalion was on the road, moving from its position south of the Fusen Reservoir back through Hamhung and around to Kapsan. Early in the morning of 24 November, as it was motoring through Hamhung, it was halted by a corps staff officer, turned around, and sent on the way to Chosin. The battalion was on the move even before the corps had time to dispatch a warning order to all units. That order went out at noon. When the 5th Marines were relieved by a unit of the 7th Division, they were to be moved west of the Hamhung Road. The airfield at Hagaru-ri was to be completed by 1 December. The 7th Division was ordered to relieve the 5th Marines east of Chosin with not less than one infantry battalion, which would be attached to the 1st Marine Division, by noon of the following day.[1] With delays due to heavy traffic through the pass, the battalion reached the 5th Marines area on the east side of the reservoir about 3 P.M. on 25 November. The following day, the 5th Marines commenced their move to Yudam-ni.

The final makeup of the Army task force was to be the 1st Battalion, 32d Infantry, and the 2d and 3d Battalions, 31st Infantry. E Company of the 2d Battalion, 31st Infantry, was to remain behind as division reserve. It would be replaced by B Company, 31st Infantry. The 57th Field Artillery Battalion, minus Battery C and D, 15th AAA-AW (SP) Battalion, minus one platoon, were to be attached. Each of these, as well as the Headquarters Company and Tank Company of the 31st Infantry and a detachment of engineers, was to proceed separately to Chosin, assemble there, and prepare to attack north to the Yalu River.

Over the next two days, the various elements of the task force assembled. Colonel Allan D. MacLean, commanding officer of the 31st Infantry and the task force commander, arrived late in the afternoon of 26 November with his command group, the intelligence and reconnaissance platoon, and a medical detachment. He established a regimental command post (CP) at Hudong. On 27 November, the 3d Battalion, 31st Infantry, the artillery, and the attached antiaircraft (AA) battery arrived late in the afternoon. The 2d Battalion, 31st Infantry, never did arrive. On the evening of 27 November, it was halted in Hamhung by corps headquarters and held there in corps reserve.

By sunset on 27 November, the task force was casually disposed in seven different locations over an airline distance of seven miles (about eleven road miles). The 1st Battalion, 32d Infantry, had taken up positions vacated by the 3d Battalion, 5th Marines, where the road north passed through a low saddle about three miles north of the mouth of the Pungnyuri River. The Chinese referred to the location as Neidongjik. The 3d Battalion, 31st Infantry, and the two artillery batteries occupied positions in an area of reasonably level low ground on the south side of the Pungnyuri River inlet identified on the map as one of the many places named Sinhung-ni in Korea, otherwise referred to by the troops as "the Inlet." The heavy-mortar company was in position about halfway between Neidongjik and the Inlet. MacLean established an advance CP nearby. The headquarters of the 57th Field Artillery (FA) Battalion, under Lt. Col. Ray O. Embree, and the attached AA battery occupied positions in a swale on the western side of Hill 1656, about a mile south of the Inlet. The rear CP remained at Hudong, on the north side of the Paegomni River. The tank company had arrived at Hudong late in the day and had remained there for the night. Arriving even later in the evening, the service battery of the 57th FA Battalion had taken up separate positions farther to the south near Sasu-ri.

Brigadier General Henry I. Hodes, assistant commander of the 7th Division, had joined the task force on 26 November to be the "eyes and ears" for Major General Barr, the 7th Division commander. He was joined shortly by Maj. William R. Lynch from the 7th Division, who was to act as his G-3 assistant. Hodes brought some information with him, but it is not known if he was aware of the Chinese counteroffensive on the Eighth Army front. Otherwise, officers of the RCT had only fragmentary information about the situation. They had learned from the 5th Marines of the patrol contacts and of the Chinese attempt to take a prisoner on the night of 25 November, and they knew there were Chinese in the village of Pungnyuri. In addition, refugees moving southward through the task force positions had told of many Chinese in the hills who intended to recapture the Chosin area in the next few days.

To follow up on some of this information, Colonel MacLean, on the afternoon of 27 November, dispatched his intelligence and reconnaissance platoon to reconnoiter up the river toward the village of Pungnyuri. The platoon was ambushed. Regimental headquarters never heard from it again, but three men managed to evade the ambush and later make their way into the perimeter of the 1st Battalion, 32d Infantry.

At Yudam-ni, the 2d Battalion, 5th Marines, with the regimental headquarters, arrived on 26 November, prepared to commence the attack westward the following morning. The 3d Battalion, which had been the farthest forward on the east side of the reservoir, arrived about noon on 27 November; the 1st Battalion did not arrive until after dark. Supporting the two Marine regiments at Yudam-ni were the howitzers of both the 1st and the 4th Battalions of the 11th Marines, together with two more batteries of the 3d Battalion—a total of thirty 105mm howitzers and eighteen 155mm howitzers. The 1st and 3d Battalions of the 7th Marines, with D and E Companies of the 2d Battalion, were holding Yudam-ni. The 2d Battalion's headquarters and the weapons company remained at Hagaru-ri, waiting for trucks to move them, while F Company had been placed in position at the top of Toktong Pass.

Intelligence Estimates
At corps and in the Marine division, information provided by the three deserters from the 60th CCF Division, captured on 26 No-

vember, did not substantially change the estimate of the enemy's defense capability. Both HQs appeared to believe that those forces had gone farther south on the west flank of the corps. In the 1st Marine Division Periodic Intelligence Report (PIR), the most probable capability was the conduct of a determined defense west of Yudam-ni with two divisions: "He [the enemy] will defend at all costs our debouchment in his rear." But the PIR also noted the capability for a strong attack in the Sinha-ri area.[2]

The corps PIR noted the resistance to the advance to Yudam-ni and the many reports of enemy to the front and flanks of the 1st Marine Division from civilians, air reconnaissance, and PWs. Thus the PIR concluded the most likely enemy capability was to defend in current positions along the line Changjin–Sachang-ni. "Because the present position of X Corps imposes a serious threat to Chinese forces he [the enemy] may be expected to counterattack to maintain his positions or to drive back X Corps forces." As he had for the previous several days, the X Corps G-2 pointed out the vulnerability of the west flank of the corps.[3]

General Oliver Smith's personal estimate was that his division would meet the Chinese in strength in the mountains to the west. He expected to encounter greater forces than his G-2 predicted, and he hoped it would occur when the 5th and the 7th Marines were still relatively close together, rather than strung out along the mountain road.[4]

Yudam-ni

Shortly after dark on 27 November, the Chinese struck in seven different places across the X Corps front. They struck at Yudam-ni from both the north and the northwest. They cut the road south of Yudam-ni. They struck the 1st Battalion, 32d Infantry, at Neidongjik and the 3d Battalion, 31st Infantry, at Sinhung-ni (the Inlet). They cut the road south of RCT 31 at Hill 1121, and they cut the road south of Hagaru-ri, between there and Koto-ri. The following night, two more locations came under attack: Hagaru-ri and, far to the southwest, Sachang-ni.

The Chinese were to make their main effort at Yudam-ni, with portions of the 89th CCF Division attacking from the west and the

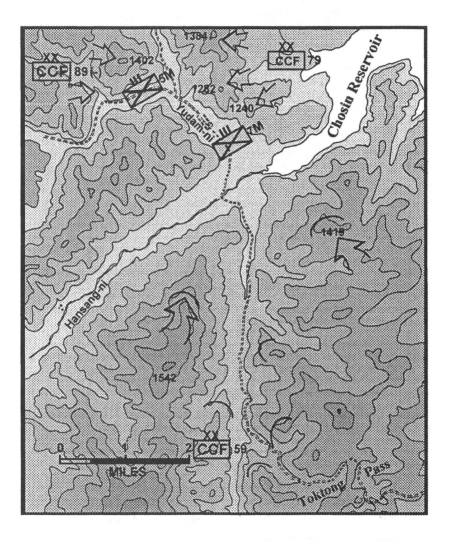

Chinese deployment at Yudam-ni, 27–28 November 1950.

79th CCF Division attacking from the north with three regiments abreast, each regiment in a column of battalions. The 59th CCF Division was to cut the road to the rear. Once the assault battalions had broken into the perimeter, the following units were to pass through and, in coordination with other CCF units, "annihilate the enemy at Yudam-ni."[5]

On the right (north), the 237th CCF Regiment was to seize Hill 1384, lightly outposted with a platoon of I/3/5. The 235th Regiment in the center was to capture Hill 1240, defended by D/2/7. The 236th Regiment on the left (south) was to take Hill 1167, which was undefended. No unit was assigned to Hill 1282, now occupied by E/2/7. The 79th CCF Division had assembled in the vicinity of Yongji, about five miles north of Yudam-ni. Assault forces began leaving their assembly area shortly after dark.

In the northwest sector of the perimeter, elements of the 89th CCF Division, having put up a determined defense during the day, counterattacked. It appears that one battalion was left in place to halt any westward movement of the 3d Battalion, 7th Marines, while a regiment concentrated the bulk of its forces to attack the 2d Battalion, 5th Marines, along the road and the lower slope of Hill 1403 and How Company, 7th Marines, on the crest of Hill 1403.[6]

At 9 P.M., a small group probed the roadblock set up by the 2d Battalion, 5th Marines, along the valley floor. Under cover of this diversion, the assault units moved into position, launching their main attack at about 9:45 P.M. The attackers broke through and forced back the right-flank platoon of F/2/5. On the right, an attack on the center of E/2/5 was beaten off. By midnight, the penetration on the right flank of F Company was sealed off and the Chinese attack tapered off. At 3 A.M., a second attack commenced. At E Company, the attack was halted. At F Company, the Chinese made a small dent in the front line but were halted. Sporadic long-range firing continued the remainder of the night.

Further to the northwest, however, the elements of the 89th CCF Division reached their objective. The attack against H/3/7 began at about 10 P.M. Initially the Chinese gained the crest of the hill and overran at least one platoon. By midnight, H Company had rallied and regained most of the lost ground. But at 3 A.M., the second Chinese attack succeeded in driving the company from the top of the hill. Permission was given for it to withdraw to the southwest and tie in with 2/5.

The withdrawal of H Company had left a gaping hole in the perimeter. Chinese forces at that point dominated the valley floor and were capable of driving a wedge through the heart of the two regiments. The 89th CCF Division halted then, made no further move to exploit the gains, and posed no further threat to the forces at Yudam-ni during the remainder of the action there.

On the north end of the ridge at Hill 1384, the 237th Regiment reached the crest of the hill without opposition early in the evening. A CCF combat patrol was pushed forward down the ridgeline toward Yudam-ni and, about 8:45 P.M., began firing on a 3/5 outpost on the ridge. After some hesitation, a larger Chinese force, estimated to be made up of two companies, was assembled. At 2 A.M., they swept down the ridge, driving in the outpost and a detail of South Korean police. Shortly thereafter the 3d Battalion, 5th Marines, organized a counterattack, regained the ridge, and began advancing toward the peak, halting just 500 yards short of the crest before being recalled. For the rest of the action at Yudam-ni, the 237th CCF Regiment held its positions but did not attack.

In darkness and on the wretchedly broken terrain approaching North Ridge, the other two CCF regiments lost their way. The 1st Battalion, 235th CCF Regiment, assigned to secure Hill 1240, veered off course to launch its attack on Hill 1282. The attack began with a probe of E/2/7 lines at 10 P.M. The assault commenced about midnight and continued until 2 A.M. In squads of eight to ten, they struck again and again at the perimeter. By 5 A.M., the Chinese had a tenuous toehold on the crest of the hill but had taken grievous losses. The defending troops had been cut to platoon size during the night, but they were reinforced by C/1/5 and a platoon of A/1/5. At daylight, the defenders counterattacked and secured the crest.

The 3d Battalion, 236th CCF Regiment, guiding on the unit on its right, also lost its way and reached the base of Hill 1240 some time after the attack on 1282 had begun. D Company, 7th Marines, held the hill. Probing began about 11:45 P.M. The full-scale attack came at 1:05 A.M. By dawn, the defenders had been reduced to sixteen men holding a line on the lower slope of the hill. Reinforced with a platoon from C/1/5, the shattered company counterattacked, gained the crest, but was again forced back. A daylong fight supported by air and artillery could not dislodge the Chinese. For two more days, the Marines and the Chinese faced each other over the crest of Hill 1240.

The 79th CCF Division continued to maintain pressure on the North Ridge until the withdrawal of the Marines southward on 1 December. It showed a tenacity not matched by any of the divisions of the 20th Army. It was the only unit that continued its attacks in the daylight, despite the presence of air support.

South of Yudam-ni, units of the 59th CCF Division had assembled in the valley running southwest from Yudam-ni toward Chang-ni. As the last aircraft departed that evening, the 59th Division began to move. The 175th Regiment climbed through the saddle south of Hill 1542, crossed the road, and took up positions in the hills east of the road. The 177th Regiment took their positions on the ridge west of the road from Hill 1542 north to 1276. The 176th Regiment moved farther south to take up positions in the Toktong Pass.[7] The defenders were in place somewhere around 9 P.M. The first Marine to learn that the road had been cut was Lt. Robert Messman of the 4th Battalion, 11th Marines. He was on a run to Hagaru-ri to pick up ammunition for the 155mm howitzers of the 4th Battalion when his Jeep was halted by a Chinese roadblock some time after 9 P.M. Messman spent the next two and a half years as a prisoner of war.

On a hill overlooking the crest of Toktong Pass, F Company, 7th Marines, had been positioned late in the afternoon of 27 November to protect the main supply route (MSR). At 2:30 A.M., what is estimated to have been a battalion of the 176th CCF Regiment launched an attack on Fox Company's perimeter. After losing some ground, the company held for the remainder of the night in very bitter fighting. By dawn, the company had lost twenty killed and fifty-four wounded. There is some evidence to indicate that the Chinese had not expected to find F Company there.

Late in the afternoon of 27 November, C Company, 7th Marines, minus one platoon, had been ordered to take up positions on Hill 1419 to protect the MSR. Arriving close to dark, the company, starting up the hill, met Chinese coming down the hill. Forced to take up unfavorable positions on the lower slopes, the company was hit hard and suffered heavily during the night. By morning, the company had suffered fifteen killed and fifty wounded.

East of Chosin

The 81st CCF Division, minus one regiment, was to seize the Chohantae and Kwangtae-ni areas on the western side of the Fusen Reservoir and cut what they believed to be the U.S. 7th Division's contact with the 1st Marine Division.[8] The 80th CCF Division, with one regiment of the 81st attached, was to destroy the units on the east side of the reservoir.[9] The probable assignment of objectives was

- Neidongjik: Against the 1st Battalion, 32d Infantry, were the 239th Regiment, 80th CCF Division, plus one battalion of the 81st Division.
- The Inlet: Against the 3d Battalion, 31st Infantry, were the 238th Regiment and two battalions of the 81st Division. CP was the 240th Regiment, 80th CCF Division.[10]

Enemy probing attacks began against the 1st Battalion, 32d Infantry, at Neidongjik at about 10:30 P.M. The main attack began at midnight. Initially the Chinese penetrated between the two front-line companies. Local counterattacks were able to restore the lines in most places. But the most serious problem for 1/32 that night was the loss of a high point at the junction of C and B Companies east of the road. By daylight, most of the 1st Battalion's position had been restored except for that particular high ground. Efforts to retake that position continued all the following day, without success. Chinese prisoners taken during the night said the attack would envelop both sides of the Chosin Reservoir. One prisoner identified the 80th CCF Division and possibly the 81st as well.

Wire communication with the artillery went out about the time of the initial Chinese probing attacks. Radio contact was reestablished some time later. Only then was it learned that the Inlet was under heavy attack. The artillery was busy defending itself and unable to answer calls for fire. Colonel MacLean, who had arrived ear-

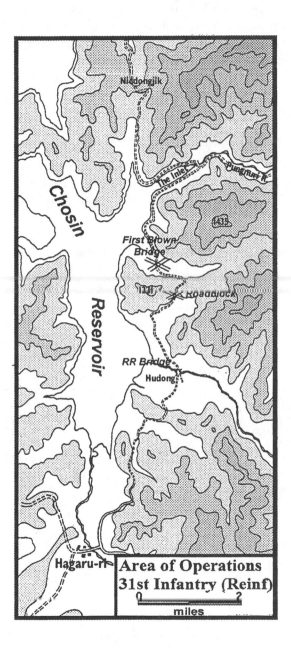

Area of Operations
31st Infantry (Reinf)

0 ───────────── 2
miles

lier in the evening and remained the rest of the night at the 1/32 command post, seemed surprised. This appears to have been the only information he had on the situation at the Inlet.

The Chinese attack at the Inlet came not long after midnight. Early in the evening, some firing was heard between the front line and a roadblock about two miles up the valley. After an extended period of quiet, the front line was suddenly hit and almost immediately penetrated. The initial Chinese attack carried it through the front lines and overran K Company, part of I Company, the 81mm mortar's position, and the battalion command post. The fragmented defenders were driven back to the positions of Battery A of the 57th Field Artillery Batallion. Eventually that position was overrun. The infantrymen and artillerymen then fell back farther to Battery B, making a stand there that held for the rest of the night. In the midst of this, a small group of M Company, the heavy-weapons unit, held out. With the exception of this and other isolated holdouts, the battalion had been penetrated and completely overrun in the initial Chinese attack.

Farther south and around the corner, Battery D, 15th AAA-AW Battalion, and the Headquarters Battery of the artillery had spent a quiet night, oblivious of the fight raging at the Inlet, until 4:30 A.M. Then the Chinese struck there. With no infantry protection, only the tremendous killing power of the self-propelled .50-caliber and 40mm antiaircraft weapons held off the Chinese.

At sunrise, the Chinese withdrew from the Inlet. The 3d Battalion was near collapse. The battalion commander, Lt. Col. William R. Reilly, had been wounded but was able to sit up and talk. His executive officer had been wounded and other members of the battalion staff had been wounded or killed. The battalion S-3 took charge and attempted to reorganize the perimeter. About 10 A.M., the artillery headquarters battery and the AA battery moved to the perimeter. Captain James R. McClymont, the AA battery commander, disposed his weapons at what appeared to be the most logical positions, providing much of the defensive strength of the battered battalion.

At the Hudong command post, four miles south of the Inlet, the 31st Medical Company arrived about midnight after an all-day motor march. Anxious to reach the forward troops, it pushed on. Where the road wound around the east side of Hill 1221, the company was ambushed by the Chinese. There were very heavy casualties and the loss of nearly all vehicles. A few survivors trickled back to Hudong to report the attack. Some survivors were able to make it north to the Inlet.

In the early morning hours, the staff at the rear CP received garbled reports of the action at Neidongjik and the Inlet, but communication with the forward units deteriorated. About 3 A.M., a brief radio contact was made between Generals Hodes and Barr, but radio reception soon faded. RCT 31 never again had radio contact with 7th Division headquarters.[11] The rear CP continued to have wire communication with the 1st Marine Division CP at Hagaru-ri, and, apparently through the 1st Marine Division switchboard, with X Corps.

During the following day, the enemy kept pressure on both perimeters with long-range fire. At Neidongjik, the troops looking to the east could see long lines of Chinese soldiers moving southward.

At Yudam-ni—Reaction to the CCF Attack

At daylight, the matter of Hills 1228 and 1240 was still in doubt. On the northwest ridge, 2/5 was holding. Hill 1403 had been lost, but the Chinese holding the hill had made no further aggressive moves. Colonels Murray and Litzenberg conferred. In such a situation, the assistant division commander would have flown in to take command, but Brig. Gen. Edward A. Craig had been ordered home on emergency leave just two days earlier. Although Col. Homer Litzenberg, the senior officer, would have been justified in assuming command, he and Lieutenant Colonel Murray chose instead to act cooperatively. According to those who knew both, neither man had the least difficulty in making his views known and understood, nor did either have the slightest difficulty in recognizing and agreeing on the immediate action needed

The first decision was to hold all units in place until the situation could be sorted out. Both officers agreed that the size and strength of the Chinese attack presented a completely new and different situation—one that justified exercising their initiative to call off the attack for the present. Their third decision was to pull back the 2d Battalion, 5th Marines, and tie it in with units on the right and left, closing the potential hole in the north sector of the perimeter. Then, with the perimeter reasonably secure, efforts could be commenced to reopen the road to Hagaru-ri and relieve C and F Companies.

Not long after daylight, the 1st Battalion, 7th Marines, began moving south on the reopening mission. It took almost until dark, and some heavy fighting, for the battalion to reach C Company. F Company was directed to fight its way toward C Company but was immobilized by wounded and remained in position. Loading the casualties on trucks, the battalion, with C Company, withdrew to the perimeter. Two attempts to reach F Company from Hagaru-ri were turned back.

Late in the afternoon, General Smith confirmed the decision to break off the attack, directing the two regiments to remain in position "until the present situation clarifies," and ordering the 7th Marines to clear the MSR between Yudam-ni and Hagaru-ri.

First Marine Division—Reaction to the CCF Attack
A collection of service units had assembled at Hagaru-ri. Supplies were being accumulated in dumps to serve the westward attack. South of the town, D Company, 1st Engineer Battalion, was working day and night on an airfield. The 1st Marine Division's advance command post had been established and was ready to take control. An Army engineer company was making preparations for a corps command post. Civilians coming into the Hagaru-ri perimeter from both the north and the west on 25, 26, and 27 November all told of being evicted from their homes by large numbers of Chinese.[12]

To defend this critical point, the 3d Battalion, 1st Marines, had arrived on 26 November. It was short G Company, left behind when there were insufficient trucks to lift the whole battalion from Chigyong. In addition, the headquarters of the 2d Battalion, 7th Marines, remained there with the bulk of its weapons company, and because of the shortage of trucks. To support the meager infantry forces, there were two batteries of artillery.

When the sun rose on the morning of 28 November, an early helicopter reconnaissance of the road south from Hagaru-ri showed it cut by roadblocks in several places. The previous night, the 60th CCF Division had moved from its assembly area in the Sinha-ri–Samdaepyong area and had taken up positions blocking the road and overlooking Koto-ri. A convoy carrying part of the division headquarters company attempting to get through to Hagaru-ri was turned back to Koto-ri. Traffic bound for the reservoir area began to pile up at Koto-ri, and a massive traffic jam developed along the main supply route.

General Smith helicoptered into Hagaru-ri to open the division CP. He ordered the 1st Marines to send patrols north from Koto-ri and south from Hagaru-ri. Both patrols failed to make progress against the Chinese. The road was firmly blocked. One of General Smith's first concerns was the defense of Hagaru-ri. He appointed Lt. Col. Thomas L. Ridge, commanding officer of the 3d Battalion, 1st Marines, as defense commander and authorized him to use whatever forces were available in Hagaru-ri to man the perimeter. Then he issued instructions to the 5th and 7th Marines to hold fast.

To the southwest, the 58th CCF Division, assembled in the area of Sucho-li and Sangpyong-ni, five to eight miles southwest of Hagaru-ri, was supposed to have attacked the perimeter on the night of 27–28 November in coordination with the attacks at Yudam-ni and east of Chosin. For unknown reasons, the attack did not occur.

During the Inchon–Seoul campaign, and earlier during the operations of the Marine Brigade along the Naktong River, units had accumulated a variety of Korean help in the way of interpreters, CIC (Counterintelligence Corps) agents, and South Korean police. In that casual fashion, an ROK officer had attached himself to the 3d Battalion, 1st Marines. The battalion was further enriched by the attachment of two South Korean CIC agents. Professional field intelligence officers are horrified at the thought of small units using makeshift line-crossers without the necessary careful vetting and training. The techniques for employing such agents are jealously guarded trade secrets of the intelligence professionals. Using such agents is, in fact, risky. But, given the situation, 2d Lt. Richard E.

Carey, the S-2 for the 3d Battalion, 1st Marines, thought it worth the risk. It was. He sent his two agents for a cruise through the surrounding area. They were able to return with information on the Chinese units, their location, and their approximate strength.

Armed with that information, the battalion commander was able to orient his sparse infantry strength in the most probable direction of the Chinese attack, the southwest, and brace the men for the coming attack. The remainder of the perimeter was covered by makeshift infantry recruited from the various service units. On the south edge of Hagaru-ri, D Company, 1st Engineer Battalion, continued working around the clock, using lights at night, to complete the airstrip to handle C-47 aircraft.

RCT 31

By daylight on 28 November, the Chinese had effectively cut RCT 31 into three separate pieces. After spending the night at the 1st Battalion, 32d Infantry, command post, Colonel MacLean returned to his own forward command post about 8 A.M. with the announced intention of moving it to the 3/31 area. In preparation for the move, he sent his intelligence sergeant, Ivan Long, south to 3/31 with a small party. Long reached 3/31 under heavy fire, losing some men on the way.[13] This was the first news that the road between the two battalions was under fire. MacLean changed his mind about moving. Instead, he moved his command post closer to 1/32. He did not yet know that the road was cut south of the Inlet.

At Hudong-ni, Capt. Robert E. Drake led his tank company, together with a provisional platoon of infantry, forward toward the site of the previous night's ambush of the 31st Medical Company at Hill 1221 in an attempt to break through the Chinese block. An all-day effort failed to do the job. Drake withdrew late in the afternoon, having lost four tanks. None of the forward units were aware of this attempt to break through to them.

At 9:50 A.M., Major Lynch phoned a situation report to corps. He reported the attack on the forward units, noting that the Chinese had penetrated the artillery positions, that the medical company had been ambushed, that the tank company had moved out to attack, and that there was no wire communication with the forward units.

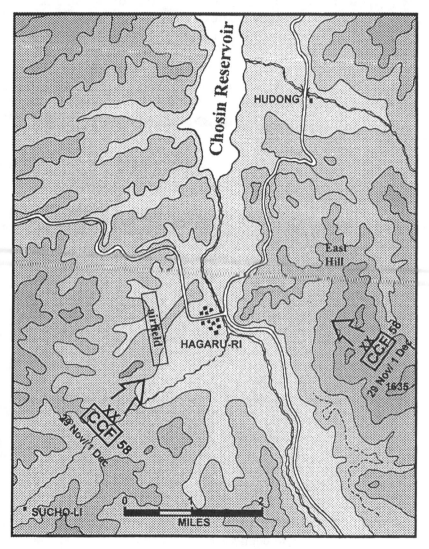

**Chinese attackers on Hagaru-ri,
November and December 1950**.

He requested ambulances for the wounded, air on station, improved communication, an air drop of small-arms ammunition to 1/32, and liaison aircraft to direct artillery fire.[14] By noon, X Corps was well aware of RCT 31's situation. At 11:20 A.M., Lt. Col. John H. Chiles, the X Corps G-3, had called the 7th Division, informed them of the RCT 31 situation, and stated that the 2d Battalion, 31st Infantry, had been released as corps reserve and ordered to rejoin the regiment without delay. Chiles then instructed Lt. H. S. Escue, RCT 31 liaison officer, to contact Lt. Col. Richard R. Reidy, commanding the 2d Battalion, 31st Infantry, and tell him to continue his move to the RCT 31 area at Chosin, not to stop at Majon-dong as previously ordered. He added that these were the instructions of the corps commander.[15]

Shortly after noon, a liaison pilot from the 57th FA Battalion, arranged by the corps artillery, was over the positions at the Inlet. He received, and relayed to X Corps, a message saying all elements had been attacked and that ammunition and medical aid were needed. The message also requested that he locate any friendly tanks in the area and drop a message to them asking them to move forward.

General Almond's Visit
At 11:30 A.M. on 28 November, presumably shortly after instructing his G-3 to have the 2d Battalion, 31st Infantry, released from X Corps reserve and sent forward, General Almond left his command post and flew to Hagaru-ri. After conferring with General Smith on the local situation, he borrowed a Marine helicopter and flew to Colonel MacLean's CP on the east side of the reservoir.[16] Together with MacLean, he jeeped forward to the 1/32 command post and conferred with Lt. Col. Don C. Faith, Jr., who reported that he had been attacked the previous evening by elements of two different Chinese divisions. Casualties had been fairly heavy; more than 100 men had passed through the aid station. It is not known if Faith identified the two Chinese divisions. He surely must have identified at least the 80th. This would have been startling information—indicating not only a new division but a new three-division Chinese Army.

Almond refused to believe the report, telling Faith: "That's impossible. There aren't two Chinese Communist divisions in the whole of North Korea."[17] Almond thought the Chinese who had attacked the previous night were part of the 124th, 125th, and 126th CCF Divisions, which had been delaying the advance for nearly a month, and that the attack had been carried out by stragglers withdrawing northward.[18] In discussions with MacLean, it appears that both Almond and MacLean agreed that with the arrival of 2/31 and the tank company, MacLean could get control of the situation and continue the advance. As he prepared to depart in his helicopter, Almond passed on encouraging words, saying, "The enemy who is delaying you for the moment is nothing more than remnants of a Chinese division fleeing north. . . . We're still attacking and we're going all the way to the Yalu. Don't let a bunch of Chinese laundrymen stop you."[19]

Almond's statements are difficult to understand. He had been at Yudam-ni the previous day and was well aware of the serious resistance that had been met. He was also aware that the Chinese were attacking in strength all across the front of the Eighth Army and that II ROK Corps had folded. Almond didn't leave the corps command post until 11:30 A.M. Lt. Col. Chiles's statement that the orders to 2/31 were those of the corps commander would seem to indicate that Almond was aware of the RCT 31 situation, but perhaps not of its seriousness. Just before reaching RCT 31, he had been at the 1st Marine Division CP at Hagaru-ri and would have been aware of the very heavy counterattacks taking place at Yudam-ni, of the road cuts, and of General Smith's decision to assume the defensive while efforts were made to reopen the MSR.

Although MacLean knew of the attack on the Inlet the previous night, he probably did not know how serious it was, and he did not seem to be aware of the attack on the artillery headquarters and AA battery, or the ambush of the medical company. So Almond may not have known how serious the situation was at the Inlet or the CCF roadblock at Hill 1221, but there was more than enough evidence to indicate a completely new and unforeseen situation that required rethinking.

With the failure of the tank attack to clear the road to the Inlet, General Hodes, still at Hudong, decided that he should go to Hagaru-ri to seek help. About noon, he departed in one of Captain Drake's tanks—to ensure both that he would get through and that he would have communication with the rear CP through the tank radio net.[20] It is not known if he was at Hagaru-ri when General Almond returned from his visit to MacLean. He would certainly have learned that there was little help to be had at Hagaru-ri.

Major Lynch and his operations sergeant followed later in a Jeep. Although they saw Chinese on the hills, they were not obstructed. At 4 P.M., Lynch reported to corps that the situation with the cut-off units was deteriorating and that they were badly in need of help. The battalions were holding their positions but were cut off from Hagaru-ri. They had a considerable number of wounded, and both tactical air control parties (TACPs) were knocked out. He requested that 2/31 and the additional battery for the artillery be moved forward without delay. They also needed another air drop; only portions of the one delivered that day had been recovered.[21]

Intelligence Estimates

By the evening of 28 November, the 1st Marine Division had information on elements of six of the CCF divisions in the offensive. At Yudam-ni, the 59th, 79th, and 89th CCF Divisions had been identified; at Hagaru-ri, the 58th and 60th had been identified; and the 80th from information furnished by RCT 31. The most-favored enemy capability was stated succinctly: "Attack the front and flanks of the 5th and 7th Marines with an estimated three divisions supported by an unknown amount of artillery," defend in the same strength, or attack the MSR in unknown strength.[22] At the corps headquarters in Hamhung, the Chinese attack was still not recognized as an all-out offensive. The corps estimated there were six CCF divisions with a strength of 35,000 troops. Additional forces were on the way. The PIR stated that the enemy action ". . . probably has as its objective the protection of the east flank [of the offensive against Eighth Army] . . . ," and that "the enemy is evidently attempting to assume the initiative in X Corps zone." The PIR listed the most probable enemy capability as "to launch attacks against the western section of the X Corps front, employing forces approximating 35,000 troops."[23] As of 28 November, seven of Song Shilun's twelve divisions were engaged.

Night of 28 November, Day of 29 November—RCT 31

East of Chosin, the 80th CCF Division and its attached regiment of the 81st renewed their attacks on the two forward enclaves of RCT 31. At the Inlet, the Chinese forces, continuing to attack from the north and east, did not seem to press their attacks as hard. More ominously, the Chinese had moved completely around to the south of the perimeter and mounted several attacks from the west. One Chinese prisoner captured during the attack said that there were 4,000 Chinese surrounding the Army forces and that their leaders had offered a great prize for each one of the antiaircraft weapons captured or destroyed.

In the 1st Battalion, 32d Infantry, perimeter, enemy attacks resumed at dark. The attacking forces quickly penetrated the 1/32 lines in several places. About midnight, MacLean authorized Faith to make his own decision to continue to hold or to fall back to the Inlet.[24] With front-line units hard-pressed and ammunition beginning to run low, Faith decided to withdraw. Hoping to reoccupy the positions the following day, Faith had his motor officer disable any vehicles left behind in a way that would permit them to be restarted.

The withdrawal started about 4 A.M. The Chinese did not seem to react by pressing closely behind. By 5 A.M., the battalion was on the road, harassed only by intermittent fire until halted by a log barricade near the bridge leading across the Pungnyuri River into 3/31 positions. The block was reduced, but the bridge remained under long-range fire. The troops started across the river ice while vehicles prepared to run for it across the bridge.

As troops prepared to cross the ice, Colonel MacLean observed a column of troops approaching the 3/31 perimeter along the road from the southwest. Troops in the perimeter were starting to fire on the advancing column, while the troops in the column returned the fire. MacLean believed that the advancing column was his 2d Battalion, whose arrival he was expecting. Fearing a bloody clash between two of his units, he shouted, "Those are my boys," and started across the ice to halt the firing. He was seen to be hit and to fall several times, then he disappeared in the brush on the far side of the Inlet. He was not seen again by friendly troops. It was learned later that MacLean had been captured by the Chinese and died of his wounds on the road north to prison camp. He was the highest-ranking Army officer killed in action in Korea.

By 9 A.M., troops from 1/32 were crossing the Inlet to the 3/31 perimeter; by noon, all had closed in the perimeter. The scene at the Inlet made an indelible impression on those who witnessed it. Major Hugh W. Robins described it: "One had only to look about . . . to confirm everything. . . . Dead and wounded GIs lay in and around the Korean mud house that served as a CP and just a few yards beyond I counted twenty dead Chinese in their now familiar quilted jackets and tennis shoes. In fact they were strewn throughout the area giving evidence of their penetration into the very foxholes of the beleaguered battalion and its command post."[25]

Captain Edward P. Stamford, the Marine forward air controller, reported: "The dead were everywhere when we joined them." Stamford said he saw dead in their sleeping bags. Captain Erwin B. Bigger, 1/32 heavy-weapons company commander, also reported: ". . . in the 31st Infantry and 57th FA . . . many men were killed by the Chinese as they slept in their bedrolls."[26]

With MacLean missing and Reilly wounded, Faith assumed command of the task force. He spent the remainder of the morning trying to find out what was left of I and K Companies of the 31st Infantry. There was no L Company left.[27] The perimeter was reorganized and consolidated. A search of the area along the edge of the reservoir revealed no trace of Colonel MacLean.

Back at the Hudong command post, Lt. Col. Barry K. Anderson, the task force operations officer, called X Corps about 4 A.M. and provided an update on the situation as he knew it. He reported that 3/31 had come under attack commencing at 7 P.M. and that the attack on 1/32 began about midnight: "All units received probing attack. Enemy buildup continues, including armor." He asked that the information be relayed to the 7th Division and reported that he was in radio contact with both infantry battalions and the artillery, but that physical contact had not been regained although attempts were being made to regain this contact.[28]

Later in the morning, the 31st Infantry Tank Company, with the assistance of a larger force of provisional infantry, made a second attempt to break through around Hill 1221. That attack also failed.

Night of 28 November, Day of 29 November—Hagaru-ri

Due to the extraordinarily accurate intelligence available, H and I Companies were alert when the Chinese attack commenced at 11:30 P.M. The 58th CCF Division plan was to attack from the southwest with the 173d Regiment, while elements of the 172d Regiment seized East Hill, overlooking and dominating the perimeter.[29]

The 173d CCF Regiment attacked with exceptional determination. That determination was exemplified by the citation for one Tang Yun, assistant platoon leader, 9th Company, 173d Regiment. He was unable to charge because of wounds to both legs, so he lay in the snow throwing hand grenades to cover the charge of his comrades-in-arms. Tang was a durable soldier, surviving through three more campaigns.[30]

The attack penetrated the center of H Company. For a time, it appeared that if the penetration were exploited, the entire perimeter might be in danger. But no effort was made to reinforce the success. Some infiltrators reached as far as the airstrip. Marine engineers, working under lights, dismounted from their equipment, took up rifles, cleared out the infiltrators, and went back to work. The attacks began to taper off by 4 A.M. A short time later, a counterattack was launched, which reduced the penetration. The defensive line was restored by 6:30 A.M. Losses to the attacking troops were extremely heavy.[31] The Chinese claim to have inflicted losses of 800 in the fighting.[32]

East Hill was held by a conglomeration of various units hastily assembled to fight as infantry. The attack there went off about midnight and immediately drove the defenders from the top of the hill. A makeshift force, about company size, attempted a counterattack. It failed to retake the crest of the hill but managed to hold a line just below the crest. In spite of the failure to reach the top, the Chinese also felt severely pressed in the bitter fighting, as shown in the following account taken from the Chinese history: "Yang Gensi, Company Commander, 3rd Company, 172nd Rgt led the 3rd Platoon of his company in defending a hilltop southeast of Height 1071.1 on the Hagaru-ri outer perimeter. On 29 November they repulsed eight consecutive fierce attacks by an enemy supported by a large number of aircraft and artillery. Just at the time a detachment was en route to reinforce and aid them, the enemy launched his ninth attack, with over 40 of them climbing upward to the position. Yang Gensi, already wounded, resolutely picked up a five kilogram satchel charge, pulled the lanyard and jumped toward the enemy group, blowing up the enemy climbing up to the position and giving up his own life."[33]

Night of 28 November, Day of 29 November—Sachang-ni

As part of the reorientation of the X Corps attack to the west, the 3d Infantry Division sent its 7th Infantry Regiment advancing westward toward Sachang-ni as flank protection for the attack of the 1st Marine Division. The main body of the 89th CCF Division, leaving one regiment with an additional battalion attached at Yudam-ni, had gone south to Sachang-ni. A portion of the 89th Division infiltrated eastward to the MSR, while the main body remained in the vicinity of Sachang-ni. On the night of 28/29 November, the Chinese launched an attack against the 1st Battalion of the 7th Infantry at Sachang-ni. After a very heavy fight, the battalion held its position and the Chinese force drew back. The 89th Division's attack on Sachang-ni was blocked.[34]

Except for the continued pressure on Hill 1282, the two U.S. regiments at Yudam-ni had spent a relatively quiet night. F Company at the pass held against another night of Chinese effort. The most urgent task at daylight was to reach F Company and carry out the division order to clear the MSR. This was a problem for Colonel Litzenberg. He was short one battalion headquarters, one weapons company, and one rifle company. He had eight of his nine rifle companies present at Yudam-ni, but only the 1st and 3d Battalion Headquarters. Litzenberg and Murray agreed to form a composite battalion. Taking Maj. Warren Morris, executive officer of the 3d Battalion, 7th Marines, as commander, the composite battalion was formed from G/3/7, B/1/7, and A/1/5.

The battalion moved out at 8 A.M. on 29 November. By 10:20 A.M., it had made contact with the enemy. Then began a slow, grinding effort with little progress. Observation aircraft reported strong enemy defenses in the hills on either side of the road. Litzenberg radioed a change in mission: Reach F Company and return by dark. But as the morning wore on, enemy groups could be seen working their way around to get behind the battalion. At 12:15 P.M., the battalion was ordered to return to the perimeter.

Task Force Drysdale
Although the initial Chinese attack on Hagaru-ri had been beaten off, the situation there was precarious. Repeated efforts failed to drive the Chinese from the crest of East Hill. Renewed attacks by Chinese reinforcements were expected. Ten miles to the south at Koto-ri, potential reinforcements for the Hagaru-ri defenders had collected. G Company, 3d Battalion, 1st Marines, had arrived there, along with B Company, 31st Infantry, various division headquarters and service units, twenty-nine Marine tanks, and the 41st Independent Commando of the British Marines. Colonel Lewis B. Puller, commanding the 1st Marines at Koto-ri, was ordered to form them into a task force under the command of Lt. Col. Douglas B. Drysdale, RM, the senior commando officer, and send them forward to Hagaru-ri.

Just a few miles north of Koto-ri, Task Force Drysdale was halted by heavy Chinese fire. Colonel Drysdale asked for instructions. General Smith, in desperate need of reinforcement for Hagaru-ri, commanded that the task force move forward in what amounted to an "at all costs" order. With the assistance of the tanks, most of the commandos and George Company got through. But the convoy was split. Some were able to return to Koto-ri, others were captured, and many trucks were destroyed in what became known as Hellfire Valley. Of the 920 officers and men in the task force, about 400 men and seventeen tanks got through shortly after dark, 300 men and eleven tanks managed to get back to Koto-ri, and about 220 were killed, wounded, missing, or captured. Later reports put the number captured at 130.

The Chinese were unable to mount an attack on the Hagaru-ri perimeter that night. Prisoners later said heavy artillery fire and air

attacks on known and suspected assembly areas located by the im-
promptu line-crossers broke up planned attacks before they could
get under way.

Reaction in Far Eastern Command

The size and scope of the Chinese attacks on the Eighth Army became clear to General MacArthur on the afternoon of 28 November. That afternoon, General Willoughby concluded that the attacks
were a full-scale counteroffensive across the entire front. He believed
the possible total of Chinese troops might be as high as 200,000, with
another 41,000 North Korean troops. This total included only 18,900
in the three divisions of the 20th CCF Army in the X Corps area. But
the scale of the Chinese effort at Chosin was not yet clear in Tokyo.
Willoughby believed the offensive at Chosin was only "sealing off"
the Chosin area with the 20th CCF Army.[35]

MacArthur acted. His first step was to summon Gens. Walton
Walker and Edward Almond for a conference in Tokyo. The next
step was to inform the Joint Chiefs of Staff. At 4:45 P.M. Tokyo time,
he sent the following:

> The developments resulting from our assault movements
> have now assumed a clear definition. All hope of localization
> of the Korea conflict to enemy forces composed of North Ko-
> rea troops with alien token elements can now be completely
> abandoned. The Chinese military forces are committed in
> North Korea in great and ever increasing strength. No pretext
> of minor support under the guise of volunteerism or other sub-
> terfuge now has the slightest validity. We face an entirely new
> war. Interrogation of prisoners of war and other intelligence
> info establish the following enemy order of battle, exclusive of
> North Korea elements, as reported by commanders in the field:
> 38, 39, 40, 42, 66, 50, and 20 CCF armies and 6 additional di-
> visions without army identification, comprising an aggregate
> strength approaching 200,000. North Korean fragments, ap-
> proximating 50,000 troops, are to be added to this strength.
> The pattern of Chinese strategy is now quite clear. Immedi-
> ately after the Inchon operation, the center of gravity of the
> Chinese forces was moved northward in China with heavy con-

centrations of their troops in Manchuria and a surreptitious movement by night infiltration of their organized forces into North Korea under the protection of the sanctuary of neutrality. After checking the United Nations advance toward the Yalu late in October, following the destruction of the North Korean forces, the Chinese partially broke contact before launching a general offensive in order to build up in overwhelming strength, presumably for a spring offensive. Their ultimate objective was undoubtedly a decisive effort aimed at the complete destruction of all United Nations forces in Korea. At the present moment the freezing of the Yalu River increasingly opens up avenues of reinforcement and supply which it is impossible for our air potential to interdict. It is quite evident that our present strength of force is not sufficient to meet this undeclared war by the Chinese with the inherent advantages which accrue thereby to them. The resulting situation presents an entirely new picture which broadens the potentialities to world embracing considerations beyond the sphere of decision by the Theater Commander. This command has done everything humanly possible within its capabilities but is now faced with conditions beyond its control and its strength.

As directed by your JCS 92801 DTG 272240Z Sept 50 [basic instructions], as amplified by your JCS 93709 DTG 092205Z Oct 50 [instructions should the Chinese intervene], my strategic plan for the immediate future is to pass from the offensive to the defensive with such local adjustments as may be required by a constantly fluid situation.[36]

This startling report clearly bucked the next decision up to the Joint Chiefs. MacArthur's third step was to get on record with the public. Less than an hour later, he issued Communiqué No. 14 for worldwide distribution, announcing that major enemy forces in total strength of more than 200,000 men were now committed against UNC forces.

> . . . Consequently we face an entirely new war. This has shattered the high hope we entertained that the intervention of the Chinese was only of a token nature on a volunteer and in-

dividual basis as publicly announced. It now appears to have been the enemy's intent in breaking off contact with our forces some two weeks ago, to secure the time necessary surreptitiously to build up for a later surprise assault upon our lines in overwhelming force, taking advantage of the freezing of all rivers and roadbeds which would have materially reduced the effectiveness of our air interdiction and permitted a greatly accelerated forward movement of enemy reinforcements and supplies. This plan has been disrupted by our own offensive action which forced upon the enemy a premature engagement.[37]

As an afterthought, he sent an addition to that communiqué to say that the situation posed issues that had to find their solution within the councils of the United Nations and the chancelleries of the world.

The radically revised figures on the Chinese strength, together with the ominous tone of the communiqué, was startling enough information to be included in the 1st Marine Division's PIR for the day. In addition to shocking America and the world with the sudden reversal of the situation, MacArthur's communiqué provided the Chinese with two very worthwhile bits of information. It told them that MacArthur's estimate of enemy strength was still only half of its actual size. And, by suggesting it was a problem for the chancelleries of the world, MacArthur was saying that the Chinese offensive might be beyond the capability of the UNC forces. Both bits of information would be highly satisfying to Mao and the Chinese.

Response in Washington
Early press reports on 27 November were not particularly alarming. It only seemed that the offensive had stalled. That afternoon, the Joint Chiefs had met briefly to go over the official reports, which were not particularly alarming. The Chiefs had based their thinking on the assumption that the situation would develop slowly, allowing for timely reappraisal. Business proceeded as usual in Washington.

MacArthur's report, arriving in the predawn hours of 28 November, was a shocker. The sudden reversal was totally unexpected and unforeseen. Bradley termed it "hysterical."[38] The press, if anything, was only slightly less so. The morning papers were screaming disaster. The official reports coming into the Pentagon were equally depressing. President Truman called for an expanded meeting of the National Security Council for that afternoon.

In preparation for that meeting, Defense Secretary George Marshall met with the Armed Forces Policy Council, a group made up of the service secretaries and the Joint Chiefs. The immediate topic was possible air and ground reinforcements. General J. Lawton Collins reported that individual replacements would be available starting in January. They might fill up the existing units sufficiently to enable them to deal with the Chinese. The only ground unit available was the 82d Airborne, and it should not be used. Otherwise no ground units would be available until March 1951.[39]

An increasingly serious concern was the Chinese air potential. Up to 300 aircraft had been assembled in Manchurian airfields in recent days. In addition, the performance of the new MiG-15s, appearing earlier in the month, had instantly made all fighter aircraft in the Far East obsolete. General Hoyt Vandenberg believed the F-84 and F-86 fighters, now being unloaded in Japan, could handle the MiG. Still, there was serious concern that the UN airfields in Korea were crowded and vulnerable to attack. The only remedy would be a strike at the Manchurian airfields, which would risk widening the war. The alternative was to withdraw the fighters to Japan. This would leave UNC ground troops vulnerable to air attack. Finding a solution for dealing with the air threat would become one of the most difficult problems in coming days.

The discussion turned to future policy on the conduct of the war. Because much of the future course of the war depended on keeping X Corps intact, its very exposed position was a worry to General Marshall. At that time, it appeared in Washington that there was a real possibility that X Corps could be cut off and the Marine division might be lost.[40] Marshall assumed that the advance forces would be withdrawn and regrouped, but he was unwilling to give MacArthur a specific order to do so. General Collins believed the UNC could hold a line, probably in North Korea, provided X Corps were not cut off. General Marshall was not quite as hopeful as

Collins about the ability of the UNC to hold a line, but he defended General MacArthur's offensive as a reconnaissance in force.[41]

On the assumption that X Corps was not cut off, and that a line could be held, the secretaries proposed some policies that formed the core of discussion for the next few days. The secretaries recommended that the United States carry out its obligation to the United Nations, localize the war in Korea, avoid general war with China, not commit any UNC ground troops in mainland China, not use any Chinese Nationalist troops, ask for additional contributions from other UN members, and accelerate the U.S. military buildup.[42]

MacArthur's report had implicitly asked for new instructions. Were new instructions needed?[43] That was the question for the National Security Council meeting with President Truman that afternoon.

The discussion ranged widely over U.S. responsibilities to the UN, the necessity to avoid expanding the war, the possibilities of a cease-fire, and the need to commence immediately the rearmament program approved by NSC 68. All comments were based on the assumption that the ground situation could be managed, that it was only a question of where the forces in Korea could hold a line.

General Omar Bradley told the president that although the situation was serious, the Joint Chiefs were doubtful that it was as much of a catastrophe as the newspapers were leading everyone to believe.[44] With the exception of the serious threat of an enemy air offensive, General Bradley's report on the military situation was cautious. The directive under which MacArthur was operating authorized him to go on the defensive. Because he had done that, it would be desirable to wait forty-eight or seventy-two hours for a clarification of the situation. The terrain through which the enemy was launching their attack was extremely mountainous, with few roads. They might have transportation difficulties sustaining their offensive. The situation could change in one or two weeks. He recommended against calling up the National Guard or other forces, saying he thought MacArthur had adequate forces at hand.

Without formal action, the council deferred action. Otherwise, the general consensus of those present was that the implementation of NSC 86 to build up the armed forces should commence soon, even if, as Stuart Symington put it, "we have to give up refrigerators and television sets." The meeting broke up with the president complaining about the campaign of political vilification that was being aimed at him, saying, "Some would rather see the country go down than for the administration to succeed."[45]

With few replacements and no formed ground units available as reinforcements, MacArthur considered Chiang Kai-shek's earlier offer of 30,000 troops. MacArthur requested the use of these forces and asked that he be authorized to negotiate directly with the Chinese Nationalists for movement of the troops. The growing tension between MacArthur and Bradley is evident in Bradley's comment that the request was profoundly disturbing.[46] Disturbing or not, the answer was evenhanded, stating: "Your proposal is being considered. It involves world-wide consequences." It went on to point out the possibility that it would disrupt the U.S. position with the UN, might extend hostilities to Taiwan (Formosa) and other areas, and might be unacceptable to other nations to have their forces deployed in conjunction with Chinese Nationalist forces.[47] No further action was ever taken.

Concern for X Corps, and especially concern for the 1st Marine Division, increased the following day. At a brief meeting of the Joint Chiefs on 29 November, Adm. Forrest Sherman was seriously concerned with the possibility of losing the Marine division. He urged the JCS to instruct General MacArthur to withdraw X Corps to a consolidated defense line. The other members were reluctant to issue such specific orders. Instead, they sent a message approving his decision to go on the defense and stated: ". . . any directive in conflict therewith is deferred. Strategic and tactical considerations are now paramount." Then he added: "What are your plans regarding the coordination of operations of the Army Eight and X Corps and the positioning of X Corps the units of which appear to us to be exposed?"[48]

MacArthur responded to the Joint Chiefs' query the following morning:

> The X Corps geographically threatens the main supply lines of the enemy force bearing upon the right flank of the Eighth Army. This threat is emphasized by thrusts from elements of the

Corps all along its west flank as far north as Mupyong-ni and as far south as the road nets west from the Wonsan section. This threat is now being met by the enemy commitment of a reported 6 to 8 divisions which otherwise would have been available for use against the Eighth Army. The enemy's penetration southward could not be safely accomplished until this threat of the X Corps is contained or nullified. Any concept of actual physical combination of the forces of the Eighth Army and X Corps in a practically continuous line across the narrow neck of Korea is quite impractical due to the length of that line, the numerical weakness of our forces and the logistical problems due to the mountainous divide which splits such a front from north to south.

The X Corps will contract its position, as enemy pressure develops, into the Hamhung–Wonsan sector. The corps commander has been enjoined against any possibility of piecemeal isolation and trapping of his forces. While geographically his elements seem to be well extended, the actual conditions of terrain make it extremely difficult for an enemy to take any material advantage thereof.[49]

MacArthur's message sparked further antagonism with the Joint Chiefs, particularly Bradley, who later wrote: ". . . This message was so utterly absurd and insulting that my faith in MacArthur . . . eroded sharply. I was outraged by this message and felt that MacArthur treated the JCS as if we were children."[50]

Commanders' Conference
By 9:30 P.M. on 28 November, Gens. Walton Walker and Edward Almond, summoned earlier, had arrived in Tokyo. Together with Gen. Doyle Hickey, acting chief of staff; Gen. Edwin Wright, G-3; Gen. Charles Willoughby, G-2; Gen. Courtney Whitney, MacArthur's military secretary; Gen. George Stratemeyer; and VAdm. Turner Joy, they assembled with General MacArthur at his residence for a four-hour discussion of the situation. No official record of the discussion was kept. General Whitney made brief mention of the conference in his book on MacArthur. Other information has been supplied by

interviews with General Almond and from messages sent subsequently to X Corps.

The thrust of the discussion was what X Corps could do to assist the Eighth Army. At that time, it was assumed that X Corps, rather than being the most threatened, was least affected by the offensive. The accumulated reports from three days of fighting in the Eighth Army section made it seem as if the Eighth was in greater danger than X Corps.[51]

When General MacArthur asked Walker what he thought the situation was and what he could do, Walker said he thought he could restore his right flank and attempt to hold along the Chongchon, but, failing that, he would fall back to Pyongyang–Chinampo and hold with defense lines to the north and east.

When asked what he could do to help, General Almond was even more optimistic. He stated that he expected the Marines and the 7th Division to continue their attack west and north, carry out the plan to cut the enemy line of communication near Mupyong-ni, and continue to the Yalu. He would reinforce the units at Chosin with 7th Division units.

Walker's optimism is somewhat understandable. When he departed Korea, he had every reason to think the Army could stabilize along the Chongchon. Further, having been thoroughly browbeaten by MacArthur over his withdrawal to the Chongchon earlier in the month, and the alleged public relations indiscretions in his Army, he was not about to voice anything but the most aggressive opinions.

Almond's optimism is a little more difficult to understand. Almond had been to both front-line units within the previous thirty hours. The X Corps Periodic Intelligence Report for 28 November reported six CCF divisions totaling an estimated 35,000 men in the Chosin area, twice what Willoughby estimated.[52] Lieutenant Colonel Robert Glass from the X Corps G-2 section accompanied Almond to Tokyo and surely must have provided him with the most current enemy information during the three-and-one-half-hour flight.

Almond later explained his thinking:

> I recall the gist of statements by Walker and myself. Neither one of us knew the strength of the Chinese. We stated so much.

Walker thought he could hold his "then position" . . . we thought for a while it was possible for the Marine division to push forward to the northwest and thereby protect the flank of the Eighth Army . . . two days earlier the G-2 of the 1st Marine Division did not give the enemy an offensive capability in the Chosin Reservoir area and that is the unit that had been in contact with what enemy forces had been discovered. The only reports that we received supported the probable presence of an unusually large number of enemy in the area which originated with local civilians whose reports had been exaggerated in all our other experiences. . . . In view of the above I agreed that we could make an effort not knowing the enemy strength—the first thing to do was "try." It must be remembered that the situation on the 1st Marine Division front was developing at the very time that we were conferring in Tokyo, and when I stated that the 1st Marine Division could assist I had done so with the possibility of an advance by the enemy coming on later.[53]

The conference discussed various measures for coping with the situation, including an attack westward by the 3d Division. Walker was anxious to be reinforced, but he wanted the pressure kept on the Chinese, who were on his right flank: "The meeting broke up after midnight on a note of confident resolution."[54] MacArthur, apparently, made no decisions and issued no instructions when the meeting concluded. The next morning, he directed Walker to defend Pyongyang but authorized him to withdraw farther if he was in danger of envelopment. Almond was instructed to concentrate at Hagaru-ri, maintaining aggressive contact with the enemy, prepared to withdraw to Hungnam.[55]

The Chinese Reevaluate Their Plans

While the situation was being discussed and reevaluated in Tokyo and Washington, the Chinese were also reviewing their options. On 29 November, after two days of fighting, Gen. Song Shilun and his staff reappraised the situation. Their offensive had not gone as expected. They believed that the forces at Yudam-ni were the 7th

Marines and two battalions of the 5th Marines. They estimated that the forces at Sinhung-ni, east of Chosin, consisted of the 32d Infantry Regiment with one battalion of the 31st, plus one artillery battalion. At Hagaru-ri, they thought the forces were one battalion of the 5th Marines, one tank battalion, and the headquarters of the 1st Marine Division. They believed the force at Sachang-ni to be the 7th Infantry Regiment. Thus, the total enemy strength surrounded at Yudam-ni, Hagaru-ri, and east of Chosin appeared to be four regiments, one tank battalion and three artillery battalions—more than 10,000 men, twice the enemy strength on which their plan was based.

General Song Shilun decided to shift his main effort. Instead of concentrating on the 1st Marine Division forces at Yudam-ni, he would concentrate additional forces to destroy the Army units at Sinhung-ni and thereafter shift his troops to destroy the units at Yudam-ni and Hagaru-ri, one after the other. The 27th CCF Army would move the two remaining regiments of the 81st CCF Division, then near the Fusen Reservoir, to join the 80th Division in the attack at Sinhung-ni. The 27th Army's reserve division, the 94th, would be prepared to assist.

To coincide with this, the 58th CCF Division and the 79th Division would carry out holding attacks on the forces at Hagaru-ri and Yudam-ni. The 59th Division of the 20th CCF Army would be attached temporarily to the 27th Army to assist in coordinating action at Yudam-ni. In the Sachang-ni area, the 89th Division would temporarily go on the defensive.[56]

Notes

1. X Corps msg 241239I, Nov. 50.
2. 1st Mar Div PIR 34, 27 Nov. 50.
3. X Corps PIR 62, 27 Nov. 50.
4. Lieutenant General O. P. Smith interview by Ben Frank, 9–12 June 1969. Papers of O. P. Smith, Archives Branch, Marine Corps Research Center.
5. Lynn Montross and Nicholas Canzona, *U.S. Marine Operations in Korea.* Vol. III, *The Chosin Reservoir Campaign* (Washington, D.C.: Historical Section, U.S. Marine Corps, 1957), 167.
6. 1st Mar Div PIR 34, 27 Nov. 50, shows that two regiments of the 89th CCF Division were identified at Yudam-ni, confirming earlier identifications of this division. However, the official map in *Chinese People's Volunteers* shows the 89th CCF Division, minus one regiment and one battalion, in the attack on Sachang-ni on 27 November. This would indicate that the 89th Division's forces at Yudam-ni totaled only four battalions.
7. 3d Bn, 7th Marines, *Special Action Report 8 Oct–15 Dec. 50.* Copy in author's possession.
8. Because of the distance and difficult terrain, no lateral contact was ever established between 1st Marine Division units at Hagaru-ri and 7th Infantry Division units on the east side of the Fusen Reservoir. This is an interesting example of the Chinese having appraised the situation in light of their own abilities to operate over such difficult terrain.
9. *Chinese People's Volunteers,* 59–64.
10. *China Today: War to Resist U.S. Aggression and Aid Korea.* Appendix II, "Chinese People's Volunteers Heroes and Models" (Beijing: Chinese Social Sciences Publishing House, 1990). Unpublished partial translation in possession of the author (hereafter cited as *Heroes and Models*).

Awards cited indicate that all of the awards for 80th Division personnel on 27 November were for action in the Sinhung-ni area. Awards were given later to members of the 242d and 243d Regiments for action at Sinhung-ni, and one to a member of the 241st for blocking the attack south from Sinhung-ni.

11. Roy E. Appleman, *East of Chosin: Entrapment and Breakout in Korea, 1950* (College Station: Texas A&M University Press, 1987), 87 and N34.

12. Montross and Canzona, *Chosin Reservoir Campaign*, 203.

13. Arthur Wilson and Norm Strickbine, *Korean Vignettes: The Faces of War* (Portland, Ore.: Artworks Publications, 1966), 123 (narrative of Ivan Long).

14. X Corps G-3 Journal J-27 0950, 28 Nov. 50.

15. X Corps G-3 Journal J-36 1120, 28 Nov. 50.

16. *Special Report—Chosin Reservoir.* X Corps.

17. Hammel, *Chosin*, 137.

18. Roy E. Appleman, *Escaping the Trap: The U.S. Army X Corps in Northeast Korea, 1950* (College Station: Texas A&M University Press, 1990), 102.

19. Blair, *The Forgotten War*, 462.

20. Appleman, *East of Chosin*, 115.

21. X Corps G-3 Journal J-76 1600, 28 Nov. 50.

22. 1st Mar Div PIR 35, 28 Nov. 50.

23. X Corps PIR 63, 28 Nov. 50.

24. Wesley J. Curtis, *Operations of the First Battalion, 32d Infantry Regiment, 7th Inf Div., in the Chosin Reservoir Area of Korea During the Period 24 November–2 December 1950.* Unpublished manuscript provided courtesy of Col. George Rasula (hereafter cited as *Curtis mss*).

25. Appleman, *East of Chosin*, 144ff.

26. Ibid., 148.

27. Ibid., 149.

28. X Corps G-3 Journal J-6 0315, 29 Nov. 50.

29. Most accounts based on PW interrogation identify the 172d Regiment as being the main attack force on the southwest perimeter. However, various citations in *Heroes and Models* show that the 172d Regiment was involved on the East Hill while the 173d Regiment was involved in the attack on the southwest perimeter.

30. *Heroes and Models.*

31. Montross and Canzona, *Chosin Reservoir Campaign*, 208ff.

32. *Chinese People's Volunteers.*

33. Ibid.

34. Ibid.

35. The figures and estimates were published in DIS 3003, 29 Nov. 50, which would reflect the G-2's thinking late in the day on 28 November.

36. FEC msg C69953, 28 Nov. 50 to JCS.

37. FEC Communiqué No. 14, 28 Nov. 50.

38. Bradley, *A General's Life,* 598–99.

39. Condit, *History of the Secretary of Defense,* 83–84.

40. General O. P. Smith was told later that General Bradley thought the Marine division was lost. Smith interview with Ben Frank.

41. Condit, *History of the Secretary of Defense,* 83–84.

42. Ibid.

43. Details of the NSC meeting contained in notes taken by Philip Jessup, *FRUS,* 1249.

44. Truman, *Years of Trial and Hope,* 385.

45. Notes taken by Jessup, *FRUS,* 1249.

46. Bradley, *A General's Life,* 602. The full quote is, "At this time we received another message from MacArthur that disturbed all of us profoundly. It suggested that MacArthur was monumentally stupid, had gone mad, or had rejected the JCS and administration policy to keep the war localized and was willing to risk an all-out war with the Chinese, regardless of the consequences."

47. JCS msg 97594, 29 Nov. 50, to CINCFE quoted in *HJCS,* 343–44.

48. JCS msg 97592, 29 Nov. 50, to CINCFE.

49. CINCUNC msg CX50095, 30 Nov. 50, to JCS.

50. Bradley, *A General's Life,* 600–601.

51. Schnabel, *Policy and Direction,* 279. No record was kept of this meeting. General Whitney later included a brief account in his book. The substance of the meeting has been reconstructed from Whitney, from messages sent later by X Corps, and from Ferguson's interview and correspondence with General Almond.

52. X Corps PIR 63, 28 Nov. 50.

53. Letter Almond to Appleman 21 Dec. 76 (Almond Papers, MHI).

54. Courtney Whitney, *MacArthur: His Rendezvous with History* (New York: Knopf, 1956), 423–24.

55. Appleman, *Disaster in Korea,* 216

56. *Chinese People's Volunteers* and Zhang, *Mao's Military Romanticism.*

13
Chosin: The First Step Back

On the 3rd the enemy ... exerted themselves to the utmost and broke out of the encirclement ... because of day after day of combat, useless ammunition and pretty heavy frostbite and combat losses....
—Chinese description of the breakout from Yudam-ni

X Corps Plans

At the 28 November conference in Tokyo, General Almond had responded with optimism to General MacArthur's questions. At midnight, when the meeting broke up, he directed the two staff officers who had accompanied him to Tokyo to alert the X Corps HQ to possible change in corps orders and to get an update on the current situation. The bulk of the corps was to be concentrated in the Hamhung–Hungnam area. The 3d Division was to launch a "demonstration" across the peninsula. General David Barr and Maj. Gen. Robert Soule, 3d Division commander, were to be at the corps command post (CP) at 4 P.M. the following day to receive instructions. The future mission of I ROK Corps was not yet firm. For the present, Almond had no new instructions for the 1st Marine Division.[1] In the next few days, General Almond's thinking underwent some rapid changes.

By the time he returned to Hamhung the following afternoon, Almond was determined to maintain an aggressive stance, drawing off or occupying Chinese forces that otherwise would threaten the Eighth Army. In a phone call from the corps, Gen. Oliver Smith was told all forces at Koto-ri and north were now under his command and were to be concentrated in a coordinated perimeter defense based on Hagaru-ri. One RCT was to be withdrawn immediately from Yudam-ni to Hagaru-ri and used to gain contact with RCT 31. And the 1st Marine Division was to open and secure the Hagaru–Koto-ri main supply route (MSR). X Corps would coordinate the movement of units south of Koto-ri.[2] A corps operational instruction confirmed these orders shortly thereafter. Under this plan, one RCT would remain at Yudam-ni.

That evening, the X Corps periodic intelligence report (PIR) stated: "The enemy is disregarding tremendous losses as he continues to press his assault on X Corps forces in the Chosin Reservoir area. Additional CCF reinforcement continue to flow into the sector as units previously identified cascade down the western flank of X Corps into the 30 mile gap which exists between the Corps and Eighth Army." The estimated enemy strength in the Chosin area was 40,000, with an additional 12,000 deployed in the south generally along the X Corps boundary and near the east-west routes of approach to Hamhung and Wonsan. Air reconnaissance reported considerable additional forces moving down from the north. The enemy was considered capable of continuing the attack to force withdrawal of X Corps units from Chosin.[3]

Situation at Yudam-ni

Late in the afternoon of 29 November, when General Smith learned of the failure of the composite battalion to clear the MSR, he instructed the 5th Marines to assume responsibility for protection of Yudam-ni, adjusting present dispositions accordingly, while the entire 7th Marines was to be employed without delay to clear the MSR.[4] General Almond's order, instructing Smith to redeploy one RCT to Hagaru-ri, had been anticipated by two hours.

The 5th and 7th Marines staffs worked through the night with unit commanders to arrive at a plan. The two regiments were so closely tied together that any move by one affected the other. Fortunately, it was a quiet night, with no significant enemy contact. The 3d Battalion, 11th Marines, received some long-range sniper fire and, in turn, fired several counter-battery missions on suspected Chinese artillery locations. But care was exercised to conserve the critically short supply of artillery ammunition.[5] By 6 A.M. on 30 November, Joint Operation Order No. 1 was ready for issue. Essentially, the 5th Marines would move southward into the mouth of the valley below Yudam-ni, forming a tighter perimeter, while the 7th Marines would attack south. It would take a day to readjust all the lines and move the supporting units.

The following day, 1 December, the plan was changed. The plan now was to concentrate the 5th and 7th Marines and RCT 31 at Hagaru-ri. The new corps operation order stated that X Corps was to maintain contact with the enemy to the maximum capability "consistent with cohesive action oriented to the Hamhung–Hungnam base of operations." In addition to concentrating at Hagaru-ri, the 1st Marine Division was to secure the Sudong–Hagaru-ri MSR in its zone.

The 7th Infantry Division was to assemble immediately in the Hamhung–Sinhung–Hungbong-ni area, establishing strong blocking positions in the Sinhung and Hungbong-ni areas; protect the corps' north and northeast flank; and provide one RCT with the division tank battalion as corps reserve. I ROK Corps was to hold its position, protect the corps right flank, and secure the east coast MSR.

The 3d Infantry Division was given a collection of tasks. It was to attack westward with a strong task force on the Yonghung–Inhung-ni axis and assist the Eighth Army. It was to protect the corps left flank and the Hamhung–Sudong MSR in zone. The remaining elements of the division, except for one battalion, were to assemble in the Chig-yong–Yonpo area. The one battalion, together with the 1st KMC Regiment, was to form a task force to protect Wonsan and the Wonsan airfield.[6]

General Soule apparently had concerns about the many different missions. About midmorning of 30 November, he met with General Almond and Col. William W. Harris, commanding officer of the 65th Infantry. It was agreed to change the attack westward to a reconnaissance in force by a reinforced battalion.

No sooner had changes been made in the 3d Division's tasks than a new directive arrived from Tokyo. General MacArthur, prodded by the Joint Chiefs' concern about X Corps dispositions, advised: "In view of deteriorating situation in Eighth Army area and the probable result of successive withdrawals to the south, it is no longer important to make your thrust to the west. Under such circumstance, and in view of latest reports of increasing buildup against your front, believe contraction of your forces becomes advisable."[7]

Situation East of Chosin

During 29 November, two air drops were received but some of the materiel fell outside the lines. Units remained short of ammunition. No 40mm ammunition was received then or later, and only about forty rounds of 105mm ammunition were received. The 40mm ammunition needed was delivered to the Hudong CP, while the 75mm ammunition Capt. Robert Drake had requested was delivered to the Inlet. No one at the Inlet was aware that Drake with his tanks and improvised infantry force was trying to break through to them.

About 4 P.M., an evacuation helicopter, arranged by Gen. Henry Hodes, arrived. The first two evacuees taken out were Lt. Cols. William Reilly and Ray Embree, both wounded the first night. The helicopter returned later and took out two more wounded. That was all.

The reorganized perimeter was quiet during the early part of the night. At midnight, the Chinese attacked from the south against the lines of 1/32. They were driven off. Later, probing attacks were made at each end of the perimeter, where the roads entered. At the west end, the enemy did overrun one machine-gun post and capture some of the crew. Otherwise, the perimeter held except for small enemy teams infiltrating to make special attacks against the antiaircraft weapons.

During the night, movement was spotted out on the ice. Illumination showed the figures to be U.S. soldiers who were guided into the perimeter. They were members of a cutoff platoon of A/1/32 who had been left behind and had managed to find their way through the Chinese.

For the remainder of the night, the Chinese limited themselves to harassing fire, flares, whistles, and bugles. The decreased enemy activity gave the troops hope that perhaps the worst was over.

Early on 30 November, another air drop provided some .50-caliber ammunition but no 40mm. A later drop arrived shortly after noon. Again, some fell outside the perimeter and could not be recovered, but an ample supply of ammunition was delivered for the 4.2-inch mortars.

At Hudong on the morning of 30 November, enemy forces could be observed building up to the south, between Hudong and Hagaru-ri. A message to the 1st Marine Division G-3 section—relayed to X Corps—reported the buildup, along with the known status of the cut-off units.[8] As the day wore on, the Chinese commenced isolated prob-ing attacks.[9]

General Hodes had arrived at Hagaru-ri late in the afternoon of 28 November. He conferred with General Smith, reported that the cutoff battalions had about 400 casualties, and said that it was im-possible for them to fight their way out, that they would need help. At that time, the only infantry troops Smith had available were the two rifle companies of the 3d Battalion, 1st Marines, and the weapons company of the 2d Battalion, 7th Marines. He was at that point work-ing on a plan with Col. Lewis Puller to organize a task force to drive through from Koto-ri with reinforcements for Hagaru-ri. With Yu-dam-ni under attack, he was unwilling to risk sending forces north to aid a task force that had more combat strength than he had at Hagaru-ri. He believed that with the strong tank force at Hudong-ni, the cutoff battalions could at least improve their situation by mov-ing toward Hagaru-ri, particularly when there was plenty of air cover to support them. General Hodes remained in Hagaru-ri, monitor-ing the situation.

On the morning of 30 November, General Barr arrived at Hagaru-ri to discuss measures to assist RCT 31. General Smith lent him a he-licopter to fly into the Inlet. Barr's appearance was a note of en-couragement to the troops, who met him at the landing site. But he brusquely waved off any courtesies and stalked off to find Colonel MacLean—only to be the first from higher headquarters to find out that MacLean was missing and Colonel Faith was in command. What transpired between Barr and Faith is unknown. At a meeting of officers the next day, Faith only said he had received no instruc-tions on what to do.[10]

With the responsibility for the rescue of RCT 31 assigned to him, General Smith, some time late in the afternoon of 30 November, de-termined to direct the forces to fight their way south. Smith reported: "Although Gen. Hodes was not in the chain of command, I asked him to draw up a dispatch in my name to Task Force Faith em-bodying my ideas. Lt. Col. Faith was advised that his command was now attached to the [1st Marine Division] and that he should make every effort to secure necessary exits and move south toward Hagaru-ri at the earliest. The dispatch further stated that he should do nothing which would jeopardize the safety of his wounded. He was authorized to destroy such equipment as would impede his movement and was advised that in view of the critical requirements for troops to hold Hagaru-ri no actual troop assistance could be furnished but that unlimited air support would be available to the task force to assist it in moving southward."[11]

Conference at Hagaru-ri

Acting on MacArthur's instructions to concentrate X Corps, General Almond flew to Hagaru-ri, arriving at 2:10 P.M. to confer with Generals Smith and Barr. The plan was changed once more. Smith was to withdraw to Hamhung. Almond stressed the necessity for speed. He authorized Smith to burn or destroy equipment or supplies and promised that he would be supplied by air drop as he withdrew. General Smith thought it unnecessary to abandon equipment. He told the corps commander that his movement would be governed by his ability to evacuate the wounded, that he would have to fight his way back and could not afford to discard equipment, and that, therefore, he intended to bring out the bulk of his equipment.

General Almond also was anxious to get the RCT 31 task force withdrawn. It appears that he agreed with General Smith that Task Force Faith could improve its situation by attacking south. In the discussion that followed, he told General Barr that if the acting regimental commander, Faith, did not attack, he should be relieved. How such a relief would be effected was not stated. Barr objected that Faith was an excellent officer in whom he had great confidence. The discussion ended with Almond directing Barr and Smith to draw up a plan for extricating the cutoff units and directing Barr to have the plan ready for him by six o'clock that evening when he returned to Hungnam.[12]

After Almond departed, Smith and Barr discussed the situation. In view of the threat to Hagaru-ri, Smith said, "We can't do anything about going up there for those people until the 5th and 7th Marines fight their way in to us. Then maybe we can do something about it." Barr agreed.[13]

General Barr took one more step. The force collected at Hudong-ni had twice failed to break through to the Inlet. As the day wore on, Lt. Col. Barry Anderson, at Hudong, reported that the Chinese buildup in the vicinity was becoming more threatening. Apparently with the concurrence of General Smith, Barr ordered the force withdrawn to Hagaru-ri. The timing of this order, and its transmission, is not clear, but it apparently occurred some time around 2 P.M. Lieutenant Colonel Anderson, and others in the Hudong force, knew that the 2d Battalion, 31st Infantry—then stalled south of Koto-ri—had been cleared by corps to advance to Hagaru-ri. Their belief was that on the arrival of the battalion, the Hudong force would be on hand to reinforce them and, with a solid tank/infantry force, could break through to the Inlet. Late in the afternoon, the Hudong force withdrew.

Smith's order for the task force to attack south, and the order to withdraw the Hudong force, which had to have been made with his approval, added to the long list of controversial decisions of the Chosin action. Smith's order appears not to have been received by the task force prior to Faith's determination to make a run for it. Two different officers have stated they heard the message transmitted in the clear on Jeep-mounted radios as the southward advance began. Had it been sent prior to withdrawal of the Hudong force, it could have been transmitted to Hudong by tank radio, then relayed via observation aircraft to the troops at the Inlet.

When the task force eventually was halted and overrun, it had reached Hudong. It is believed that if the Hudong force had remained in position, the bulk of the task force might have been saved. Alternatively, the Hudong force could well have been destroyed in the meantime by the gathering Chinese. Lieutenant Colonel McCaffrey, X Corps deputy chief of staff, was present when General Almond asked Barr about it. Barr replied that he could not see any good coming from losing more men on behalf of those already lost.[14] Not long afterward, Barr was replaced.

That evening, Almond began a series of daily reports to General MacArthur, giving his personal estimate of the situation. Almond reported two CCF armies in the Chosin area with a possible third army on the west flank of X Corps, fifty miles from Yonghung. He believed they had a far greater degree of training and capacity for infiltration and night operation than those of the 124th Division, previously encountered. He gave an upbeat report on the status of RCT 31, saying, "Two battalions of the 7th Infantry Division, isolated by the enemy drive east of Chosin Reservoir, have 400 wounded which must wait for slow helicopter evacuation, then these two battalions can drive through enemy road blocks assisted by the 5th and 7th Marine Regiments now withdrawing to Hagaru-ri."[15]

The corps intelligence estimate that evening reported a steady buildup of forces in the Chosin area and along both sides of the MSR south of Hagaru-ri, but it offered the opinion that diminishing contact with enemy forces in Yudam-ni and Hagaru-ri suggested the possibility that enemy force there might have disengaged in order to continue their advance to the south.[16]

Defense of Hagaru-ri

At Hagaru-ri, the crest of East Hill was still in Chinese hands on 30 November and remained so despite a stubborn all-day effort by G Company, 1st Marines. That night, the Chinese launched a renewed attack on East Hill. G Company was driven back and had to be reinforced by the commandos, then further reinforced by whatever additional men could be found in the vicinity of the 3d Battalion, 1st Marines, command post. By 9 A.M. on 1 December, the situation had been contained but the Chinese still held the crest of East Hill.

To the southwest, the Chinese commenced again with probes around 11:30 P.M. At midnight, the Chinese 173d and 174th Regiments, reinforced with some troops from the 176th Regiment of the 59th Division, launched another attack aimed principally at Item Company. This time the attack was beaten off without any penetration of Marine lines. Losses to the Chinese were estimated to be between 500 and 750 KIA. The Marines had two killed in action.

In the three-day attempt to seize Hagaru-ri, the estimated Chinese losses in the 58th CCF Division were 3,300 in the 172d Regiment and 1,750 each for the 173d and 174th Regiments. In the 59th CCF Division, the 176th Regiment was believed to have lost 1,750 men. The 58th CCF Division was, for all practical purposes, finished as an effective combat organization.

On 1 December, advance elements of the 26th CCF Army began arriving in the vicinity of Hagaru-ri, having been ordered southward from the Munak-ni and Mio-ri areas, north of Changjin Town, to take over the 20th Army's task of attacking Hagaru-ri. The main body of those units took several more days to reach Hagaru-ri. The 58th and 60th CCF Divisions were to move southward to the Hwangcho Pass (Funchillin Pass).[17]

The Advance from Yudam-ni
Following General Almond's urging for speed, General Smith sent a message to the 5th and 7th Marines the evening of 30 November, telling them to expedite Joint Operation Order No. 1 and the combined movement of both RCTs to Hagaru-ri, preparing for further withdrawal southward. With a few alterations, Joint Operation Order No. 1 was converted to Joint Operation Order No. 2, ready for execution the morning of 1 December.

The 3d Battalion, 7th Marines, would lead off by attacking and securing the two dominating heights on either side of the valley south of Yudam-ni. The 3d Battalion, 5th Marines, would then pass through down the road while the 1st Battalion, 7th Marines, moved overland to the east in a flanking movement to reach Fox Company at Toktong Pass. The 1st and 2d Battalions, 5th Marines, would deploy across the valley, facing north to hold off pursuing Chinese. They, in turn, would pass through 3/7, which would then come off the hills and bring up the rear.

The 3/7 attack did not go well. H Company, on the left, was to seize Hill 1419. In a daylong effort fiercely resisted by the Chinese defenders, in spite of intense artillery and air support, the company was unable to reach the top of the hill. Late in the day, portions of 1/7 were committed. The hill was finally secured by sunset. Across the valley, I Company, then G Company, and finally a provisional company of artillery and headquarters people made very slow progress along the ridge toward the commanding heights of Hill 1547.

Without having possession of Hill 1547, 3/5 began its advance down the road, while 1/7 passed through 3/7 on the left, picked up H Company, and commenced an arduous night march across the frozen hills that became one of the great feats of the Korean War. The 1/7 envelopment was a decisive factor in breaking the Chinese resistance and won Lt. Col. Raymond G. Davis, the battalion commander, the Medal of Honor for his leadership. Temperatures ranged from −20°F to −30°F. As the heavily laden men advanced, the trail became packed and slick with ice. Burdened with extra ammunition, men stumbled and strained to keep their footing. At one point, the column began to veer to the right toward the Chinese positions. At another point, Chinese took the column under fire, but the rear guard was able to fight off the threat. Davis said later that the cold and exhaustion of the march made it so difficult for him to concentrate that he made his unit commanders repeat to him whatever orders he had given. At one point, Davis had to halt the column from sheer exhaustion. Finally, at 11:25 the next morning, the column reached Fox Company. There was now a battalion with five understrength but still effective companies behind the Chinese opposing the advance of the main column.

By the morning of 2 December, the 3d Battalion, 5th Marines, was meeting very heavy opposition and taking casualties at an alarming rate. Colonel Homer Litzenberg radioed the division that the situation looked grave. He estimated there were two full Chinese divisions dug in on the high ground and attacking the column from all sides. At noon, the column reached a blown bridge and was halted there while engineers under fire cleared a bypass. The advance continued against determined opposition until two o'clock the following morning, when it halted for the night just 1,000 yards short of F Company.

To the rear of the force, the situation was uncertain. The 2d Battalion, 5th Marines, holding positions to the west of the road, was hit by the Chinese about 1 A.M. on 2 December. The battalion lost some ground and was able to hold, but it never regained portions of the line. At 4:30 that morning, Chinese descending from the crest of Hill 1547 counterattacked G and I Companies of 3/7, driving them back until they reached a line lower on the hill, where they were able to hang on precariously. From their position on the hill, the Chinese were able to snipe at the column from long range, but they were unable to do any real damage. Then, at 9 P.M., the 1st Battalion, 5th Marines, was attacked, but it managed to hold.

On the morning of 3 December, the 1st Battalion, 7th Marines, moved out to clear the remaining positions at the top of the pass. In so doing, it dislodged a battalion of Chinese, who withdrew northward, right into the path of the advancing troops of 3/5. The result was the greatest slaughter of Chinese in the Yudam-ni breakout, probably eliminating an entire Chinese battalion.

By 1 P.M., the two forces made contact. The column halted only long enough to load aboard the wounded from F Company. The 1st Battalion, 7th Marines, then led the advance toward Hagaru-ri, while 3/5 held the top of the pass until midnight on 3 December. In the rear, 1/5 passed through 3/7, followed by 2/5. The 3d Battalion, 7th Marines, was ordered to hold its position until dark; then, with nothing behind them but pursuing Chinese, they moved briskly toward the pass as the rear guard. There were no stragglers that night.

By 7 P.M. on 3 December, the point reached the Hagaru-ri perimeter. There was a brief halt as those still on their feet closed up, fell in, and marched in cadence. It was an emotional event. It was not until 2 P.M. on 4 December that the last man in 3/7 closed on the perimeter. No one had ever doubted the troops from Yudam-ni would make it, but there was always a question of how *many* would.

Chinese Reaction

The 177th CCF Regiment retained control of Hill 1542 and the highest ground west of the valley throughout the action. Lower on the slopes of 1542, the action is described in a Chinese account: "Zhou Wenjiang—Chief of staff, 2nd Bn, 177th Regt—Led a vanguard company in holding a position and was in heavy fighting for seven days and seven nights, with the most enemy counterattacks for a single day being more than ten." And "Wang Xingji—political instructor, 2nd Bn, 177th Regt—Charged at the head of his men, enhanced morale and insured the troops held their positions for seven days and seven nights satisfactorily completing blocking attack tasks."[10]

To the east the 175th CCF Regiment held the key hill, 1419, for most of the day on 1 December. The action of one CCF soldier in defense of Hill 1419 is described in the register of heroes: "Wang

Yunge—Squad Leader, 4th Company, 175th Rgt—In Dec 1950, in a counterattack at Hill 1414.2 [1419] during the second campaign, after the soldiers in his squad were wounded and he was alone without ammunition among many enemy, he fought on alone and threw the few hand grenades he had at the enemy, killing more than 30 of them and holding the position."[19]

The Chinese history gives a grim picture of the overall action: "On 1 and 2 December 27th Army units and 59th Div engaged in heavy fighting in the Wonsu-ni [south of Yudam-ni] and Sayong Pass [Toktong Pass] area. On the 3rd the enemy, aided by the Hagaru-ri enemy, under cover of more than 50 aircraft and led by a tank group, exerted themselves to the utmost and broke out of the encirclement. They fiercely attacked our positions on Sayong Pass, Changhyang-ni and Sohung-ni lines. Our 59th Division was attacked by enemy from two sides and did all it could to resist, inflicting heavy casualties on the enemy; however, finally, because of day after day of combat, useless ammunition and pretty heavy frostbite and combat losses, the enemy broke through."[20]

The "tank group" referred to in the Chinese account consisted of one M-26 tank from D Company, 1st Tank Battalion, which had been sent to Yudam-ni as a pilot tank to see if additional tanks could make it over the road. The lone tank formed the point of the attacking column.

Destruction of RCT 31

East of the reservoir, the situation was grim. Captain Edward Stamford had a busy day directing air strikes on 30 November. Planes repeatedly struck the high ground and ridges surrounding the perimeter. There appeared to be no shortage of targets. Song Shilun's revised plan was under way. Reinforcements from the 81st CCF Division were arriving. Colonel Faith and his S-3 worked out a plan to counterattack penetrations in any part of the perimeter. Wire communication within the perimeter was improved and ammo was redistributed. The troops had hope that a relief force would reach them. But, as the hours ticked off, it became apparent no relief force would reach them that day. As darkness came on, the word was passed: "Hold out one more night and we've got it made."

The enemy attacks renewed earlier than usual, and with more determination. Snow began to fall. The approach to the perimeter across ice from the north was a favored enemy avenue. The 4.2-inch mortars attempted to break the ice there, but it was too thick. The intensity of the enemy attack built up toward midnight, yet no penetration had been made. Increased mortar fire fell in the perimeter, including 120mm mortars, and with increasing accuracy. Then the enemy penetrated the east side, held by the skeletal 3/31. Other attacks came from the road to the west. The perimeter was penetrated at five different points. Local counterattacks were able to halt the penetrations but not always to restore positions. In the early morning hours, there was doubt the perimeter could hold out until daylight. When daylight came, enemy attacks subsided, but the enemy did not pull back as they had done previously. They remained in the low ground, in contact with the perimeter.

First light showed a dishearteningly low ceiling, precluding air support. But about 10 A.M., a lone Corsair penetrated the overcast and buzzed the perimeter. Through Captain Stamford's radio, the pilot reported that some improvement was forecast. As soon as weather permitted, he would lead a flight of planes to the perimeter. Lieutenant Colonel Faith started making plans to break out for Hagaru-ri. By 1 P.M., planes were on station. All trucks were unloaded and loaded with wounded. Gas tanks of inoperable vehicles were drained for fuel. The little ammunition left was redistributed. Unfortunately, the 40mms were out of ammunition and ammunition for the quad .50s was very limited. Both weapons had played a decisive role in keeping the perimeter from being overrun.

Headed by the 1st Battalion, 32d Infantry, the column began its advance. Then a prematurely released napalm tank from supporting aircraft hit at the point of the column, killing several soldiers and injuring others, demoralizing and disorganizing the advance units. But the same attack suppressed Chinese resistance. The column lurched forward. Major Wesley J. Curtis, S-3 of 1/32, described the situation: "At the initial success of the breakout a sort of hysterical enthusiasm seized the troops. They flooded down the road like a great mob and tactical control broke down almost immediately. Officers and NCOs tried frantically to reestablish control and to order men up on the high ground where they could protect the truck column, but every man seemed to want to reach the head of the column and thereby increase his chances of reaching safety. Enemy small arms fire was encountered all the way, but men attacked and over-ran enemy positions frontally with seeming disregard for basic tactical principles and their own safety."[21]

Under heavy small-arms fire, the column proceeded. As troops took cover from time to time, units became intermingled and increasingly disorganized. Because of the loss of key officers and NCOs, effective control slipped away. It became a battle of individuals and small groups.

The column halted at the first blown bridge. Each truck had to detour across a marshy area and through a bypass. Some trucks stalled and required help. Chinese fire took its toll of drivers. Others were prepared to pull dead or wounded drivers from the cab and drive themselves. The tortuous passage of the low area was dominated by Chinese on Hill 1221 to the south, the hill that had foiled Captain Drake's efforts to break through to the task force. Once past the first blown bridge, the convoy was again halted by another roadblock at the hairpin turn on the east side of Hill 1221. While Faith took personal charge of efforts to break this block, other officers and NCOs, individually and with whatever small group they could recruit, attacked Hill 1221. At the same time, Chinese were closing in on the tail of the column from their positions to the north on Hill 1435.

The crest of Hill 1221 was reached and the roadblock was broken, but Faith was killed and a misdirected air strike strafed the soldiers on Hill 1221. From the hill, some men continued down to the road again, while others veered to the west onto the ice of the reservoir. The truck column was again halted south of Hill 1221 by a second blown bridge. Agonizing efforts were made to continue southward by driving the trucks across a railroad bridge. Some trucks succeeded but were finally halted completely by Chinese in the vicinity of Hudong-ni. Some who had stayed with the trucks remained to the last possible moment, then made their way individually and in small groups out onto the ice and toward the Marine perimeter at Hagaru-ri. The Chinese wreaked havoc upon the wounded in the stalled truck convoy.

On the night of 1 December, survivors of RCT 31 began coming into Hagaru-ri across the ice—wounded, exhausted from five days of continuous combat, half frozen, hungry, and often disoriented and suffering from shock. The appearance of the survivors at the Marine perimeter presented a startling scene that made an indelible impression on the Marines who first saw them. The earliest arrivals nearly came to grief within sight of help when they started through the Marines' defensive minefield. The wounded and those with severe frostbite were treated and, as quickly as possible, taken to the newly completed airstrip and evacuated. Others were collected, fed, and organized into provisional units.

The following day, pilots flying over the area reported a single file of wounded coming across the ice. Another pilot flew over the trucks and saw wounded who tried to wave.[22] Over the next two days, Lt. Col. Olin L. Beale, commanding officer of the 1st Motor Transport Battalion holding that sector of the perimeter, improvised rescue efforts to bring in others, some of whom had collapsed on the ice. Beale and others managed to reach some of the stalled trucks, but by that time, they found only dead.

Precise figures on losses in RCT 31 are not readily available. Appleman estimates that, including the forces at Hudong-ni, there were about 3,200 men in RCT 31, including KATUSA (Korean Augmentation Troops, U.S. Army). Other estimates ranged as low as 2,500. Out of those reaching Hagaru-ri, 1,137 were evacuated with wounds or frostbite. There remained 385 members of the RCT who, with other available Army troops at Hagaru-ri, were formed into a provisional battalion under Lieutenant Colonel Anderson and served with the 1st Marine Division on the breakout to Hamhung. This would indicate between 748 and 1,448 killed or captured.

No reliable estimate of the Chinese losses can be made. Nevertheless, they were horrendous, as much or more from air attack as from ground fire. The 80th CCF Division was identified, briefly, in the perimeter protecting the evacuation of Hamhung. Otherwise, the 80th and 81st CCF Divisions, like the remaining divisions of the 9th Army, were not identified in combat again until early April.

The Enemy Situation

All four of the divisions of the 20th CCF Army had been identified, as had the 79th and 80th Divisions of the 27th Army. There were believed to be substantial but as yet unidentified reserves north of

Chosin. Colonel William Quinn believed that the new arrivals would compensate for the casualties inflicted by UN air and ground action and could actually represent an increase in total Chinese strength. The 1st Marine Division PIR believed the additional forces moving south from Changjin were the rest of the 27th Army and the 24th Army. Each of the three armies of the 9th Army Group had been reinforced with an additional division from yet another army. It did cause some confusion.

On 30 November, the X Corps PIR had noted the slackening pressure on the Yudam-ni perimeter and suggested that enemy forces might have disengaged in order to advance farther south. A threatened advance southward from the Fusen Reservoir to Sinhung (northeast of Oro-ri) was noted. That theme was developed more fully the next day. The X Corps G-2 believed the Chinese practice of double envelopment indicated the possibility of an attack on Hamhung along three axes: down the Hagaru-ri–Hamhung main supply route, south from the Fusen Reservoir, and from Sachang-ni to Chigyong. The elimination of resistance east of Chosin enabled the release of one or two divisions either to attack Hagaru or to move south between the Fusen and Chosin Reservoirs for a deep envelopment or an attack on Hamhung. In the west, the withdrawal of the Marines from Yudam-ni would allow enemy forces there to move south toward Sachang-ni, join the 89th CCF Division, and attack Hamhung from that direction.

Developments in these areas were watched closely over the next few days. By 4 December, it appeared there was a substantial buildup in the Sachang-ni–Huksu-ri area, following the withdrawal of the 7th Infantry. The X Corps G-2 believed that these developments were preparatory to an attack on the Hamhung–Hungnam complex and stated: "It is probable that renewed attacks will soon be made . . . toward Hamhung before friendly forces can be fully established."[23]

The X Corps Situation
Given the extended deployment of X Corps and the G-2's estimate, there was a real possibility the Chinese would engage the 1st Marine Division and hold it in place while other elements slipped around both sides to attack Hamhung directly. If that were to happen, there

would be terrible losses. In a conversation with General Soule, Gen. Clark Ruffner, the X Corps chief of staff, told Soule: "I don't know whether we will be able to save the Old Man's corps." Lieutenant Colonel McCaffrey, deputy chief of staff, was also concerned, as were many of the X Corps staff.[24] The possibility of losing most of the 1st Marine Division was real.

Although General Almond wanted to maintain an aggressive stance, his first and greatest concern was to secure the Hamhung–Hungnam base of operations. Then, and only then, could attention be given to doing something about the Marines. With units spread over a distance of 400 miles in regiment- and battalion-size packets, and with a limited number of trucks (many without tire chains for the icy roads), concentrating the corps at Hamhung would be difficult and time-consuming.

When the Chinese offensive commenced, the 7th Infantry Division in the northeast was preparing to move to new positions dictated by Corps Operation Order No. 7 for the attack westward. The 26th ROK Regiment, attached to the 7th Division, was to take up positions from Hyesan-jin to Samsu and Kapsan. When relieved by the ROKs, the 17th Infantry, with all three battalions present, was to move south of Kapsan and protect the Kapsan–Pukchong MSR. The 32d Infantry was to move to Pukchong as division reserve.

In a strange and little-known incident, General Barr had already ordered one unit, Battery B, 31st Field Artillery Battalion, pulled back from Kapsan to below Pungsan. Barr had received a message sent by a relay of runners from the headman of a village downstream (to the west) from Hyesan-jin that CCF troops were crossing the Yalu into Korea in huge numbers. Based on this information, Barr ordered the withdrawal of the battery. The G-3 told the artillery commander that General Barr, based on his experience in China as adviser to Chiang Kai-shek, was convinced that there was no terrain the Chinese troops could not cross, regardless of the weather. Barr wanted the heavy howitzers clear of the roads in the event a further pullback was required. The message Barr received obviously referred to units of the 27th CCF Army crossing the river at Linjiang. There is no record of this information's having been passed on to X Corps—or that it was given any credence if it was passed on.[25]

On receipt of Corps Operation Order No. 8, the 7th Division prepared to withdraw. The 26th ROK Regiment, with one battalion of the 32d Infantry attached, would take up positions in the vicinity of Pungsan. The 17th Infantry would pull back through that covering force and the remaining 7th Division units would follow, with the 26th ROK Regiment bringing up the rear.

On 30 November, the 3d Division was moving toward Hamhung to concentrate. One battalion was in Wonsan; one was in corps reserve; two were defending between Sachang-ni and Huksu-ri; and the remainder were assembling in the Yonpo–Chigyong area, as directed by the X Corps order. In his report to MacArthur that evening, Almond noted his plan to concentrate the 3d and 7th Divisions at Hamhung. Wonsan would be abandoned.[26]

Those plans were thrown into turmoil by MacArthur's reply. He directed Almond to accelerate concentration of X Corps, "keeping Third Division in Wonsan repeat Wonsan." The concentration was to include pullback of ROK units, with the region northeast of the waist of Korea ignored except for strategic and tactical considerations "relating to the security of your command."[27]

The 7th Division was still working its way southward from Hyesanjin. With the 3d Division moving south to Wonsan, Hamhung would be wide open, except for the one battalion of the 7th Infantry then in corps reserve. Nevertheless, Almond dutifully ordered the 3d Division south. His previous instructions were rescinded. Without the 3d Division, not only was Hamhung vulnerable, but there was also a long stretch of road not covered between Chinhung-ni and Hamhung.

Learning that the 17th Infantry was moving south without enemy opposition, Almond, in desperate need of those forces in the Hamhung area, ordered the 7th Division to employ, without delay, not less than one RCT on the Oro-ri–Toksangwan lines. He urged the 7th Division to expedite its withdrawal. With icy roads, truck breakdowns, and fatigue, the main body did not reach Pukchong until 4 December. There it was forced to pause to give the drivers a rest. Finally, by the evening of 5 December, the majority of the 7th Division had reached Hamhung. Haste had taken its toll. Much equipment that should have been destroyed was left behind intact. Even more distressing, there were reports that stragglers and isolated elements of the division, including men who had been wounded, were inadvertently left behind.[28]

Almond reported to MacArthur that he had ordered the 3d Division to assemble in Wonsan. He said the situation in the Marine division, although extremely serious, was not critical: "Although 7th Division units will assist in protecting the southern half of the Marines' axis of withdrawal, the division is still confronted with a serious fight the entire way south to Hamhung." He gave details on the fate of the cutoff battalions of the 7th Division. In uncharacteristically blunt language, he protested the instructions for the 3d Division, stating, "As indicated during my visit to GHQ on 29 Nov, this corps must be assembled in the Hamhung–Hungnam area to adequately support the 1st Marine Division previous to further employment. The 3rd Division by its isolation at Wonsan may become involved before we could go to its assistance."[29] That same morning, he had sent Col. Edward H. Forney and Lieutenant Colonel Quinn from his staff to Tokyo to argue for the return of the 3d Division.

The mission to Tokyo was successful. At three o'clock the next morning, FEC teleconned to X Corps: "3rd US Division released to CG X Corps for employment as he desires. CinC has no particular interest in Wonsan area. Will be confirmed by separate message."[30] The 3d Division was quickly ordered northward again, with one RCT to concentrate in the Chigyong area and one around Oro-ri.[31] For some of the troops, it would be their third trip by open coal train between Hamhung and Wonsan. Almond was able to report, with some satisfaction: "3rd Infantry Division concentrated in Hamhung–Yonghung area 24 hours after ordered to do so as I stated at the conference on 29 November in Tokyo could be done."[32]

Probably the low point in the campaign was 2 December. The 5th and 7th Marines were finding heavy going in their attack southward. Two infantry battalions and one artillery battalion of the 7th Division had been destroyed. Hamhung was wide open and the 3d Division had been taken away. By 4 December, things looked somewhat better. The Marines had reached Hagaru-ri—bruised but in good spirits and fighting trim. The 3d Division had been returned to Hamhung and the bulk of the 7th Division was approaching. One dark cloud was at Huksu-ri. The 1st Battalion, 7th Infantry, had drawn back from Sachang-ni, backstopped by the 3d Battalion. But both were being pressed backward toward the MSR by building Chinese forces.

Unknown to either side, the successful consolidation of the 1st Marine Division at Hagaru-ri secured the survival of that division and the successful withdrawal of the units at Chosin. There was much hard fighting left, but the initiative now lay with the Marines.

At Yudam-ni, the 79th CCF Division had exhausted its limited supply of ammunition and suffered terrible casualties as well as frostbite. It took no further part in the action. East of Chosin, the Chinese had succeeded in overrunning and scattering RCT 31, but they were reduced to uselessness in doing so. RCT 31, in fighting to destruction, had kept the Chinese from concentrating two more divisions at Hagaru-ri. Thus, three of the four divisions of the 27th CCF Army were so battered they could take no further effective part in the battle. The fourth division, the 94th, for some reason was never identified in combat. In the 20th Army, the 58th Division had effectively destroyed itself in the unsuccessful attempt to take Hagaru-ri. The 59th Division had been virtually destroyed by the 5th and 7th Marines. The 60th Division and 89th Divisions still were in fair shape but had shown little aggressiveness.

Chinese reserves were now moving down from the north in a desperate effort to regain control of the situation, but, as with the other units, weather and U.S. aircraft were taking a heavy toll. All Chinese accounts talk of problems of frostbite, probably a euphemism for outright freezing to death. And, although the Chinese had shown great skill at using the cover of night for stealthy movement, tactical and operational imperatives required them to move during daylight hours, exposing them to devastating air attack. One prisoner captured at Hagaru-ri on 5 December, probably from the 88th CCF Division, said that his division had never been in contact but had heavy losses from air attack.[33]

Oddly, it was at this very point in the campaign—when the first faint rays of hope appeared in the field—that the mood in Washington reached its lowest point, almost to the edge of panic.

Notes

1. Telecon 663 CINCFE–X Corps 29 282400, Nov. 50. That telecon also stated that RCT 31 had identified two separate CCF divisions in their zone, believed to be the 80th and the 70th.
2. X Corps Operational Instruction (OI) 19 292046I, Nov. 50.
3. X Corps PIR 64, 29 Nov. 50.
4. CG 1st Mar Div msg 1750, 29 Nov. 50.
5. 7th Marines Unit Report, 25 Nov.–2 Dec. 50 (copy in author's possession).
6. X Corps Operation Order No. 8, 30 Nov. 50.
7. CINCUNC msg C50106, 30 Nov. 50 to X Corps.
8. X Corps G-3 Journal J-53, 30 Nov. 50 (time not noted).
9. *Command Report—Chosin Reservoir 27 November 1950–12 December 1950.* "Action of 7th Infantry Division Units at Chosin Reservoir from 24 November 1950 to 12 December 1950." 7th Division, n.d.
10. Appleman, *East of Chosin,* 176.
11. O. P. Smith *Aide-Memoire.* There is a question of when this message was drafted and when it was sent. The 1st Marine Division G-3 journal apparently has no record of it. Because General Smith refers to Task Force Faith in his diary, kept contemporaneously, it probably was sent during the afternoon of 30 November. It could have been sent to the rear command post of RCT 31 at Hudong either by wire or tank radio until 4 P.M., when the Hudong force began to withdraw to Hagaru-ri. Survivors of the Army forces report that the message was not received until 1 December, when it came in the clear over at least two of the Jeep radios in the withdrawal column.
12. O. P. Smith diary, Papers of O. P. Smith, Archives Branch, Marine Corps Research Center.
13. O. P. Smith interview with Ben Frank, 9–12 June 1969.
14. Appleman, *East of Chosin,* 186 (quoting letters and interview with General McCaffrey).
15. X Corps msg X13481 to CINCFE, 30 Nov. 50.
16. X Corps PIR 65, 30 Nov. 50.
17. *Chinese People's Volunteers.*
18. *Heroes and Models.*

19. Ibid.

20. *Chinese People's Volunteers.*

21. *Curtis MSS.*

22. X Corps G-3 Journal J-115, 2 Dec. 50.

23. This portion from X Corps PIRs 69–71, 4–6 Dec. 50.

24. Appleman, *Escaping the Trap,* 268 (quoting interviews with Ruffner and McCaffrey).

25. Ibid., 271.

26. X Corps OI 20 011636I, Dec. 50.

27. CINCUNC C-50215, 1 Dec. 50, to X Corps.

28. X Corps G-3 Journal J-91, 7 Dec. 50. Available sources do not indicate the number of missing in the various regiments. However, X Corps reported a total of 2,505 missing in action in the 7th Division. RCT 31 is estimated to have had a strength of some 3,200. Of these, 1,500 were evacuated due to wounds and frostbite. Another 385 were fit and made their way out with the 1st Marine Division. This would indicate a total of about 1,315 missing from RCT 31, leaving nearly 1,200 missing from other 7th Division units during the operation.

29. X Corps X13610 to FEC, 2 Dec. 50.

30. X Corps–FEC telecon 668, 3 Dec. 50.

31. X Corps OI 24 031927I, Dec. 50.

32. X Corps X13741, 5 Dec. 50, to FEC.

33. 1st Mar Div PIR 42, 12 Dec. 50.

14
Washington and Tokyo:
To the Edge of Panic

...responsibility and authority clearly resided right there in the room.... We owed it, I insisted, to the men in the field and to the God to whom we must answer for those men's lives to stop talking and to act.
—Lt. Gen. Matthew B. Ridgway
to the Joint Chiefs of Staff, 3 December 1950

Debate with MacArthur
For the next few days, the Joint Chiefs of Staff continued their "wait and see" mode. No new directives were issued. MacArthur's basic instructions were still in force, except for the "temporary suspension" of any directive in conflict with his assumption of the defense. Early on 30 November, a new situation report from MacArthur increased the apprehension of the JCS:

> The Chinese Communists continue the buildup of their forces in North Korea despite all interdiction of our Air Command. Red troops located in Manchuria less than a week ago are now definitely indicated on our front and the two Army Groups, 4th and 3rd, are operating in our two sectors. The North Korean Command has been practically swept aside.
> Troops from the neutral international border can reach the front in two night marches. This condition provides for a continuous and rapid buildup, as the enemy potential strength immediately available for prompt reinforcement comprises several hundred thousand troops which in turn are subject to replacement from other Chinese sectors. As a result, it is quite evident that the Eighth Army will successively have to continue to replace (sic) to the rear.
> Everything leads to the conclusion the Chinese forces have as their objective the complete destruction of United Nations forces and the securing of all Korea.[1]

General Bradley labeled this as more hysteria.[2] He had doubts about this as well as the previous message saying X Corps threatened Chinese supply lines. Such a threat, he thought, was ineffective. He also questioned the assertion that X Corps had engaged between six and eight Chinese divisions. The Joint Chiefs' immediate concern was the widening gap between the Eighth Army and X Corps. In a briskly worded but diplomatic reply message, they expressed that concern:

> Your plan for withdrawal of X Corps into the Hamhung–Wonsan sector as enemy pressure develops and your anticipation of probable future successive displacement to the rear by the 8th Army are causing increased concern here. Experience to date in Korea, particularly during the last few days, indicates that enemy can operate strong forces through difficult mountain terrain. The developments of a progressively widening gap between your forces on the east and west coasts would afford the enemy opportunity to move considerable forces southward between the 8th Army and X Corps. We feel that the elements of the X Corps must be extricated from their exposed positions as soon as practicable and that then the forces on the two coasts should be sufficiently coordinated to prevent large enemy forces from passing between them or outflanking either of them. The JCS hope you will take the foregoing into consideration in the formulation of your further plans. In amplification of our JCS 97592 regarding the mission assigned you by the UN the entire region northeast of the waist of Korea should be ignored except for strategic and tactical considerations relating to the security of your command.[3]

Prompted by this message, MacArthur radioed X Corps to accelerate concentration of the corps, including the pullback of ROK forces, and directed that Korea, northeast of the waist, should be ignored except for strategic and tactical considerations relating to the security of X Corps.[4]

Panic Among the Allies
At the United Nations, Gen. Wu Xiu-zhuan, the long-awaited rep-

resentative of the People's Republic of China, arrived and was invited to speak on the Formosa (Taiwan) issue on 28 November. He delivered a blistering attack condemning U.S. policies in Taiwan and Korea. Other anti-American speeches by representatives from the USSR and its satellite nations followed. The spate of speeches was capped by a Soviet-sponsored resolution claiming that U.S. forces had invaded and occupied Taiwan, that armed aggression by the United States against China and armed intervention in Korea had shattered the peace, and that the UN condemned the United States for these criminal acts and demanded the complete withdrawal of U.S. forces from Korea and Taiwan.

The resolution was easily defeated, but a U.S. counterproposal condemning China for aggression horrified European allies. They were unwilling to endorse any measure that would further inflame the Chinese or their Soviet sponsors. Secretary of State Dean Acheson reported the virtual state of panic that seemed to exist among America's allies in New York. Many complained that the U.S. leadership had failed and that the existing difficulties were the fault of General MacArthur's action. Acheson was distressed that they were blaming the United States, not the Communists.

To provide some reassurance to the allies, President Truman held a news conference on 30 November. He said the United States would continue to work for action to halt aggression in Korea, would take steps to strengthen its own defense, and would aid its allies to do the same. He repeated assurances that America had no aggressive intentions toward China. He also said MacArthur had done a good job and had not exceeded his authority.

Responding to a question, Truman stated: "We will take whatever steps are necessary to meet the military situation. . . ." Asked if that would include the atomic bomb, he said that included "every weapon we have." There followed this brief exchange: Q. "Mr. President, you said, every weapon that we have, does that mean there is active consideration of the use of the atomic bomb?" A. "There has always been active consideration of its use. . . ."

In response to further questions, Truman blundered by suggesting that the decision on use of the bomb was in the hands of the military, possibly the commander in the field, General MacArthur.[5]

Flashed around the world, that news was received with apprehension and dismay. Instead of restoring confidence, Truman's mis-statement had heaped fuel on the flames. Use of the atomic bomb in Korea would most likely trigger a Soviet response. The Chinese were not the only ones who believed that they fought under the pro-tection of the Soviet nuclear "umbrella." The thought of Korea es-calating to a general war, and of that war becoming a nuclear war, was terrifying in the United States. It was even more so in Europe, where people were only then beginning to recover from some of the effects of World War II. A belated attempt to "clarify" Truman's re-mark—stating that only the president can authorize the use of the atomic bomb and that no such authorization had been given—was faint reassurance.

MacArthur chose the same unfortunate time to go public with what came to be called his "posterity papers." Over the next several days, in response to inquiries from newsmen, he complained about the restrictions on his actions. To *U.S. News and World Report,* he said the order forbidding him to strike across the Manchurian border had been ". . . an enormous handicap, without precedent in military history." To Hugh Baille, president of the United Press, he accused European leaders and newsmen of a "somewhat selfish though most short-sighted preoccupation with NATO and the safety of Western Europe at the expense of the Far East." He reiterated his belief that the battle for Europe would be fought out in Asia. Other similar state-ments went to the International News Service (INS), the London *Daily Mail,* and the Tokyo press corps.[6]

Truman was infuriated. He later wrote: "Within a matter of four days he [MacArthur] found time to publicize in four different ways his view that the only reason for his troubles was an order from Wash-ington to limit hostilities in Korea . . . [and] . . . made it plain that no blame whatsoever attached to him or his staff. . . . I should have relieved him then and there."[7]

He didn't. The political uproar would have been tremendous. Tru-man says that he didn't want it to appear that MacArthur was being relieved because the offensive had failed. He also didn't want to rep-rimand him. Instead he issued an order to all State and Defense De-partment activities, but aimed at MacArthur, requiring prior clear-ance of any statement of U.S. policy.

MacArthur's statements heightened the concerns of America's European allies. Distrust of MacArthur grew. Not without reason, they believed he had exceeded his authority. The thought of him with his hand on the atomic button was frightening. Equally frightening was the thought that the United States would become tied down in Korea, unable to assist the Europeans—who, at that time, were dangerously vulnerable to Soviet aggression. British Prime Minister Clement Attlee, after conferring with other European UN members, came flying across the ocean to discuss the situation with Truman.

To deal with the allies' concern, Acheson, General Marshall, the Joint Chiefs, and other senior personnel met at the Pentagon on 1 December. Acheson said the need was to present to the allies a plan that the military could support. One option would be a firm line across Korea. Was there one that the United States could expect to hold? For the first time, the possibilities of asking for a cease-fire or withdrawing from Korea were raised.[8]

The Joint Chiefs could give no assurance that there was any line that could be held. There was some confusion and disagreement between General Marshall and the JCS. While the Chiefs had expressed concern about the gaps in the middle, between X Corps and the Eighth Army, General Marshall told Acheson that the kind of line he was considering was not a practical proposition. He felt it might be possible to hold on the east and the west, but it was not possible to be certain at that point. It depended on X Corps, which was so widely dispersed. Marshall felt that since ports were available, perhaps as much as three-fourths of X Corps might get out. The situation needed a firsthand look. General Lawton Collins agreed to go.

Acheson wondered whether the Chinese might agree to withdraw back into Manchuria if the United States offered to withdraw from Korea.[9] General Walter Bedell Smith, CIA director, announced that a new estimate in preparation indicated that the Soviets were much closer to war than was previously thought. Smith felt that the Soviets would never accept a Korea in hostile hands, and that it was important to get out right away, although that would not solve the problem.

In discussing a possible cease-fire, Gen. Omar Bradley agreed that would be acceptable provided there was not too great a price to pay.

Robert A. Lovett, General Marshall's deputy, summarized the wide-ranging discussion by saying he thought consensus had been reached on two points: (1) Korea was not a decisive area for the United States; (2) The loss of Korea might mean the loss of Japan, but that would be preferable to the loss of Western Europe. Only General Collins disagreed, his point being only that losing Korea did not necessarily mean the loss of Japan.

"Wait and See" Turns to Alarm

The critical state of X Corps became clear on 2 December. That evening, Acheson, Marshall, and Bradley met with the president. General Marshall reported that the situation looked very bad. He thought a decision would have to be made within forty-eight hours and could not wait for the first meeting with Attlee. Bradley stated that the situation would reach "crash" (crisis?) state in two to three days. He thought the 7th Division could get out and the 3d Division might be saved; X Corps could be evacuated in five days. Implicit in the discussion, although not specifically stated, was the likelihood of abandonment of all supplies and equipment, as well as abandonment of the 1st Marine Division. With two regiments fighting their way from Yudam-ni seventy miles away, and with Chinese blocking the road south of Koto-ri, there was no possible way the Marines, with or without equipment, could reach the coast in five days, if at all.[10]

General Marshall said that if the Chinese launched an air attack, even a Dunkirk-type evacuation might not be possible. In that case, Acheson suggested that a decision to counterattack the Manchurian airfields should be made solely on the basis of whether it would help or hurt the troops, not as retaliation for a Chinese attack or for the purpose of holding Korea. It would require very fine military judgment—which had to be made in Washington, not by General MacArthur.[11]

The meeting went on to discuss the very heavy price that might have to be paid for a cease-fire. The least the Chinese might ask for would be withdrawal to the thirty-eighth parallel. Probably they would ask for much more, such as total withdrawal of all UN troops from Korea, a seat in the United Nations, the surrender of Taiwan, and, perhaps, participation in the Japanese peace treaty. General Marshall was concerned about both saving the troops and protecting America's national honor. We could not abandon the South Koreans. The conferees talked about implementation of NSC-68 and declaration of a national emergency. At the conclusion of the meeting, President Truman agreed to proceed with the rearmament plan and said he would issue a declaration of national emergency that would bring home the seriousness of the situation to the American people.

That was on Saturday night. By Sunday morning, 3 December, the atmosphere in Washington was even more grim. James C. Reston of the *New York Times* reported the mood in a dispatch filed that day: "Every official movement in the capital today, every official report from Tokyo, and every private estimate of the situation by well-informed men reflected a sense of emergency and even of alarm about the state of the United Nations Army in Korea. Not even on the fateful night twenty three weeks ago when the Korean War started was the atmosphere more grim."[12]

The overnight telecon from Tokyo gave a critical report of the situation. An estimated nine CCF divisions were attacking the forces in the Chosin Reservoir area. The cutoff battalions of the 7th Division were overrun. The withdrawing 5th and 7th Marines were being attacked on three sides by four enemy regiments. Colonel Homer Litzenberg's estimate that he was facing a grave situation reached Washington. Hostile units continued to block the main supply route south of Hagaru-ri, while strong enemy elements were approaching the MSR south of Koto-ri on a twelve-mile front. Air reconnaissance reported that roads in the Yangdok area, twenty-five miles west of Wonsan, were jammed with enemy troops moving east toward Wonsan.[13]

If that was not depressing enough, a long and pessimistic estimate by General MacArthur, responding to the Joint Chiefs' expression of concern about the situation in X Corps, arrived that morning:

> The X Corps is being withdrawn into the Hamhung area as rapidly as possible. The situation within the Eighth Army becomes increasingly critical. General Walker reports, and I agree

with his estimate, that he cannot hold the Pyongyang area and under enemy pressure, when exerted, will unquestionably be forced to withdraw to the Seoul area. There is no practicability, nor would any benefit accrue thereby, to attempt to unite the forces of the Eighth Army and the X Corps. Both forces are completely outnumbered and their junction would, therefore, not only not produce added strength, but actually jeopardize the free flow of movement that arises from the two separate logistical lines of naval supply and maneuver.

As I previously reported, the development of a defense line across the waist of Korea is not feasible because of the numerical weakness of our forces as considered in connection with the distance involved; by the necessity of supplying the two parts of the line from ports within each area; and by the division of the area into two compartments by the rugged mountainous terrain running north and south. Such a line is one of approximately 120 air miles with a road distance of approximately 150 miles. If the entire United States Force of seven divisions at my disposal were placed along this defensive line it would mean that a division would be forced to protect a front of approximately 20 miles against greatly superior numbers of an enemy whose greatest strength is a potential for night infiltration through rugged terrain. Such a line with no depth would have little strength and as a defensive concept would invite penetration with resultant envelopment and piecemeal destruction. Such a concept against the relatively weaker North Korean forces would have been practicable, but against the full forces of the Chinese Army is impossible.

I do not believe that full comprehension exists of the basic changes which have been wrought by the undisguised entrance of the Chinese Army into the combat. Already Chinese troops to the estimated strength of approximately 26 divisions are in line of battle with an additional minimum of 200,000 to the enemy rear and now in process of being committed to action. In addition to this, remnants of the North Korean Army are being reorganized in the rear and there stands, of course, behind all this the entire military potential of Communist

China. The terrain is of a nature to diminish the effectiveness of our air support in channelizing and interrupting the enemy supply system; it serves to aid the enemy in his dispersion tactics. This, together with the present limitations of international boundary, reduces enormously the normal benefit that would accrue to our superior air force. With the enemy concentration inland, the Navy potential is greatly diminished in effectiveness; amphibious maneuver is no longer feasible and effective use of naval gunfire support is limited.

The potentials, therefore, of our combined strength are greatly reduced and the comparison more and more becomes one of relative combat effectiveness of ground forces.

It is clearly evident, therefore, that unless ground reinforcements of the greatest magnitude are promptly supplied, this command will be either forced into successive withdrawals with diminished powers of resistance after each such move, or will be forced to take up beachhead bastion positions which, while insuring a degree of prolonged resistance, would afford little hope of anything beyond defense. This small command actually under present conditions is facing the entire Chinese nation in an undeclared war and unless some positive and immediate action is taken, hope for success cannot be justified and steady attrition leading to final destruction can reasonably be contemplated.

Although the command up to the present time has exhibited good morale and marked efficiency, it has been in almost unending combat for five months and is mentally fatigued and physically battered. The combat effectiveness of the Republic of Korea Forces now at our disposal is negligible; for police and constabulary uses they would have some effectiveness. The other foreign army contingents, whatever their combat efficiency may be, are in such small strength as to exercise little influence. Each United States division at my disposal other than the First Marine Division, is now approximately 5,000 men under strength and at no time have they achieved their fully authorized numerical complement. The Chinese troops are fresh, completely organized, splendidly trained and equipped and apparently in peak condition for actual operations. The general evaluation of the situation here must be viewed on the basis of an entirely new war against an entirely new power of great military strength and under entirely new conditions.

The directives under which I am operating based upon the North Korean Forces as an enemy are completely outmoded by events. The fact must be clearly understood that our relatively small force now faces the full offensive power of the Chinese communist nation augmented by extensive supply of Soviet materiel. The strategic concept suitable for operations against the North Korean Army which was so successful is not susceptible to continued application against such power. This calls for political decisions and strategic plans in implementation thereof, adequate fully to meet the realities involved. In this, time is of the essence as every hour sees the enemy power increase and ours decline.[14]

The casualty count added to the gloom. To this point, casualties for the Eighth Army in the aborted offensive totaled more than 11,000. Losses in the 2d Division alone were more than 6,300. The Turks had lost a thousand out of their 5,000 men.

It was this gloomy message and the attendant gloomy situation that faced Secretaries Marshall and Acheson, the Joint Chiefs, and a State Department delegation when they met at 9:30 A.M. Sunday, 3 December, at the Pentagon. The running discussion of the situation, which had continued for five days, continued some more. Reflecting the tension between them, Bradley later commented he thought MacArthur had ". . . lost control of the battlefield and possibly his nerves." He thought it disgraceful. MacArthur should have gone to Korea and rallied the troops. Instead of going himself, MacArthur had sent his acting chief of staff and his G-3.[15]

General Ridgway briefed the situation. The ability of X Corps to withdraw was questionable. The Eighth Army could probably withdraw to the line west from Changdo, but Ridgway was not sure they would be able to reach Seoul. He said if the troops could get into beachhead areas of Inchon, Hungnam, and Pusan, they could hold for some time, time enough for a decision to be made on evacuation.

In the next few hours, the discussion ranged over a wide variety of questions: The need for a cease-fire and the cost that might be extracted; whether or not to withdraw from Korea or be forced out; measures to take against the Chinese if we were forced out; the possibility of Soviet intervention; and the need for immediate mobilization. Although consensus was reached on a number of items, no firm decisions were made.

At one point, General Ridgway began to lose patience with the discussion. As he later put it: "No one apparently was willing to issue a flat order to the Far East Commander to correct a state of affairs that was going rapidly from bad to disastrous. Yet the responsibility and authority clearly resided right there in the room." Displaying the concern for the troops that made him such an admired leader by those who served under him, Ridgway secured permission to talk and broke in on the discussion. In his words: "I blurted out—perhaps too bluntly but with deep feeling—that I felt we had already spent too damn much time on debate and that immediate action was needed. We owed it, I insisted, to the men in the field and to the God to whom we must answer for those men's lives to stop talking and to act."[16]

Ridgway received no response to his plea, other than an appreciative note from a Navy colleague. Dean Acheson commented that this was the first time someone had expressed what everyone thought—that the emperor was wearing no clothes.[17] The meeting droned on. The only decision made as a result of the meeting was to send a message to MacArthur, in reply to his latest estimate: "We consider that the preservation of your forces is now the primary consideration. Consolidation of forces into beachheads is concurred in."[18]

Notwithstanding the lack of firm decisions, the State and Defense Departments were narrowing their focus to certain basic principles that would form the basis of policy decisions in the near future. Aside from that, further decisions were held off until the conclusion of talks with Attlee, scheduled to begin the following day.[19]

At the State Department, Acheson met with his staff, saying he thought the military leaders were dejected. It was imperative to take a military stand in Korea to buck up the allies. Otherwise they might seek accommodation with the USSR. He leaned toward trying to find a place to hold and fight the Chinese to a standstill. In pursuit of this thought, Acheson called General Marshall, who agreed with the plan, with two provisos: (1) It was first necessary to see if X Corps could be successfully withdrawn; (2) America could not dig herself into a hole without an exit.[20]

Basic Policy Decisions Take Shape

General Ridgway had reason to be impatient with the extended and apparently aimless discussions. But at least consensus was being reached on basic questions; the policy framework gradually was taking shape. Underlying those policy decisions was the belief that war with Russia was much more likely. The CIA estimate of 2 December believed that the Soviets and the Chinese both intended to render the UN position in Korea untenable; that the Soviets intended to support the Chinese effort with materiel, possibly with volunteers; that the Soviets could intervene directly in the event of major U.S. action against Chinese targets; and that both had become involved with an acceptance of the risk of general war. Evidence of Soviet intentions to initiate global war was inconclusive, but it was anticipated the Soviets could be prepared to accept that global war if it should result from their action.[21]

Given those conditions, the basic U.S. policy was that Europe was more important than Asia; the defense of Japan was more important than Korea. The loss of Korea may or may not mean the possible loss of Japan. But the loss of Japan obviously would seal the fate of Korea. Preservation of the existing ground forces in Korea was vital— not only to ensure the defense of Japan but also because they represented the major share of existing U.S. ground forces. That led to the question of whether or not the United States should withdraw from Korea or wait to be kicked out. President Truman and his advisers believed it would be unconscionable, dishonorable, to depart Korea voluntarily and leave the Korean government and army to the depredations of the victorious Communists. More practically speaking, it would certainly reduce confidence in America's friendship. Contrasted to this was the vital need to preserve the forces in Korea, the only intact ground forces the United States had. Above all, whatever action or decisions the United States made, they needed to remain strictly within the UN framework, keeping the allies together.

With that background, other questions that remained unresolved were whether or not to support efforts for a cease-fire and what action to take if attacked by Chinese or Soviet air. The joint State and Defense Department meeting on 3 December had resolved to wait until the conclusion of talks with Clement Attlee, scheduled to begin on 4 December. The questions requiring military action—could X Corps get out, and how or where to make a stand—would have to await the return of General Collins from Korea.

The Chinese Have Decisions to Make

By 1 December, the situation looked almost as murky in Beijing as it did in Washington. The news from both the Chongchon and the Chosin fronts was encouraging. One concern for Mao and the Central Military Commission (CMC) in Beijing was the U.S. 7th Infantry Division. It appeared as if the 7th Division might be commencing a westward movement, down the Yalu, which could develop into a threat to Chinese supply lines between Huchang and Changjin. The 26th CCF Army had two divisions stationed at Huchang. Mao ordered one eastward to halt the 7th Division's movement.[22] The following day, after receiving reports from the New China News Agency (Xinhua) that the 7th Division was withdrawing from Hyesan-jin, Mao canceled that order and directed that the division be moved south, leaving one unit as flank protection.[23]

When it became clear in Beijing that the Eighth Army had pulled back from the Chongchon River line, Mao and the CMC believed it would make a strong stand at Pyongyang. It would take time to organize an attack. Mao authorized Peng Dehuai to break off pursuit of the Eighth Army, take several days to reorganize, then prepare to deal with Pyongyang. His suggested plan was to penetrate the Sunchon–Sukchon line, then hold that position with one army while the remainder of his forces moved south and east to flank Pyongyang and to secure the remainder of the Pyongyang–Wonsan line.[24]

In the east, Mao initially believed the 9th Army Group had won a great victory. In addition to its surrounding the 5th and 7th Marines at Yudam-ni, he thought it had destroyed more than one regiment of the 7th Division, as well as most of the 1st Marines and other reinforcing units at Hagaru-ri. He believed the only potential relief forces for the surrounded units were one regiment of the 7th Division and two ROK divisions. He urged Gen. Song Shilun to move the 26th Army southward, prepared to destroy any relief forces.[25] Two days later, Mao received information that led him to believe an attempt would be made to withdraw the 5th and 7th Marines from Hagaru-ri by air. He urged Song Shilun to seize the Hagaru-ri airfield as soon as possible.[26]

Late on 4 December, Mao learned that the Eighth Army was withdrawing from Pyongyang. Both Mao and Pcng believed that the Eighth Army was pulling back to the prewar fortifications along the thirty-eighth parallel. This opened up unexpected opportunities. Mao thought it possible that UN forces would attempt to negotiate a cease-fire. He told Peng that China would negotiate only if the enemy agreed to withdraw from Korea, but that he would not even discuss it until they had withdrawn to the thirty-eighth parallel.[27]

Kim Il Sung, who had arrived in Beijing that day to discuss war plans, urged Mao to pursue. This was an opportunity to end the war by driving the UN forces completely from Korea. Mao saw the opportunity, but he also saw the possibility that the war could become protracted. After some discussion, Peng started south in pursuit of the Eighth Army on 5 December with three of the six armies he had on the western front, while Song Shilun continued his increasingly difficult effort against X Corps.

The Chinese armies had suffered heavily in the campaign. The 38th, 39th, and 40th CCF Armies on the western front each needed 10,000 replacements. The 42d, 50th, and 66th Armies each needed 5,000. The 9th Army Group on the eastern front needed 60,000 replacements.[28]

A Ray of Sunshine

General Collins arrived in Tokyo on 4 December, talked briefly with MacArthur, and flew on to Seoul, arriving there at dusk. The Eighth Army was withdrawing from Pyongyang, planning to move south to the Imjin River line to protect Seoul. General Walton Walker told Collins that he did not think he could hold the Seoul area for long; the Eighth Army might be threatened with envelopment. But the

Eighth Army could not be backed into a beachhead at Inchon; a forced evacuation through the limited Inchon port facilities, with their extreme tides, would be slow and costly. Walker believed, however, that with the help of X Corps, he could hold the old Pusan perimeter indefinitely.[29] This was a more optimistic appraisal than Collins had heard up to that point.

At X Corps, Collins found more optimism. The unexpected success of the 5th and 7th Marines in reaching Hagaru-ri had restored General Almond's confidence. The 3d Division, having reassembled in the Hamhung area, was preparing to attack north to clear the road to Chinhung-ni, opening the withdrawal corridor for the Marines. The future definitely looked more cheerful. There was a real chance the Marine division would get out, that he could hold the Hungnam beachhead for an indefinite period, and that X Corps could be withdrawn with no great difficulty if and when ordered to do so. Collins agreed.[30]

The view in Tokyo was different. Colonel James H. Polk, Willoughby's executive officer, reported that General Headquarters had the blues. A few days ago, he said, they believed " . . . the whole thing was going to end in a victorious flourish and now no one can see the end."[31]

MacArthur's view was equally pessimistic. Collins proposed three scenarios, asking MacArthur's view of each:

1. The CCF continue to attack, MacArthur is forbidden to mount air attacks against China, there is no blockade of China, no reinforcement by Chinese Nationalist forces, no substantial increase in MacArthur forces until April 1951, and no possible use of the atom bomb in North Korea. MacArthur's response was that that essentially represented a surrender. With or without a cease-fire, UNC forces would have to be withdrawn from Korea. UNC forces could safely be withdrawn from Pusan and Hungnam with or without an armistice.

2. The CCF attack would continue but there would be a naval blockade of China, bombing of China, Chinese Nationalist forces used to the maximum, and the atom bomb used if tac-

tically appropriate. In that case, MacArthur said he should be directed to hold positions in Korea as far north as possible. He would move X Corps to Pusan to join the Eighth Army.

3. The CCF agree not to cross the thirty-eighth parallel. Under those conditions, MacArthur felt the United Nations should accept an armistice. The conditions of the armistice would preclude movement of North Korean and Chinese forces below the thirty-eighth parallel and require withdrawal of North Korean guerrillas. The Eighth Army would remain in position covering the Seoul–Inchon area and X Corps would withdraw to Pusan. A UN commission should supervise the armistice. This would be the best condition if those in alternative 2 could not be implemented.[32]

Regardless of his answers to Collins's assumptions, MacArthur remained fixed in his view that without reinforcements, the command should be evacuated "as soon as possible"—only with materiel and timely reinforcement could the UN Command withdraw in successive positions, as necessary, to the Pusan area. MacArthur felt that the United Nations, having committed itself to the support of the Republic of Korea, should not fail to accept the new challenge of Chinese aggression. He urged that the full power of the UN be mobilized to support the relatively small UN force committed and oriented toward an entirely new and undeclared war.[33]

General Collins departed for Washington on 6 December. That same day, the Far Eastern Command, including the naval and air forces, began planning for evacuations of Korea.

On 8 December, just as the meeting with Clement Attlee was concluding, General Collins reached Washington. He briefed the Joint Chiefs, the president, and Attlee. He said that if Walker were not tied to Seoul or any particular spot, he could gradually withdraw in an organized way to Pusan. It was an excellent port. The Eighth Army was not in danger. Collins thought they could hold below the Han River or at the Naktong. He reported that the situation of the Marines was serious but not critical.[34] His recommendation: "If the United Nations decision is not to continue an all out attack in Korea and if the Chinese Communists continue to attack, MacArthur should be directed to take the necessary steps to prevent the destruction of his forces pending final evacuation from Korea."[35]

In Washington, General Bradley greeted Collins's report and the recommendations as "a ray of sunshine. We now had options to discuss other than catastrophe."[36]

In Beijing, Mao received a garbled version of Collins's report and passed it on to Peng Dehuai with some considerable satisfaction:

> Secret information: US Army Chief of Staff [J. Lawton] Collins has been instructed to visit Japan and the Korean front. After his meetings with [Douglas] MacArthur, [Walton H.] Walker, and other high-ranking generals of the American armed forces, Collins believes that the situations of the United Nations' and America's forces in Korea has become hopeless. According to Collins' opinion, under the current conditions of the speed and scale of the Korean People's Army and the Chinese People's Volunteers' offensive, the American forces cannot organize a protracted defense because the American forces have suffered very heavy casualties, great losses of equipment, and an extreme deterioration in morale. Collins has reported the above situation and his opinion to the US Joint Chief of Staff. The above Collins' report shows that he has already given some appropriate instructions to MacArthur, ordering him to prepare ships and assemble troops around certain seaports, in order to get ready for a withdrawal, and so on. According to the reports of foreign news agencies, Seoul is being prepared for a withdrawal. It may not take long before one can be certain whether the above information is correct or not. It should be clear no later than when our 13th Army Corps reaches Kaesong and other areas, and begins pressing on Seoul. Do not pass down the above information in order to avoid having our troops relax their efforts.[37]

Attlee Conference

Clement Attlee's initial concern about the use of the atom bomb grew into concern about general war with the Soviets. He wanted hostilities with the Chinese to end. The war in Korea threatened to expand—absorbing U.S. energies, giving the Soviets great advantage, and leaving Europe open to attack. Concessions should be made to China. It was possible they would respond. There was Titoism in China. They were not Soviet puppets. Attlee wanted a cease-fire without strings. The Chinese Communists should have Formosa. It was part of China. They should have a seat in the UN. And, finally, Chinese role in the Japanese peace treaty would not be so bad. President Truman said that he was not prepared to proceed on that line.[38]

Although Attlee's point of view was also strongly held by the French and other European countries, as well as most of the other UN member states, Truman had little political support at home or abroad. He was under constant attack from critics who said his policy in Asia was weak and vacillating. Truman could not agree with Attlee under such pressure. Scarcely nine months earlier, the administration had considered stepping aside if the Chinese Communists went for Taiwan. Now such action was unthinkable. Dean Acheson said the United States was not prepared to surrender in the Far East to please some of America's allies, then cooperate with them in Europe. He insisted that U.S. foreign policy would not be divided into two compartments. U.S. policy on Korea began to solidify into five points:

1. Fight as hard as we can.
2. If someone proposes a cease-fire, accept it if we don't have to pay for it.
3. If a cease-fire collapses or is not accepted, fight again the best we can, but we can't run out.
4. If thrown out, harass the Chinese with a blockade or such other action.
5. Never give up Formosa as a condition to settle.[39]

To this should be added implacable opposition to a seat in the United Nations for the Communist Chinese. The idea of two Communist nations on the Security Council was unthinkable.

The four days of talks netted the British little; there was, after all, little Truman could afford to give. The meeting concluded on the following points:

- The forces in Korea were sent there by the United Nations. The United States and Great Britain will continue to carry out the mission assigned by the UN.
- There will be no thought of appeasement.
- The U.S. is ready to negotiate an end to the hostilities.
- The U.S. and Britain differ on the question of a seat in the UN for China.
- The future of Taiwan is up to the United Nations.
- With regard to the atom bomb, the U.S. hopes not to use it. The president desires to keep the prime minister informed at all times of developments that might bring about a change in the situation.[40]

Prime Minister Attlee asked if Truman would put that last point in writing. Truman refused: "If a man's word isn't any good it isn't made any better by writing it down."[41]

The remaining unstated agreement was that the United States and Great Britain would pursue the unification of Korea by political means. Essentially, this meant ending the war on the basis of the thirty-eighth parallel.

Notes

1. CINCFE msg C-50107, 30 Nov. 50, to JCS, *FRUS*, 1260.
2. Bradley, *A General's Life*, 600.
3. JCS msg 97772, 30 Nov. 50, to FEC.
4. CINCUNC msg C-50215, 1 Dec. 50, to X Corps.
5. Blair, *The Forgotten War*, 522.
6. Ibid., 524.
7. Truman, *Memoirs*. Vol. II, *Years of Trial and Hope*, 384.
8. Jessup notes on meeting with JCS, *FRUS*, 1276–77.
9. Ibid.
10. In an interview with D. Clayton James, on 25 August 1971, General Smith says that General McGee, then on the joint staff, had been told by General Bradley that the 1st Marine Division was lost.
11. Memorandum by Jessup, *FRUS*, 1312.
12. *New York Times*, 4 Dec. 1950 (Reston column).
13. DA Telecon 4088, 3 Dec. 50, to FEC.
14. FEC msg C-50332, 3 Dec. 50, to JCS, *FRUS*, 1320.
15. Bradley, *A General's Life*, 604.
16. Ridgway, *Korean War*, 71–72.
17. Acheson, *Present at the Creation*, 475.
18. JCS msg 97917, 3 Dec. 50, to CINCFE.
19. Jessup Memorandum, *FRUS*, 1323.
20. Acheson, *Present at the Creation*, 477.
21. CIA Estimate 3 Dec. 50, *FRUS*, 1308.
22. Mao Telegrams, No. 31, 1 Dec. 50.
23. Mao Telegrams, No. 33, 2 Dec. 50.
24. Mao Telegrams, No. 34, 2 Dec. 50.
25. Mao Telegrams, No. 35, 3 Dec. 50.
26. Mao Telegrams, No. 37, 4 Dec. 50.
27. Zhang, *Mao's Military Romanticism*, 121.
28. Ibid., 123.
29. Collins, J. Lawton, *War in Peacetime: The History and Lessons of Korea* (Boston: Houghton Mifflin, 1969), 230.
30. Blair, *The Forgotten War*, 530–31.
31. Toland, *In Mortal Combat* (quoting Polk letter), 351.
32. Schnabel, *Policy and Direction*, 284.

33. CINCFE Memorandum for General Collins 4 Dec. 50.
34. Collins Report, *FRUS*, 1468.
35. Schnabel, *Policy and Direction*, 285.
36. Bradlcy, *A General's Life*, 607.
37. Mao Telegrams, No. 43, 11 Dec. 50.
38. Memorandum of meeting, *FRUS*, 1382.
39. Ibid.
40. Memorandum of meeting with Attlee, *FRUS*, 1476.
41. Memorandum of meeting with Attlee,

15
The End in North Korea

You can't retreat or withdraw when you are surrounded.
The only thing you can do is break out, and when you
break out, that's an attack.
—General Oliver P. Smith, USMC

The Eighth Army Abandons Pyongyang

On 1 December, while the 5th and 7th Marines in northeast Korea commenced their attack southward to Hagaru-ri, the Eighth Army in northwest Korea had stepped back far enough to break contact with the pursuing Chinese. The gap between advance units of both forces now widened to nearly a hundred airline miles. Isolated clashes occurred the following day in the 1st Cavalry Division sector on the eastern portion of the Eighth Army line. For the next three weeks, the Eighth Army had no further contact with the Chinese.

Early on the morning of 2 December, with the approval of Mao and the Central Military Commission, Gen. Peng Dehuai had given orders to his armies to halt the pursuit, mop up the battlefield, and rest four or five days in order to reorganize and resupply with food and ammunition.[1] The Chinese objective was to reach the Pyongyang–Wonsan line. Focused on that objective, Mao and Peng believed the Eighth Army would put up a determined defense of Pyongyang. Seizure of Pyongyang would require careful preparations. Peng's plan was to make a holding attack on the Sukchon–Sunchon line with one army while the remainder of the available forces moved around the flank.

The Eighth Army had taken a serious bruising. The only fully combat-ready units were the 24th Infantry Division, the 27th Commonwealth Brigade, and the 29th British Brigade. The 25th Division had serious losses in both the 24th and the 27th Infantry

Regiments. The 1st Cavalry Division had substantial losses in the 7th Cavalry. The 8th Cavalry was still not fully recovered from its beating at Unsan a month earlier. The 7th and 8th ROK Divisions were in need of a complete refit and reorganization. The 6th ROK Division was also in need of refit and reorganization, but it was employable as a regimental combat team (RCT). The Turkish troops and the 2d Infantry Division were both in need of complete refit and reorganization.

The Far Eastern Command (FEC) estimate on 2 December painted a grim picture, estimating that 429,381 Chinese and North Korean troops were in contact or on the immediate front of UN forces. The remaining Chinese forces along the Yalu, consisting of eight Chinese armies with twenty-four divisions and two artillery divisions, totaling 204,000 troops, were available as a strategic reserve.[2] Air reports of troop columns moving southward were believed, erroneously, to be some of these reserve units moving forward to reinforce the Chinese drive.

At the conference in Tokyo on 28 November, General Walker had told MacArthur he planned to defend Pyongyang. To do so, he had also counted on having the 2d Division, the Turkish Brigade, and at least portions of some of the divisions of II ROK Corps. Now, damaged as the Eighth Army was, out of contact with the Chinese who now were not pursuing, and believing he faced a still-huge Chinese force being continuously reinforced, Walker did not believe he was capable of either defending an enclave at Pyongyang or holding a line across the peninsula. He decided to withdraw south to the Imjin River line, then to the Inchon–Seoul area. On 1 December, he assembled his staff and announced: "I have not been able to get MacArthur's HQ to advise me of their intentions. In the absence of instructions, I shall assume that the tactical integrity of this army, on which the entire defense of Japan depends, is my paramount objective. I will give up any amount of real estate if necessary to prevent this army from being endangered."[3]

The following day, Gens. Doyle Hickey and Edwin Wright from the Far Eastern Command visited Eighth Army Headquarters, reviewed the situation with Walker, and approved his decision.

On 3 December, the FEC's intelligence summary reported heavy troop movements in the Yangdok area as well as in the gap between Eighth Army and X Corps. This would enable the Chinese to seize the road south from Yangdok to Singye, limiting the road net available to the Eighth Army and narrowing its withdrawal corridor. More ominously, Chinese forces could advance along this axis, seize Kaesong, and cut off the Eighth Army from Seoul.[4]

With this threat in mind, Walker hastened the southward movement of the Eighth Army. The evacuation of supplies from Pyongyang was rushed. Quantities of supplies and equipment were destroyed or, in some cases, left behind. On the morning of 5 December, the last bridges across the Taedong River were blown. With the 1st Cavalry Division reinforced by the Commonwealth Brigade as rear guard, the Eighth Army began moving southward to an intermediate position about twenty miles south of Pyongyang, prepared to continue south to the Imjin River line.

Unbeknownst to Walker, there was no need for haste. The CCF in western Korea was not prepared for either an attack on Pyongyang or pursuit of a withdrawing Eighth Army. After two major offensives in little more than thirty days, both with little preparation, the Chinese People's Volunteers (CPV) troops were close to their limit of endurance. Casualties had been heavy; ammunition and food were exhausted. There was an urgent need for rest, resupply, and reorganization. Peng Dehuai needed 45,000 replacements—30,000 for the 38th, 39th, and 40th Armies, and 5,000 each for the 42d, 50th, and 66th Armies. He believed it would take three months to get the needed reinforcements to the front.[5]

After grossly underestimating the size of the Communist Chinese Forces, the Eighth Army G-2 now failed to note the weakened condition of the CCF. Roy Appleman, who has studied the campaign in western Korea in detail, believes that Walker's failure to defend Pyongyang was one of the greatest tactical mistakes of the war. The pursuing Chinese were in no condition to meet the armor and artillery of the Eighth Army. They were dispersed, out of touch with each other—many unsure of their positions or those of adjoining or supporting units—and very, very tired. It became clear later in the war that the Chinese could not sustain an offensive for more than two to five days. With the port of Chinampo open and abundant logistical support available, the Eighth Army—with armor, artillery, and unchallenged air support at hand—could have taken up defensive positions, fought the Chinese to a standstill, then counterattacked and turned them back. There is no evidence that Walker ever considered this possibility.[6]

Advance to the South

In northeast Korea, while the 20th and 27th Armies advanced to the attack, the 26th CCF Army had been held in reserve along the Huchang River. Mao had urged Song Shilun to deploy the 26th Army close to Chosin. But the flimsy Chinese logistics system was unable to support it that far forward. It had to remain close to the railhead at Linjiang. With the attack on Hagaru-ri having failed, the two Marine regiments at Yudam-ni about to break through, and the 80th and 81st CCF Divisions exhausted, Song Shilun, on 2 December, ordered the 26th CCF Army southward to take over the attack on Hagaru-ri. The 26th would relieve the 58th and the 60th CCF Divisions, which would then move south to block the Funchillin Pass. The 89th CCF Division would join this effort, moving eastward from its position at Sachang-ni. Song hoped to have the 26th Army in position to attack Hagaru-ri on the night of 6 December.[7]

The 26th CCF Army had about a hundred miles to go. Marine and Navy air immediately picked up the movement and began continuing attacks. There was concern that those troops moving south were not only the 26th CCF Army but possibly the 24th Army as well.[8]

In Beijing, Mao and the Central Military Commission were confused about the situation at Chosin. Mao believed that the 9th Army Group not only had destroyed more than one regiment of the 7th Infantry Division at Sinhung but also had destroyed most of the 1st Marine Regiment and several other units in the Hagaru-ri area. He was anxious for the 26th CCF Army to reach Hagaru-ri in time to intercept reinforcements that he believed were coming forward to aid the 5th and 7th Marines at Yudam-ni. He gave elaborate instructions to Peng to have Song refrain from complete destruction of the surrounded troops so reinforcements could be enticed forward to their destruction. He was unaware for several days that the 5th and 7th Marines had successfully broken through and reached Hagaru-ri.[9]

At Hagaru-ri, the tired and frozen but triumphant troops from Yudam-ni were given a day to rest and reorganize. All galleys operated around the clock, stopping only to clean up for the next round. But General Smith, aware of approaching enemy reinforcements and mindful of his orders to expedite, did not plan to tarry long.

The most pressing problem was caring for the casualties. The fight through from Yudam-ni, the defense of Hagaru-ri, and the defeat of RCT 31 had resulted in far more casualties than estimated—from both frostbite and enemy action. Foresightedly, work had begun on 18 November on an airstrip at Hagaru-ri. By 1 December, it was only 40 percent complete, just 2,900 feet long. But with the casualties threatening to overwhelm the ability of the medical installation at Hagaru-ri, a test landing was authorized and succeeded. By the evening of 5 December, a total of 4,312 casualties had been evacuated aboard Air Force, Greek, and Marine aircraft.

General Almond came up to Hagaru-ri on 4 December to award the Distinguished Service Cross to General Smith, Col. Homer Litzenberg, and Lt. Cols. Raymond Murray and Olin Beale. General Smith described Almond as weeping, but not sure why. Almond had reason to weep in gratitude. The determination, and good fortune, of the Marine forces at Yudam-ni and Hagaru-ri had very possibly saved his X Corps from destruction. That evening, Almond reported to General MacArthur that he had conferred with Smith, Litzenberg, and Murray at Hagaru-ri and with Col. Lewis Puller at Koto-ri. He reported they were ". . . resolute. . . . They proposed to succeed, but the rifle companies of all Marine Regiments have lost from 40 to 50 percent of their strength from enemy and weather causes."[10] There was a shadow of doubt. The Marines still had fifty-eight miles to go.

Major General William H. Tunner of the Far Eastern Air Force (FEAF) Combat Cargo Command flew into Hagaru-ri with a solution. Tunner's planes had been ferrying out the casualties. With the evacuation of casualties complete, he proposed to General Smith that, with the planes he had, he could haul out all the remaining troops. Smith declined. He pointed out that as the number of troops became smaller, the perimeter would shrink to the point where the airfield could not be protected. Planes would not be able to land to take them out and they would not have the strength to fight their way out on foot.[11]

One serious obstacle to the attack southward was the Chinese force still holding East Hill, dominating Hagaru-ri and the road to the south. A mixed group of Marine and Army troops had only a precarious toehold on one small corner of the hill—which had to be secured before the division could move. The division plan was to have the 5th Marines hold the perimeter and secure East Hill. The 7th Marines would secure a key hill to the south of the airport and lead the attack south. All division service units were divided up into two trains. Train One would be attached to the 7th Marines and follow the regiment down the road. Train Two, protected by the 5th Marines, would follow. The remainder of the 5th Marines would bring up the rear. The division objective was Hamhung. Koto-ri was only an intermediate objective.

A small group of reporters had arrived at Hagaru-ri on the incoming cargo planes. General Smith took time to brief them on his proposed plan of attack. A British reporter asked if this wasn't a retirement or retreat. In his typical quiet and scholarly manner, Smith explained, "You can't retreat or withdraw when you are surrounded. The only thing you can do is break out, and when you break out, that's an attack."[12] Smith's explanation, correct as it was, became hyped and was repeated around the world as, "Retreat, hell; we are just attacking in a different direction."

Preparations for the Marine attack southward were under way as the main body of the 26th CCF Army began arriving in the area east of Hagaru-ri on the night of 5 December. The first unit to arrive was the 76th CCF Division. The 229th and 227th Regiments of that division relieved the units of the 58th CCF Division on East Hill, while the 228th Regiment took up positions farther to the south near Pusong-ni, relieving elements of the 60th CCF Division blocking the road.[13] The Chinese reinforcements were a day late. In addition to heavy attacks from aircraft, parts of the 26th Army had become lost in a snowstorm.[14]

At Hagaru-ri, the last act of the Chosin battles began at first light on 6 December. Concurrently with the attack southward by the 7th Marines, the 2d Battalion, 5th Marines, advanced to clear the Chinese from East Hill. The 76th Division units in place on East Hill defended tenaciously, but by early afternoon, the hill had been secured with the capture of 220 prisoners. That night, the Chinese launched a massive attempt to retake East Hill, desperate to halt the withdrawal. When the attack was finally halted and driven back, more than 1,000 Chinese dead lay in front of the Marine lines.[15] If the usual wounded-to-killed ratio prevailed, the possible Chinese casualties amounted to more than 4,000. Additional units of the 26th CCF Army arrived too late to block the southward move of the Marines. The Chinese history explains: ". . . because the distance was pretty far and movement was slow, they were unable to launch their attack on time. When they were ready to make their attack the night of the 6th the enemy had already broken out of the encirclement. . . ."[16]

South of East Hill, the 228th CCF Regiment stubbornly resisted the advance of the 7th Marines. By dusk, the Marine column had advanced only 5,000 yards. Finally breaking through the block late in the afternoon, the column commenced moving. Throughout the night—in what veterans remember as a chaotic running fight—the advance continued in fits and starts. The column would halt to reduce a roadblock or to cut a bypass around a blown bridge. Chinese units that had been bypassed, or units newly arriving, attempted to cut the column. Marine squads, platoons, or companies would peal off to deal with infiltrating Chinese, then leapfrog down the road as they were relieved by other units. As the night wore on, units in the column became more and more intermingled.

Elements of the 77th CCF Division, arriving near Hagaru-ri on 6 December, continued southward that afternoon and evening. Some were able to establish hasty roadblocks, which halted the column for various periods. Others closed in on the flanks of the column after the advance guard had passed. Still others continued south to relieve the remaining elements of the 60th CCF Division, which had encircled Koto-ri. The running fight with the Chinese failed to halt the column. In the early morning hours of 7 December, the advance guard of the 7th Marines reached Koto-ri. By dark, all elements of the 1st Marine Division had closed.

The 88th CCF Division, added to the 26th Army just before leaving Shanghai, had followed the 76th and the 77th Divisions southward. According to a prisoner captured near East Hill, the 88th had taken a terrible beating from air attacks. The 77th CCF Division had reached Koto-ri but never was able to launch an attack. Severe air attacks, artillery, cold, fatigue from the long forced march south, and losses on 6 and 7 December had rendered both divisions ineffective. In the march south and the attempt to defend East Hill, the 76th CCF Division was virtually annihilated. Altogether two, and possibly three, divisions of the 26th CCF Army had been defeated. The Chinese history reports: "After the Hagaru-ri enemy fled southward, our 20th Army immediately relied on positions already held [Funchillin Pass] to carry out successive blocking attacks. The 26th Army was in hot pursuit of the enemy."[17]

There were now some 14,000 Marine and Army troops with a full complement of artillery and more than fifty tanks assembled at Koto-ri, ready for the last leg. General Smith later said: "It may have appeared to some that there was considerable cause for apprehension over an enemy attack at Koto-ri. For my own part, upon arrival at Koto-ri my feeling was that we were in."[18]

General Smith's optimism was not reflected by the intelligence reports, which spoke of additional reserves moving south. Colonel Bankson T. Holcomb, Jr., the 1st Marine Division G-2, confirmed that the 26th Army, made up of three or four divisions, was present in the area. He said that consistent reports over the previous week of convoy and troop movements to the Chosin Reservoir area—and indications of regrouping of forces originally here—pointed to an enemy force of at least ten divisions, with a possible reserve of several additional divisions. He believed the enemy was fast approaching the point where he would be capable of accomplishing his mission, "that of destroying UN forces and equipment immediately to his front."[19]

Colonel William Quinn, at X Corps, was no less pessimistic. He reported that nine divisions had been identified, four more were possible. He reported elements of the 20th, 26th, and 27th CCF Armies in contact, with the possibility of the 24th and the 30th. In addition, there were large reserves north of the Chosin Reservoir. One prisoner, supposedly from the 84th CCF Division, mentioned the possible presence of either the 30th or the 28th Army; both were known to be in Manchuria. Quinn believed the new identifications and the large unidentified reserve to the north indicated preparations for a major enemy effort against the Hamhung–Hungnam complex.[20]

MacArthur Changes His Mind

While the 1st Marine Division with attached Army forces prepared to attack southward, the staff at the Far Eastern Command was preparing new instructions. On 5 December, COMNAVFE commenced planning for evacuation of forces from Korea. Two amphibious groups were organized, one for the east coast and one for the west coast. The Far Eastern Air Force had a plan ready for mass evacuation by air: If two additional twelve-plane squadrons of four-engine C-54s were available, together with thirty R4Ds (Navy designation for the C-47), 16,000 people per day could be withdrawn from Korea in good weather, 12,000 per day in poor weather.

General Wright summed up the evacuation situation. At Inchon, the Eighth Army could be loaded out in five days, provided they left all supplies and equipment behind. With equipment, it would take six days to load one division. Wright had learned from the experience of the 1st Marine Division in outloading from Inchon. The limitations of that port were apparent. It was a slow, dangerous, and inefficient use of surface lift. Only LSTs could beach at Inchon, and then only for two four-hour periods each day. The trips from Inchon to Japan would be longer. Pusan could handle more ships at once (up to twenty-eight at a time), could handle heavy lifts, and could move units and equipment much faster, in one-fourth of the turnaround time.

Air support was spotlighted as a key factor. If evacuation from Inchon were chosen, that would mean the loss of the southern airfields and the support they provided. If evacuation from Pusan were chosen, with the Eighth Army delaying in successive positions, the rear airfields could be protected, guaranteeing full air support as long as possible.

Wright concluded his recommendations: "By early junction of our forces we have the capability to delay and punish the enemy enormously, retain our status in Korea and be better prepared to meet the eventual political decisions to be formed."[21]

Across the peninsula, General Walker, on 6 December, pausing at the intermediate line below Pyongyang, realized he needed to build up forces on his right flank. There were three untried divisions of III ROK Corps at hand, together with the remnants of II ROK Corps. He began moving them into the area of Chorwon–Pyonggang (as differentiated from Pyongyang), in early attempts to build a line.[22]

After arguing vigorously against a line across the peninsula, MacArthur changed his mind. Exactly why is not known. Some circumstances had changed. Most important, it was now apparent that the bulk of X Corps could manage to withdraw more or less intact. The additional ROK divisions were a factor. The realization that it was necessary to protect the airfields for continued ground support and air defense may have been the decisive factor. In contrast to his decision to land at Wonsan, opposed by most of his staff, MacArthur now listened. On 7 December, he issued a warning order. The Eighth Army would withdraw in successive positions, if necessary, to Pusan, holding Seoul for the maximum time possible short of risking envelopment. X Corps would be withdrawn and joined with the Eighth Army.[23] CINCUNC Operation Order No. 5, issued the following day, amplified the warning order and delineated nine lines across the peninsula. Line 1 was the temporary position of the Eighth Army south of Pyongyang from Kyomipo–Chunghwa–Yul-li–Singye.[24]

CINCUNC Operation Order No. 5 was followed by one of General Willoughby's most pessimistic intelligence estimates of the war. He gave as the most probable Chinese capability "continued reinforcement by Chinese Communist units." The second capability was offensive operations across the entire front. The third capability was penetration and envelopment in the area between X Corps and the Eighth Army.

Willoughby had been assuming the strength of each CCF division as 8,000. Now, based on PW and other reports stating that some divisions had as many as 12,000 men, he settled on 10,000, with another 5,000 nondivisional troops. He suggested the presence of two new CCF armies, the 24th and the 30th. In addition, he believed that another two, the 25th and the 37th, would soon appear. All told, Chinese forces in contact with UN troops had a strength of 268,000, with another 160,000 North Korean troops potentially available. In a second echelon along the Yalu were 550,000 troops of the First, Third, and Fourth Field Armies, with another 200,000 en route to Manchuria from various parts of China. From this information, he believed that ". . . over a million CCF ground troops are poised as a threat to UN ground forces." This, he said, pointed to the ". . . probability of unlimited Chinese commitment." The Chinese were willing to accept war by overtly provoking hostilities that might provoke world conflict.[25] In the daily telecon for 7 December, Willoughby reported: "The bottomless well of CCF Manpower in Manchuria continues to overflow into Korea with an unrelenting surge."[26]

In fact, no Chinese reinforcements had entered Korea since the arrival of the twelve divisions of the 9th CCF Army Group in November. No more would arrive until March and April of the following spring.[27] And the twelve divisions of the 9th Army Group would soon be out of action for several months, leaving only the eighteen divisions of the 38th, 39th, 40th, 42d, 50th, and 66th Armies—badly battered, tired, and short of supplies—to continue pursuit. It was from these eighteen battered and exhausted divisions, short on supplies and numbering only about 180,000 effectives, with little or no artillery, that the Eighth Army was withdrawing.

Nevertheless, Willoughby's estimate was alarming to Walker. Believing that the Chinese in force were moving southward along the Yangdok–Singye–Kaesong axis, Walker dared not remain long on Line 1. Substantial forces to his right rear would cut him off from Seoul and force him westward onto the Ongjin Peninsula, with no airfield for support and no port for supply and evacuation. Simultaneously with receipt of Operation Order No. 5, Walker ordered further withdrawal to Line 2: Haeju–Sinmak–Singye–

Ichon–Pyonggang–Kumhwa. I Corps moved south along Route 1: Chunghwa–Sariwon–Haeju. IX Corps took Route 33 south along the line Yul-li–Singye–Sibyon-ni.

Seizure of Funchillin Pass

The ten-mile stretch from Koto-ri to Chinhung-ni was potentially the most hazardous section of the entire breakout. Six or seven miles of that would be down a tortuous road exposed to enemy fire from high ground on both sides. With the road cut into the sides of steep hills, there was no cover. On the one-way road, a single vehicle, unless shoved over to the side, could block all movement. To complicate matters further, the road was already cut by the huge penstocks carrying water from the Chosin Reservoir to the power plants in the valley below. Where the penstocks crossed the road, they were covered by a gatehouse. The road was carried around the outboard side of the gatehouse by a bridge that the Chinese had blown, leaving a twenty-four-foot gap to span.

Successfully reaching the valley floor from Chinhung-ni to Sudong would not eliminate the possibility of Chinese ambush. By 6 December, elements of the 89th CCF Division were advancing westward from Sachang-ni to the vicinity of Chinhung-ni. There was the possibility of further reinforcement of the 89th Division by units coming south from Yudam-ni. The road from Chinhung-ni south to Majon-dong ran through a narrow gorge. Damage could be done by the Chinese. But with expeditious movement, it was possible to reach the valley and clear the narrow gorge before the pursuing forces could occupy the dominating hills on either side of the pass.

The remainder of the 60th CCF Division had occupied Hill 1081 and other positions overlooking the key part of the pass. To the west, remnants of the 58th CCF Division had taken up positions near the top of the pass. The remnants of the 79th CCF Division from Yudam-ni were moving south through Sachang-ni and east toward Hungnam in a deep enveloping move, attempting to cut off the withdrawing forces.[28]

Hill 1081 was critical. With it and the higher Hill 1452 in friendly hands, the route down the pass, hugging the sides of the hills to the east, was reasonably safe. Chinese on the hills to the west, without artillery and with few mortars, would be unable to take advantage of their dominating hilltop positions. The 1st Battalion, 1st Marines, then at Chinhung-ni, could attack north and secure 1081 while withdrawing troops attacked south to secure 1452 and the pass itself. But the road north from Majon-dong would have to be secured and 1/1 would have to be relieved of its defense of Chinhung-ni.

X Corps ordered the formation of Task Force Dog, under Gen. Armistead Meade, the 3d Infantry Division's assistant commander. Its mission was to secure the road from Majon-dong to Chinhung-ni and relieve the 1st Battalion, 1st Marines. The task force was made up of the 3d Battalion, 7th Infantry; the 92d Field Artillery (SP) Battalion with 155mm howitzers; a company of engineers; two sections of the deadly self-propelled quad 50s and twin 40s; and a detachment of trucks. Alerted to be ready to move any time after 6 A.M. on 6 December, they started north at 11 A.M. on 7 December. Without opposition, the task force reached Chinhung-ni by 2:20 P.M. that day and relieved 1/1.

Daylight on 8 December filtered through a steady snowfall. Visibility was sharply curtailed, banishing all hope of air support as the troops moved to their attack positions. The plan was a three-pronged attack—one from the south, two from the north. From the south, the 1st Battalion, 1st Marines, began climbing through the snowstorm at 2 A.M. in order to reach their attack positions by 8 A.M. Their objective was Hill 1081. By dark, all of Hill 1081 except the summit was in Marine hands. From the north, the 3d Battalion, 7th Marines, the western prong, led off, advancing to secure key terrain on the west side of the MSR. The 1st Battalion then would pass through, secure the saddle at the very top of the pass, then secure the bridge site. The eastern prong, the 5th Marines, would secure Hill 1457, the highest hill dominating the pass.

The 5th Marines, with the assistance of the provisional army battalion, secured Hill 1457 by 3:30 P.M. On the right, the Chinese put up a bitter fight against the 3d Battalion, 7th Marines. The 2d Battalion was committed to assist, but at dark both battalions were halted short of the objective. The 1st Battalion, however, had passed through and reached the saddle at the top of the pass.

That night the temperature dropped. Wind funneling through the pass drove the windchill factor to new lows. When the advance was resumed at daylight, there was little resistance. Many Chinese were found frozen to death in their foxholes. Others were so incapacitated with frozen feet and hands that they were incapable of resisting. The site of the broken bridge was secured by noon. At Hill 1081, the final peak was secured by 3 P.M.

The twenty-four-foot gap was the final obstacle, but the division engineer was prepared. Fortuitously, four Brockway trucks, specially designed for installing Treadway bridge sections, had been sent to Hagaru-ri prior to the Chinese attack to assist in construction of an advance headquarters for X Corps. Unfortuitously, there were no bridge sections with it. Lieutenant Colonel John H. Partridge, the division engineer, inquired of the Combat Cargo Command: Could they load and parachute some bridge sections to him? They had never before done such a thing but were willing to try. After one test drop (which indicated a need for improved technique), eight sections, providing 100 percent backup, were dropped at Koto-ri. Six of them were serviceable. Shortly after noon on 8 December, the bridge sections were in position and work began. By 3:30 P.M., with the help of some Chinese prisoners, the bridge was in and the division trains started to roll. Shortly thereafter, a crucial mishap damaged the bridge. Expedient measures were taken and the trains rolled again. A steady stream of vehicles continued down the pass during the night and through the following day.

At 2:30 A.M. on 10 December, troop movement began down the pass, led by the 1st Battalion, 7th Marines. As units of the 5th and 7th Marines moved off their protective positions, they were relieved by elements of the 1st Marines leapfrogging southward from Koto-ri. Some time after midnight on 10 December, when the tanks bringing up the rear cleared the bridge, orders were given for it to be blown. By 1 A.M. on 11 December, the last units had cleared Chinhung-ni, and by nine o'clock that night, all 1st Marine Division units closed in their assembly area near the Yonpo Airport. At 2 P.M. on 11 December, Task Force Dog had begun withdrawing from Chinhung-ni, having kept the road open for the withdrawing Marines. That evening, the 3d Infantry Division's daily operations report stated: "Successfully extracted the 1st Marine Division."

The Chinese Attempt Pursuit

From 7 December onward, the Chinese movements were a series of random, hastily extemporized, and uncoordinated actions. Communications had been strained to the breaking point. Air action had delayed and disrupted the movement of reinforcing forces. Cold, fatigue, and lack of supplies had drained many units of their combat capability. Still, the Chinese were able to strike some blows at the withdrawing forces. Elements of the Chinese 89th Division made several attempts to attack the route through the valley between Chinhung-ni and Sudong. One attempt succeeded in temporarily halting traffic but was beaten off. The Chinese lacked the reserves to reinforce these attacks sufficiently to pose a serious threat to the southward movement.

The remaining major threat to the withdrawing units was the 78th CCF Division of the 26th Army. While the 76th, 77th, and 88th Divisions of that army had moved directly south toward Hagaru-ri, the 78th CCF Division had made a wide flanking move down through the valley of the Fusen Reservoir toward Oro-ri. As early as 2 December, the 1st Marine Division G-2 had noted a buildup south of the Fusen Reservoir and smaller units in the Oro-ri and Sinhung-ni areas. On 7 December, the 65th Infantry, defending the route south from the Fusen Reservoir, made contact with the 78th CCF Division. Over the next several days, air attacks broke up further Chinese advances there.[29]

As the 1st Marine Division was moving down the pass, the division G-2 again expressed concern that the enemy was still collecting reinforcements and would soon be in position for a coordinated attack against Hamhung. Both the division and the corps G-2s believed the Chinese forces were much larger than had been identified previously. There was a belief that only a portion of the available divisions had been employed and that substantial additional forces were assembling for an all-out assault on the Hamhung perimeter. The 1st Marine Division after-action report stated the belief that the 9th Army Group consisted of the 20th, 24th, 26th, 27th, 30th, 32d(?), and 33d Armies, with a total of eighteen and perhaps twenty-one divisions: "There is positive evidence to support the presence of elements of all of the above armies but the 33rd in the Chosin Reservoir–Hamhung area prior to the final withdrawal of UN forces on 24 Dec 1950, although it is not presumed that the entire strength of these armies had arrived or had been committed."[30]

The report also stated the belief that ten and probably twelve divisions of three of the armies saw action at Chosin.

Departure from Hamhung

As early as 5 December, with renewed confidence that the 1st Marine Division would successfully reach Hungnam, and in anticipation of a prolonged defense of the Hamhung–Hungnam enclave, X Corps issued Operation Order No. 9-50 for defense of the Hungnam area. It established a semicircular perimeter stretching from shore to shore, with a final defense line having a radius of about seven miles. From east to west, sectors were assigned to I ROK Corps, 7th Infantry Division, 3d Infantry Division, and 1st Marine Division.

MacArthur's order to withdraw changed that. General Almond decided that the 1st Marine Division, having taken the heaviest casualties of the campaign, should be the first to outload. The 7th Marines were the first to embark, beginning on 11 December. The filthy and exhausted troops were greeted aboard ship by round-the-clock galleys serving steak and tomatoes and evaporators running at warp drive to provide hot showers. By 14 December, all Marine units had been outloaded.

The remnants of RCT 31 were next to embark. The remainder of the 7th Infantry Division took up positions on the north side of the perimeter while the 3d Infantry Division covered the perimeter from Oro-ri west to Chigyong and south to the Yonpo Airport. Corps planned to have the perimeter shrink in three phases. In the first backward step, the 3d Division would withdraw north from Yonpo to the north side of the Tongsongchon River. The 3d Division would then establish a defense line behind the 7th Infantry Division and I ROK Corps. The latter two would then withdraw through the 3d Infantry Division and embark. In the final phase, the 3d Division would thin out its line—withdrawing battalions from each regimental zone, then companies, and finally the remaining platoons. The entire defense of the beachhead would be supported generously by naval gunfire from ships offshore.

At General Almond's evening staff conference on 10 December, the plan was reviewed. The X Corps staff estimated it would take ten days to clear the port from the date outloading began, provided no serious enemy intervention occurred. The rate of loading would be determined by the speed with which the ships could be loaded. Enemy pressure permitting, all possible materiel and equipment would be evacuated.[31]

General MacArthur arrived at Yonpo for a brief conference on 11 December. He reviewed the plans for evacuation, then held a private conference with General Almond. Almond was offered his choice: return to Tokyo and resume his duties as chief of staff or remain with X Corps, report to General Walker, and serve under him in the Eighth Army. Almond chose to remain as commander of X Corps, despite personal friction between Walker and himself. MacArthur then proceeded to Seoul to confer with Walker. The following day, he reported to the Joint Chiefs of Staff:

1. Withdrawal of X Corps from northeast Korea has been initiated with 3rd ROK Div now enroute by water to Pusan.

2. Plan for evacuation of Hungnam area provides for three phase successive withdrawals to contracting perimeters centered on port area. 7th Marine Regt now embarking for water lift to Pusan. Next unit to embark will be ROK Capital Div which will move via LSTs to Samchok to assist Eighth Army's right flank. Subsequent units will move to Pusan in following order: 1st Mar Div, 7th Inf Div, 3rd Inf Div.

3. Plan now being implemented is based on current estimate of enemy capability to interfere and current availability of water and air lift. Plan will accomplish orderly withdrawal and complete evacuation of all personnel and organic equipment, and consumption or evacuation of all supplies in Hungnam base. X Corps can clear Hungnam 25 December and close Pusan 27 December.[32]

The gathering Chinese forces were a source of apprehension to X Corps. On 10 December, a force believed to be as large as

20,000 was reported building up in the Sinhung area, indicating a possible attack on Hamhung either via Oro-ri or moving southeast to attack the right flank of X Corps.[33] Thereafter followed a lull with no enemy contact. Interrogation of PWs captured earlier spoke of the effects of weather and air attacks, with some units being depleted to the point of ineffectiveness. Others reported a very high incidence of frostbite and failure to resupply food. On 14 December the PIR reported an attack on Oro-ri and other movements indicating preparations for a full-scale operation. Colonel Quinn believed that as many as four CCF armies were gathering around Hamhung—the 27th Army to the northwest of Hamhung; the 32d Army to the northeast, with the 26th Army in the center along the Hamhung–Hagaru-ri axis; and possibly the 42d Army on the left flank, with possibly another army in reserve in the Hagaru-ri area. The tempo of CCF probes increased on 15 December.

On 15 December, the 9d Infantry Division withdrew from the outer line, contracting the perimeter. Quinn believed the withdrawal threw the enemy off stride, but he felt that the Chinese would react within twenty-four hours and that the likelihood of an enemy attack would increase as the perimeter contracted. But by 17 December, no such attack had materialized. As the days passed, even Chinese reconnaissance activity declined, although there were continuing indications of reinforcements arriving.[34]

By 19 December, the 3d Division had occupied the second of the corps defense lines. Units from the 7th Division and I ROK Corps were moving to the beach and commencing embarkation. By 23 December, the 3d Division had reached the final defense line and was commencing to embark. On Christmas Eve, the last units embarked and withdrew.

In reality, the Chinese 9th Army Group was a much-battered remnant of the force that launched the attacks on the night of 27 November. It was incapable of effective sustained action on any significant level. The deputy commander of the Chinese People's Volunteers had a realistic view: ". . . after the enemy retired to the Hungnam harbor, fire support from naval warships could give support. They used sea, air and land fire power to form a close fire net and a wall of fire. Under these conditions Chief Peng ordered 9th

Army Group to halt pursuit and to conduct an on-the-spot surveillance of the enemy."[35]

Hong Xuezhi reported that the 9th CCF Army Group had suffered "severe non-combat reduction of personnel" due to lack of experience in preventing frostbite. Mao stated that the 9th Army Group lost as many as 40,000 men due to cold weather, lack of supplies, and the fierce fighting. He sent a cable to express his "deepest sorrow" for those who died of bitter cold.[36] Peng Dehuai asked for 60,000 replacements for the 9th Army Group.[37] That would represent 40 percent of the original 150,000 in the group. The 9th Army Group was so badly damaged that, for a while, Mao considered sending it back to Manchuria for rest and replacement. He believed that six armies on the western front would be adequate with the rebuilt North Korean People's Army (NKPA). No elements of the 9th CCF Army Group were again identified in combat until early April.

Like the withdrawal from Pyongyang, the withdrawal from Hungnam was premature and unwarranted. The Chinese forces in the east were in even worse condition than those in the west.

Further Debate in Washington

As a result of the early December conference with Clement Attlee, President Truman made some basic decisions. He determined not to leave Korea voluntarily. If kicked out, he would make sure that he took the officials of the ROK government and as many ROK soldiers as possible. The other basic decision was to abandon the objective of reunifying Korea by force. It was believed at the time that only by massive commitment of additional forces, with the risk of all-out war with China and the Soviet Union, could North Korea be cleared out and the country pacified.

That brought up the urgent question of the part the United States would play in asking for a cease-fire. With the British we agreed that we would not ask for one but would support one if the conditions were reasonable. The question became pressing during the second week in December, when thirteen Asian and African countries in the United Nations began preparation of a cease-fire resolution. The National Security Council met and agreed to support the effort. The Joint Chiefs of Staff agreed, with some reservations. Their concern was that the conditions should not put the UN Command forces at a disadvantage. The resolution was passed in the UN General Assembly on 14 December. A week later, it was rejected by the Chinese. Zhou Enlai announced that it did not include, as prerequisites, withdrawal of UN forces from Korea and Formosa (Taiwan), a seat for the People's Republic of China (PRC) in the UN, and no involvement by the United States or the United Nations in Korea's resolution of its political future. He also declared that the UNC invasion of North Korea had obliterated forever the thirty-eighth parallel as a demarcation line of political geography. Now the PRC would produce the unification of Korea by force. As a final salvo, he declared the resolution illegal, because it had been adopted without the participation of the PRC.

Rejection of the cease-fire resolution was not unexpected in Washington, where the situation looked dismal. General Collins's report of his visit to Korea had been encouraging. Still, MacArthur believed that the UN and the United States eventually would be forced from Korea. The increasingly pessimistic intelligence estimates from the Far Eastern Command reflected that view. That raised the question of when we should go: Should we go now? Admiral Forrest Sherman and Gen. Hoyt Vandenberg were of the opinion that it was unwise to wait and perhaps have to attempt an evacuation under enemy pressure. We should go now and concentrate our efforts in Europe. Generals Bradley and Collins were concerned about the defense of Japan. If we waited too long and had to withdraw under severe pressure, much equipment would be lost. We might get the troops out, but they would be of little use in defending Japan without equipment. General Bradley thought that MacArthur might even be able to spare a division or two from Korea now for the defense of Japan.

Coincidentally, General MacArthur was also giving thought to the defense of Japan. On 18 December, he requested that the four National Guard divisions that had been mobilized be sent to Japan to complete their training. MacArthur argued that because it was questionable that the existing force in Korea could hold out for long, and that any reduction in forces in Korea would encourage further Communist attacks, no forces could be spared from Korea. He further argued that the four divisions in Japan would contribute more to the ultimate security of the United States than would a similar deployment to Europe.

The Joint Chiefs did not accept the argument. MacArthur was informed that he would have to get along with the troops that he had. His previous request for Chinese Nationalist troops was also turned down.

The Chinese Decide to Pursue

When the Chinese occupied Pyongyang on 6 December, the situation of the 9th Army Group was still uncertain. Given the condition of the Chinese Army and the uncertain situation with the 9th Army Group, Peng was reluctant to pursue. It appeared that a portion of the six armies in western Korea might have to turn east to complete seizure of the line Pyongyang–Wonsan. In Beijing, Mao had met with Kim Il Sung and discussed the situation. Kim was anxious to pursue and exploit the Chinese victory to drive UNC forces completely out of Korea. Mao was uncertain, recognizing the possibility that the war could become protracted.

Two events combined to change his mind. On 2 December, Kavalam Panikkar, the Indian ambassador to Beijing, informed the Chinese that thirteen African and Asian nations were discussing the possibility of a cease-fire. On 11 December, Mao obtained the information that General Collins believed the situation of the UNC forces had become hopeless, that a protracted defense could not be organized because of casualties and loss of equipment.[38] On 13 December, Mao told Peng that the United States and Great Britain were asking for a cease-fire north of the thirty-eighth parallel so they could reorganize troops to continue the war. It was vital, he felt, that the Chinese cross the thirty-eighth parallel.[39] Two days later, at a meeting of commanders, Peng told the group: "Because of political considerations the central leadership requires us to cross the 38th Parallel. Therefore we are obliged to do so. . . ." He doubted if such an action would compel the enemy to withdraw from Korea.[40] The Chinese began to move southward with portions of the reconstituted North Korean Army on their left flank, opposing the ROK forces in the eastern flank of Eighth Army.

Death of General Walker and New Instructions

The Eighth Army continued to move southward during December, out of contact with the main Chinese force. By 16 December, General Willoughby was concerned with the lack of information on the whereabouts of the Chinese. Aerial reconnaissance and the reports of agents provided fragmentary and incomplete information. The Eighth Army was ordered to conduct strong patrols northward in an effort to locate the Chinese main body, but they encountered mostly reconstituted North Korean units. Willoughby believed the Chinese might be assembling for a further offensive behind a North Korean screen.

By 23 December, the Eighth Army was nervously positioned along the Imjin River and its eastward extension, Line 4 in MacArthur's operation order—roughly along Line B, as it came to be known in Eighth Army reports. Portions of the line coincided with defensive positions prepared before the war. But the eastern portion was sketchily held by the arriving ROK forces.

That same day, Gen. Walton Walker, driving north from Seoul, was killed when his Jeep collided with a truck. As a contingency plan, Gen. Matthew Ridgway had been designated as Walker's successor. Ridgway arrived in Tokyo on Christmas Eve, was briefed by MacArthur the following day, and arrived at the Eighth Army command post late on 26 December.

In Washington on the evening of 26 December, Marshall, Acheson, and Bradley met with President Truman. Now that X Corps has been successfully evacuated from northeast Korea, the president wanted to know if a military position could be held in Korea. Acheson opposed the idea of a withdrawal and urged staying in Korea to test Communist strength. He was concerned that so many changes had been made that MacArthur might be confused by his directives. Marshall agreed that MacArthur's directive should be rewritten.

By 29 December, the Joint Chiefs had a new draft ready. They radioed it to MacArthur, asking for his comments:

This message has been handled here with the ultimate of security and it is suggested that the contents thereof be confined, for the present, to you and your Chief of Staff and General Ridgway and his Chief of Staff. Message follows:

"It appears from all estimates available that the Chinese Communists possess the capability of forcing United Nations Forces out of Korea if they choose to exercise it. The execution of this capability might be prevented by making the effort so costly to the enemy that they would abandon it, or by committing substantial additional United States Forces to that theater thus seriously jeopardizing other commitments including the safety of Japan. It is not practicable to obtain significant additional forces for Korea from other members of the United Nations. We believe that Korea is not the place to fight a major war. Further, we believe that we should not commit our remaining available ground forces to action against Chinese Communist Forces in Korea in face of the increased threat of general war. However, a successful resistance to Chinese–North Korean aggression at some position in Korea and a deflation of the military and political prestige of the Chinese Communists would be of great importance to our national interest, if this could be accomplished without incurring serious losses.

"Your basic directive to furnish such assistance to the Republic of Korea as may be necessary to repel the armed attack and to restore international peace and security in that area requires modification in the light of the present situation.

"You are now directed to defend in successive positions, as generally outlined in your CX 50635, inflicting such damage to hostile forces in Korea as is possible, subject to the primary consideration of the safety of your troops. Every effort should be continued to mobilize the maximum Korean contribution to sustained resistance, including both conventional and unconventional means.

"Since developments may force our withdrawal from Korea, it is important, particularly in view of the continued threat to Japan, to determine, in advance, our last reasonable opportunity for an orderly evacuation. It seems to us that if you are

forced back to positions in the vicinity of the Kum River and a
line generally eastward therefrom, and if thereafter the Chinese
Communists mass large forces against your positions with an
evident capability of forcing us out of Korea, it then would be
necessary under these conditions to direct you to commence
a withdrawal to Japan.

"Your views are requested as to the above-outlined conditions
which should determine a decision to initiate evacuation, particularly in light of your continuing primary mission of defense
of Japan for which only troops of the Eighth Army are available.

"Following receipt of your views you will be given a definite
directive as to the conditions under which you should initiate
evacuation."[41]

For a month, President Truman, the National Security Council,
and the Joint Chiefs of Staff had agonized over the new situation—
an entirely new war, as MacArthur called it. They had at last arrived
at a decision and prepared new instructions. For several days thereafter, MacArthur and the Joint Chiefs quibbled about the meaning
of certain phrases. But even as they quibbled, the instructions were
becoming obsolete. A new general taking command of the Eighth
Army was about to create totally new conditions.

A new phase of the war was about to begin.

Notes

1. Zhang, *Mao's Military Romanticism*, 116.

2. DA Telecon TT4099, 6 Dec. 50.

3. Blair, *The Forgotten War*, 503 and n74, 1037.

4. FEC DIS 3007, 3 Dec. 50.

5. Zhang, *Mao's Military Romanticism*, 123.

6. Appleman, *Disaster in Korea*, 314.

7. *Chinese People's Volunteers.*

8. 1st Mar Div PIR 39, 2 Dec. 50.

9. Mao Telegrams, No. 35, 3 Dec. 50.

10. X Corps 13687, 4 Dec. 50, to FEC. General Almond reported to MacArthur that he had awarded the DSC "in your name." That is one of the few recorded instances when Almond, while commanding X Corps, used his authority as chief of staff of the Far Eastern Command.

11. General O. P. Smith interview with Ben Frank.

12. Ibid.

13. 1st Mar Div PIR 42, 5 Dec. 50.

14. Chai Changwen and Zhao Yontain, *A Chronicle of the War to Resist America and Assist Korea* (Beijing: CCP Historical Materials Press, 1987). Unpublished partial translation in author's possession (hereafter cited as *Chronicle of the War to Resist America*).

15. Montross and Canzona, *Chosin Reservoir Campaign*, 293.

16. *Chinese People's Volunteers.*

17. Ibid.

18. O. P. Smith Diary.

19. 1st Mar Div PIR 44, 7 Dec. 50.

20. X Corps PIR 71, 6 Dec. 50.

21. G-3 FEC Memorandum to Chief of Staff 6 Dec. 50.

22. Mossman, *Ebb and Flow*, 156.

23. CINCFE msg CX 50635, 7 Dec. 50, to Eighth Army and X Corps.

24. CINCUNC Operation Order No. 5 CINCUNC 50801, 8 Dec. 50.

25. FEC DIS 3012, 8 Dec. 50, and 3013, 9 Dec. 50.

26. DA Telecon 4105, 7 Dec. 50.

27. Zhang, *Mao's Military Romanticism*, 142.

28. *Chinese People's Volunteers.*

29. DA Telecon 4110, 8 Dec. 50; X Corps PIRs 10–12 Dec. 50.

30. *Special Action Report for the Wonsan–Hamhung–Chosin Reservoir Operation, 8 Oct.–15 Dec. 50.* 1st Marine Division. Annex B—Intelligence, 15.

31. *Special Report–Hungnam Evacuation: 9–24 Dec. 50.* X Corps, 2.

32. CINCFE CX 51102, 12 Dec. 50, to JCS.

33. X Corps PIR 75, 10 Dec. 50.

34. X Corps PIRs 81–88, 16–23 Dec. 50.

35. Hong, *Recollections.*

36. *Chronicle of the War to Resist America.*

37. Zhang, *Mao's Military Romanticism*, 123.

38. Mao Telegrams, No. 43, 11 Dec. 50.

39. Mao Telegrams, No. 44, 13 Dec. 50.

40. Zhang, *Mao's Military Romanticism*, 125.

41. JCS 99935 to FEC re Future Planning, 29 Dec. 50.

16
Looking Back

In order to hook a big fish you must let the fish taste your bait.
—Peng Dehuai

Plumes of black smoke rising skyward from burning supply dumps and long lines of exhausted and dispirited soldiers trudging southward marked the finish of the first Korean War, the one we lost. The United States, as the agent for the United Nations, had aimed for forcible reunification of Korea, had been denied that objective, and had been driven back when the Chinese unexpectedly intervened.

The Communist Chinese, good students and worthy successors to Sun Tzu—huge in number but primitively organized and equipped, apprehensive about fighting a modern military force—had resorted to that most ancient and effective resource: guile.

General Douglas MacArthur, the Joint Chiefs of Staff (JCS), and the Central Intelligence Agency (CIA) had been deceived and led into a trap by one of the most well-planned and coordinated deception campaigns American forces had ever encountered.

The Chinese Deception Plan
General Peng Dehuai had something in mind when he told his assembled officers: "In order to hook a big fish you must let the fish taste your bait."[1] His scheme was a well-executed combination of stealth, misdirection, and misinformation.

The movement of the first echelon of Chinese People's Volunteers (CPV) into Korea without the knowledge of the UN Command was a masterful accomplishment requiring careful planning and draconian march discipline. The stealthy deployment of the follow-up echelon, the 9th CCF Army Group, was an equally remarkable achievement.

Bogus prisoners were part of the disinformation effort. A review of the prisoner-of-war (PW) reports from the Eighth Army seems to show that those giving the code identification of their unit tend to have been soldiers who identified closely with the Communist Party. They also seem to have been the most convincing to Eighth Army intelligence officers.

The broadcast from Sinuiju Radio saying the Chinese troops were a Volunteer Corps for Protection of the Suiho Hydro-electric Zone gave the impression the Chinese force was small, with a limited aim. This was further reinforced by reports that the Chagang-do Redoubt was being established, both to maintain a North Korean government and to protect the hydroelectric facilities.

The Chinese delegation to the UN that left Beijing on 16 November was an effective bit of misdirection. Encouraged by Indian ambassador Kavalam Panikkar's report that the delegation had wide authority to discuss the entire situation, the United States and the other UN members were lulled into believing that a settlement was possible. It does not seem accidental that the delegation's slow progress from Beijing to New York distracted U.S. and UN attention long enough to permit the Chinese People's Volunteers to complete their preparations for attack.

Bogus radio traffic appears to have played a major role in the Chinese deception plan. Historical records on the activities of Army Security Agency units in the Far East have not been released. There were five Army Security Agency units located in the Philippines, Okinawa, and Japan. Beginning in early November 1950, steps had been under way to augment them with three additional fixed-station units of about 650 men each, releasing smaller mobile units for theater operations. Information from these units was available for production of theater intelligence.[2] The proposed augmentation would seem to indicate the listening posts were having some success. In addition, the 226th Provisional Communication Service Company, the usual designation for a radio intercept unit, and a 2d Communication Intelligence Unit were attached to X Corps.[3]

Information from communication intelligence was very carefully handled. The information itself might be used under certain circumstances, but the source would never be identified. The 24 October edition of the Daily Intelligence Summary (DIS) identified twelve Chinese armies with forty-four divisions in Manchuria, with another six armies with eighteen divisions possible. Radio intercepts are the most likely source for this order of battle information—information that greatly exaggerated the Chinese strength in Manchuria at that time.

The last element of the deception plan was the general Chinese withdrawal starting on 7 November. General Omar Bradley was not the only one to gain the impression that the Chinese had only intervened in moderate numbers and that these few had suffered such a bloody nose that they may have lost the taste for battle. The DIS of 25 November stated: "[There are] some indications which point to the possibility of a withdrawal of Chinese Communist Forces to the Yalu River or across the border into Manchuria. In unconfirmed reports, heavy casualties and the lack of a will to fight are given as possible reasons for such a move. The lull in fighting along most of the front, and the actual loss of contact in some sectors might well be indications that such an operation is underway."[4]

The DIS noted that other equally unconfirmed reports suggested that the withdrawal might be connected to political factors—obviously referring to the imminent arrival of the Chinese delegation at the United Nations. The source of the "unconfirmed reports" was not stated, but radio intercepts were the most likely origin.

The final touch in the deception effort was the release of twenty-seven American PWs. General Charles Willoughby thought their release could be interpreted as a possible indication that the Chinese had plans to withdraw from Korea. Later releases of American prisoners were found to be a prelude to renewed Chinese offensives.

MacArthur Takes the Bait

UN forces, under American command, "tasted the bait" first and foremost due to American hubris. The North Koreans had been whipped and the Chinese were poor fighters. We "understood the Oriental mind." The extent to which the subservient and colonialized Oriental mind had been changed by Communism and nationalism was known by some but believed by few. Those who did believe were considered fellow travelers, sympathizers at best, for the favorable reports they had written on the Chinese Communist movement. Further, Chinese entry into the war at this stage of the game was not logical, therefore they shouldn't be there. But what was not logical from the American viewpoint was not necessarily illogical from the Chinese viewpoint. Supplementing these viewpoints was the "pursuing a beaten enemy" mindset. All added to flawed evaluation of the material at hand, which in turn contributed to flawed decisions.

Just what intelligence triggered MacArthur's decision to go for the Manchurian border rather than halting at his preapproved stop line? One factor may have been the 12 October CIA estimate, which concluded that Chinese intervention was not probable in 1950. If they should intervene, it stated, they could do so effectively but not decisively. Despite statements by Zhou Enlai, troop movements to Manchuria, and propaganda charges, the CIA did not believe there were any convincing indications of an intent to intervene on a large scale. In his order to go for the border, MacArthur reminded his commanders that the previously approved stop line had been established only in view of a possible enemy surrender. Kim Il Sung's radio address on 16 October said North Korea would fight to the death. There would be no surrender. Information on the plans for the Chagang-do Redoubt began to gather. The C. L. Chen report of 18 October, saying the Chinese had decided to enter the war, was startling information but accepted as authentic. The Chinese were not in Korea yet, but they might be soon.

If the DIS was correct, the Chinese, with eighteen armies, sixty-two divisions, then in Manchuria, had more than enough capacity to defeat the UN Command (UNC) forces. If, as MacArthur apparently believed, they were preparing to cross into Korea, the only possible course of action to prevent total defeat of the UNC forces would be to reach the crossing sites ahead of the Chinese. In his reply to the Joint Chiefs of Staff inquiry, MacArthur hinted darkly about tactical hazards that might occur had he not taken such action. Massive entry of the Chinese was that possibility.

The problem was that there were not eighteen armies in Manchuria at that time. Of those both confirmed and tentatively identified, presumably from radio intercepts, seven were never in Korea then or later, and may never have been in Manchuria. Five of those identified may have been in Manchuria but were not deployed into Korea until the following spring. But, unbeknownst to MacArthur and his G-2, of the remaining six armies, the major portions of four of them were already in Korea, with two more close behind.

Initial contact with the Chinese forces was a surprise in both the east and the west. It was automatically assumed that the total Chinese force must be quite small if it had escaped detection by air reconnaissance. With that frame of mind, information obtained in the following days from prisoners of war and other sources was evaluated optimistically. The inclination was to make the information from prisoners and other sources reconcile with prior assumptions.

Were the Chinese formations in contact only smaller units, task forces, the advance forces of larger units? Or were they fully formed units? The PW reports were contradictory. In the Eighth Army and at the Far Eastern Command (FEC), they were accepted as task-force elements, the total size modest. In I Corps, Col. Percy W. Thompson thought they were fully formed units, the total size much larger. No one seemed to comment on the fact that the damage inflicted on the Eighth Army was out of all proportion to what could be expected from a small and primitively armed Chinese force.

There has to have been another factor not stated in the available intelligence reports. There had to be information from radio intercepts that tended to confirm the more modest estimates of Chinese size. MacArthur had the resources available. He had great success with radio intercepts during the Pacific Campaign.[5] During the early days in Korea, communication intelligence had been very helpful in allowing the Eighth Army to move reserves to meet North Korean threats. Raw communication intelligence would not have appeared in the DIS, which was only classified as secret. But conclusions based on that intelligence would have been included.

The Chinese were well aware of the UNC's capability to intercept radio traffic. As early as 1 September, Mao had sent a cautionary message to Chen Yi, ordering him to use wire instead of radio telegrams for all confidential telegrams. Only nonclassified information could be sent by radio. The rule was to be applied to the Party, the government, and the military.[6] So, knowing or believing the UNC was reading their radio traffic, there can be little doubt the Chinese made deceptive radio traffic a mainstay of their deception campaign, using American technology against us.

Nor was MacArthur the only one deceived. The CIA estimate of 14 November also seems to have fallen victim to the same disinformation campaign.

Chinese Intelligence Collection

The extent to which the Chinese benefited from the espionage efforts of the notorious British spy trio of Kim Philby, Guy Burgess, and Donald Maclean has yet to be revealed. The full damage assessment has never been released by the CIA and may never be released. The CIA maintains that to do so might jeopardize intelligence methods. That could be methods used either by us or against us. We may never know. Perhaps the Russians may eventually release some information. But the capacity of the trio for damaging UN interests in Korea was enormous. Dean Acheson is supposed to have said that what we knew the Philby trio knew.

There were a number of incidents that point to information available to Philby or Burgess that appears to have been passed on to the Chinese. The first of these was the warning to the Chinese that the UNC forces were to cross the thirty-eighth parallel. President Truman approved the National Security Council (NSC) recommendation on 11 September 1950. MacArthur was informed on 15 September. New instructions to MacArthur were issued on 27 September. Zhou Enlai's warning in his speech on 1 October, and his specific and pointed reiteration of that warning to Ambassador Kavalam Panikkar in the early morning hours of 3 October, would seem to indicate that the Chinese had information on the planned crossing by 1 October, and by 3 October they were aware of the actual orders to do so.

Philby or Burgess would seem to have been the source of that information. Maclean did not take over his duties on the American desk in the British Foreign Office until 1 November, but from then until the next spring, he saw virtually everything that came in. A strong indication that information was coming from one of the three, either from Washington or London, is a Mao telegram of 11 December to Peng and others giving purported details of the report

Gen. Lawton Collins made to the JCS on his return from an inspection trip to Korea.[7]

Then there is the question of who told the Chinese we would not bomb north of the Yalu River. As MacArthur argued, the Chinese would not have dared to assemble such concentrations of troops and supporting elements in Manchuria close to the border if they believed they would be bombed. The "Manchurian sanctuary," as it was later labeled, was a vital asset to the Chinese. Their belief it would not be bombed could have come from the same source that revealed MacArthur's instructions. In any case, the information would almost have to have been known to the Chinese prior to 20 October and probably would have been an important factor in their decision to intervene.

From some source, Mao was aware of the U.S. intelligence estimates. On 30 October, he reported to Peng: "The enemy, however, has not yet received clear information about our side. It only knows vaguely that our army has 40,000 to 60,000 men." On 18 November, he reported: "The enemy still believes our forces are approximately 60,000 to 70,000 men. . . ."[8] The Chinese appear also to have had a source in ROK Army headquarters. On 21 and 22 October, Mao gave Peng details of current locations and planned movements of the ROK forces that seem as if they could only have come from someone at a relatively high level.[9]

One other incident that appears to indicate espionage is the situation at Hagaru-ri and Yudam-ni on 27 November. The Chinese believed that there was one regiment between Hagaru-ri and the east side of the reservoir when they planned their attack. That is essentially the situation that existed on 24 and 25 November—the 5th Marines on the east side and the 7th Marines pushing toward Yudam-ni. That would have been reported in the daily telecon, which had fairly wide dissemination.

UN members and allies also deliberately or inadvertently provided the Chinese with some useful information. It appears that Indian prime minister Jawaharlal Nehru might have confirmed the *Newsweek* story carrying the proposed stop line for UN forces in North Korea. On 24 November, in an article in the Communist Party newspaper, Zhou Enlai wrote: ". . . Nehru told me that the UN forces would stop

40 miles short of the Yalu River after crossing the 38th Parallel. . . ."[10] The fortieth parallel would be a rough approximation of the approved stop line. The Indians would have obtained that information through their UN contacts, or they may have been specifically supplied with it as a way of reassuring the Chinese.

MacArthur himself, through his communiqués, provided the Chinese with some quite useful information. In his "massive compression" communiqué, he inadvertently let the Chinese know that the bulk of their forces had not been discovered—information they doubtless found reassuring. In his "new war" communiqué on 28 November, he stated that the Chinese forces were in excess of 200,000: "The situation . . . poses issues beyond the authority of the United Nations military council—issues which must find their solution within the councils of the United Nations and the chancelleries of the world." The first statement practically told the Chinese that the UN Command was not yet aware of their total strength. The latter statement told them they had won this battle.

Gambling on Continuing the Advance

Reassured in the belief that the Chinese strength in Korea was small but the reinforcement potential huge, and believing that his air had actually isolated the battlefield and kept reinforcements from crossing, MacArthur elected to continue the advance.

He knew Lin Biao commanded the Fourth Field Army and believed him to be the commander of the Chinese troops entering Korea. We know now that Lin opposed entry into Korea. With the Chinese forces in Korea at that point of moderate size, MacArthur figured it might be possible to continue the offensive, deal them a sharp setback, and convince them not to intervene. He was aware the Chinese had much larger forces at hand, but his "home for Christmas" statement indicated he was gambling that those forces would not be committed. Lin Biao might be bluffed out. The wild and reckless plan to send the 1st Marine Division westward across the mountain divide to cut the Chinese line of communication was meant only as a bluff. It could only succeed if the Chinese were bluffed into withdrawing. If the Chinese didn't withdraw, they would react long before that offensive progressed very far. They did.

MacArthur's statement in his memoirs comes as close as anything
to explaining his reasoning at that point. Having met the Chinese,
he states he could go forward, remain in place, or withdraw. As he
says, the Chinese could overwhelm the UN forces were they committed to a fixed defense. Withdrawing was against his orders (although he could have reported a changed situation and asked for
new instructions, which is what he did later). He says he chose to go
forward as a way of determining the strength of the Chinese. Later,
he called it a reconnaissance in force. He implied as much at the time
in his message C68465 of 7 November to the Joint Chiefs, announcing his intention to resume the advance: "Only through such
an offensive effort can any accurate measure be taken of enemy
strength." It was that, but also an attempt at bluffing.

When the Chinese offensive began in the west on the night of 25
November and spread to the east on 27 November, MacArthur knew
his bluff had failed. This would explain why, at the Tokyo conference
with Generals Almond and Walker on 28 November, MacArthur was
quicker to react to the Chinese offensive and more realistic about it
than either of his field commanders. Not only was he facing new
armies only now identified; he was potentially facing huge reinforcements from the armies assembled in Manchuria, including the
"ghost" armies, forces capable of driving the UN forces from Korea.
The "ghost" armies of Manchuria were the last and perhaps the most
successful element of the Chinese deception plan.

Given those circumstances. MacArthur's very pessimistic reports
to the JCS following the Chinese attack were not quite as pessimistic
or "hysterical" as General Bradley characterized them. MacArthur
believed the Chinese intended to commit most of the forces in
Manchuria. He told the U.S. Senate committee the following May
that he believed China was maintaining the "maximum military force
of which she is capable" in the Korean campaign.[11]

Interestingly, MacArthur claimed that the "reconnaissance in
force" revealed the Chinese buildup that was intended to launch an
all-out offensive in the spring. This was the initial Chinese plan. His
knowledge of the Chinese plan would indicate that he had sources
of information not published in the DIS. Those sources might have
provided more details on the internal debate on intervention that

was taking place in the Politburo. He may have known of the Soviet refusal to provide air cover, and he may have known of Lin Biao's opposition, believing that Lin was to be in command of the Chinese intervention forces. All this would have provided a basis for taking a truly calculated risk in advancing rapidly toward the border.

Douglas MacArthur was a man with a towering ego. In his book, the lack of rationalization for continuing the advance on 24 November is completely uncharacteristic. The only reason for not presenting a detailed justification for his most serious mistake must be that the information on which that decision was based was still highly classified as of 1964, when he wrote the book.

Consequences

The risk to the United States created by MacArthur's order to advance to the border on 24 October was enormous. In October 1950, the United States had the equivalent of eleven active infantry divisions and one armored division to meet its entire worldwide commitments. Seven of these—nearly two-thirds of the entire U.S. ground forces—were in Korea. MacArthur abandoned the stop line across the Korean Peninsula and sent these seven divisions in an uncoordinated rush toward the border of a hostile nation that possessed an army of more than 5,000,000 in 253 divisions, with 700,000 of these, including 200,000 well-trained combat troops, in Manchuria. All this was done in the face of explicit Chinese warnings not to do so and in defiance of orders from the Joint Chiefs of Staff. Granted that the available information was not sufficient at that time to form a firm conclusion on Chinese "intentions," their "capabilities" were enough to justify considerable caution in putting at risk two-thirds of America's ground forces.

The difference between a very serious reverse and a total disaster was a near thing. The most crucial battle was in the northeast, at Chosin. In concentrating twelve CCF divisions against the three U.S. and two ROK divisions of X Corps, with the major portion of that force directed against the 1st Marine Division, Peng Dehuai obviously expected decisive results. Loss of the 1st Marine Division would have resulted in the loss of a substantial portion of X Corps. Instead, X Corps was withdrawn intact, while inflicting such damage upon the twelve divisions of the 9th Army Group that they were out of action until the last days of the following March. With the reinforcement by X Corps, and with the absence of nearly 40 percent of the total Chinese strength, the Eighth Army was able to hold in the south.

General MacArthur agreed that this was the decisive battle. In commenting on a study by the Marine Corps Board, he wrote: "The Marine Corps Board of Study rightfully points out that the campaign of the 1st Marine Division with attached Army elements in North Korea was 'largely responsible for preventing reinforcement of CCF forces on Eighth Army front by 12 divisions during a period when such reinforcement might have meant to Eighth Army the difference between maintaining a foothold in Korea or forced evacuation therefrom.' . . . I think it might have gone further. The diversionary attack which pinned down an estimated 12 CCF divisions, preventing them from exerting that much additional pressure on the Eighth Army front or executing a flanking movement to the east, saved the Eighth Army from a much more imminent threat of destruction when it uncovered Red China's surreptitious build-up operations."[12]

MacArthur was certainly right when he called it "an entirely new war." The battles in North Korea changed the course of the war. In the first Korean War, the United States had hoped for reunification of Korea, the first return to freedom of land that had come under Communist domination. That war ended in defeat when the Chinese entered. In the new war, after two and one half years of stalemate, we settled for a return to the status quo ante and an ensuing fifty years of armed tension. Communist China—until then considered to be a rogue regime of doubtful legitimacy—became a power with which to be reckoned.

Korea has been called "The Forgotten War." There was a good deal to forget. It was a war we stumbled into unexpectedly—unplanned and woefully unprepared. Some of America's senior leaders, successful commanders in World War II, had difficulty dealing with this limited war. Certainly the Chinese Communists were not as well known and understood as our antagonists in World War II had been.

In the end, this second Korean War was finally brought to an end to put a stop to the growing losses of men. Mao was right. It did depend on how many Americans he could kill.

One wonders if Ho Chi Minh was watching and learning.

Notes

1. Zhang, *Mao's Military Romanticism*, 110.

2. Letter, Chief ASAPAC to CINCFE 9 Nov. 50, re proposed expansion plans.

3. Annex A, Task Organization, to X Corps Operation Order No. 6, 14 Nov. 50.

4. FEC DIS 2999, 25 Nov. 50.

5. Edward J. Drea, *MacArthur's ULTRA: Codebreaking and the War Against Japan* (Lawrence: University Press of Kansas, 1992).

6. Mao Telegrams, No. 5, 1 Sept. 50.

7. Mao Telegrams, No. 43, 11 Dec. 50.

8. Mao Telegrams, No. 24, 18 Nov. 50.

9. 46 Telegrams, Nos. 28 and 31.

10. Goncharov et al., *Uncertain Partners*, 193–94.

11. *Military Situation in the Far East*, 171.

12. Letter MacArthur to Snedeker 17 Oct. 56.

Appendix 1:
The People's Liberation Army

Power grows out of the barrel of a gun. The Party controls the Army. The Army will never control the Party.

—Mao Zedong

The huge size of the Chinese Communist Army in the summer of 1950 did not necessarily reflect its strength. The organization, equipment, training, and combat efficiency of the Chinese Communist Forces (CCF) varied greatly from unit to unit. Many of the units were made up of combat-seasoned soldiers who had been fighting either the Guomindang (GMD) or the Japanese for years. Others were made up of former Nationalist units that had surrendered individually or had been integrated into the CCF by entire divisions. Some senior officers were highly experienced veterans of the Long March; others were led by officers who were politically reliable but militarily inefficient. As a result, only about half of the more than five million men and 250 divisions were considered to be reliable combat units.

Out of the 125 or so reliable combat-effective divisions, thirty were to be employed initially in Korea—twelve during the Chinese attack in late October 1950, and those same twelve plus an additional eighteen during the offensive in late November. At the peak in 1952, a total of fifty-five divisions—nearly half the effective strength of the People's Liberation Army (PLA)—was tied down in Korea.

The first two Army groups sent to Korea were part of the general reserve. Because the PLA high command followed the militarily prudent course of keeping some of the better units in reserve, those units initially selected for service in Korea were some of the best in the PLA. They were selected based on their strength and their political reliability as well as the quality of their weapons, equipment training, and experience.

The Fourth Field Army, under Lin Biao was generally believed to be the best of the five field armies. The 38th, 39th, 40th, and 42d Armies came from the Fourth Field Army and were said to be especially strong; they had the honorary title of "Iron Troops." They had fought successfully in the Chinese Civil War against better-equipped Nationalist armies. Chiang Kai-shek had committed many of his American-trained and -equipped divisions in the defense of Manchuria. Lin Biao had captured large numbers of these well-trained troops in 1949 and had incorporated them into his forces to supply some of the skills lacking in his guerrilla army. Some were inducted directly into the PLA. Others, when possible, were given several months of indoctrination before being inducted into the PLA.

There were relatively few new recruits in these armies. An important exception was the 50th Army. It was a former Nationalist Army that defected as a unit during the civil war and was taken over virtually intact. The 66th Army was well regarded because of its reputation for political trustworthiness. It was looked upon as a bodyguard unit for Mao Zedong because it had been stationed in Beijing.

Lin Biao's troops from Manchuria were accustomed to cold weather. General Song Shilun's troops, employed in northeast Korea, were mainly from eastern China and not used to the cold. It is one of the ironies of the Chinese plan that those troops were employed around the Chosin Reservoir, where the temperatures were extremely cold, while the Manchurian troops were employed in western Korea, where the temperatures were somewhat milder. The losses from cold were devastating. It was an unfortunate error brought on by the hasty and extemporized nature of the Chinese intervention.

The Third Field Army as a whole was not rated as particularly strong, but the 26th Army, part of the 9th Army Group, was a crack unit. The 9th Army Group had taken Shanghai. The commander, Gen. Song Shilun, was considered the best commander in the Third Field Army. About forty years old at the time, he had been a student of Zhou Enlai at the Whampoa Military Academy when it was run by Chiang Kai-shek. He had been fighting since he was seventeen years old—first with guerrilla bands and then with organized units. He was a veteran of the Long March in 1934–35, when he commanded a regiment.

In terms of equipment, the Chinese Communist Army of 1950 was primitive by any standards. It has been compared to an army of 1914, without the trucks and the artillery, primarily an army of infantrymen. There were few trucks, little artillery, very limited communication (particularly via radio), no air support, and no antiaircraft defense. Logistical support in the civil war had been provided by the local population. When the PLA entered Korea, it was fighting outside of its home territory for the first time. Eventually a reasonably effective system of logistical support was devised, but in the first few months after intervention, it was barely adequate.

Divisional Organization

The Chinese division was a bare-bones organization made up of three infantry regiments, an artillery battalion, and miscellaneous troops. Each regiment had three battalions plus, sometimes, an artillery company, a mortar company, a transportation company, a guard company, and a reconnaissance and signal unit. The infantry battalion was made up of three rifle companies. Each rifle company had three rifle platoons, a heavy-weapons platoon with 60mm mortars and rocket launchers, and three machine-gun squads. There may or may not have been some 82mm mortars at the battalion level. There often was considerable variation in division organization, depending on the division's previous location and experience.

The nominal strength of a division was around 10,000 men, a regiment about 3,000, and a battalion about 850. The strength of many of the divisions fell below that, although those divisions that were designated for the invasion of Taiwan had more than 10,000 men. This would include the 20th, 26th, and 27th CCF Armies of the 9th Army Group.

There was also a great variation in equipment. Some of it was U.S. equipment taken from the Chinese Nationalists; some was Japanese, captured during the war; some was Czech, purchased on the open market. Through a mutual-security pact concluded with the Soviets in the fall and winter of 1949, Russian advisers had traveled to China to help reorganize and train the Chinese Army. Reorganization was commencing along the Soviet model, and modern equipment had been promised but not yet received.

Not only was there considerable variation in organization and equipment; there was a broad range in quantity of equipment. Some infantry regiments had as few as 400 rifles and carbines, 180 pistols, and 200 submachine guns. Prisoners reported that as many as two-thirds of the front-line infantry might have no weapons other than hand grenades. They would be expected to pick up weapons from a dead or wounded comrade, or from the enemy.

In a division there might be six 105mm howitzers, or 76mm guns, in the artillery battery of the artillery battalion, between four and six 37mm antitank guns, and four 120mm mortars. Within the regiment there would be three 75mm pack howitzers in the artillery company, 135 light machine guns, eighteen heavy machine guns, and eighteen 60mm mortars. The divisions initially sent in to Korea left behind nearly all of their artillery, as well as most of their heavy mortars. Transportation for the other crew-served weapons and ammunition was by pack animal.

Communication within the division was even more primitive. In some divisions, radio extended down to regimental level. In all divisions, communication from regiment downward was by telephone, or by runners. There would normally be only one field telephone at each battalion headquarters, none below that. Bugles, whistles, and runners were the communication means between battalions and companies, and within companies.

Political Organization
Mao Zedong's dictum was that "Political power grows out of the barrel of a gun." The Army was the "gun," so it was vital that the Communist Party maintain absolute control of the military. In some respects, the Party was the Army. The PLA provided many of the senior leaders of the People's Republic of China (PRC). The result was a system of joint leadership by military commanders and political commissars. To a great extent, the military commanders and the commissars were interchangeable at the senior levels. The commanders were as politically dedicated and knowledgeable as the commissars, and the commissars were experienced and capable military com-

manders. In some cases, such as in the 9th Army Group, Gen. Song Shilun served in both capacities, as did Gen. Zhang Yixiang, commander of the 20th CCF Army.

Control was extended through Party committees at each level of Army organization down to and including the company. Within the company, the political organization extended down to the rifle squad, with a "three by three" organization within the squad—each man assigned to watch the others, and each aware he was being watched. Even when one of them went to the head, the other two would follow.

The three-by-three squad organization may have been devised principally as a measure of political control. Nevertheless, it was highly effective in fostering close comradeship and cooperation within the squad. The effectiveness of that organization so impressed Maj. Evans F. Carlson when he observed the Chinese Communist Army in the late 1930s that he adopted the three by three organization for his raider battalion in the early days of World War II, along with that well-known Marine Corps motto, "Gung ho." It was one of the bases for adoption of the Marine fire team organization.

To further ensure Party control, the government aimed to have a reliable Party man in command of all units down to and including the subsquad level. It was a fundamental government belief that there were no limits to what a Communist could accomplish provided his political ideology was strong enough. But government officials also believed that even a good state of political health on the part of the most dedicated Communists was subject to abrupt lapses and even total reversal. So while a close watch was kept on all soldiers, an extra-close watch was kept on Party members and cadres.

The Chinese Soldier

The appearance of the Chinese soldier was not impressive. A U.S. recruiter would have turned away most of them. That would have been a mistake. They were short, scrawny, thin-legged men, but they were tougher than leather. The bulk of them had been recruited from the hardy rural peasantry. They were accustomed to hardship, indifferent to discomfort, generally in good physical condition, and capable of long and sustained marches. The individual soldier was poorly educated and often illiterate but reasonably intelligent. He was an excellent night fighter. Although the average soldier lacked a great deal of imagination, he bore the hardships and dangers of war with a certain degree of stoicism and was willing to close with his enemy in combat. But he was not indifferent to danger or death.

There was no conscription, by that name, in the Chinese Army. All were "volunteers." Quotas would be assigned to each village. Volunteers would then be obtained by a combination of persuasion, propaganda, and organized social pressure. Given the benefits and dignity the Communists had brought to many of the poorer peasants, it was often not necessary to apply pressure. Preferential economic treatment was given to families who provided a "volunteer." Both family and volunteer were made to feel it was an honor to join the Army. There was no fixed term of service. All were in for the "duration" unless discharged earlier because of wounds or illness. The length of the "duration" was not defined.

Soldiers seldom had an opportunity for leave. There was concern that soldiers going home would become dissatisfied with army life, so it was considered better to isolate soldiers from their families. To keep the soldiers further isolated from outside influences, only those of higher rank (usually colonels and above) were permitted to marry.

The soldiers were reasonably well clothed under ordinary conditions. Under the severe weather conditions of the Chosin Reservoir campaign, however, the Chinese clothing proved totally inadequate. The rubber-and-canvas tennis shoes worn by the Chinese provided no protection against the cold and resulted in extremely heavy rates of frozen feet. Few had gloves, so many suffered from frostbitten or frozen hands. Many soldiers froze to death in the extreme cold.

According to prisoner reports, the one thing many soldiers did like about the CCF was that they had a chance "to fill their belly." Under normal conditions, the troops were well fed. Particular pains were taken to provide the troops with an especially good meal before going into combat. Prisoners complained they had not had this opportunity in Korea.

In contrast to the behavior of the North Koreans, there are few known incidents of deliberate atrocities committed by the Chinese.

During their campaigns in China, prisoners were considered an asset. They were indoctrinated and inducted into the ranks to help swell the size of the PLA. In Korea, prisoners of war were considered to be important political and propaganda assets. To the extent possible, given the situation, prisoners were treated reasonably. In most cases, conditions considered outrageous by the prisoners were considered normal by the Chinese soldier. In the initial phases of the Korean War, the Chinese were no better prepared to take care of prisoners than they were of their own people.

The huge numbers of former Nationalists integrated into the PLA posed particular difficulties. As the Chinese Civil War progressed, the problem of dealing with defeated Nationalist units became pressing. It would not do to release them on parole; the resources to guard, house, and feed such huge numbers did not exist. Mao decided to integrate them into the CCF to compensate for losses, to safeguard against the danger of released prisoners joining a guerrilla force, and to make use of their military skills. Three criteria were applied:

1. Those units that negotiated a surrender of the entire group without putting up a fight at all were included intact into the CCF with minimum alteration of their officer corps, but with the addition of Communist commissars.

2. Those units that surrendered after offering some combat but surrendered by means of an armistice negotiation were retained intact, but gradually their officers were replaced with Party members. The remaining officers were indoctrinated and "retrained," then sent to other units, usually at a lower rank. Eventually these units were broken up and their members were parceled out as replacements to other units.

3. Those units that fought determinedly and surrendered only because they were overpowered were considered the least reliable and were broken up. Their members were distributed to other units and the officers became privates.

Between 50 and 70 percent of the members of the units sent to Korea in the initial intervention were made up of former Nationalist soldiers, including the noncommissioned officers and junior officers.

All prisoners being integrated into the PLA were subject to intensive sessions of "thought reform." It was an adaptation of the *chen feng* or *hsi-nao* method, which the Communists used in training their own Party cadres. The enlisted men underwent a period of indoctrination that varied from two weeks to three months. If they responded properly, they would not continue to be regarded as reactionary, but they were made to feel that they owed a special debt to the Party and the country for the leniency they had received. It was a debt to be repaid by extraordinary devotion and service, especially in combat. Most Nationalist prisoners adapted reasonably well. But, with few exceptions, former Nationalists never were fully accepted. Some prisoners reported that former Nationalists were not permitted to handle crew-served weapons.

Captured Nationalist officers were subjected to much more severe treatment. Some who were considered dispensable were shot. However, the Communists were in need of trained junior officers. These were sent to a "Military-Political University" where they were given a much more intensive program of thought reform, which could last from three to six months. The method might be described as "group therapy," as opposed to intensive individual psychotherapy.

The techniques used were self-examination, group criticism, morale surveillance, isolation, and application of intense pressure—methods that have been refined and are used today in cults worldwide. The aim was to transform the individual subject into a dedicated Communist. The object was to repress, rather than simply suppress (and the distinction is important), undesirable and reactionary thoughts. The pressures were extremely intense. Some subjects who did not respond were executed as a lesson to others. Some went mad. Occasionally there would be "field trips," where the students would observe concrete situations. A former Nationalist officer described one of these in which the class attended a "people's court" trial of an old peasant woman—a rich peasant, and therefore a reactionary—and her subsequent stoning to death.

Truly converted former Nationalists and dedicated Communists were described as "beets." Those who feigned conversion and simply suppressed any overt criticism were "radishes." The beets were red throughout, the radishes were just red outside, still white inside.

All prisoners, as well as the regular recruits, were given political indoctrination, a milder and continuing form of *chen feng*. The program succeeded in achieving good discipline and performance in combat. But political indoctrination, to succeed, has to be reinforced continually. Interrogation of prisoners and their subsequent behavior while in prisoner camps indicated there was widespread dissatisfaction in the CCF. The discipline and indoctrination did not deter the individual soldier, or junior officer, from surrendering when the situation dictated. He was a realist. And, without the constant reinforcement, his political dedication faded. That was clearly demonstrated two and a half years later, when, given the chance, more than 14,000 out of some 21,000 elected to go to Taiwan rather than return to China.

Discipline and Morale

Basic discipline in the PLA was boiled down to two slogans, "The Three Imperatives" and "The Eight Points of Attention":

The Three Imperatives
1. Obey orders in all your actions.
2. Don't take a needle or a piece of thread from the people.
3. Turn in everything you capture.

The Eight Points of Attention
1. Speak politely.
2. Pay fairly for what you buy.
3. Return everything you borrow.
4. Pay for any damage.
5. Don't strike the people.
6. Don't damage the crops.
7. Don't take liberties with women.
8. Don't mistreat captives.

Political officers at all levels were responsible for the morale of the men in their units. To the extent possible, they kept a particularly close watch on the state of morale and the ideological commitment of the troops. Any defect in behavior or failure in performance was considered to be the result of ideological and political deficiencies. If a man took some private problem to his political officer, he might be criticized for not having the proper ideological dedication, for being an "individualist." A typical response might be: "You are not firm in ideology yet. You have not a strong will yet. In military life you must dismiss all worldly thoughts and devote yourself solely to military duties." Worst of all, one could be called corrupt or reactionary, a serious political risk.

To monitor the ideology and morale of the soldiers, subsquad and squad leaders and platoon leaders reported twice a week to the political officer. There also was constant and covert surveillance by representatives of the regimental political section. The troops were well aware of it and were uncomfortable with it. Consequently, those who were politically unsympathetic suppressed any evidence of it. Anyone disaffected was isolated, not daring to comment or question.

Recruits were promised that they would not be beaten or mistreated in the CCF. And they were not. But any failure was subject to group criticism at squad meetings twice a week. If the man did not confess to any mistake or failure, a fellow soldier would accuse him. If a fellow soldier who knew of some minor transgression did not report it, he was considered an accessory. If a transgressor didn't mend his ways after three attempts, he would be held up to group criticism at a platoon meeting. Everyone was required to participate. Anyone who didn't participate—either by confessing mistakes or criticizing others—was considered an "ideological reactionary." As one former Nationalist master sergeant put it, "No one was beaten or cursed . . . in practice, however, one was punished through self-criticism meetings which were many times more horrible than beatings or cursing. . . ."

Unquestionably, the system did effect a change in the behavior of most individuals. In those individuals not politically converted, it succeeded in getting them to watch their own behavior very closely. The system of surveillance extended particularly into combat. As one soldier put it, "If the men feared to advance, the political officers gave us combat enforcement holding their pistols."

Leadership

There were no ranks in the CCF, and few distinctions other than "soldier" or "officer." Individuals were distinguished only by the billet they held, such as "squad leader" or "battalion commander." Officers wore the same uniforms as the troops, distinguished only in some cases by red piping. Officers were careful to share exactly the same conditions as the soldiers.

This was a heritage of both the guerrilla background of the PLA and its proletarian ideology. Under conditions of guerrilla warfare, when units were scattered, equipment was simple, and the men were truly volunteers, military ranks and distinctions meant little. As all armies have learned, discipline could be maintained through the close and prolonged association of respected leaders and ordinary soldiers. The truly revolutionary feature was comradeliness and unity between the soldiers and their leaders, with compliance obtained by the method of instruction and patient persuasion. It coincided with the Communist ideal of a classless society.

Accordingly, junior leaders were rated as to political reliability according to their occupational and socioeconomic background. Workers and peasants were preferred. In 1950, the government published a regulation differentiating class status; it listed twelve occupational classes—starting with "poor peasant" and ending with "landlord" and "rich peasant"—as a presumed means of estimating political reliability.

The problem the CCF faced was that there were not enough men who were both dedicated Communists and competent military leaders. They settled on using a large number of experienced former Nationalist officers as junior leaders—subject to very close political supervision.

Leaders at all levels, but particularly at the lower levels, faced a serious dilemma. Decisions in combat (and elsewhere) not only had to be militarily or tactically correct; they also had to be politically correct. Leaders at all levels knew that any failure or shortcoming would be criticized as much or more for their not being firm in ideology—something that could be more serious than criticism for a faulty tactical decision. There is little question that this was a serious hindrance to the exercise of initiative on the battlefield and resulted in the loss of many opportunities for exploitation. The Chinese reliance on the "set-piece battle," and their inability to extemporize as opportunities occurred, had as much to do with ideology as it did with their limited communication.

All the political indoctrination did not keep the Chinese soldier from willingly and truthfully telling whatever he knew when captured and interrogated. In the political effort to infuse the individual soldier with enthusiasm, a special effort was made to keep him informed of "the big picture." He often knew more about the plans of higher units than our own troops would ordinarily be expected to know. The result was some excellent intelligence information. But U.S. officers were often quite skeptical of the details such prisoners supplied.

War Indoctrination
Before crossing into Korea, the Chinese troops were subjected to particularly intense political indoctrination. The CCF had never fought on foreign soil. It required explaining and, in the Communist thinking, justification to themselves and the troops.

The major effort at justification was to explain the legitimacy of their intervention. These points were stressed:

- South Korea had started the war by invading the north.
- A civil war between the two Koreas then commenced.
- North Korea was about to win when the aggressive, imperialist United States sent in overwhelming forces and drove back the North Korean Army.
- The United States has aggressive designs on China and plans to attack Manchuria.
- North Korea is a "brother" country of China.
- North Korea helped the Chinese Communists win their struggles against the Japanese, so the CCF should help North Korea in its present struggle against the reactionary forces of Syngman Rhee, the U.S., and its puppets.

There were other justifications:

- The U.S. is attempting to follow in the footsteps of the Japanese, who first invaded Korea, then used it as a stepping-stone to invade Manchuria and China to enslave the Chinese people.
- The U.S. has aggressive plans against the Far East as a whole, against Russia, and against the whole world if its plans for China are not thwarted.
- If the U.S. aggressors are not stopped, they will attack other "democratic" states, which will resist, and World War III will break out.
- The U.S. is already guilty of aggression against China by bombing Manchurian territory and by occupying Taiwan.

An intense effort was made to whip up hatred of the United States by using examples like this:

> The United States is the paradise of gangsters, swindlers, rascals, special agents, fascist germs, speculators, debauchers, and all the dregs of mankind. This is the world's manufactory and source of such crimes as reaction, darkness, cruelty, decadence, corruption, debauchery, oppression of man by man, and cannibalism. This is the exhibition ground of all the crimes which can possibly be committed by mankind. This is a living hell, ten times, one hundred times, one thousand times worse than can be possibly depicted by the most sanguinary of writers. Here the criminal phenomena that issue forth defy the imagination of human brains. Conscientious persons can only wonder how the spiritual civilization of mankind can be depraved to such an extent.

Prospects for a quick and easy victory were talked up by the Chinese political officers. The troops were told that the United States had only 50,000 troops in Korea, that their weapons were not particularly good, and that the Americans lacked perseverance and were tired of the war. The mere appearance of the CCF would put them to rout. The Americans would withdraw to Pusan and flee to Japan.

The impression given to the troops going to Korea was that they would win as they had won before, with the same weapons and tactics, and that nothing new was required.

Given all of these factors, the Chinese government fielded a force of light infantry that was highly motivated and extremely well disciplined but without the weapons, equipment, organization, training, and support services to meet the conditions of sustained combat in modern war. Further, although the senior leaders of the CCF had extensive experience in maneuvering large bodies of infantry, they had no experience with or understanding of the complexities of modern mechanized warfare and had never really faced a well-trained and well-armed modern army.

American leaders knew this. As a result, the initial successes of that primitive army in the coming battles came as a shocking surprise— probably as much of a surprise to the Chinese leaders as it was to U.S. leaders.

Tactics

The movement of more than 300,000 men undiscovered into the mountains of North Korea was a superb military feat. For that accomplishment alone, the CCF deserved respect. That it had bloodied the nose of a modern army warranted even more respect. How did they do it? What tactics and methods had they used?

Chinese tactics were shaped by the strengths and weaknesses of the Chinese Army and its history. Because the PLA had originated as a guerrilla army in southern China, the guerrilla mind-set—concerned with secrecy, mobility, and surprise, and the willingness to trade space for time—figured heavily in the tactical and strategic thinking of its leaders. The great strength of the Chinese Army was in the availability of huge supplies of manpower. Its great weakness was in arms equipment and logistical support.

To the Communist mind, correct thinking, correct adherence to doctrine, is the key to success. The correct doctrine was to be found in the writings of Mao Zedong.

The basic policy of the Chinese Communist Army was carefully laid out in Mao Zedong's book *On Protracted War*: "Because the enemy force, though small, is strong (in equipment and the training of officers and men) while our own force, though big, is weak (only in equipment and the training of officers and men but not in morale), we should, in campaign and battle operations, not only employ a big force to attack from an exterior line a small force on an interior line, but also adopt the aim of quick decision."

Chinese operations attempted to attack units that were on the move and to resist the temptation to attack strongly held positions. Again, as Mao stated: "To achieve a quick decision we should generally attack, not an enemy force holding a position, but one on the move. We should have concentrated, beforehand [and] under cover, a big force along the route through which the enemy is sure to pass, suddenly descend on him while he is moving, encircle and attack him before he knows what is happening, and conclude the fighting with all speed. If the battle is well fought, we may annihilate the entire enemy force or the greater part of it. Even if the battle is not well fought, we may still inflict heavy casualties."

This principle was applied in the initial attacks on 25 October 1950, then was applied again in the attacks against the Eighth Army on 25 November and in the attacks against X Corps on 27 November. The 5th and 7th Marines at Yudam-ni, as well as the 31st Infantry units east of Chosin, were attacked while they themselves were disposed for attack. Hagaru-ri was attacked because of its crucial importance, but the Chinese lost heavily. On the other hand, Koto-ri was never attacked, even though the Chinese had built up considerable strength around it. It was too well defended.

A recurring theme in PLA military doctrine was "Numerical superiority will defeat the better weapons of the enemy." The aim was to use the tremendous manpower of the PLA to absorb the enemy firepower, exhaust his ammunition, and overrun key tactical positions by sheer numbers of men. As one former Nationalist put it, "Men were to be used as weapons of attack."

Without heavy equipment or vehicles, a Chinese division, moving on foot, was not restricted to established road networks, thus making it unusually mobile. But without good communication, it was slow to react to a changing situation. To avoid enemy artillery and air attack, it depended on night movement and night attacks to close with enemy before superior firepower could take its toll. Without artillery of its own it depended for success on close combat and the shock of surprise.

All of this resulted in Chinese operations that were typified by set-piece battles carefully planned ahead, using tactics that made the most of movement by stealth, of surprise, of overwhelming numbers. The aim was for quick success in annihilating the enemy, which meant killing or capturing the enemy force. The great weakness was the inability to sustain an action for more than a few days, and an inability to react flexibly to unexpected or changing situations.

Precombat Briefing

A thorough precombat briefing of all CCF troops was an essential part of both the political indoctrination and the tactical plan. It included composition, character, weapons, and morale of the opposing unit; the relation of the forthcoming action to large objectives; the difficulties likely to be encountered; and the grounds for believing that the PLA would be successful. Interrogators of captured Chinese found it difficult to believe that the ordinary soldier was so well informed. The information they provided was often discounted, but eventually it proved, in most cases, to be quite accurate.

The precombat briefing was also used to whip up hatred of the enemy. The Chinese had launched an extensive "Hate America" campaign among the military as well as the civilian population. Chinese soldiers were told they could expect to be facing Japanese, South Korean, Chinese Nationalist, and American troops. They understood that any soldier who surrendered would be immediately decapitated. Soldiers were induced to sign the "Pledge to Kill":

A Solemn Pledge to Kill the Enemy

We eight members of the squad hereby solemnly promise to be determined to kill the enemy by helping the leader in this combat and achieve merits to our most glorious honor.

1. I will fight bravely without being afraid of enemy fire and make our firearms effective to the greatest extent.

2. I will overcome every difficulty. I will not be afraid of great

mountains to cross or of long marches. I will fight bravely as usual even when I have nothing to eat for a full day.

3. We will be united and help one another, observe one another, so that we may not retreat even a step.

4. We eight members of our squad without fail will kill and wound more than three enemies for the people of China and Korea and for our leader.

5. Should we fail to do this, we wish to be punished. [In the case of a Party man, he adds, "I will be faithful to the Party as a Party member."]

Squad Leader_____Thumb Print
                    Signature
Vice S. Leader_____Thumb Print
                    Signature
Private_____Thumb Print
                    Signature

Movement of the Troops
The initial successes of the Chinese in North Korea were based on their ability to move very large forces quickly and secretly through some very difficult terrain. The PLA's ability to move rapidly and over long distances on foot was legendary.

All major movements on entering Korea were made at night. The march started about 7 P.M. and ended at 3 A.M. By daylight, all troops and equipment were to be under cover and completely hidden or camouflaged. Korean houses were used as shelters, with as many as forty or fifty men to a room. If not disturbed, they stayed inside, out of sight of aircraft, leaving just before day's end to organize the night's activities. If attacked by aircraft, they would remain inside unless or until a direct hit was made on their own shelter. During daylight hours, only small scouting parties moved ahead to select the next night's bivouac area.

If the situation required daylight movement, all men were required to "freeze" if an enemy aircraft approached. Troops would kneel or squat, giving the impression from the air of rocks or stumps.

If strafed, they would immediately fall in their tracks as if wounded. Some had white camouflage uniforms or a cape, which they could pull over themselves to make it appear as if they were small haystacks or other snow-covered features. Officers were authorized to shoot at once anyone who disobeyed.

Oddly, the Chinese seemed to make little attempt to conceal tracks and trails, which indicated use around and leading up to the native shelters or other places of concealment.

A Chinese division could move eighteen to twenty miles in a night and keep up that pace for several days. On the march, a division might take up eighteen to twenty miles of road space.

The march objective was an assembly area from which attack preparations could be made. Efforts were made to select an assembly area that was beyond range of enemy artillery—that is, some seven to ten miles from the known enemy positions but within a distance that could be covered in approximately three hours of rapid movement. Coincidentally, this distance would also put them just beyond the range of most friendly patrols, because most patrols did not extend beyond the range of supporting artillery.

In China, the troops had depended upon their own knowledge of the country and upon a friendly population. In its movements in Korea, the CCF made substantial use of local guides—some willing, some unwilling.

Scheme of Maneuver

The favored scheme of maneuver for the Chinese was the "inverted-V" formation, the "Hatchi Shiki"—what Americans would call a double envelopment. It was usually executed by divisions or larger units, but it was adaptable to smaller units in appropriate circumstances. In that scheme of maneuver, one unit would attack frontally to hold the enemy in place, or to panic the enemy and force them to withdraw, while two additional units would attempt to work their way around both flanks to fold in the flanks of the defending force, to sever supply lines and isolate, intercept, and surround the withdrawing enemy—eventually destroying the enemy piecemeal. Because the enveloping forces were, like the rest of the Chinese Army, composed of light infantry, and because they were able to disregard normal logistic support, at least temporarily, the enveloping forces could move over routes of approach that otherwise would be considered unusable, consequently achieving considerable surprise and success.

According to Chinese manuals, the attack had to be in depth: "Using the triangle formation, the force advancing toward the enemy front must not be composed of more than two-thirds of the strength, or two of the three echelons. The forward units must carry all the weapons and grenades possible."

Reconnaissance

In Korea, the Chinese used Korean-speaking Chinese dressed in civilian clothes to move through the lines with refugees in order to obtain information on enemy dispositions. They also made extensive use of local informants and guides.

Attack—General

The overriding concern of Chinese attack tactics was to move their lightly armed troops through the zone of defending fire with as few losses as possible so they could close in close combat with the defenders, where the fighting would be man to man, where their superior numbers would prevail, and where the superior firepower of the defenders would be minimized. To accomplish that, almost all attacks were made at night, so the attackers could move forward under cover of darkness.

After dark, the attacking forces would move forward from the assembly areas. The main attack would generally be preceded by probing attacks carried out by an infiltration group, each member of which carried six to eight concussion grenades—either similar to the Japanese hand grenades or the potato-masher (stick-grenade) type—but no small arms. The objective of this initial probing attack would be to cause friendly forces to reveal their positions. On occasion, the Chinese would use white phosphorus mortar shells to mark the defending positions. In one case, they used burning, oil-soaked rags to outline the defense lines. This initial probe often had the effect of causing the defending forces to withdraw any local outposts, so there would be little or no warning of a follow-up main attack.

The main attack would generally follow within half an hour, more or less. The attacking forces would move forward in a column, following natural and often predictable routes of approach. Pre-planned fires on these routes of approach were often very effective. Artillery attacks on suspected assembly areas and routes of approach may have kept the Chinese from mounting a full-scale attack on Koto-ri.

If not discovered, the attacking force would attempt to work its way forward by stealth to a point as close as possible to the defending lines. Then, on signal, the troops would commence the assault.

If the attacking force was discovered, the men would continue to move in column formation until coming under small-arms fire; then they would deploy in combat groups and move forward in rushes during lulls in the firing, until they were within assaulting distance.

If the defending troops moved to alternate or supplementary positions after dark, or after the initial probe, the Chinese would often be confused. If the defending dispositions were known, the Chinese would attempt to infiltrate smaller groups deep into the defending position—to the command posts, supply installations, or artillery—in an attempt to create panic and confusion.

The attack was usually on a company or platoon front and made in depth with the following units continuing to push forward. The objective was to punch a hole in the defending line—preferably at some weak point—then exploit that penetration.

The Assault

On signal, the assault would commence with a volley of grenades, followed by whistles, bugles, gongs, cymbals, more grenades, shouting and screaming, and submachine gunfire. It was classic shock action, aimed at unnerving the defending troops, confusing them, creating panic, and overrunning them in the first rush. Once the assault began, there was no letup. If the first attack failed to dislodge enemy troops, it would be followed by successive groups of shock troops. The attack would often be prosecuted with an apparent total disregard for human life, group after group pressing onward. Illumination seemed to have no effect on the attackers, and attacking troops frequently would press forward, totally ignoring the effect of mortar and artillery fire.

The persistence of the Chinese assault was amazing. The basic idea was that if the position was not overrun in the first assault, continuing the attack in depth would eventually cause the defending troops to run out of ammunition, enabling the position to be overrun and taken. This was the "short attack." As described by Lin Biao, it ". . . is like sticking a long sharp-pointed knife into the enemy's weak spot." The key was an attack in depth with additional units following and reinforcing the advance unit. Basically, it was a matter of pushing enough men on a narrow front against a defense so that some would, eventually, break through.

If the first attack and the continuing assault did not succeed, it would soon be followed by another unit moving into position and taking up the attack. The rigidity of Chinese plans and their slowness to react to changing situations often resulted in a unit's continuing the attack long after there was any hope of success.

If the attacks had not succeeded by sunrise, the Chinese, under most circumstances, would break off and withdraw to avoid air attack.

A defender might be faced with multiple "short attacks" on one portion of his front. Some called it a human wave, but it wasn't a "wave" as such. It was more nearly typified by large numbers of small groups working their way forward. Excited descriptions of the Chinese attack led to the term *hordes*. As one Marine put it, "How many hordes in a Chinese platoon?" And another one described it this way: "Saw three hordes, shot two and captured one." Well-dug-in troops, adequately alerted, could generally hold out. One problem described by platoon leaders was "trigger fatigue." Trigger fingers became tired.

Exploitation

If the attack was successful, the Chinese did not often stop to reorganize and defend the position; they continued the attack. The result was that they were vulnerable to counterattack. In addition, they sometimes stopped just to plunder the position—to take whatever weapons and ammunition they could find and, in the cold weather, to confiscate any warm clothing.

The Chinese often had problems continuing the attack and exploiting any break-in. On a number of occasions, they succeeded in making a substantial break-in to defending lines but were unable to exploit it because of a lack of grenades and small-arms ammunition. In one instance, a Chinese running through a position ran into and knocked down a defending Marine. The Marine got up, pulled the pin on a hand grenade, and handed it to the Chinese—who ran off with it with fatal results.

Junior leaders in particular were reluctant to exercise any substantial initiative in a changing situation for fear of being criticized as "incorrect." This fear, together with limited communication, made the Chinese fail to exploit some good opportunities.

Defense

On defense, the Chinese preferred not to defend on the ridgeline but took up positions down the forward slope, or on the reverse slope. In moving from one to another, they would go around the ridgeline rather than over it. They defended obvious avenues of approach and based their defense on the assumption that U.S. forces would attack only during the day. Some predawn attacks were able to penetrate positions in which the enemy was found asleep without even normal security posted.

Logistics

The logistical inability to sustain combat for more than a few days was a serious problem for the Chinese. The problem was partially solved by replacing whole divisions in the line with fresh divisions. This may have accounted for the exceptionally large reserves held out in the initial attacks. Of the twelve divisions available to the 9th CCF Army Group, only six were used in the initial attacks.

Upon crossing the Yalu River, the Chinese forces employed in the initial attacks were given four or five days' worth of cooked rations and between forty and eighty rounds of ammunition. The rations were rice, millet, soybeans, or cooked peas. General Nie Rongzhen admitted that the troops initially relied only on food and ammunition they carried with them, and that this supply could only last a week. After that, they depended on whatever support they could requisition from the countryside, plus what could be captured from the defenders and what could be brought forward. Captured supplies were a major source for the Chinese. Some prisoners said they preferred to fight against Americans because of all the good loot they could find. The Chinese were particularly good at battlefield salvage.

An attempt was made to bring supplies forward by truck to within thirty miles of the front-line units, with men or animals packing forward from there. The 9th Army Group command recruited an army of coolies to carry supplies forward, but many of the coolies froze to death. In addition, providing supplies to feed the coolies themselves was a problem. It might require all the food a coolie could carry to feed himself on the trip to the front.

Unlike most of China, North Korea was a sparsely populated area with little in the way of agricultural resources. The few small villages raised and stored enough rice to support themselves through the winter, but they had little to spare. The winter's rice supply for a small village might feed a Chinese division for a day, or perhaps two, but probably not more. The Chinese did levy requisitions upon the population. The looting of civilian rice supplies by the Chinese was a major cause of the mounting number of refugees encountered later. Throughout the operation, there were conflicting reports on the adequacy of the food supply. Apparently some units fared much better than others.

Medical evacuation and treatment of the wounded were minimal, sometimes nonexistent. In the extremely cold weather that prevailed, a wounded Chinese soldier was often a dead soldier. There is some evidence that Communist Party members were given preferential medical treatment. According to one account given by a captured CCF officer who later refused repatriation, Party members had a special insignia inside their jacket. Aid men were told to look first to see if a wounded man had such an insignia. If so, he was saved if at all possible. It didn't matter about the others—if they were unable to walk, they were either left or shot.

Notes

This section is based upon the writer's personal experience as a battalion intelligence officer during the Korean War and on discussions with a variety of other experienced officers at the time and in later years. In addition, the following published works, listed in the bibliography, were consulted: William C. Bradbury, *Mass Behavior in Battle and Captivity;* Gerard Corr, *The Chinese Red Army;* Alexander George, *The Chinese Communist Army in Action;* John Gittings, *The Role of the Chinese Army;* Samuel B. Griffith, *The Chinese People's Liberation Army;* Robert J. Lifton, *Thought Reform and the Psychology of Totalism;* Nie Rongzhen, *Inside the Red Star;* Lt. Col. Robert B. Rigg, *Red China's Fighting Hordes;* William W. Whitson, *The Chinese High Command;* William W. Whitson (ed.), *PLA Unit History.* Also consulted were various intelligence reports and combat bulletins from the Eighth Army and X Corps, as well as Annex B, Intelligence, of the *Special Action Report—Wonsan–Hamhung–Chosin Reservoir Operation, 8 Oct.–15 Dec. 1950,* 1st Marine Division.

Appendix 2:
Order of Battle, Chinese People's Volunteers (CPV)

Headquarters, Chinese People's Volunteers

Commander: Peng Dehuai (and concurrent political com-
                    missar)
Deputies: Deng Hua (and concurrent deputy commissar)
                    Hong Xuezhi
                    Han Xianchu
Chief of Staff: Xie Fang
Political Director: Du Ping

38th CCF Army

Commander: Lian Xingchu
Commissar: Liu Xiyuan
Deputy Commander: Jiang Yonghui
Chief of Staff: Guan Songtao
Political Director: Wu Dai

112th CCF Division
113th CCF Division
114th CCF Division

39th CCF Army

Commander: Wu Xinquan
Commissar: Xu Binzhou

Deputy Commander:	Tan Youlin
Chief of Staff:	Shen Quixian
Political Director:	Li Xue (and deputy commissar)

115th CCF Division
116th CCF Division
117th CCF Division

40th CCF Army

Commander:	Wen Yucheng
Commissar:	Yuan Shengping
Deputy Commander:	Cai Zhengguo
Chief of Staff:	Ning Xianwen
Political Director:	Li Boqiu

118th CCF Division
119th CCF Division
120th CCF Division

42d CCF Army

Commander:	Wu Ruilin
Commissar:	Zhou Biao
Deputy Commander:	Hu Jicheng
Deputy Commissar:	Guo Chengzhu
Chief of Staff:	Liao Zhongfu
Political Director:	Ding Guoyu

124th CCF Division
125th CCF Division
126th CCF Division

50th CCF Army
| Commander: | Zeng Zesheng |
| Commissar: | Xu Wenlie |

Chief of Staff:	Shu Xing
Political Director:	He Yunhong

148th CCF Division
149th CCF Division
150th CCF Division

66th CCF Army

Commander:	Xiao Xinhuai
Commissar:	Wang Zifeng
Deputy Commander:	Chen Fangren
Chief of Staff:	Liu Su
Political Director:	Zhang Liankui

196th CCF Division
197th CCF Division
198th CCF Division

9th CCF Army Group

Commander:	Song Shilun
Commissar:	Song Shilun
Deputy Commander:	Tao Yong
Chief of Staff:	Qin Jian
Deputy Chief of Staff:	Wang Bin
Political Director:	Xie Youfa

20th CCF Army

Commander:	Zhang Yixiang
Commissar:	Zhang Yixiang
Deputy Commander:	Liao Zhengguo
Deputy Commissar:	Tan Youming
Chief of Staff:	Yu Binghui
Political Director:	Qiu Xiangtian

58th CCF Division
     Commander: Huang Chaotian
     Commissar: [unknown]

59th CCF Division
     Commander: Dai Kelin
     Commissar: He Zhensheng

60th CCF Division
     Commander: Peng Fei
     Commissar: Yang Jiabao

89th CCF Division
     Commander: Yu Guangmao
     Commissar: Wang Zhi

26th CCF Army

Commander: Zhang Renchu
Commissar: Li Yaowen
Deputy Commander: Zhang Zhixiu
Chief of Staff: Feng Dingsan

76th CCF Division
     Commander: Chen Zhongmei
     Commissar   Cao Punan

77th CCF Division
     Commander: Shen Ping
     Commissar: Wei Boting

78th CCF Division
     Commander: Qu Anju
     Commissar: Zhang Jian

88th CCF Division
     Commander: Wu Dalin
     Commissar: Gong Jie

7th CCF Army

Commander:	Peng Deqing
Deputy Commander:	Zhan Danan
Commissar:	Liu Haotian
Chief of Staff:	Li Yuan
Deputy Commissar:	Zeng Ruqing
Political Director:	Zhang Wenbi

79th CCF Division

Commander:	Xiao Jinghai
Commissar:	Xiao Jinghai

80th CCF Division

Commander:	Rao Huitan
Commissar:	Zhang Yingbo

81st CCF Division

Commander:	Zhang Duanfu
Commissar:	Zhang Duanfu

94th CCF Division

Commander:	Guan Junting
Commissar:	[unknown]

Bibliography

National Archives

Records of the Korean War are found in several different record groups in the National Archives, Archives II, at Adelphi, Maryland. The records have been shipped to record retention centers at various times by the original and by successor organizations, and then moved again. I understand that as of this writing, the archivists are attempting to collect them together. Consequently, the following guide may or may not be of help to subsequent researchers. Contrary to usual practice, I have not identified the source and location of each document. Instead, I have chosen to follow the practice used in preparation of the official Army histories. The following, from my notes, indicates the general locations of documents referenced.

Far Eastern Command (FEC)/United Nations Command (UNC)

	Record Group	Boxes
Command Reports Nov. 1950–May 1951	472	75
History of Korean Conflict	472	95
Command Reports w/ staff report	338	336–42, 369
Command and Staff Section Reports (includes G-3 Journals with a separate file for Top Secret items)	338	17–23
Daily Intelligence Summaries (DIS)	407	364–67

Eighth Army	**Record Group**	**Boxes**
War Diaries	407	1081–1127
War Diary	472	58–63

444

I Corps	Record Group	Boxes
War Diary and Command Reports	338	646–652, 692–700

X Corps	Record Group	Boxes
G-3 Journals	338	90–94
Periodic Intelligence Reports (PIR)	338	11086–96

7th Infantry Division	Record Group	Boxes
War Diary and Journals	407	3173–75

MacArthur Library, Norfolk, Virginia

Although not as comprehensive as the National Archives records, this library has an unparalleled collection of material on Gen. Douglas MacArthur and many items on the Korean War not found, or not easily found, in the National Archives. Particularly valuable for the Korea researcher are the materials in Record Groups 6, 7, 9, and 38. Some of the materials, such as the Daily Intelligence Summaries (DIS), are available on microfilm and can be obtained through interlibrary loan.

Marine Corps Sources

Marine Corps material is available at the Marine Corps Historical Center, Washington Navy Yard, or from the Archives Branch, Marine Corps Research Center, Quantico, Virginia.

Published Sources

Acheson, Dean. *Present at the Creation: My Years in the State Department.* New York: W.W. Norton, 1969.

Alexander, Bevin. *Korea: The First War We Lost.* New York: Hippocrene Books, 1986.

Appleman, Roy E. *East of Chosin: Entrapment and Breakout in Korea, 1950.* College Station: Texas A&M University Press, 1987.

———— *Disaster in Korea: The Chinese Confront MacArthur.* College Station: Texas A&M University Press, 1989.

————. *Escaping the Trap: The U.S. Army X Corps in Northeast Korea, 1950.* College Station: Texas A&M University Press, 1990.

————. *South to the Naktong, North to the Yalu: U.S. Army in the Korean*

War. Washington, D.C.: Center of Military History, U.S. Army, 1992.

Biographies of PLA Generals. Beijing: Liberation Army Publishing House, 1984–89.

Blair, Clay. *The Forgotten War: America in Korea, 1950–1953.* New York: Random House, 1987.

Borg, Dorothy, and Waldo Heinrichs, eds. *Uncertain Years: Chinese-American Relations, 1947–1950.* New York: Columbia University Press, 1980.

Bradbury, William C. *Mass Behavior in Battle and Captivity: The Communist Soldier in the Korean War.* Chicago: University of Chicago Press, 1968.

Bradley, Omar N., with Clay Blair. *A General's Life: An Autobiography.* New York: Simon and Schuster, 1983.

Chai Changwen and Zhao Yontain. *A Chronicle of the War to Resist America and Assist Korea.* Beijing: CCP Historical Materials Press, 1987.

Chassin, Lionel Max. *The Communist Conquest of China: A History of the Civil War 1945–1949.* Cambridge: Harvard University Press, 1965.

China Today: War to Resist U.S. Aggression and Aid Korea. Appendix II: "Chinese People's Volunteers Heroes and Models." Beijing: Chinese Social Sciences Publishing House, 1990.

Chinese Academy of Military Science. *The War History of the Chinese People's Volunteers in the War to Resist U.S. Aggression and Aid Korea.* Beijing: Military Science Press, 1988.

Clubb, O. Edmund. *Twentieth-Century China.* New York: Columbia University Press, 1965.

Collins, J. Lawton. *War in Peacetime: The History and Lessons of Korea.* Boston: Houghton Mifflin, 1969.

Condit, Doris M. *History of the Secretary of Defense.* Vol. 2, *The Test of War: 1950–1953.* Washington, D.C.: Office of the Secretary of Defense, 1988.

Corr, Gerard. *The Chinese Red Army: Campaigns and Politics Since 1949.* Reading: Osprey Publishing, 1974.

Cumings, Bruce. *The Origins of the Korean War.* 2 vols. Princeton, N.J.: Princeton University Press, 1981.

Domes, Jurgen. *Peng Te-huai: The Man and the Image.* Palo Alto, Calif.: Stanford University Press, 1985.

Drea, Edward J. *MacArthur's ULTRA: Codebreaking and the War Against Japan.* Lawrence: University Press of Kansas, 1992.

Fehrenbach, T. R. *This Kind of War: A Study in Unpreparedness.* New York: Macmillan, 1963.

Feis, Herbert. *The China Tangle: The American Effort in China from Pearl Harbor to the Marshall Mission.* Princeton, N.J.: Princeton University Press, 1953.

Field, James A. *History of U.S. Naval Operations: Korea.* Washington, D.C.: Government Printing Office, 1962.

George, Alexander. *The Chinese Communist Army in Action.* New York: Columbia University Press, 1967.

Gittings, John. *The Role of the Chinese Army.* London: Oxford University Press, 1967.

Goncharov, Sergei N., John W. Lewis, and Xue Litai. *Uncertain Partners: Stalin, Mao and the Korean War.* Palo Alto, Calif.: Stanford University Press, 1993.

Goulden, Joseph C. *Korea: The Untold Story of the War.* New York: McGraw-Hill, 1982.

Griffith, Samuel B. *The Chinese People's Liberation Army.* New York: McGraw-Hill, 1968.

Hammel, Eric. *Chosin: Heroic Ordeal of the Korean War.* New York: Vanguard Press, 1981.

Handbook on the Chinese Communist Army. D.A. Pamphlet 30-51. Washington, D.C.: Department of the Army, 1952.

Hastings, Max. *The Korean War.* New York: Simon and Schuster, 1987.

Hong Xuezhi. *Recollections of the War to Resist U.S. Aggression and Aid Korea.* Beijing: PLA Publishing House, 1990.

Jian, Chen. *China's Road to the Korean War: The Making of the Sino-American Confrontation.* New York: Columbia University Press, 1994.

Kahn, E. J. *The China Hands: American Foreign Service Officers and What Befell Them.* New York: Viking, 1975.

Karig, Walter, Malcolm W. Cagle, and Frank Manson. *Battle Report: The War in Korea.* New York: Holt Rinehart, 1952.

Kennan, George F. *Memoirs: 1950–1963.* Boston: Little, Brown, 1972.

Khruschchev, Nikita. *Khruschchev Remembers.* Trans. Strobe Talbott. Boston: Little, Brown, 1970.

Lautensach, Hermann. *Korea: A Geography Based on the Author's Travels.* Berlin: Springer Verlag, 1988.

Lifton, Robert J. *Thought Reform and the Psychology of Totalism: A Study of "Brainwashing" in China.* Chapel Hill: University of North Carolina Press, 1989.

Liu, F. F. *A Military History of Modern China, 1924–1949.* Princeton, N.J.: Princeton University Press, 1956.

MacArthur, Douglas. *Reminiscences.* New York: McGraw-Hill, 1964.

MacDonald, Callum A. *Korea: The War Before Vietnam.* New York: Macmillan, 1987.

Mao Zedong. *Selected Military Writings of Mao Zedong.* Beijing: Foreign Language Press, 1963.

Marshall, S. L. A. *The River and the Gauntlet: Defeat of the Eighth Army by the Chinese Communist Forces, November 1950, in the Battle of the Chongchon River.* New York: William Morrow, 1953.

McAleavy, Henry. *The Modern History of China.* New York: Praeger, 1967.

Military Situation in the Far East: Hearings Before the Committee on Armed Services and the Committee on Foreign Relations, United States Senate, Eighty-second Congress, First Session. 5 vols. Washington, D.C.: Government Printing Office, 1951.

Montross, Lynn, and Nicholas Canzona. *U.S. Marine Operations in Korea.* Vol. III, *The Chosin Reservoir Campaign.* Washington, D.C.: Historical Section, U.S. Marine Corps, 1957.

Mossman, Billy C. *Ebb and Flow November 1950–July 1951.* U.S. Army in the Korean War Series. Washington, D.C.: Center of Military History, U.S. Army, 1990.

Nie Rongzhen. *Inside the Red Star: The Memoirs of Marshal Nie Rongzhen.* Beijing: New World Press, 1988.

Panikkar, Kavalam M. *In Two Chinas: Memoirs of a Diplomat.* London: Allen and Unwin, 1955.

Rees, David. *Korea: The Limited War.* New York: St. Martin's, 1964.

Ridgway, Matthew B. *The Korean War: How We Met the Challenge.* New York: Doubleday, 1967.

Rigg, Robert B. *Red China's Fighting Hordes.* Harrisburg, Pa.: Telegraph Press, 1951.

Rusk, Dean. *As I Saw It: Dean Rusk as Told to Richard Rusk.* Ed. Daniel S. Papps. New York: W.W. Norton, 1990.

Salisbury, Harrison. *The Long March: The Untold Story.* New York: Harper and Row, 1985.

Schnabel, James F. *Policy and Direction: The First Year.* U.S. Army in the Korean War Series. Washington, D.C.: Center of Military History, U.S. Army, 1988.

Schnabel, James F., and Robert J. Watson. *History of the Joint Chiefs of Staff: The Joint Chiefs of Staff and National Policy.* Vol. III, *The Korean War.* Part 1. Wilmington, Del.: Michael Glazier, 1979.

Sebald, William. *With MacArthur in Japan: A Personal History of the Occupation.* New York: W.W. Norton, 1965.

Service, John Stuart. *Lost Chance in China: The World War II Despatches of John S. Service.* Ed. Joseph W. Esherick. New York: Random House, 1974.

Snow, Edgar. *Red Star Over China.* New York: Grove Press, 1968.

Spurr, Russell. *Enter the Dragon: China's Undeclared War Against the U.S. in Korea, 1950–51.* New York: Henry Holt, 1988.

Stanton, Shelby L. *America's Tenth Legion: X Corps in Korea, 1950.* Novato, Calif.: Presidio Press, 1989

Toland, John. *In Mortal Combat. Korea, 1950–1953.* New York: William Morrow, 1991.

Truman, Harry S. *Memoirs.* 2 vols. (vol. 1: *Year of Decisions;* vol. 2: *Years of Trial and Hope*). Garden City, N.Y.: Doubleday, 1955–56.

Tsou, Tang. *America's Failure in China: 1941–1950.* Chicago: University of Chicago Press, 1963.

U.S. Department of State. *Foreign Relations of the United States: 1950.* Vol. VII, *Korea.* Washington, D.C.: Government Printing Office, 1976.

U.S. Department of State. *United States Relations with China with Special Reference to the Period 1944–1949 with Letter of Transmittal.* Washington, D.C.: Government Printing Office, 1949.

White, Theodore H., and Annalee Jacoby. *Thunder Out of China.* New York: William Sloan Associates, 1946.

Whiting, Allen. *China Crosses the Yalu: The Decision to Enter the Korean War.* Palo Alto, Calif.: Stanford University Press, 1968.

Whitney, Courtney. *MacArthur: His Rendezvous with History.* New York: Knopf, 1956.

Whitson, William W., ed. *The Chinese High Command: A History of Communist Military Politics, 1927–71.* New York: Praeger, 1973.

Willoughby, Charles A., and John Chamberlain. *MacArthur: 1941–50.* New York: McGraw-Hill, 1954.

Wilson, Arthur, and Norm Strickbine. *Korean Vignettes: The Faces of War.* Portland, Ore.: Artworks Publications, 1996.

Wilson, Dick. *China's Revolutionary War.* New York: St. Martin's, 1991.

Zhang, Shu Guang. *Mao's Military Romanticism: China and the Korean War, 1950–1953.* Lawrence: University Press of Kansas, 1995.

Periodicals

Cohen, Eliot A. "Only Half the Battle: American Intelligence and the Chinese Intervention in Korea." *Intelligence and National Security* 1 (January 1990).

Farrar-Hockley, Gen. Anthony. "Reminiscence of Chinese People's Volunteers in Korea." *The China Quarterly* 98 (June 1984).

Xiaobing, Li, Wang Xi, and Chen Jian (trans.). "Mao's Dispatch of Chinese Troops to Korea: Forty Six Telegrams, July–October 1950." *Chinese Historians* 5, no. 1 (spring 1992).

Xiaobing, Li, and Glenn Tracy (trans.). "Mao Telegrams During the Korean War: October–December 1950." *Chinese Historians* 5, no. 2 (fall 1992).

Other Sources

An Evaluation of the Influence of Marine Corps Forces in the Course of the Korean War (4 Aug 50–15 Dec 50). 2 vols. U.S. Marine Corps Board, 1952.

Command Report—Chosin Reservoir 27 November 1950–12 December 1950. 7th Division, "Action of 7th Infantry Division Units at Chosin Reservoir from 24 November 1950 to 12 December 1950." n.d.

Command Report: November 1950. Chapter I. GHQ Far East Command/United Nations Command, n.d. *History of the Korean Conflict,* Part 2, Vol. 1, "GHQ Support and Participation 25 Jun 50–30 Apr 51." Far Eastern Command, Tokyo, n.d.

Special Report on Chosin Reservoir: 27 November to 10 December 1950. X Corps. n.d.

Special Report—Hungnam Evacuation: 9–24 Dec 50. X Corps, n.d.

Special Action Report—Wonsan–Hamhung–Chosin Reservoir Operation, 8 Oct–15 Dec 1950. 1st Marine Division, May 1951.

Smith, Oliver P. *Aide-Memoire.* Marine Corps Historical Center, n.d.

PLA Unit History. Ed. William W. Whitson. Office of the Chief of Military History, Washington, D.C., n.d.

Interview: Lt. Gen. Edward M. Almond by Capt. Thomas G. Ferguson, 29 Mar 1975. Almond Papers. U.S. Army Military History Institute, Carlisle, Pennsylvania.

Interview: Lt. Gen. O.P. Smith by Ben Frank, 9–12 June 1969. Papers of O.P. Smith. Archives Branch, Marine Corps Research Center, Quantico, Virginia.

Index

Casualties; 31st Infantry, 347; 9th
CCF Army Group, 394; at
Kunu-ri, 293; CCF Phase 2, 383;
CCF at Hagaru-ri, 340; CCF esti-
mates, 84; CCF from cold, 389;
CPV, 369; Eighth Army, 364;
NKPA, 75
Cease fire efforts, 81, 394
Central Intelligence Agency, 216,
218; opinion on Chinese inter-
vention, 63
Central Military Commission, 90,
153, 376; meeting to discuss
intervention, 71; preparations
for war, 84; timing of Chinese
intervention, 83
Central People's Government
Council, 87; Mao report to, 69
Central Soviet Area, 91
Chagang-do Redoubt, 119, 132,
143, 364
Chai Chengwen, 71
Changdian, 147
Changjin, 179, 232
Changpyong-ni, 258
Changsha, 90
Chen Feng, 36
Chen Yi, 72, 88
Chen, C. L., 118
Chengchou (See Zhengzhou)
Chiang Kai-shek, 3, 14, 32, 34, 37,
79, 102
Chien Chang-san, 161
Chiles, Lt. Col. John H., 312
China Hands, 24
Chinaman's Hat, 278, 279
Chinampo, 64, 127
Chinese Communist Party, 7th
Party Congress, 35; anti-foreign
outlook, 16; base areas, 38;
Central Soviet, 35; formed, 33;
initial uprising, 14; land reform,
38; military political universities,
36; Moscow influence, 35; orga-

nizing the villages, 37; party rec-
tification, 35; policies, 15; sinification, 35; United Front in
1936, 42; Yanan, 35
Chinese air action, 202, 323
Chinese apprehensions, 80; meeting at Wake Island, 108; Pacific
defense line, 19, 46; Syngman
Rhee aggresiveness, 81; U.S.
domestic debate, 46
Chinese deception measures, 402;
bogus prisoners, 403; concealed
movement, 229; delegation to
UN, 215-216; release of U.S.
POWs, 234; "volunteer" designa-
tion, 197
Chinese Eastern Railway, 49
Chinese grievances, century of
shame, 31; unequal treaties, 41;
western concessions, 31
Chinese intelligence collection,
143, 169, 234, 295, 322, 407
Chinese Nationalist Ministry of
Defense, 110
Chinese People's Volunteers (See
CPV)
Chinese strategy, moral force, 36;
people's war., 85; time for entry,
83
Chinese Worker's and Peasant's
Army, 91
Chinese warnings, 86, 99;
Burmese report, 218; C. L.
Chen, 118; Nie Rongzhen, 100;
Zhou Enlai speech, 87; Zhou
Enlai to Panikkar, 103
Chinese view of U.S., 31, 142, 213;
U.S. as the most dangerous
enemy, 47
Chingwantao (See Qinhuangdao)
Chinhung-ni, 182, 387
Chitose, 110
Chohantae, 304
Chokyuryong - Kangnam

Index

Index

May 4th Movement, 33
Mazu (Matsu), 50
McCaffrey, Lt. Col. William J., 339
McCarthy, Joseph, 23
McClymont, Capt. James R., 306
Mead, Brig. Gen. Armistead, 388
Messman, 1st Lt. Robert, 303
Middle Kingdom, 41
Milburn, Maj. Gen. Frank W., 172, 174, 290
Mildren, Lt. Col. Frank T., 180
Missed opportunity in China, 44
Molotov, 48
Mongolia, 48
Morehouse, RAdm. Albert K., 249
Morris, Maj. Warren, 318
Muchon-ni, 258Mukden, 63
Mukden (See also Shenyang), 39
Munsan, 293
Mupyong-ni, 169, 235
Murray, Lt. Col. Raymond L., 296, 307
Myohyang-san, 143, 151, 275

NSC-68, 24, 58
Naktong River, 56, 74
Nangnim Mountain Range, 128
National Revolutionary Army, 91
National Security Council, 207, 213, 323; basic policy decisions, 366; council deferred action, 324; debate on unficationof Korea, 57-58; discuss withdrawal, 366; exposed position of X Corps, 323
Nehru, Jawaharlal, 81, 229
Neidongjik, 265, 297, 299, 304, 307
New China News Agency (Xinhua), 100, 106
Newsweek, 65; MacArthur line, 64,82
Nie Rongzhen, 71, 85, 88, 98, 100, 105

Ningxia, 90
North Atlantic Treaty Organizatiom, 4
North Korea; border barrier, 131; communication routes, 130; population, 134; resources, 135; roads and railroads, 135, 137, 136, 128
North Korean Army (NKPA), 58; deterioration of, 115; initial attack, 56; offensive stalled, 74; return of Koreans in PLA, 87
Northeast Frontier Force (NEFF), 74
Northeast Military Region, 74
Northwest Military Field Army, 92

Ongjin Penninsula, 386
Unjong, 149, 151, 190, 100
Oro-ri, 150

Paegomni River, 297
Paik Sun Yup, Maj. Gen., 165, 196, 284
Pak Il-yu, 149, 153
Pakchon, 156, 166
Panikkar, Kavalam M., 102, 215; warning from Nie Rongzhen, 100; warning from Zhou, 103
Peng Dehuai, 34, 72, 84, 88, 145, 158, 163, 283, 402; appointed to command, 89; background of, 89; difficulty in control, 158; efforts to stablize the situation, 163; estimate of U.S. force, 146, 146, 145; Phase 1, 169-170
Peng Deqing., 235
People's Liberation Army, 40; central reserve force, 73; early growth, 38; modernization of the army, 92; short attack, 42, 93; size and organization, 72; tactics, 82
People's Political Consultative

Index

attempt to reassure Chinese, 81; authorize use of U.S. ground forces, 71; crisis meeting, 360; debate on unfication of Korea, 57; decision not to withdraw voluntarily, 394; news conference, 357; use of A bomb, 357; U.S. policy toward China, 45
Tshu Tsei-chiang, 170
Tsingtao (See Qingdao)
Tunner, Maj. Gen. William H., 380

UNC/FEC; exploitation of Inchon, 60, 83 ; military objective, 58; Operation Order 4, 117, 119; Operation Order 5, 385; Operation Plan 9, 123; order to advance to the border, 120; plan for renewed offensive, 240; planning for evacuation from Korea, 386
Ungi River, 240, 249
United Nations, 80, 214; proposed resolution on China, 215; resolution on crossing 38th Parallel,102; resolution to assist ROK, 55; responsibility for Korea, 9
Unsan, 149, 151, 161, 164, 275
U.S. foreign policy, 191; concern with Communist takeover in China, 20; containment policy, 4; Far Eastern policy, 4, 20; reappraisal of China, 43; relations with China, 13
U.S. ground forces, prewar status of, 7
U.S. military policy, air power, 6; atomic weapons, 86; Pacific defense line, 5
U.S. occupation of Korea, 8, 100; withdrawal from, 10
U.S. reaction to Chinese intervention, 168, 170, 175, 178, 206, 254
U.S. remobilization, 24
U.S. view of China, 19; capabilities, 191; opinion of Chinese soldiers, 123, 187
U.S.SR, 43, 98, 113, 216; air forces in Siberia, 62; interest in Manchuria, 85; military aid to China, 71, 88, 94, 141; occupation of Manchuria, 39; renege on aid, 142

Viet Nam, 46, 50, 78
Vincent, John Carter, 123
Vladimirov, P. P., 93

Wake Island meeting, 61-62
Walker, Lt. Gen. Walton, 57, 158, 163, 166, 168, 172, 174, 195, 280, 282, 286, 326; death of, 397; orders general withdrawal, 285; orders withdrawal to Chongchon,176
Walpo-ri, 287
Wang Yunge, 343
Wang Jing-wei, 70
Wang Xingji, 343
Ward, Angus, 18, 110
Wawon, 280, 283
Weather, 133; effect on equipment, 134; effect on men, 133
Webb, James E., 104
White Paper, 21, 46
White Terror, 33
White, Theodore, 38
Whitney, Maj. Gen. Courtney, 80, 326
Willoughby, Maj. Gen. Charles A., 26, 108, 175, 180, 191, 320, 326
Wilson, Brig. Gen. Vennard, 279
Wilson, Woodrow, 32
Withdrawal by air, 381
Withdrawal from Pyongyang, 378

Index

Index